Gendering the Vertical Mosaic

Feminist Perspectives on Canadian Society

Second Edition

Roberta Hamilton

Queen's University

PEARSON

Prentice
Hall

Toronto

National Library of Canada Cataloguing in Publication

Hamilton, Roberta
    Gendering the vertical mosaic : feminist perspectives on Canadian society / Roberta Hamilton.—2nd ed.

Includes bibliographical references and index.
ISBN 0-13-147371-9

    1. Feminism—Canada. 2. Women—Canada—Social conditions. 3. Feminist theory. I. Title.

HQ1453.H35 2005   305.42'0971   C2003-907166-9

0-13-147371-9

Vice President, Editorial Director: Michael J. Young
Executive Acquisitions Editor: Jessica Mosher
Senior Marketing Manager: Judith Allen
Associate Editor: Patti Altridge
Production Editor: Richard di Santo
Copy Editor: Alex Moore
Proofreader: Lu Cormier
Production Coordinator: Anita Heyna
Page Layout: Jansom
Art Director: Mary Opper
Cover Design: Anthony Leung
Cover Image: Corel Photo Library

10 11 12 CP 15 14 13

Printed and bound in Canada.

In memory of my parents
Elizabeth Freedman Russell (1919–2001)
and B.M. (Cy) Russell (1913–2000)

Table of Contents

Preface to the First Edition

In December 1976, when I sent my first manuscript to the publisher, I began my acknowledgments by recognizing my debt to the women's liberation movement. Today, my acknowledgment is similar, though in deference to the times, I invoke the collective work of generations of feminists who created the immense, diverse scholarly literature and intellectual environment that made possible critical research on gender, racism, sexuality, class—the list continues. Like the late poet and feminist activist Bronwen Wallace, I feel strongly that mine "is only one voice in a huge community" (1983, 295). In an interview with Janice Williamson in February 1989, only six months before she died, Bronwen stressed that this community included the dead as well as the living. For this reason, she started every public reading with a poem by someone who had died recently.

It is with great deliberation, then, that I recall Bronwen Wallace, her political commitment, her sensibilities, her power to evoke the best in others. In my copy of *The Stubborn Particulars of Grace*, she wrote what she must have written in many other copies: "For Roberta. Grace. Woman to woman through our own stubborn particulars." Bronwen told Janice that her book was "an attempt to begin to talk about spiritual matters in a political context and to say that if we're going to live in a state of grace, if we're going to live with wholeness or integrity in the world, we have to pay attention to the particulars and politics of where we are going." In writing *Gendering the Vertical Mosaic*, a book that presumptuously deals with so much, I keep Bronwen's vision in view, as well as her healthy scepticism toward academic feminism. My illustrations are intended to remind readers (and myself) that complex theoretical ideas need to be understood through the prism of the small events of everyday life and evaluated in terms of their ability to illuminate, rather than obfuscate, our own stubborn particulars.

This book was written over the course of several years while I taught a large introductory class in sociology. My primary commitment as a teacher is to encourage students to understand their society and the social relationships in which they participate by using a range of theoretical perspectives—intellectual tools, as it were. I have never thought that this meant simplifying complex systems of thought. Indeed, this approach would provide a false sense that knowing is an easy matter, hardly worth the trouble. But conveying complexity, ambiguity, contradiction, and open-endedness puts the onus on the teacher to interact with students in accessible and challenging ways. Convincing my students that there is no simple formula for understanding the social world, and encouraging them to see this as intellectually exhilarating, rather than an occasion for regret, is great fun, and many of them have responded in kind, engaging in critical discussions with me, with each other, and, from what they tell me, with their housemates, friends, and partners.

In writing this book, I have tried to pursue a similar course. This proved far more difficult than teaching in a classroom where perplexed faces, body language, hands in the air, nodding heads and closing eyes, people lined up at the microphones, and the odd shout provide ongoing indications about the level of clarity and comprehension. Moreover, students find their way to my office and challenge me to explain, justify, or recant. But I have written this book with an eye to making complex ideas comprehensible. Many times I have sat before my keyboard imagining myself in front of two hundred and fifty undergraduate students, most of them less than half my age, waiting to be convinced (or at least entertained). And I have written for them. I trust that this book will be useful to introductory students in sociology, women's studies, and political studies. And because the ideas that animate this book are complex, I believe that it may be helpful as well to those who have considerably more background.

Because this book has taken so long to write—and even longer not to write—there are many people who contributed to making my environment supportive and stimulating. First, I must express my deepest gratitude to Barbara Tessman of Copp Clark. She persuaded me to write this book; she gave me a great deal of help; she was patient; and she shared my feminist convictions. The book would not have been written without her, and now, at the end of the project, I can say that I am very happy that she was willing to endure the wait. She deserved a more disciplined author, and she got me. But for my part, I am eternally grateful to have had the opportunity to work with this knowledgeable, competent, and indefatigable editor. I also want to thank her colleagues, Brian Henderson and Jeff Miller. Brian helped launch the project, and Jeff provided crucial support about halfway through.

I am grateful to several readers of the first chapters of the manuscript and especially to Dawn Currie who provided a thorough and incisive critique. Pat Armstrong and Deborah Gorham reviewed the whole manuscript, and I want to thank them very much. Not only were their comments very helpful, saving me from many errors, overgeneralizations, and excesses, but I appreciate that their schedules are frantically busy without such time-consuming additional tasks. I am also grateful to Karen Dubinsky for reading chapter 6, and to Jessica Hamilton, Elizabeth Russell, Susan Russell, Emma Whalen, and many graduate students in my feminist theories seminar for reading and commenting upon chapter 1. Two of those students, Adam Givertz and Alison Forrest, started the journal *left history* the year after taking that seminar. They invited me to submit an earlier version of chapter 1 for their inaugural issue, and it appeared as the first article. The response that I received helped spur me on to finish this book, and I am very grateful to them for going to such lengths to offer support! Another former student, Phyllis Bray, provided me with an amazing newspaper clipping service and much encouragement.

My research assistants have served me very well indeed. Patti Phillips offered critical readings of several chapters; Lore Fredstrom gave me the benefit of her rich and extensive background while doing a prodigious amount of research for several chapters; and Shelley Reuter made it possible for me to meet my final deadlines. Like all good researchers, she was a wonderful detective; she provided insightful response to all the chapters, and saved me from many an inappropriate turn of phrase. My great thanks to all of them.

During the 1990–91 academic year, I was fortunate to be associated with the Beatrice M. Bain Research Group at the University of California, Berkeley. In particular, I am grateful to Ilene Philipson and Carla Golden who provided warm friendship as well as critical readings of an earlier version of chapter 1. Janor Tuck and Ted and Susan Wright gave me wonderful places to stay in the Bay Area. I thank all of them for making my sabbatical a happy and productive time.

At Queen's University, I am very fortunate to have many colleagues in sociology and in women's studies whose personal support and encouragement for this project have sustained me through times happy and sad. In particular, for friendship and kindnesses over many years, I want to thank Rob Beamish, Annette Burfoot, Beverley Baines, Elspeth Baugh, Roberta Lamb, Colin Leys, Haideh Moghissi (now at York), Christine Overall, June Pilfold, Vincent Sacco, Terri Easter Sheen, Pamela Dickey Young, and (my Diana)

Mary Morton. My new friends and colleagues in the Faculty Office have been so kind and supportive, as well as tolerant of my obsessive desire to finish this book; in particular I thank Natalie Forknall for helping in the preparation of the manuscript.

Jane Errington has been an ongoing source of love and confidence. Her perseverance, resilience, and scholarship are worthy of emulation, and I have tried. Olga Kits chose me to be her supporter when things were tough, and I am very happy she did. She taught me some new lessons about patience and possibility and loyalty. In an earlier incarnation, my colleague and friend, Karen Dubinsky, was my student. It is a sweet thing when intellectual and personal interests become so intertwined, as indeed they have with my own mentor and dear friend, Hubert Guindon. I have relied on all these relationships during all the machinations of personal life and university politics, and they make possible the finding of time and energy for writing.

For a person who has been so unremittingly critical of family in contemporary society, I have been remarkably blessed in my own familial relationships. In particular, I want to acknowledge how much I have learned from my son Joe and my daughters Susan and Jessica. Their experiences—as seen through my eyes—have long provided illustrations for my lectures, and they have never completely stopped speaking to me for this. They have worked hard to try and keep me informed about themselves and about life. They tease me about all that I don't seem to know and don't seem to want to know. Their interventions alone would save me from dogmatism about masculinity, racism, aerobics, music, sexuality, popular culture, work, and play. I have written much of this book with them in mind: Could I explain and justify what I have written to Joe, Susan, and Jessica? When the answer seemed to be no, the delete key on my computer was activated. Their support for me and for this project moves me greatly. Because they are my children, I don't suppose that they will ever know how much this mattered. They must have learned a lot about support from their father, Neville Hamilton. I am also thankful for the close relationship I have with my brother, Jim Russell, and our sister, Susan, who is cited more than once in the pages that follow. I have learned so much from them both.

Finally I want to mention my partner, the irrepressible and loving Geoffrey Smith. Shulamith Firestone wrote that successful lovers give each other another window on the world. Looking through that other window has helped me see connections that I would not have seen (and may not be there), to shift my gaze, to reflect again. Living with someone who is politically and intellectually engaged, in ways different but not usually incompatible, may not have rushed this book along, but it altered the content, in ways subtle and various. Certainly living with Geoff has helped destabilize categories. As a dog lover, he often barks at dogs on the street; they often bark back. Once I went to the Syracuse Airport to pick him up. When I couldn't find him, I went to the Information Desk. The attendant picked up the Intercom: "Would Geoffrey Smith please come to the Information Desk." Seconds later, I heard barking from the other side of the airport. "Did you know it was me?" Geoff asked later. "Oh no," I replied. "There were lots of people barking." After that incident, I realized that I live with a man who thinks he's a dog, and a dog, Tuborg the Dog, who thinks he's a man. Together they have helped me write this book, although only Geoff did some serious proofreading. What can I say? They make me happy when skies are grey.

In the fall of 1962, I was a student in John Porter's course, "Class, Stratification and Power" at Carleton University. In retrospect, it is clear that his lectures became the basis of *The Vertical Mosaic* (1965). I wish that I could say that I realized, as a student, that he had not gendered his vertical mosaic. Looking back, I am flabbergasted by how much I didn't see what was to become—starting in the revolutionary winter of 1970—a central preoccupation in my life. This helps explain, I suppose, why one of the great joys of teaching for me has been introducing students to the ways of thinking that had not been presented to me, ways of thinking that turned out to be so important for every aspect of my life, including, and especially, my return to sociology as a graduate student ten years after my course with Professor Porter.

It is with humility and delight that I borrow John Porter's title for this book. I want to speculate briefly on what he might think about contemporary politics in Canada. For Porter, the way forward was to dismantle the vertical part of the vertical mosaic by providing equality of opportunity. The primary route would be access to education, particularly university education, and the precondition for this was a reasonable standard of living for all. What we are witnessing today in Ontario and much of the rest of the country is the dismantling of the educational opportunities in place since *The Vertical Mosaic* appeared. This is part of a larger agenda which, whatever the motivation, is most assuredly making the rich richer, the middle class smaller, and the poor poorer and more numerous. This agenda has been made acceptable precisely by declaring that more and more people have, to paraphrase Judith Butler, "bodies that don't matter" (1993). Declared outside the realm of the worthy are the poor, those on welfare, especially mothers and children, those with a physical or mental disability, mothers who work and mothers who don't work, fathers who don't work, and persons who are incarcerated. Not far removed are those who work for government whether in offices, classrooms, hospitals, universities, many of whom will be joining the ranks of the former. We must find ways to name this process of savage othering for what it is, a mean-spirited, racist, and misogynist rationale for buttressing existing privilege and power. We need to resist the hegemonic, multimedia message that each person stands alone, and that the best anyone can do is cling to a place inside the loop. Feminists have much to contribute to mobilizing resistance at every level to this absurd and unjust conception of social life, and I hope that *Gendering the Vertical Mosaic* makes this clear.

Acknowledgments to the Second Edition

Jessica Mosher encouraged me to undertake a second edition, and Patti Altridge inspired me to do more than I intended. Perhaps they feel like the Boy Scout who helped an elderly woman across the road. His good turn took a very long time, he explained, "because she actually hadn't wanted to go."

As I reach the other side of the road, however, I can sincerely express my gratitude to them both. Preparing this text meant that I read ten times more than I would have; shifted my line of vision on many issues; changed my mind about things familiar; and encountered new perspectives: in a sense nothing stayed the same. Feminist-inspired research, theories, critiques, and visions of the future proliferate in all areas of the world, in every discipline, in social movements, everywhere. My crash self-taught course on global restructuring provided dramatic counterpoint to the dominant messages in the media, and renewed my belief that feminists throughout the world gain a great deal from their ongoing conversations and alliances. I want to thank the six anonymous reviews of the first edition for providing much guidance, and to Alex Moore who copy edited the manuscript with great finesse, to Lu Cormier for careful proofreading, and to Richard di Santo for his help in completing this project.

Encouragement came from unexpected sources. In 2002 I was returning to Canada from California with two large prints wrapped in brown paper which my partner had inherited from his parents. Since I didn't know what fate awaited them by mail, I risked trying to sweet talk these vastly over-sized packages onto planes. Airline officials, each of whom began by saying "absolutely not," became accommodating once I launched (at length) into stories of deaths in the family. In Ottawa I lined up at customs, the last hurdle. Were they valuable? I didn't know or care since they were destined for our living room wall. But did customs care? The young woman eyed me and my six-foot-high package, took my passport, and studied it long enough for me to wonder what was up. Then she looked up: "Are you an academic?" I confessed. "Are you Roberta Hamilton, who wrote *Gendering the Vertical Mosaic*?" I nodded, in disbelief. "I loved that book," she said. "We read it in Women's Studies at Western." She continued to talk but I was stunned: my package and I had arrived safely. The one customs officer in the country (I think) who had read *Gendering* was standing there waiting to welcome me home. There are many reasons to write books, and I had just found another.

After using *Gendering* in a course, Judith Blackwell generously sent me a package of student responses which she thought would cheer me. They did, and I thank her very much. Jill Smith, whom I first met in a consciousness-raising group in Montreal in 1971, has been equally encouraging. It is a pleasure to thank Michelle Teixeria for taking the time to talk to me about third wave feminism, and to introduce me to the 'zines that she finds the most stimulating. On quite another note, just as I finished chapter 5, my spirits were lifted by Susan Belyea who built me the best birthday present ever, complete with her own beautiful glass windows.

In preparing this text I have been sustained by all of the usual suspects whom I thanked eight years ago: children, friends, family, colleagues. I remain grateful to them all. But there are also some particular debts. Krista Robson helped me come to terms with the task ahead, finding and organizing material systematically and creatively. During the last months, Cindy Halligan responded energetically and cheerfully to outlandish requests for material, and without her I would have (as we used to say) lost my cool long ago.

Joan Westenhaefer prepared this manuscript, giving up many evenings, weekends, and, at times I fear, peace of mind. She also organized my day job, saving me from a multitude of errors, as she has done for several previous heads of department. She has no idea how good she is; nor does she believe any of us when we tell her. Still, it gives me pleasure to record how much her judgement, loyalty, and friendship mean to me.

In writing this book I asked several scholars for help and their warm response was gratifying. In particular, I want to thank Monica Boyd, Annette Burfoot, Fiona Kay, Catherine Krull, and Laureen Snider. Special thanks go to my confidante Beverley Baines for providing me with a copy of her excellent forthcoming article "Using the Canadian Charter of Rights and Freedoms to Constitute Women." My colleagues in the Department of Sociology provide a supportive and pleasant working environment. Thank you to Michelle Ellis for help with this manuscript, and Lynn O'Malley for her ongoing assistance. My gratitude goes to Vincent Sacco for many years of warm friendship and collegial support, never more so than in the past few months, when he gave up some of his discretionary time so that I could bury myself in this manuscript.

All the things that I said about my partner Geoff Smith in the first preface remain true except that this time he also edited the last chapter, and helped me to finish more quickly. All he asked in return was that I pay homage to his dogs: Tuborg the Dog lived a long life and, after a respectful hiatus, he was succeeded by The Dog Forest who wrote many of the additions to this book, or would have if he had had the time.

Tuborg was not the only important being in my life who died since the publication of the first edition. The departure of my parents and Hubert Guindon, my mentor, so close to each other, seems to have left me, after years of resistance, as the grown-up. Never too late, my mother might have said. The first edition of *Gendering* was dedicated to my parents, this edition to their memory. I keep with me my father's admonition to 'Go canny,' and my mother's steadfast belief that we owe each other a better world.

In 1972 I arrived to do an MA in sociology part-time at Sir George Williams University, three small children in tow, and two years of feminist consciousness raising under my belt. Upon hearing my plans to understand women's subordination, the head of department explained to me, not unkindly, that the place for my interests—with which he was most sympathetic—was on the street, not the university. But a year later I met his colleague, Hubert Guindon, who gave me the green light and untold support, though he confessed later that once he realized I was not planning to study women's movements—the only sociological project he could imagine involving women—he had no idea what I was going on about. When he first mentioned a doctoral degree, I paid no attention; he wasn't pushy, but he didn't stop either. At some point, I don't know when, it stopped sounding crazy. I don't believe that he ever realized that his support for me—considering my sex and my feminist politics—was so unusual. How he came to be this person of such generous spirit, with the sort of confidence that only delights in the success of others is a good question. Given that my work has been a source of immense satisfaction, I do know that I was blessed to have had him as my mentor and dear friend.

About the Author

Roberta Hamilton was born in London, England, in 1942, and grew up in Canada. She first became involved in feminist politics in 1970 in Montreal, where she worked for several years at The New Woman Centre. In 1983, she accepted a position at Queen's University where she helped found and served as the first coordinator of the Women's Studies Program. Since 1986 she has been a member of the Department of Sociology, where she teaches a large introductory course and a graduate seminar in feminist theory.

The first edition of *Gendering the Vertical Mosaic: Feminist Perspectives on Canadian Society* was published in 1996 and has been required reading in Women's Studies courses for years. Her other publications include *The Liberation of Women: A Study of Patriarchy and Capitalism* (Allen & Unwin, 1978) and *The Historiography of New France* (Langdale Press, 1988). She co-edited (with Michele Barrett) *The Politics of Diversity* (Verso, 1986) and (with John McMullan) a collection of essays by Hubert Guindon under the title *Tradition, Modernity and Nation* (University of Toronto, 1988). In 2002, she published *Setting the Agenda*, a biography of Jean Royce, registrar at Queen's University from 1933 to 1968.

She has a son and two daughters, and lives with her partner and dog in Kingston, Ontario.

INTRODUCTION

This book provides an introduction to Canadian society from feminist theoretical perspectives. Yet it must be said immediately that neither *Canadian* nor *feminist* are used
as though their meanings were self-evident. Controversies about the nature of
Canadian society abound, and there is little agreement among scholars, activists, and
citizens about just what this society is, or if it exists at all. Canadian society is not simply "there" awaiting feminist interpretation, nor is there any agreement on what might
constitute feminist perspectives. As a result, my approach throughout this book is to
examine critically the very concepts that constitute the book's themes, namely
Canadian society and feminist perspectives.

Through this approach, I hope to encourage readers to critically analyze the interpretations offered here. Writing this book involved a constant process of selection,
ranging from the questions posed and the interpretations presented to the research
discussed. Readers must realize that textbooks—no less than other books—reflect the
judgments, conscious and unconscious, informed and not-so-informed, of the
authors. This book needs to be read critically, not for the major points in each chapter, but for the viability of interpretations. How do these interpretations stand up
against other books you have read and the ideas presented by your professors? To
what extent do they confirm or challenge your own experience, your mother's, your
daughter's, or what you read in the newspaper? This book is intended, in line with the
spirit of much feminist scholarship, to open many subjects for discussion rather than
to provide some new received wisdom.

Most feminist scholarship proceeds from an understanding that knowledge is not
prepackaged, that it is never simply a given. Rather, feminists seek to demonstrate that
what passes for knowledge is historically specific and enmeshed in discernible ways
with existing relations of power. Feminists have argued that men of the elites have had

privileged access to creating knowledge—that is, to developing the descriptions and inter-pretations about the world that are deemed important for educated people to know. This means that dominant groups have also had the power to omit, to ensure that what they have deemed trivial has been omitted from the list of indispensable works—the *canons*—of various disciplinary knowledge. These omissions constitute the corollary, or underside, of knowledge—that which is too irrelevant to formulate, to pass on, or to explain. When those who do not share the belief in their triviality question such omissions, both the omissions and their advocates are often dismissed as too subjective, emotion-laden, or narrow.

Feminists have addressed what has been left out, filling in the silences. In this process, they depose, from its privileged location, that which was previously considered knowledge, and they call into question the assumptions and methods through which that knowledge has been created and shared. This point may be elaborated by looking more closely at the title of this book—*Gendering the Vertical Mosaic: Feminist Perspectives on Canadian Society*.

In 1965, Carleton University sociologist John Porter published a book entitled *The Vertical Mosaic*. A long-standing cliché comparing Canada and the United States described the former as "mosaic," the latter as "melting pot." This distinction drew attention to the idea that the many peoples from all over the world who had populated Canada maintained their various cultural identities. In the United States, the emphasis was upon assimilation: regardless of origin, all peoples would become American, not only in citizenship but in their way of life. Without commenting on the viability of the comparison—which has been contested by critics in both countries—Porter drew upon nearly two decades of research to demonstrate that Canada's ethnic mosaic was hierarchically arranged. In his words:

> Because the Canadian people are often referred to as a mosaic composed of different ethnic groups, the title "The Vertical Mosaic," was originally given to the chapter which examines the relationship between ethnicity and social class. As the study proceeded, however, the hierarchical relationship between Canada's many cultural groups became a recurring theme in class and power....The title...therefore seemed to be an appropriate link between the two parts of the book ["The Structure of Class" and "The Structure of Power"]. (xii–xiii)

Although Porter's evidence on the nature of the relationship between ethnicity and power has been the subject of controversy within sociological literature (see chapter 4), many of his findings have been confirmed. Porter's book was also the first full-scale study to demonstrate that Canada was a class society; indeed, the media seized on the study as a news story, thus helping to dispel the common myth that nearly all Canadians were middle class, or just about to be.

The concept of a vertical mosaic also proves an apt metaphor for Canada as a racialized country. Indeed, the most enduring and dramatic divisions in Canadian society—which Porter mainly subsumed under "ethnic" differences—are those informed by the ways in which certain sectors of the population have been racialized. The term *race* becomes a code for *non-white*. Recent scholarship attends to the ways in which *whiteness* is constructed as the other side of *non-whiteness*, and how distinctions referred to as "race" shape power relations and the distribution of resources. My borrowing of the phrase *vertical mosaic*, therefore, also draws attention to a central theme of this book, namely the intersection of class and racialized hierarchies in Canada.

Let me turn to the first word in the title of this book—*gendering*. Porter's vertical mosaic acknowledged that the Canadian population came in two sexes. In particular, he called attention to the relationship between education, professional opportunities, and gender: "It is [women's] traditional exclusion from the higher professions which is a measure of the society's intellectual wastage" (179). Nonetheless, writing before the second wave of feminism, the Royal Commission on the Status of Women, and the explosion of feminist scholarship, Porter did not consider how the vertical mosaic was gendered in all of its manifestations.

Gender is a word that many feminist scholars use to indicate that sexual difference and sexual hierarchies are socially constructed. By using gender as a verb—*gendering*—I indicate that gender is not a thing but a process. Gender cannot be added on, as in "Gender *and* the Vertical Mosaic." Rather, gendering may be understood as ongoing action that plays out on every terrain from the psychic structures of individuals to the ways in which power is deployed in all organizations, institutions, and relationships. Gendering focuses on masculinity and femininity as continuously shifting social phenomena that intricately and variously inform all social interaction. Gendering the vertical mosaic involves using feminist perspectives to study Canadian society.

This brings us to the first words of the subtitle of this book. *Feminist perspectives* offer various, sometimes competing, explanations for the pervasiveness of relationships of domination and subordination between men and women, for different perceptions of the relevance of class, racial, and ethnic differences among women, and for a range of understandings about the changes required to redress exploitative and oppressive relationships. Feminists have explored the nature of reproductive labour and male control of female sexuality searching for the roots of male domination and female subordination. They have refashioned Marxism in their attempts to understand the relation between class and gender. Feminists of colour have insisted that white feminists acknowledge and dismantle their own racism, including the racism inherent in the theories that they have developed. Psychoanalytic theories have been reread for what they reveal about power, control, misogyny, and internalized oppression. Lesbians and gay men have put the oppressive system of heterosexism on the agenda and have related it to male privilege, racial stereotypes, and class exploitation. Feminists have taken up critical issues raised within the transgender movement to show the arbitrariness not only of sexual assignment at birth but also the assumptions about the fit between biological sex and gender. Feminists have been drawn to the theories of poststructuralism and deconstructionism and have turned them into powerful ways of examining how language creates, sustains, and constrains our sense of who we are and, at the same time, how language, by its volatility and flexibility, may open up the spaces for challenges to dominant discourses. Taken together, feminist theories involve a massive critique of every aspect of societies, past and present: relationships, institutions, behaviours, discourses, thought, and ideas.

Chapter 1 presents an overview of the current feminist theoretical perspectives that were used to develop the subsequent chapters on Canadian society. By first presenting the theoretical discussions, my aim is to provide readers with sufficient theoretical background to anticipate and appreciate the kinds of challenges that feminists have raised about Canadian society. In addition, the theoretical discussions should enable readers to understand and critically assess the particular interpretations of Canadian society offered in this book. Which theoretical questions are used to raise issues about Canadian society? Which questions are ignored? All selections involve exclusion, but to what extent have spaces been created to permit readers to consider for themselves what has been excluded? Readers may also raise the reverse question. To what extent do the historical and contemporary interpretations of Canadian society offered here suggest theoretical roads not followed in this text? I hope that readers who are encountering feminist theory for the first time will be attracted by the range of questions and perspectives that may be used to explore the areas of social life that most interest them.

Feminist theories offer to make visible, analyze, and critique the hierarchical social relations between men and women in all societies and in every aspect of society from the level of macroeconomics and international politics through to sexuality and the intimate social practices of everyday life. They expose the socially constructed nature of those relations and try to explain how they are sustained at the intra-psychic and inter-subjective levels. Feminist theories always offer an explicit or at least implicit critique of relations of domination and subordination. If these theories can explain why and how things are as they are, they also provide the possibility of transformation to societies no longer informed by exploitative and oppressive relations between the sexes.

In the subsequent chapters of this book, my task is to use feminist theoretical questions to study major aspects of *Canadian society*, the last part of the book's subtitle. But this task is more difficult than it may at first appear: there is no entity known as Canadian society that can simply be assumed to exist. Just as feminists have disagreed (at some point about almost everything), so have those historians, political scientists, sociologists, journalists, and bureaucrats who have written about Canadian society. Not only have their interpretations changed over the decades, but there are complex and ongoing debates about the nature of this society. Is Canada a land of opportunity for all (men) or a class-divided society, rent further by racism and ethnocentrism, a society that reserves its positions of power and wealth for self-perpetuating elites? Do the regional disparities reflect the vagaries of nature or the actions of political and economic leaders? Are we composed of one nation? Or two, as many Québécois would have it? Or at least three, as Aboriginal peoples argue? Or many, as some versions of multiculturalism would suggest? Are we a nation at all? Do the differences between Canada and the United States amount to little more than political fiction?

These profound disagreements about the nature of Canadian society mean that a feminist interrogation of the literature must also decide which (prefeminist) interpretations appear the most viable, which are most worth critiquing, elaborating upon, and appropriating. The voluminous prefeminist literature on Canadian society—including, for the most part, Porter's *Vertical Mosaic*—has generally taken the relations between the sexes as given, natural in some sense. Feminist questions undercut these assumptions and, as a result, the original interpretations are revealed more as sexist descriptions than explanations. The old interpretations do not completely disappear, however. It is rather like turning a kaleidoscope. There is familiarity about the new image, but the pieces are arranged quite differently, and, more especially, some that were hidden in the first arrangement come into full view in the second.

There is truly no aspect of life in Canada that has not been, or could not be, subjected to feminist interrogation, to a turn of the kaleidoscope. How then to decide what to discuss in this book? What criteria would be used for selection? My decision has been to organize the chapters around some of the major themes and issues that have been raised within women's movements in Canada in the last century, but primarily within the last 35 years. After all, women's movements offer the sustained challenges to the sexual hierarchies that pervade social relationships in Canada, as well as providing the initial and often continuing impetus for feminist research and theoretical development (Adamson, Briskin, and McPhail 1988).

Chapter 2, therefore, provides an interpretation of women's movements in Canada, with most of the attention given to events since the late 1960s—what has been called second wave feminism. The description of "first" and "second" wave feminism resonates with two major periods of public feminist mobilization in Canada and elsewhere. Retrospectively, the term *first wave* encompasses the period from 1850 when Elizabeth Cady Stanton and other women convened at Seneca Falls after being relegated to the balcony at an anti-slavery convention in London, England a decade earlier (Eisenstein 1981, 148). During the next 75 years women mobilized to alter their legal status as the property of men, especially fathers and husbands, and to gain equality in the public arena. The movement is often seen to culminate and recede with the granting of female suffrage after World War I. The *second wave* describes the period from the late 1960s, although there is controversy about whether it has been superseded by a third wave, by "post feminism," by a backlash, by more diverse, localized and international activity, or perhaps by all of the above.

The "waves" appear so real—great undulations of water (people) proceeding in the same direction before receding—that their metaphorical status disappears. Yet this language also shapes our understanding of women's movements in ways that limit our vision. Women's studies student Natasha Pinterics suggests that if a water metaphor is necessary "tides might be more apt with their ebb and flow. Waves surge and recede too dramatically and with too much finality to seem accurate to the pace of emancipatory change that feminism" inspires (2001, 20). The wave metaphor also obscures the conflicts, controversies, and un-evenness within each period; renders flat and uninteresting the period between waves; anticipates a third wave as a matter of course; and suggests by the numbering system something like progress. "These waves are really suspect," asserts Afshan Al: "I mean, who is deciding when the new surf's up?" (Wench Collective 2001, 71).

My discussion of women's movements in chapter 2 and throughout the book uses the wave metaphor at times while seeking at other moments to make visible that which it obscures or assumes. What have feminist activists in Canada heralded, through their mobilizations, as the most important themes and issues? Once again, the reader is called upon to assess the answer to this question as well as to judge the way that the issues have been constructed in the succeeding chapters. By presenting the women's movement as a chapter in itself, I intend to provide the reader with a broad historical interpretation as well as some grounds for assessing the process of selection. Chapters 1 and 2 provide the questions, the analysis, the broad subjects, and the particular issues that are explored in the last five chapters of the book.

Chapters 3 and 4 discuss feminist challenges to the Canadian state. Perhaps the primary reason why we speak about Canadian society is because of the internationally accepted legal set of relations encapsulated in the Canadian state. The Canadian state is generally treated as having the legitimacy to organize social and political relations within the territory recognized as Canada. There is a country called Canada on the map of the world. It is, however, a slippery slope from here to the concept of Canadian society.

Feminists have disagreed profoundly about the nature of the Canadian state, and about just what might be expected from this socio-political set of relations in terms of remedy for past injustice and inequality. Despite these disagreements, feminists have continually pressured the state for change. In the early twentieth century, the women's movement campaigned for suffrage, rights to property and child custody, and access to politics, education, and professions. From the late 1960s feminists struggled for birth control, abortion, daycare, equity in employment and pay, and an end to violence against women and to discrimination on the basis of sexual desires and practices. Understanding these campaigns involves an appreciation of the various feminist theories of the state. Liberal feminists have held that the state is pluralist in nature, open to the lobbying of pressure groups, and thereby avoiding capture by any particular set of interests. If feminists mobilize sufficiently, laws and policies will be altered to reflect their interests. Although Marxist feminists have not rejected such tactics, they hold that, in a capitalist society, the state will promote primarily the interests of capital and those who own and control that capital. Socialist and radical feminists have argued that the state is patriarchal in conception and interests, formulating laws and policies that systematically privilege men and disadvantage women. Chapter 3 deals with these feminist theories of the state and the kinds of campaigns and issues that feminists have directed towards the state.

During the past two decades women from many different locations have emphasized that gender oppression intertwines with other forms of oppression in complicated and various ways, focusing in particular on the exclusions and brutalities wrought by racism, poverty, western dominance, and environmental degradation. Often the feminist label is not attached to political positions, cultural displays, protests, or demands—and sometimes the label is explicitly spurned. Yet we might ask: would the desired outcomes be articulated, let alone possible, without feminist assumptions about the value of women's lives? Chapter 4 continues the discussion about the Canadian state by documenting the challenges that have been offered to the very legitimacy of that state by Aboriginal peoples, the Québécois, and people of colour. In all of these locations, women have worked alongside men to further shared political goals. At the same time, they have organized independently to challenge their subordinate status within each of these political formations. The criterion for inclusion in this chapter is whether women seek to undo their historic and contemporary disadvantage in their own communities, even as they demand more autonomy and/or resources for those communities from the Canadian state. The struggles of women in all of these locations have challenged feminists to recognize racist, class, and national barriers to transforming the relations of domination and subordination between the sexes. There is, therefore, ongoing dialogue and debate among the various feminist challenges to the state.

Feminists from all over the political and social map have challenged the Canadian state, especially during the past 35 years. Feminist nationalists in Quebec want that province to separate from Canada; Aboriginal women are among the vocal proponents of self-determination for their peoples; Canadians and immigrants disadvantaged by racism argue that their children remain destined for second-class status; many people, poor for generations, have ceased to imagine a better life; and feminists have argued that the October 1929 decision of the Judicial Committee of the British Privy Council recognizing women as "persons" (thus overturning the decision of the Supreme Court of Canada) has never been delivered in law or in practice (Baines 1993, 253–58).[1]

In their efforts to transform the organization of social life in Canada, feminists have challenged the gendered division of labour, how women (and men) are represented or portrayed, and how women and men perceive themselves, their characteristics, abilities, and goals. These three aspects of life—activity, representation, and subjectivity—are densely interrelated, and they can only be untangled for analytical and political purposes. These themes—what we do, how we are portrayed, and how we experience ourselves—constitute the tapestry of daily life. They are discussed in chapters 5 and 6.

Chapter 5 discusses feminist challenges to the sexual division of labour in the paid labour force, in the family, and in the community. Feminists have insisted on women's right to access to all areas of paid and unpaid work. They have challenged prevailing definitions of what constitutes work and have revealed how work has been gendered, sexualized, racialized, and differently valued depending on the ascriptive characteristics of those doing the work. They have demonstrated the fundamental incompatibility between the current organization and practices of the workplace on the one hand, and the requirements of childbearing and the needs of children on the other. Feminists, among others, have also dwelt upon the contradictions between profit making and the imperatives for sustained life on the planet.

During the past two decades federal and provincial governments have lowered taxes and reduced social spending, thus vastly increasing the numbers of poor Canadians, especially women and children. Feminist gains in many areas have been notoriously easy to reverse. In particular, long-standing forms of discrimination against women raising children alone that had been widely discredited were rehabilitated during the 1990s in ways that ripped certain aspects of feminist thought out of context. Mothers on welfare were forced to take up waged labour even while the conventional nuclear family (read mom at home) was revalorized (Little 1998). Chapter 5 elaborates upon many of the issues raised by feminists, and explicates the relationship between various theoretical perspectives and the issues that are constructed and perceived as most salient.

In chapter 6, the focus shifts to issues of representation and subjectivity, and feminist challenges to the sexual objectification of women. We look at just what seemed to be at stake in the various issues around sexual objectification and the ensuing debates among feminists. By examining the perspectives on sexual objectification that have been articulated at various times by Aboriginal women, black women, women with disability, older women, and lesbians, the diverse positions within feminism come into bold relief.

The feminist interest in representation has been linked with concerns about how girls and women understand and feel about themselves, the kinds of work they can imagine doing, the kinds of partners and relationships they dream of having, and how they think about and live their sexuality. All these questions have been encapsulated in explorations of gendered socialization: how do we come to think of ourselves in profound ways as male or female, as lesbian, gay, bisexual, or heterosexual? Many young women and girls have invented new ways to rail against old prejudice. Analyses of these issues in chapter 6 are drawn primarily from feminist appropriations of psychoanalysis and poststructuralist understandings of gender and sexuality. In these theories we find provocative understandings of masculinity and femininity as constructions and performances that buttress not only misogyny but also homophobia, hostility to transgendering, and racism.

It is very difficult to write of many things all at once. As a result, we divide up the indivisible so that we may proceed in some sort of systematic fashion. It will be the reader's task to relate many of the different subjects in this book to each other. The concept of Canadian society disappears before our eyes as we focus upon the conflicting interests of Aboriginal and non-Aboriginal peoples, the English and the French, the rich and the poor, men and women, heterosexuals and gays and lesbians, the young and the old, the able-bodied and those with disability, and those who are advantaged and disadvantaged by racism. Yet I continue to use the words *Canadian society*, both as shorthand and as a sign of hope that by acknowledging and appreciating diversity, justice, and equality we might work towards such a reality. Feminists of many persuasions provoke ongoing challenges to oppressive and exploitative relations that exist within and beyond the geopolitical borders of Canada.

There is always a utopian aspect to these challenges: things could be better, much better. At the beginning of the twenty-first century women organize in virtually every country in the world and form international coalitions to resist the conditions that they find oppressive, to remove discriminatory practices that affect themselves and their daughters, and to fight economic and social injustice. Sometimes they define themselves as feminist, often with various hyphenated prefixes, sometimes they choose other labels, especially in countries where feminist activity may be actively repressed. All these movements reflect, correspond to, and resist the processes now commonly referred to as globalization. In the last chapter we examine some of the aspects of globalization that have intensified the hardships of women's lives: the intrusion of huge multi-national corporations, the resulting loss of land and other traditional means of support, and economic restructuring, as seen in the policies and practices of the World Bank and the International Monetary Fund.

Since the mid 1990s in Canada, as elsewhere, the right-wing agenda—whatever its motivations—is most assuredly making the rich richer, the middle class smaller, and the poor poorer and more abundant. Feminist theories and strategies make links between the macro-politics of the Canadian state and the gendered socialization of children, yet such thinking remains marginalized to dominant political rhetoric in Canada.

This book presents a feminist introduction to Canadian society. The presenting questions are drawn from feminist theories, broadly considered, the issues from women's movement activists in many spheres. My hope is that it will encourage readers who are introduced to this material for the first time to engage in their own lines of questioning, and those who have pondered many of these issues before to continue to ask feminist questions and seek feminist solutions to the problems that beset those who live in Canada and elsewhere.

NOTES

1.   We should note here that this case concluded that women should be treated as persons for the purposes of membership in the Senate. This case did not extend a *carte blanche* invitation to personhood. For a history of women's claim to legal personhood see Baines (1993), 246–58. Baines concludes her analysis with this statement: "Women are not yet perceived as persons, always and everywhere" (258).

chapter one

Feminist Theories

Theory is a word that sends most mortals rushing from the room, convinced that what is coming is too rarefied, too pretentious, too difficult, or completely irrelevant. But I want to argue three things: first, that theory is very much intertwined with how we make sense of the world in an ordinary, day-to-day way; second, that we can gain something from being more systematic and probing about this activity of making sense; and third, that feminists have made very good use, indeed, of this more systematic process.

In seeking to understand gender hierarchies and how they might be transformed, some writers have recently turned to various metaphors. A metaphor is a figure of speech that helps us get a grip on something that seems intangible by comparing it to something that we can picture. Judith Butler invoked the concept "performativity," likening social life to a play (1993). "All the world's a stage, And all the men and women merely players," Jaque proclaims in William Shakespeare's *As You Like It* (Act II, Scene 7). Butler is not suggesting that we can take our gender and sexual identities on and off with our clothes and new lines, as actors must do. But she does want to disturb the idea that "we are who we are——men or women, gay or straight."

When you came to university you may have found yourself behaving differently than you had in high school. In a new milieu it was easier to act in new ways—funnier, quieter, more gregarious—because unlike your old friends, your new acquaintances didn't assume they "knew" you. Once away from home, some find they behave differently; for example, some "discover" that they are attracted to those of the same sex, others finally feel free to act on their feelings. The idea of performativity loosens things up, allows us to question the idea of the "real me," allows us to see past stereotypes to the behaviours of those we observe and with whom we interact, and to imagine other possibilities. In Susan Foster's words "conceptualizing gender as performance" provides the opportunity to produce a "critical diagnosis of gender's influences and effects while holding out the possibility for social change" (1998, 1).

Foster argues that this critical project is well served by invoking the metaphor of choreography. Choreography focuses "on the unspoken, on the bodily gestures and movements, that along with speech, construct gender identity" (4). Readers who are dancers will appreciate her detailed analysis of the relationship between the choreographer who must work creatively within particular traditions and the dancer who translates "choreography into performance" yet also modifies it in various ways to "make it their own" (9).

Nature-lovers may find Susan Hekman's metaphor of the riverbed (borrowed from philosopher Ludwig Wittgenstein) helpful in contemplating the seemingly implacable nature of gender relations. The water may flow slowly or quickly but the riverbed changes ever so slowly, by human reckoning in any case. Hekman asks: what are the best strategies for changing the riverbed—that is the seemingly rock-solid (hierarchical) relationships between men and women (1999)? Abigail Bray and Claire Colebrook borrow the metaphor of thermodynamics from Gilles Deleuze to suggest that anorexia nervosa, for example, may have as many versions as there are those who display the symptoms, thus challenging those feminists who argue that there is a primary cause, rooted in oppressive cultural representations of women (1998, 63).

Trying to understand the nature of social life, and how to transform inequitable social relationships has, then, taken many forms. Feminists have produced an enormous, diverse, and eclectic range of interpretations in their attempts to explain how sexual hierarchies are created and sustained as well as to provide strategies for confronting these hierarchies. Taken together, these interpretations constitute an unprecedented historical challenge to the organization of social life and the categories through which that life previously has been apprehended. This challenge involves examining the ways in which sexual oppression informs and is informed by the many social practices through which people are privileged and disadvantaged, included and excluded, wield and submit to power. Feminist literature in its diversity, complexity, internal debates, and many languages defies summary. Yet all of it is provoked by unease with current social arrangements. My concern is that we not lose sight of its origins within feminist movements that seek to transform our relationships to each other on the intimate, local, and global levels. This chapter delineates the contours of contemporary feminist theories and their relationship to each other, and emphasizes their collective indebtedness to past and present feminist movements.

Let us begin by examining the proposition that we all use theory and, further, that our lives would be well nigh impossible to live if we did not. In making decisions, in our interactions with others, in carrying out our activities, we proceed on the basis of past experience and some form of conscious or unconscious speculation or prediction about the future. Through this process, we provide ourselves with explanations about why things turned out as they did, and whether and how future outcomes will be similar or different.

In such ways, we navigate our way through our relationships with parents, friends, children, teachers, store clerks, employers, employees, as well as through what we have come to think of as bureaucratic red tape: applications for university, jobs, and employment insurance, returns for income tax, and so on. We make decisions about whether to study or go to the movies; whether to start, continue, alter, or end relationships; whether to use contraception, terminate a pregnancy, or have a child; whether to cook a meal or eat out. We don't do all of this blindly, although we may often wonder why we did what we did. We know what will irritate our parents, and why; what will enrage our children, and what will give them some reason to believe they are understood. We have some understanding of why there are deadlines for university applications, and what kinds of marks or skills are needed for admission. When we approach the job market, we have some idea of what sort of work we will be offered. To make all these decisions, we have at our disposal diverse sets of experience, information, and interpretations ranging from ideas about why we behave as we do through to explanations about how goods, services, and power are distributed in our society.

Often, however, we feel perplexed. We wish we knew more so that we could feel more confident about our decisions. Often we may not comprehend how people behave or how "the system" works. In these situations we have choices: to allow the world to remain a mystery, to accept "common sense" understandings that are readily available in our own milieu, or to engage in a more conscious and coherent process of observing, researching, reading, thinking, discussing, and interpreting. If we choose this third way, we will encounter a body of literature—whether about the physical world, power and politics, human psychology, bureaucracy, law, ethics and morality, or sexuality—that others have produced. The answers we find will always be tentative, and we may have to choose between very different answers or interpretations. Sometimes controversy will have given way to consensus. For a very long time, people believed the world was flat; then some iconoclasts came along and made the perfectly ridiculous statement that the world was round. Imagine the surprise of those who once prosecuted these people as heretics if they were to find out that everyone, including present-day members of the same church that conducted the prosecutions, now believes that the earth is round.

Sometimes you may ask a question that no one seems to have asked before. And if there haven't been any questions, then there will not be any answers. You may be a pioneer. More likely, however, some people will have asked the questions before, but they may not be the ones who wrote the books; they may not be those who were in a position to decide that they were "good" questions. Further, those who are in a position to decide may have a good deal to gain if *nobody* asks those questions. They may even prosecute those who do as heretics, dissenters, or enemies of the state. The famous Norwegian playwright Henrik Ibsen wrote a play entitled *An Enemy of the People* (1882) about a doctor who worked in a small town known for its healing baths that brought visitors from everywhere. When Dr Stockmann discovered that the waters were contaminated, that "the whole Bath establishment is a whited poisoned sepulchre,...the gravest possible danger to the public health," he was condemned by the powerful as a traitor. But he first had to ask the question:

> Last year there were a number of curious cases of sickness among the visitors....[T]yphoid and gastric fever....It was thought at the time that the visitors had brought their infections with them. But afterwards...during the winter...I began to have other ideas. So I carried out a few tests on the water.... (Ibsen 1967, 43)

The same author wrote another play called *A Doll's House* (1879). At the end of that play, the heroine, Nora, thoroughly disillusioned with her husband, prepares to leave him and their two children. To her incredulous husband she declares: "I must try and educate myself—you are not the man to help me in that. I must do that for myself. And that is why I am going to leave you now" (1967, 64). Until then, conventional wisdom proclaimed that a woman who did such a thing was crazy, immoral, or both. Ibsen caused a scandal by making emotional, intellectual, and political sense out of Nora's decision.

As Gertrude Stein lay dying, she apparently sat up suddenly and asked "What is the answer?" When she received no answer, she rose one last time to ask, "What then is the question?" The key to viable and convincing answers is in the question. Although there is more to theory making than asking, "What is the question?" it is a reasonable place to begin. Karl Marx asked, What is the innermost secret of capitalism? If people get paid for what they *make,* where do capitalists get their profit for further investment? The innermost secret, according to Marx, was that people do not get paid for what they produce. That they do is an assumption; it seems to be true, but it is not true. They actually get paid for selling their ability to labour—Marx called it *labour power*—to someone who owns the factory or the mine—the *means of production*—for the going wage rate. Capitalists try to keep this wage as low as possible in order to maximize their profits. Over time, Marx argued, the wage cannot fall below *subsistence*—below what it takes to keep body and soul together—for working people as a whole, or workers would die and never reproduce a new generation. Workers do what they can, through collective action, to raise the wage above subsistence. But workers will be paid for their ability to labour, not for what they have actually produced: this is the form of exploitation that defines capitalist relations of production.

Unravelling this secret of capitalism formed an integral part of Marx's theoretical enterprise: his task was to understand how capitalism worked, what it was that brought workers together to resist exploitation, and how capitalism itself might be superseded by socialism. But the theory didn't just come out of his head. He studied history; he read what economists and philosophers had already written; he observed contemporary German, English, and French society; he participated in politics; he read newspapers. People have been arguing about the viability of different aspects of his observations and predictions—his theory—ever since. But many agree that, at the very least, his questions took us a giant step forward in understanding our economic system and capitalist society.

So theory writing (about human society) has been about constructing informed interpretations of what has been, of how we arrived where we are, of the meaning this has for different participants and then, on that basis, attempting to draw informed predictions about possible outcomes and their consequences. Theory writing can also be about trying to break with the past, to imagine new ways of living with each other (Ackelsberg 1997; Perkins 2002; Raddon 2002), as expressed in Michèle Barrett's book title—*Imagination in Theory* (1999). Like fiction and other forms of creative writing, writing theory, she posits, is about *how* we write, the art of persuading, revealing, imagining, about creating rhetorical strategies for casting doubt on accepted beliefs, and invoking alternative values, hopes, desires, emotions, ways of being. "Theories" about human life lurk within many forms of writing that have not been considered "theoreti-

as Barrett demonstrates through reading Virginia Woolf's novels for their subtle
'ions to question, for example, everyday understandings of madness and sanity
, 186–204).

ding the past whether through explicit theorizations of social life, novels, or histo-
never foretells the future. What actually happens—or does not happen—will
contingent, for it will depend on what people *choose* to do.

Sociologist Philip Abrams (1982, xiii) chose the expression "the paradox of human agency" to convey the idea that what people choose to do is never straightforward. We live in particular times and places and face varying sorts of constraint and possibility; even what we can imagine we would like to do is shaped by these circumstances. This may not seem like a contestable proposition. But this way of understanding the individual and society actually stands against the ideology of the rational, autonomous individual "man" that has dominated Western thought in the past two or three centuries. These dominant ideas had their origins in the Enlightenment and have had powerful adherents throughout this age of capitalism, never more so, perhaps, than in its present neo-liberal incarnation that seeks to privatize the public sector, reduce the scale and scope of government spending, and throw each of us on our own resources (Leys 1996, 18). Marx's challenge to this ideology is encapsulated in his famous passage, "Men make their own history, but they do not make it just as they please; they do not make it under circumstances chosen by themselves, but under circumstances directly encountered, given and transmitted from the past" (Marx 1969 [1869], 398). As Marx indicates, we are born into particular, if always shifting, sets of relationships, within families and households, communities and states. Such relationships confer obligation and responsibility and shape access or lack of access to everything from economic power and privilege to care and intimacy.

Feminists have had different ways of conveying the important idea that we are born into particular arrangements that shape all aspects of our lives. Indeed, the question of who and what constrains, oppresses, and subordinates women, and how, not only unites feminists but also divides them.

FEMINISTS AND THE DEBATE ABOUT HUMAN AGENCY

There are many proliferating and overlapping feminist perspectives (Shanley and Narayan 1997, xxi). My intention is not to contribute to the drawing of firm boundaries between them, boundaries that may only imitate conventional disciplinary boundaries and make it more difficult to ask questions about the origins and perpetuation of hierarchical relations between the sexes. Yet for students of feminist scholarship, it is necessary to know something about the history of these differences. The labels have been used a good deal and, even when labels are increasingly abandoned, it is important to know what is being abandoned and why.

Let us return to Marx's statement and see how feminists of differing persuasions—liberal feminists, socialist feminists, radical feminists, lesbian feminists, lesbian separatists, black feminists, and feminists of colour—would elaborate, modify, or overturn it. We also have to consider the ways in which feminists (who might also be in one or more of the above categories) have drawn on the insights of psychoanalysis, poststructuralism, and discourse analysis in considering this question of (wo)men making their own history but not under conditions chosen by themselves.

Liberal Feminism

Feminism's history is intertwined with the individualistic ideology of liberalism. When Mary Wollstonecraft (1759–97) wrote *A Vindication of the Rights of Woman* in 1792, she was in broad agreement with the liberal democratic slogan—Liberty, Equality,

Fraternity—of the French Revolution. She argued that women, like men, are rational beings with the potential to be fully responsible for their own lives. Although she wrote in scathing terms about men's treatment of women, and provided them with reasoned arguments to treat women as their equals, she also lambasted aristocratic and middle-class women for exchanging "health liberty and virtue" for food and clothing (147), that is for a life of dependence on fathers and husbands.

She urged women not to be taken in by chivalry. Women "constantly demand homage as women though experience should teach them that the men who pride themselves upon paying this arbitrary insolent respect to the sex, with the most scrupulous exactness, are most inclined to tyrannize over, and despise the very weakness they cherish" (146).

For her, and for the liberal feminists who came after her, including those of our own time, the circumstances that shaped women's lives were the laws and prejudices (shared by men and women) that excluded them from the public sphere and from the right to earn their own living on an equal footing with men. (See Box 1-1.)

BOX 1-1	**Mary Wollstonecraft: The Rights of Women and the Complications of Love**

"What can I say about love?" So begins Canadian author Helen Humphreys' recent novel, *The Lost Garden* (2002). Like the rest of us, poets and novelists try to answer the "unanswerable questions...most often," as one reviewer noted, adding that "wisely" Humphreys "does not make love an answer" (Solie 2002, 10, 15). Wollstonecraft had something to say about love, and she urged women not to make love an answer—certainly not *the* answer, even as she struggled to follow her own advice.

In *The Vindication* she warned women about the perils of letting love and sexual passion dominate their lives. She critiqued the great treatises on girls' education (especially Jean-Jacques Rousseau's *Sophie*) for their argument that "the whole tendency of female education ought to be directed towards making girls and women 'pleasing'" (1992 [1792], 110). Their words had borne fruit for, she observed, "[t]he civilized women of the present century, with a few exceptions, are only anxious to

inspire love, when they ought to cherish a nobler ambition, and by their abilities and virtues, inspire respect" (79).

She acknowledged that "[t]o speak disrespectfully of love [constituted] high treason against sentiment and fine feelings," and she assured her readers that she was not trying "to reason love out of the world" (110). But there were serious consequences for women who devoted themselves to loving and pleasing a man. "The woman who has only been taught to please," she observed, "will soon find that her charms are oblique sunbeams [without] much effect on her husband's heart when they are seen every day, when the summer is passed and gone" (110–1).

In *The Vindication* she addressed women as "rational creatures"—especially those of the middle class who were not ruined by (unearned) aristocratic wealth, or ground down by poverty. She exhorted those of her "own sex...to acquire strength, both of mind and body." She sought "to convince them that the soft phrases, susceptibility of the heart, delicacy of sentiment, and refinement of taste, are almost synonymous with epithets of weakness" (81–2).

Although most identified with liberal feminism and the public road to emancipation, her biographer Miriam Brody argues that Wollstonecraft's approach "considers all aspect of women's condition, economic, psychological, cultural as inter-related" (59). Certainly in her life pregnancy, childbirth, childcare, and the unequal investments of men and women in love, posed obstacles for attaining what she believed were women's best hopes: economic independence and the habit of thinking rationally (Brody 1992; Eisenstein 1981; Snitow 1990; Sydie 1991).

Wollstonecraft lived against the grain of her society, falling in love with the improbable Gilbert Imlay, bearing his child, and following him around Europe, baby and nursemaid in tow, long after he had lost interest in her. Her letters to him, in the words of Miriam Brody, tell a story of "painful, almost tragic incompatibility" (14). While she "had met the various crises in her struggle for economic independence with characteristic resilience and determination...Imlay's infidelity and all that it implied of her misplaced trust left her desperate." One night, after leaving instructions for the care of her daughter, Fanny, Mary found "a secluded spot along the Thames where, making sure her clothes were heavy with water...she leapt from a bridge." A passerby saved her by dragging her unconscious body from the river.

"Perhaps," Brody suggests, "the suicide attempt exhausted the worst of her despair...for she was able at long last to resolve to forget Gilbert Imlay and [begin] to make plans for her own and her daughter's future." She went on to establish a happy relationship with the political writer William Godwin. Both of them believed that the "marriage contract was an artificial bond which two virtuous individuals did not need," but they married while Wollstonecraft was expecting their child. She died delivering this baby, her second daughter.

Her death—from "one of the oldest scourges of women"—together with her life as lover and unmarried mother became news of the day. For years following her death, it was "not the argument of *The Vindication* which formed the basis of the controversy surrounding it, but the personal life of the author" (Brody 1992, 58). For over a century most feminists did not invoke her name, concerned that the association with her "scandalous" life might harm their cause.

Wollstonecraft's life and work continue to motivate important theoretical questions for feminism: Under what circumstances does love contribute to the subordination of women? What are the consequences of definitions of womanhood and femininity that stress the pleasing of others? Do love and rationality need to be counterposed?

During the twentieth century, feminist writers Simone de Beauvoir, Shulamith Firestone, and Jessica Benjamin, among others, have put their minds to these questions. De Beauvoir claimed to have had a mutually sustaining love relationship with Jean-Paul Sartre but her novels (1954) and her biographer paint a bleaker picture (Bair 1990). Like Wollstonecraft, Firestone warned of the oppressive nature of romantic love for women (1970). Benjamin draws on psychoanalysis to explain how love can become inscribed as (gendered) relations of domination and subordination (1988). Despite many changes since Wollstonecraft's time, women still seem to be expected to invest more in love (and marriage) than men.

During the next 200 years, with much ebb and flow, women struggled for the right to higher education, entrance into the professions, the right to own property and hold public office, and for suffrage, the right that came to symbolize full citizenship. For liberal feminists, the laws that decreed that women were lesser beings than men were a product of ignorance. The expectation was that as men and women educated themselves on this subject, these laws and the prejudices that underwrote them would gradually be replaced by extending equality of opportunity to women. As will become evident in this chapter, liberal feminism has been subjected to many criticisms. But several feminist theorists, notably Martha Nussbaum (2001), have recently reworked liberalism in their attempt to show that feminist goals can be accommodated within the paradigm.

Marxism and the Woman Question

The issue of economic independence figures prominently in Marx and his collaborator Friedrich Engels' theory on the subordination of women. Like other socialists, they conceptualized this as the "woman question." The problem was important, but clearly secondary to the central issue of social class.

Engels argued that our early ancestors lived in a state of primitive communism: everyone had to labour to survive and all that was available was shared. With the invention of cultivation and animal husbandry, people created the possibility of accumulating surplus. This development was of monumental importance in human history. It opened up the possibility of longer, more secure lives. But the underside was that this surplus could be controlled by some and used in the interests of the few against the many. The surplus would be claimed by the few as their private property. Some would labour so that others might prosper. Those men with a surplus wanted their own children to inherit the wealth they had amassed. But how would men know who were their own children? Only women have this assurance. The solution was to turn women themselves into private property. If a man owned a woman, she would labour for him, and she would be permitted to have sexual relations only with him. Thus the idea of *legitimacy* was born. Legitimacy means that a man's legal children are the biological children of his wife. They are assumed to be his biological children because he owns their mother.

In this interpretation, class society and male dominance enter onto the world stage together. For Engels these developments constituted the "world historic defeat of the female sex" (1948 [1884], 57). It followed, then, that with the abolition of private property (under communism), women would be emancipated. Under capitalism, Engels detected a first step towards women's emancipation, as economic desperation forced working-class women to become wage labourers, and hence propelled them into *de facto* equality with their husbands. Economically dependent bourgeois women, on the other hand, remained the property of their husbands. For Marxists, then, the circumstances that shape women's lives are the relations of private property and, in our era, capitalist relations. They are the same relations that shape the lives of men, albeit in different ways.

Historically, liberal feminism and the Marxist perspective on the woman question not only had different explanations for, and solutions to, the subordination of women but also occupied different, and sometimes hostile, political territory.[1] Marxists accused feminists of being "bourgeois," interested only in ensuring that women would share in the privilege (or destitution) of their class. Feminism was potentially dangerous to working-class struggles because sex-specific ideas about oppression would pit working men and women against each other and might create (false) grounds for class collaboration between upper- and working-class women. Feminists, for their part, often accused left-wing men and their political parties of being as uninterested, if not as hostile, as their class enemies to the rights of women.

Not until the late 1960s did another feminism develop that put liberal feminism and the Marxist perspective on the woman question into dialogue with each other and made fully visible the hitherto unexplored fragments in Wollstonecraft's writings. For this feminism launched a critique not only of the public world but also of the private world—the world of family, love, sexuality, pregnancy, and childcare. Furthermore, these feminists argued that the interconnections between public and private worlds were pivotal for understanding the sexual hierarchy. Women's liberation, therefore, depended upon the transformation of both worlds.

But this feminism soon divided along political and theoretical lines into those calling themselves *socialist feminists* and those calling themselves *radical feminists*. For the purpose of this discussion, the difference between them centred upon the question of explanation: who and what oppressed women and why.

Socialist Feminism

Socialist feminists argued, with Marxists, that the relations of capital, and therefore class relations, are pivotal for understanding women's oppression. But they differed from Marxists in insisting that the oppressive relations between the sexes are not simply derivative of class. They argued that the interconnections between sex oppression and class exploitation had to be addressed. In other words, for socialist feminists, it was no longer enough to talk only about the woman question, and they did not assume that the basis for women's oppression would disappear automatically with the overthrow of capitalism. These feminists focused upon the ways in which the labour done by women in the household—which they called *domestic labour*—helps to sustain the capitalist system. On both a daily and generational level, women contribute to the reproduction of labour power by having and rearing children and by looking after husbands between their wearying days (or nights) in mines and factories (Armstrong and Armstrong 1994; 2002; Hamilton 1978; Luxton 1980; Luxton and Corman 2001; Vosko 2002). As a result, both capitalists and individual men benefit from the unpaid and personal service of women in the home.

Socialist feminists analyzed the interconnections between the public sphere of capitalist and state relations and the private sphere of the family/household. Not only did the complex range of tasks done in the home prop up the capitalist edifice and allow the system to function at a fraction of its real cost, but in many ways the *appearance* of the distinction between private and public created and sustained the unequal relations between men and women throughout society. Challenging the dominant interpretation that men in the work force "bring home the bacon" and that nurturing women at home provide sustenance, socialist feminists uncovered the historically specific development of this relationship during the rise of industrial capitalism. Men of capital, together with middle-class philanthropists and social reformers and the better-paid male skilled workers, engaged in diverse, but mutually reinforcing, strategies to push women out of the labour force with promises of a family wage for male workers. For women, the results of this long historical manoeuvre were doubly exploitative and oppressive. First, denied access to higher education and the professions, women were also pushed out of the better-paying jobs; only the worst-paid and least-protected jobs remained open to them. Second, most men never earned a family wage but were nonetheless expected to support a wife and children. Women compensated for inadequate wages by increasing household labour, taking in boarders, laundry, and other people's children, and putting the needs of others before their own. Third, men earned the (main) wage, and this relative privilege reinforced their power over their wives and children. Men were exploited in the work force, and many responded by flexing their muscles, literally and figuratively, at home.

Socialist feminists pointed to the final irony that when men deserted their families, women, encouraged from birth to believe that men would care for them and their children, had to earn a living in the capitalist marketplace with "one hand tied behind their back" (Liddington and Norris 1978). Most women had no marketable skills, they were denied access to education and better-paying jobs, and they had no social supports for childcare. The family wage, portrayed as a form of security for working-class people, was unmasked as a fraud. Primarily, the *idea* of a family wage functioned as a rationale for excluding women from better-paying jobs and secure incomes, for paying them less, hiring them last, and firing them first (Connelly 1978). It served as a justification for women's sole responsibility for childcare and housework coupled with a lifetime of personal service to a particular man. No wonder that sociologists and socialist feminists Pat and Hugh Armstrong wanted to call *The Double Ghetto* (their path-breaking book on women's work in Canada) *Everyone Needs a Wife*.

During the 1970s, socialist feminism developed through heated debates and open dialogue with radical feminism, quickly taking up many of its insights while eschewing many of its explanations.

Radical Feminism

Radical feminists did not dispute the exploitative nature of capitalist relations, but they argued that, buried deeper in human society, both historically and psychically, are the relations of domination and subordination between the sexes. Writing at the dawn of the contemporary women's movement, Shulamith Firestone (1970) located these differences between men and women in nature's unequal allotment of reproductive tasks. Women bore, suckled, and raised children, while men had the time and opportunity to develop social institutions—including the family—through which they were able to appropriate power and control over women and children. The bottom line was that men oppress women. Overthrowing that oppression constituted the primary struggle in which feminists should engage.

Radical feminism was neither static nor monolithic. As its critique developed, many radical feminists began to locate men's power over women in their ability to control women sexually and to develop the institutions that ensure continuing control (Eisenstein 1984). Adrienne Rich (1980) coined the famous phrase *compulsory heterosexuality* to encapsulate the social and cultural imperatives that close off all sexual options for women except monogamous heterosexual permanent coupling, usually called marriage. In a world of unequal power relations between men and women, compulsory heterosexuality ensures not only women's sexual dependence upon men but also their economic, social, and psychological dependence. From this perspective—sometimes called *lesbian feminism*, though it was by no means confined to lesbians—women's lives in patriarchal society are shaped by the myriad legal institutions and cultural messages that enjoin women (from the time they are young girls) to look to men for sexual satisfaction, personal validation, and life-long companionship, and to accept their subordination to men in general and their husbands in particular as part of the bargain (Martindale 1995; see also *Resources for Feminist Research* 1990). From this critical position, some lesbian feminists took the short but dramatic step to a lesbian separatist position that women should no longer try to change the whole society but rather find ways to live apart from men and build a society alone (Rudy 2001).

More generally, early radical feminism was eclipsed by what has been called *cultural feminism*—overlapping with, but not confined by, a separatist perspective (Echols 1989). Women should build their own institutions from health clinics and women's shelters to small businesses, art galleries, publishing houses, and magazines. The rationale for these developments varies widely: for some it is a way of building a permanent women's world; for others it is a refuge from the pain of day-to-day struggle with men; for still others such autonomous organizing is intended to build a power base from which the whole society could be transformed (Rudy 2001).

What is key for the discussion on human agency is that radical, lesbian, and cultural feminists argue that women are born into arrangements that force them to live their lives in subservience to men. These feminists might alter Marx's statement to something like "*Men make their own history; women have no history of their own.*" Socialist feminists agree that most men of all social classes have the opportunity in both their intimate and work lives to dominate and oppress women. Yet they also argue that men's and women's lives are shaped by the relations of capital, which privilege a few at the expense of the many.

Anti-racist Feminisms

For over a century feminists argued that for women sex (and class, for socialist feminists) constituted the most important and sustaining form of oppression and exploitation. Within dominant feminist discourses this became self-evident, and much effort went into charting the long and varied history of patriarchal relationships.

From the 1980s women of colour and Aboriginal women began publicly challenging the universalism inherent in liberal, radical, and socialist feminism, all of which ignored— or at best sidelined—the histories of colonialism and imperialism, the legacies of slavery and genocide, and the systemic racism that produced lives of brutality and exclusion for some, and lives of unearned and unrecognized privilege for others (Brand 1984; Dua 1999; Carty 1999; Tynes 1987; 1990). By claiming to speak for all women, white feminists denied their social and economic advantages, perpetuated racism in their own theories, failed to make their movements relevant to women of colour, and excluded the struggles against racism from the histories of feminism.

These challenges led in different directions. Some feminists began to intertwine an analysis of racism with the Marxist focus on class and the radical feminist focus on the sexual hierarchy. Such a perspective is prominently announced in the titles of books and courses—"Race, Class and Gender" (Brand 1984; Vorst 1989; Creese and Stasiulis 1996), and this formulation has motivated a good deal of important scholarship and political campaigns. The race-class-gender list, however, presupposes the possibility of coherent theoretical perspectives that can grapple with the interconnections between these three dimensions of inequality, and this is no easy matter. Michèle Barrett has argued that "existing theories of social structure, already taxed by attempting to think about the inter-relations of class and gender, have been quite unable to integrate a third axis of systemic inequality into their conceptual maps" (1988, xii).

Going further, Vijay Agnew has declared "that the mantra of 'race, class and gender' [had been] repeated so routinely that all its force as a critique of mainstream feminism had been lost" (1996, 3). The point is that mainstream feminism can hardly be left intact once interrogated for racialist assumptions. For the assumption of universalism—that a sexual hierarchy constitutes the most basic and important form of inequality for all women—is revealed as a racist assumption for writing so many women and their experiences out of feminist scripts while remaining silent on the privileges of whiteness.

Feminists from across the spectrum have responded to anti-racist feminisms and redrawn their theoretical perspectives and political agendas. For example, by looking at the lives of men and women in particular historical and social contexts, many feminists have abandoned the question of whether class, race, or sex is the more salient relation for analysis in favour of understanding the historical specificity of complex relations of power (Adamson, Briskin, and McPhail 1988; Dua 1999). The "circumstances directly encountered, given and transmitted from the past" must include those relations that are the living legacy of colonialism, imperialism, and slavery. Furthermore, they have argued—in opposition to the radical feminist perspective on sexual hierarchy—that, while these relations of racism shape the lives of men and women differently, they do not necessarily privilege men over women (Feminist Review; hooks 1988; Lorde 1984; Silvera 1986; Williams 1991). Disavowing universalistic assumptions in favour of historically specific interpretations opens space for women in different social locations to address the most pertinent forms of oppression in their lives. Many African Canadian and Aboriginal women insist that racism has been the force that most constrains and brutalizes their lives. Not surprisingly then, historically they struggled against racist practices while struggles for gender equality went "glaringly missing" (Dua 1999, 12). Feminist thought did not speak to their lives and its program for equality was (silently) predicated on the perpetuation of racialized privilege for white women.

Women in Canada are now studying the lives of their forebears from the African diaspora and Asia "to provide some answers to questions of how they experienced oppression and exploitation [and] what priority they gave to different struggles at different periods of time" (Agnew 1996, 27). The emergence of anti-racist feminists push us, in Enakshi Dua's words, "to rethink Canadian society from the standpoint of women who have been racialized as dangerous, as alien, as hyphenated Canadians" (1999, 28).

Many feminists now agree that the "circumstances directly encountered, given and transmitted from the past" include those racialized relations that are the living legacy of colonialism, imperialism, and slavery (Hooks 1988; Lorde 1984; Silvera 1986; Williams 1991; Agnew 1996; Carty 1999; Dua 1999). This challenge initially seemed to create irreconcilable differences among feminists. Michèle Barrett, for example, argued that the proposition that racism must have equal billing with class and sex dislodged the claim of socialist feminists to have a coherent theory of inequality. "Existing theories of social structure, already taxed by attempting to think about the inter-relations of class and gender, have been quite unable to integrate a third axis of systemic inequality into their conceptual maps" (1988, xii).

Feminism and Psychoanalysis

Some feminists have turned to psychoanalytic theories to explain how resolutely we are born into particular arrangements (Mitchell 1974; Benjamin 1988, 1994; Chodorow 1978, 1989, 1999; Barrett 1992; Gardiner 1992; Hamilton 1997). Starting from Freud's assertion that "women are made, not born," the focus is upon how infants become gendered, how their sexual preference is shaped, and how they take their place within the hierarchical gendered order. What is particularly pertinent here is how we come to feel ourselves to be men or women as an intrinsic part of our being. This means that we are not just forced to be dominant or submissive, but that we are complicit in our subordination; we collaborate because it feels more comfortable than it would to resist. To put it more strongly, women who resist feel anxiety and therefore guilt, and women who resist make men feel anxious about their masculinity (Benjamin 1988).

Freud's emphasis was upon the key role played by the Oedipus complex in the making of male identity. Little boys take their mothers (because they are the primary caregivers) as their first love object. When they realize unconsciously that these feelings bring them into potential conflict with their fathers, they experience great anxiety—castration anxiety—that their stronger and more powerful fathers will do them some injury for daring to compete with them. In the typical Freudian formulation, the small boy gives up his love for his mother, incorporates his father's standards within himself (the superego), and is bought off, if you like, by the promise of a woman of his own when he grows up. Freud (1965) was much less sure about what happened to the girl child during this period but, nonetheless, he came to believe that little girls also have their first love affair with their mother. They soon realize, however, that they cannot possess the mother because they lack the necessary organ, the penis. Hence Freud's famous, even notorious, insistence that women's identity is shaped profoundly by penis envy.

Feminists working with the insights of psychoanalysis have not simply accepted Freud's formulations. Rather, they have situated them within a societal context that announces to girl and boy children alike that one needs a penis to have power in a patriarchal world. They argue that all children desire everything—penis, breasts, to have a baby (a wish often expressed by little boys as well as girls). Only in a patriarchal world will the desire for a penis become overvalued, and the desire for breasts and pregnancy become undervalued (Hamilton 1986; 1996; Horowitz 1977). Feminists have also reworked psychoanalysis to show that other forms of social inequality—especially class and racialized hierarchies—also become internalized and are therefore reproduced generationally (Abel 1990; Spiller 1987; Hamilton 1997).

Some feminists, following the work of French psychoanalyst Jacques Lacan, have located the formation of masculine and feminine identities not in the process of bodily maturation and Oedipal complexes, but in the child's introduction to what Lacan called a *Symbolic Order* (Mitchell 1974) "which designates the totality of signs, roles, norms and rituals of that society" (Hird 2002, 38). This symbolic order includes language—for words are the symbols through which we name everything around us, and are perhaps the most important way in which we communicate with others. What conveys power in this symbolic order is not the penis as such but rather its symbol, the phallus. For the boy child the phallus represents the power that he comes to realize will accrue to him because he is male; the girl child's identity is designated by the boy child (and by her) by what she "lacks." In the Lacanian perspective, boys' "identification with their fathers means a complete internalization of the Symbolic Order" while girls are *"excluded...*relegated to the margins" (Hird 2002, 39).

Several feminist theorists have offered sustained critiques of what they call the phallocentricism of the Lacanian system. French feminist Luce Irigaray re-plots the entry of the girl child into social life by placing her bodily organs at the centre of her story and female sexuality as there for itself, rather than as derivative from the male body. In this version the girl does not "lack" anything: her challenge—which is monumental according to Irigaray—is to find a way to express herself in a patriarchal society (1985a; 1985b). Judith Butler offers a more sweeping challenge to the Lacanian system in an analysis that she calls "The Lesbian Phallus." Here she demonstrates, from within psychoanalytic theory itself, that many different parts of the body can become the riveting focus of sexual pleasure (1993).

Although prefeminist psychoanalytic theories insist correctly that gender is made not born, they tend, nonetheless, to "invoke a language of binaries to explain child development" (Hird 2002, 39). That is, once gender is established, and these theories portray this as a necessary and normal accomplishment, masculinity and femininity become givens, and patriarchal power appears virtually unchallengeable.

But these binaries—men and women (as well as others like gay and straight)—that have been seen as so basic are not standing up well. They have been challenged within social movements, and within the daily lives of many people who have developed new words and concepts to describe themselves: transgender, transsexual—sometimes just "trans" (Hausman 2001, 448; Devor 1997; MacDonald 1998, 5). Some of these challenges appear to re-inscribe sex categories as a kind of ontological truth (what I "really" am). Yet the traffic between male and female not only shakes up the categories but also some of these challenges provoke the question, in Eleanor MacDonald's words, "of how those categories are established [and] maintained [and how] the boundaries of what is normal is 'policed'" (1998, 9). In subsequent chapters we turn to these dramatic challenges to binary assumptions, but here we focus on the central theoretical challenges poststructuralist theories pose to binary thinking.

Poststructuralism is indebted, in part, to theories about discourse and about how language works. We tend to think that what we say conveys something that is already there, in our mind, awaiting verbalization. When teachers tell their students: "don't worry about how you say something, just get your ideas down on paper" they contribute to this belief. Our common sense notions tend to hold that language is simply a tool for expressing an underlying reality or fully developed thought. But, as Susan Heald puts it, "[P]oststructuralism begins from the perspective that it is language which makes meaning possible, that words do not name pre-existing differences but inform us about what differences are visible and matter in any given situation" (1997, 32).

We need to notice, however, that words do not simply describe or identify. Words make distinctions and create oppositions. They tell us what is encompassed in a symbol and, by implication, what is not. Think of the words *hot* and *cold*. These words structure how we describe everything from soup to sex. Yet, as we know, temperature comes on a continuum, and hot and cold are always relative. Hot and cold, when applied to sexual activity, still carry with them the connotations of lust and evil that have so informed Western civilization and the presumed identities of men and women. Medieval Catholic writers depicted women as full of lust, waiting to tempt unsuspecting men into a life of sin. Later, Protestant writers developed a language about women that described them as asexual; it was men who had to control their own lust (Hamilton 1978). Opposing concepts like hot and cold, rational and irrational (emotional), or aggressive and passive serve to distinguish men from women by depicting each sex as either one way *or* the other, and ignoring all the points on the continuum that are in between. In this way "we can only know what 'man' is through its opposition, 'woman.' The female is everything that is absent from the male and vice versa" (Hird 2002, 23).

Language together with gestures and all the other symbols that convey meaning make up fields of thought that are called discourses. Any discourse makes some thought possible and others less possible or impossible. Contemporary feminists have drawn heavily on the work of Michel Foucault who showed through several historically engaged studies how discourses "bring the true into existence" (Barrett 1991; Butler 1993; Westlund 1999). Their analyses reveal that discourses are not only thoroughly informed by prevailing power relations—of class, race, sex, age, and sexuality, among others—but also by a common-sense rationale for accepting those power relations as given, as the only way things could be (Belsey 1980).

Prevailing discourses also provide the possibilities and constraints for constructing our own identities, identities that are not fixed—as in the expression "the real me"—but rather are fragmented, changing, and contradictory. Freud argued that our psyches are a kind of lifelong battleground among the id, ego, and superego—or, put differently, among desire, possibility, and conscience. More recent theories of discourse accept Freud's idea of the fragmented self. But they shift the ground for explanation away from the body as such to the way that the body—including need and desire—is constituted by the discourse, again as a lifelong, fragmented, contradictory, illusory process. Why illusory? Because discourse can never capture "reality." This is an impossible task for two related reasons. First, the terms of a discourse are always time-bound, space-bound, culture-bound, bound by the multiplicities of power relations that inform daily life. Second, there is no "pure" reality outside of what is represented in discourse. There is no "something" outside of that which is already interpreted, except that which is to be interpreted in some future moment. As one of my students wrote in her honours thesis on "femininity" and "feminism," beauty magazines suggest that "femininity is natural but in constant need of improvement and intervention" (Wakelin 2003, 38). In this sense, discourse does not represent reality; it shapes and creates that-which-is-believed-to-be-reality.

Using this kind of analysis, feminists have argued that identities are not fixed, but rather are continually constructed in particular times and places. They are not unified, but rather are fragmented: in some circumstances, we feel ourselves to be strong and powerful, in others weak and fragile, in others perhaps creative, stupid, lackadaisical, determined—the list is yours to make and remake. If this is so, the argument goes, how can we then talk about women and men as if these categories mean something that we can all agree upon? Our language helps create the sense that our identities are not only fixed, but gender-determined. When feminists hold this language up for scrutiny, they open the space for consideration of identities that are not bound by biological sex, race, age, sexuality, ethnicity, or any other category that we use to fix and freeze identities.

If we say that men are aggressive, we are comparing them directly and indirectly to those—women—who are not. In like manner, if men are rational, women are irrational; if men independent, women are dependent. The point is not that men and women "really" are this way, although in particular times and places they may behave so or they may be believed to be so. Let us reiterate that the discourse does not convey "reality"; rather it constitutes what appears to be reality. Furthermore, women who are not perceived to be passive and emotional may be defined as "not real women," and men who are not perceived to be aggressive may be called effeminate. In such ways, the discourse permits acknowledgment that men and women do not always conform to these oppositions. But the point is that this acknowledgment is made only in the terms of the discourse itself: the categories are retained, but the individual people are labelled as deviants. In this sense, we can speak of discourses as "closed systems"; they make thought that is not consonant with the prevailing discourses difficult.

In her pathbreaking book *The Gender of Breadwinners*, Joy Parr explained why feminists need poststructuralist analysis. The task, she wrote, is to

> unmake the chain of binary oppositions—masculine/feminine, market/non-market, public/private, waged/non-waged—and rethink the categoricalism that cantonizes gender, class, race, ethnicity and nationality, so as to see past the conceptual signage, which has illuminated the previously invisible but now threatens to obstruct our view of the living space beyond. (1990, 8)

Her argument here is two-pronged. She acknowledges that it was necessary for feminists to use the category of woman in order to "illuminate the previously invisible." Women had been invisible, present only in what was left unexamined, unexplored, unstated. But her main point is that this process of making visible must "see past the conceptual signage." We must not simply recapitulate the pattern of androcentric perspectives and continue to use the categories men and women as though they really described the world.

For by doing this, we fall into three errors. First, we perpetuate the categories of the discourse that once left women invisible. We refer to women and men as if we knew what they were, and we perpetuate the oppositional character of those identities. Women still are defined by what men are not, even though we may now place more value on what-men-are-not. Second, we assume that when we use the word woman we are referring to all women; we collapse the differences among women that accrue from class, racism, heterosexism, imperialism, even the idiosyncrasies of taste and talent. In this way, the theoretical challenges to feminism from women of colour, disabled women, lesbians, bisexuals, and older women converged with those of poststructuralism. The command is "do not tell me what I am."

Third, the male/female binary makes the assumption that biologically there really are only two sexes despite the evidence that intersexuals may account for as many as 4 percent of all births (Anderson 1996, 334; Fausto Sterling 1993). Medical practitioners in North America treat children born with ambiguous genitalia "in such a way that they conform as soon as possible to the two-sex model of sexual dimorphism in order to relieve the psychological trauma and suffering" (Anderson 1996, 345) that is believed to accompany this condition. But this response also stems from the strong cultural belief that "all bodies should conform to the binary classification of male/female" (346). If you read carefully you can see that this is a circular argument: the belief in *social* difference drives the impetus to ensure that all of us are male *or* female. Yet if you ask—why is there a social difference between men and women?—the answer will be: biology. Poststructuralism helps analyze how the categories of male and female are kept afloat in the face of medical and historical evidence that reveals a much more complicated state of affairs (MacDonald 1998). (See Box 1-2.)

Let us return then to the question of how feminist poststructuralists might respond to the issue of human agency, and in particular to Marx's statement that we make our history "under circumstances directly encountered, given and transmitted from the past." The dif-

---

BOX 1-2	Sex, Gender, and Transgender

The term "transgender" has only very recently come into popular and political use, and its definition is critical to the politics that it engenders. The term, as I use it, includes all those people whose internally felt sense of core gender identity does not correspond to their assigned sex at birth or in which they were raised. This includes people who identify with the gender other than that assigned at birth as well as those who do not identify with any gender at all. It includes those who present themselves in their originally assigned sex, as well as those who present themselves in the sex which coheres with their actual identity (and therefore may include non- and pre- and post-operative transsexual people), and those who move back and forth between self-presentation as women and men. It also includes those whose gender presentation is ambiguous in ways which don't permit them to present as either gendered male or female. In this usage, the term does not include those who are both physically and emotionally comfortable in their assigned sex and gender, even while they are challenging the social meanings that have been traditionally assigned to that sex and gender. What is radical, then, to the definition of "transgender" is its origin in a problem, a disjunction between one's feelings of who one is or is not, and how one is (or has once been) perceived, recognized, and understood by others.

Gender and sex are both complex terms, whose complexity is not acknowledged in their daily usage. Sex includes, at a minimum, chromosomal sex, gonadal sex, hormonal sex, internal reproductive organs, external genitals, assigned sex, and gender role.... Much scientific evidence not only points to the non-congruence of all these variables in all cases, but also to their non-binary nature. Despite this, it is customary to presume the presence of two and only two fully congruent and "opposite" sexes, male and female. Moreover, external genitalia remain the primary factor in attributing sex.

Gender, in turn, is expected to cohere unproblematically with sex. But gender too involves a rich complex of variables, including gender assignment (which generally takes place at birth, after which it is considered immutable); roles (specific social activities which are assigned masculine and feminine status); identity (one's internally felt or experienced sense of being either male or female); status (social rank which is accorded to males and females or those performing masculine or feminine roles); relations (socially appropriate behaviours evinced by males or females in relation to other males and females); attribution (perception of others of one's sex that takes place in all social interaction); behaviour (use of the gestures, mannerisms, language, clothing, comportment considered appropriate to one's biological sex); and biology (genetic or sexual-physical predeterminants of any of the above).

What transgender identity is about is identity as the incoherence of these elements, as the felt incoherence of self and body; it is identity as non-identity of the self, according to one of the principal means by which the coherence of the self is supposed to be unconsciously achieved. For some transgendered people, the experience of a non-coherence of body and self is a permanent condition; for others, this coherence is achieved as a conscious, very often medicalized process.

Source: Eleanor MacDonald, "Critical Identities: Rethinking Feminism Through Transgender Politics." *Atlantis* 23(1) 5–6. www.msvu.ca/atlantis.

ference from Marx could be located in the definition poststructuralists might give to "circumstances": they want to look at the process through which the categories of male/female, black/white, work/home, public/private are constituted in time and place, and how those categories, as they are defined at any particular time, contribute to the range of possibility and constraint. Furthermore, unlike Marx and most feminists before them, they argue that the ways in which male and female are defined are also implicated in all other categorization, whether of class, race, or sexual preference. How, for example, has "working class" as a category in the language informed shifting definitions of masculinity and, through inclusion and exclusion, shifting definitions of femininity? At the same time, how do notions of class infuse gender definitions?

Language appears innocent, in that it appears simply as an instrument through which our ideas can be expressed. Let us take a familiar example to see how language does not express our pre-existing thought, but actually shapes that thought. The term *working mother* has come into the language in the last 20 years with the great influx into the formal waged economy of women who have children. Embedded in the phrase, implicitly, are a whole host of shifting, value-laden, gendered, and classed characters. Counterposed to working mother are *women who don't work* (and who "just" keep house and look after children) and the victims of working mothers, *neglected children* (those whose mothers do not "just" look after them). Implicit in the phrase working mothers is a cast of male characters. Whoever heard of a *working father*, or children who were neglected because their father worked? Working mother can also designate those women who take jobs away from men, therefore contributing to the category *unemployed men*—fathers who don't work and therefore are, by definition, *bad fathers*. Furthermore, working mother is more likely to be used with reference to women who do certain kinds of *class-related* occupations that have relatively low monetary rewards and little status. Women who work in other sorts of class-related occupations may be defined as *professionals* rather than working mothers. Here we see the operation of a kind of implicit override clause: sometimes gender terms take precedence, other times class terms, or racist terms, or terms referring to women's sexual lives (see chapter 5, Box 5-1).

Consider also the ways in which social movement activists and cultural radicals take words that have been used to humiliate, ridicule, or authorize discrimination, and fashion them for their own use—as displays of irony, resistance, even badges of honour. So successfully did gays and lesbians redefine the word "queer" that "queer theory" now stands for sophisticated approaches to sexuality and identity and lends its name to conferences, academic journals, and courses. (See chapter 6, pages 168–170.)

In the late 1980s I discovered that high school girls used the word slut as a derogatory word to describe girls outside their own circle (and one could easily fall out) who were believed to have any sexual experience (Currie 1999, 234–36). In my introductory course in sociology I asked if there was a "boy" version of slut—or whether the double standard still prevailed. A male student brought the house down with the words "male whore" as an equivalent. Everyone got it: he needed to invoke a pejorative label for a woman to come up with a phrase suitable for a male. Equally interesting as a form of resistance is how "seemingly outrageous...unruly and ironic play with and on, female sexuality via various verbal...twists on words like 'slut,' 'bitch,' 'chick,' and 'whore' have now become staples of third wave feminists" (Diner 2001, 76). They circulate their ideas in small noncommercial magazines called zines, on Web pages, in feminist anthologies and among themselves (Ferris 2001; Bell 2001). Even the word "girls" changed spelling and took on new meaning in the movement "Riot Grrrls" comprising "young female punks who were fed up with the overwhelming maleness of punk rock [and] with sexism in general" (Jacques 2001, 64; Brasile 2001). Words, as you can see, do not just say what they appear to say; they carry and create shifting identities, possibilities, and constraints.

Feminist Theories and Social Change

Feminist theories about human society are also, explicitly or implicitly, theories about the possibilities for social transformation and, in particular, for emancipation for the subordinated, oppressed, exploited, and excluded. Indeed, these theories play a role in producing or complicating their own predictions about the future. This is because theories that present ideas confirming peoples' sense of grievance also help to legitimate their resistance. For example, Marx's theories provided people throughout the world with an ideological legitimation to engage in revolution. Catholics in Latin America intertwined their religious beliefs with an understanding of Marxism to argue that the church should be on the side of the oppressed in this life as opposed to simply promising them an eternal reward after a life of suffering—"the preferential option of the poor" (Baum 1986). This complex set of beliefs, called *liberation theology*, contributed to widespread forms of social protest as a new generation of church workers challenged the church's age-old admonition that entrance into heaven depended upon acceptance of the hierarchy of this world. While few theories—perhaps none—have unsettled the powerful as much as Marxism, feminism arguably is running a close second. As women the world over increasingly question their subordination, victimization, and exclusion, they appropriate, revise, and develop theoretical perspectives to legitimate their struggles.

Social theories, then, address the question of how things change. Included in such theories is consideration of the role of conscious human intervention—*agency*—in bringing about social change. Marxist theory argues that the working class has the potential to become a conscious agent of liberation. The initial site for the development of a shared consciousness of exploitation is the point of production—that is, the workplace. But socialist feminists have argued that women's collective and specific oppression is located in the private sphere and in the interrelationship between private and public. This suggests that Marxism, left to its own devices, does not provide sufficient legitimation, let alone an adequate strategy, for the "rising of the women" (Tax 1980). Socialist feminists insist that women organize around their own interests in the workplace and that their demands address their interests as mothers and wives as well as their interests as waged workers.

These considerations involve a critique not only of relations between workers and employers but also of the relations between men and women in both public and intimate spaces.

Some radical feminist theorists draw such an unyielding account of women's subordination and victimization that they have difficulty explaining how women ever came to resist, indeed how the women's movement itself could ever have mobilized. Where was the space for the development of rebellious ideas, let alone the possibility for acting upon them? In a similar way, those feminists who have drawn upon, elaborated, and critiqued Lacan's idea of the child's linguistic entrance into the symbolic order seem, at times, to create a closed system, impervious to change. Luce Irigaray has argued that women are excluded from the discourse of the symbolic order. If we are to glimpse what women think or feel, we must attend to the silences in their discourse, to the ways in which they may parody what men say. As a theorist, Irigaray repeats what male theorists have written, playing on their words to make her subtle point. From this perspective, we may have access to what women imagine, but even these triumphs of imagination are, necessarily, entangled within masculine discourse (Berg 1991). Does such a perspective leave a space for women's resistance?

Some other feminists have also accused feminist poststructuralists of pulling the rug out from under the women's movement (Brodribb 1992; Hartsock 1990; Modleski 1991). From her studies of Islamic fundamentalism, Haideh Moghissi argues persuasively that if we jettison gender-based politics and feminism, "we will end up excluding women of developing societies from the movement's emancipatory goals and ideas," thereby producing "a new form of ethnocentrism" (1999, 94). If identities are fractured, if the categories women and men must be deconstructed rather than accepted as given, what are the grounds for a feminist movement? If people are going to mobilize politically, they have to mobilize around something. In the women's movement the mobilization has been—it sounds self-evident to say it—around and about and for women. What happens when the rallying cries about women's oppression, their common interests and needs, indeed their victimization, are invalidated?

Although recent theoretical developments informed by poststructuralism challenge the concept of identity, and therefore of woman, in ways that appear, to some, to shake the foundations of the women's movement, the questions about what a woman is inform older perspectives as well. The category woman—what she is and what she should do—lies at the heart of most feminist analysis, albeit in different ways (Marshall 2000, 68). Liberal feminists, dating back to the eighteenth century, argued that if women appeared less rational, less interested in the world, less given to philosophical thought and political activity, the explanation resided in the ways in which women were denied the opportunity for education. Women would be as rational as some men (and as irrational as some others) if they were treated similarly in social terms. Genetic makeup, biology, or reproductive capacities accounted for the essence of woman no more than for the essence of man. In the terms of the times, therefore, Mary Wollstonecraft challenged the category of woman and, also, although less systematically, that of man. Men, Wollstonecraft lamented, were disappointing in their inattention to love and emotional life. Contemporary liberal feminists argue that there are no tasks in the public sphere—including armed combat roles in the military—for which women are unsuitable. At the same time, they have argued for parental leave for fathers after birth, adoption, and in the case of children's illness. To the extent that we are defined by what we do, and what we have the capacity to do, liberal feminists have challenged dominant notions about women and men. Far from being discrete categories, women and men are more likely to overlap in their motivations, goals, and talents.

Socialist feminists go further than liberal feminists in challenging the concept of woman as a universal category. Following Marx, they argue that the consciousness of human beings reflects the activities in which they engage and the accompanying relationships they create. Women in different historical periods and different social classes are not only different from each other, but in some respects share more with the men of their time and station than they do with other women. Furthermore, by analyzing the interconnections between the private and public sphere, revealing and challenging the attempts to relegate women to the first, insisting that the tasks done in the household constituted "more than a labour of love," and renaming that activity domestic labour or work, socialist feminists challenged the dominant idea that held that male and female nature and identities were discrete.

Early radical feminists like Shulamith Firestone argued that the differences between men and women resided only in their different roles in reproduction. While these differences had been crucial in creating social inequality, increasing control over pregnancy and birth as well as the promise of reproductive technology could (and should) eliminate the social consequences of these differences. The categories of woman and man would cease to matter after the socialist feminist revolution. Some later radical feminists reclaim the category woman, suggesting that it possesses certain qualities and attributes that distinguish it in important and irreconcilable ways from the category man. At the same time, many radical feminist analyses increasingly address the question of diversity among women, diversity resulting from class, racism, age, ethnicity, religious conviction, and sexuality.

As we have seen, some of the most trenchant criticisms of the assumption that there is a category called woman that may be used in theoretical discussions and political mobilization come from women of colour in the first world and women in non-Western societies. Their analyses expose the chasms between dominant ideologies about "woman" and the lives that women lead, the assumptions of white feminists about female exploitation and oppression, and the centrality of racism, imperialism, and cultural specificity in structuring people's lives in ways that privilege them if they are "white" and disadvantage them if they are not.

Paradoxically—paralleling the air-tight categories of man and woman created by some radical feminists—some of these writers produce discrete racialized identities of their own: categories of white and black, women of colour and white women. The title *Black Feminist Thought* implies another category, white feminist thought (Collins 1990). But most of these writers have an explicit goal: to challenge racism and the ways in which racism creates hierarchical categories of white and black. In their challenges to white feminists to confront their own racism, they insist that identities based on racial difference are politically and socially created. Race, as Rhada Jhappan insists, "is one of the central organizing principles of the modern world," but this does not mean that human beings should be essentialized as black or white, and indeed most of the efforts to do this have come from white supremacists. Instead Jhappan forwards the concept "contextual essentialism" because this would permit "us to stress one or several aspects of our identities according to the axis of oppression" in any particular circumstances (1996, 52–53).

Seen in this light, the feminist poststructuralist assault on the concept of fixed identity of any sort—woman/man, white/black, straight/gay—does not go against the grain of most previous feminist analysis. In her history of the concept "gender," Barbara Marshall concludes that "to simultaneously recognize the fiction of gender while treating it as concrete...is what historically feminism has always been about." In this usage "gender" refers to "relational and thoroughly social processes," which means that it is "constituted differently across historical and political contexts" (2000, 161).

When Denise Riley (1987) writes that there are times when we need to mobilize "as if" there were women, she puts into words an implicit assumption underlying much previous feminist analysis and action: women should not be defined by their biology; their life chances should not be defined by their relationships to men; the social constraints that have been legitimated by biological difference from men—whether women's size and physical strength or their role in reproduction—must be challenged.

Perhaps the differences between poststructuralists and other feminists over the concept of identity have been overdrawn. Yet that is not the whole story. Poststructuralism does not focus on identities as the properties of human beings, but rather considers how identities are animated within and through discourses. The focus of analysis shifts from the subject in history and the relationships between people to an analysis of how different discourses enable the production of various subjectivities—but not others. As I discovered, this might be easier to see in the past than in the present. In writing a biography of Jean Royce, the influential registrar of Queen's University during the mid decades of the twentieth century when women were not encouraged to have "careers," I wondered whether "certain behaviours, deliberate or not, [made] it possible, in an institution governed by men, for a woman to be treated seriously, yet remain unthreatening" (2001, 8). All of us become "ourselves" by negotiating a thicket of constraints and possibilities, and understanding these processes involves attending to how the structure of language informs thought and constructs identities. Not only what is said, but what is not said; not just what is said but how it is said; not just what can be said but that which cannot be said: this is what constitutes the focus for poststructuralist analysis. When Riley critiques the subject of woman in history, it is in the context of a perspective that dislodged the very concept of subject from a privileged place in social analysis.

Many argue that this does not pose any deterrent to feminism. In Cornelia Klinger's words "what women have in common and what constitutes the basis of feminist theory and practice does not reside in a feminine identity" but rather results from "certain still-valid rules of how societies are constructed." With globalization producing a "drastic deterioration [of the] actual conditions and prospects of women all over the world" these "rules," she notes, show little sign of disappearing (1998, 341). Gender is (still) used as a criterion for defining the division of labour in society, for excluding some and including others from different spheres, and for allocating "potentials and resources of all kinds" (1998, 340; see also Bannerji 1999, 269). As long as all this is so—and only so long as it is so—"feminism remains the theory designed to study these rules of construction and the women's movement is the practice designed to change them" (1998, 341).

The remarkable and exponential development of feminist scholarship, perspectives, theories, and creative writing in the last 35 years originates with the questions, demands, and goals of the contemporary women's movement. Understanding this important convergence is also a theoretical/ historical undertaking. In seeking answers, feminists have taken up the question of the origins of gender hierarchies, not just the contemporary questions about "in whose interest" such hierarchies are sustained, but also questions about ultimate origins. How contingent are the categories man and woman? To what extent do they encapsulate and describe biological and sociological realities? How do we begin to answer those who claim that feminists are tampering with the laws of God and nature when they critique and seek to transform the relations between men and women? How serious a challenge to hitherto existing, androcentric knowledge do feminists pose?

Origins of Gender Hierarchy

In seeking to explain the pervasiveness, and therefore the origins, of female subordination, feminists confront vast multicultural, theological, biological, archeological, and anthropological literatures that assume and justify gender hierarchy in terms of biological differences, sexual temperaments, divine ordinance, and natural proclivities. The argument about biological difference has been the most difficult to combat because such differences seem to be irreducibly natural. Indeed, a challenge to biological difference has often appeared ridiculous, a joke guaranteed to elicit laughter. In their practices and claims to domination, men appeared to have nature on their side. While assumptions about biological differences were once much easier to make, they are not without their vocal proponents today, both among the powerful and those with little power, among men and women.

Physical Size and Male Bonding Let us look then at two different kinds of biological arguments—or rationalizations—for gender hierarchy that continue to enjoy broad consensus. On average, and in any particular society, men are bigger and physically stronger. This has led to a set of explanations that have insisted that men are more aggressive, and even that they have been genetically programmed to act collectively—through what has been called male bonding—in order to impose their will on women (Tiger 1969).

Such ideas, which attempt to explain gendered social practices in terms of biological differences—part of the whole field of *sociobiology*—tend to be used to confirm rather than question the socio-historical relations between the sexes. As a result, feminists have tended to reject not only the specific findings of sociobiology but the whole field of inquiry (Hubbard 1990). Sociobiologist Sarah Hrdy has argued that this is short-sighted and that there is a great deal to be learned from sociobiology about the evolution of human society (1981, 198). Sociobiology is not inherently sexist, she argues; rather its practitioners have been sexist: when the evolution of the female differs from the evolution of the male, the female is treated as an irrelevant deviation from the norm.

A good example, Hrdy argues, is the female potential to be multi-orgasmic. Sociobiologists have regarded this as an aberration, with no importance for the survival of the species. Hrdy argues that if they took their own precepts seriously—that there are no genuine flukes—they would have had to explore the reasons for this adaptation. What is germane here is her argument that the female of the species has evolved in a way to maximize her survival and the survival of her children. This has involved the development of competition as an adaptation to environment. Males, she demonstrates, have no genetic monopoly on competitive forms of behaviour.

Feminist archaeologists and anthropologists have been in a good position to argue that the usual assumptions of sociobiology are the assumptions of an ideology of male supremacy. By approaching societies with a set of critical questions about the distribution of resources, the relations of power, and the division of labour, feminists have discovered that in many human societies women provide, in one way or another, most of the food necessary for the survival of themselves, the men, and their children.

The differences in physical size between men and women and the surmised differences in genetic aptitude for bonding have not impressed feminist researchers trying to explain the near universality of sexual hierarchies. But there is another set of biological differences that feminists have taken more seriously in their quest for explanations: namely, those differences related to the reproduction of the species.

The Sexual Division of Reproductive Labour Women do almost all reproductive work. Men's role has been necessary, but so invisible that uncovering their participation was a rather late development in human history. That our early ancestors managed to link two events—conception and birth—that come nine months apart and are of such different order is quite mind-boggling. Most children, quite sensibly, do not believe it when they are first told how babies are made.

The process of pregnancy, childbirth, and lactation has meant that if women do not do the reproductive labour, it will not be done. Reproductive differences have underwritten an assumption that this natural division of reproductive labour has an autonomous life of its own, impervious to the social environment in which it occurs. Further, these differences have provided a point of departure for arguing that the hierarchical relations between men and women derive from this division of labour. There are several major problems with the leap that takes us first from "women have the babies" to "therefore women's lives are grounded in nature's imperatives," and from there to "therefore women are destined to be subordinate to men."

First, only women *can* have babies, but not all women choose to do so. Throughout the ages women have tried to control their fertility, and religious teachings, law, and the suppression of information often thwarted these attempts (Gordon 1976). In Canada it was illegal until 1969 for doctors to provide their patients with birth control information and for pharmacists to sell contraceptive devices (McLaren and McLaren 1986). Women have remained celibate for life or for periods of time; they have loved women rather than men; they have developed and practised methods of birth control; they have self-aborted or sought help from others. African women, on board slave ships en route to America, are known to have killed their newborns rather than have them live the lives to which they were destined.

Second, while some women have refused to bear or suckle children or have been coerced or persuaded to do so, others have been encouraged or forced not to reproduce. The racist policies of the Canadian state only permitted single women with no children to come to Canada under various domestic labour programs (Agnew 1996, 35). Ironically, their job was to care for the children of affluent Canadians. State regulations have sometimes stipulated that women be sterilized before qualifying for social welfare; third-world women have been the subject of dangerous experimentation by first-world pharmaceutical companies engaged in contraceptive research. Many women choose not to suckle their babies. In Europe wet nursing was common, and in the twentieth century breastfeeding faced a new competitor in high-quality infant formula, now a multi-million dollar business (Altergott 1999).

Third, the assumption of the naturalness of women's reproductive role neglects the enormous variations in the conditions under which women in different historical periods, cultures, and social classes have children (Armstrong and Armstrong 2002). Sometimes the economic and political organization of the society facilitates their reproductive work;

other times there are enormous obstacles. In most cases, no special privileges greet pregnant women: if they are living in destitution, they will bear their children in destitution; if they live in countries at war, they will remain at risk; if they are subject to racist ideologies and practices, pregnancy will not alleviate them. Also, infanticide has been a widespread practice in many societies. We know little about how women have felt about this, but what we do know suggests that there is always a level of economic or political coercion involved in their decision. In Canadian society, generally pregnancy was considered sufficient grounds for dismissal from paid employment until recently.

Fourth, there has been a related assumption that women's reproductive labour linked them more with the animal kingdom than with the productive labour of (primarily male) human beings. Mary O'Brien was the first to argue systematically that although women who carry their infants to term do not have a choice about engaging in reproductive labour, this does not mean that they do not actively and consciously engage in this labour. Through this labour, women mediate their relationship with their children, and more generally between the generations and continued life on the planet. Reproductive labour is human labour, actively entered into and, like productive labour, it shapes the consciousness of women so engaged (O'Brien 1981).

Fifth, although the link between women and childbearing was produced by nature, the link between women and childcare (outside of lactation) is humanly created. Men may actually do very little of the world's nurturing work. Their biology is not the reason; rather their biology has been invoked as the rationale for this lack of participation. Enough men have done enough of this work to indicate that their relative absence from this line of work is not a result of genetic programming.

Sixth, the link between childbearing and female subordination is clearly an invention— a highly ingenious invention—developed in most, though perhaps not all, human societies (Gough 1973; Leacock 1981). That the forms of female subordination are neither universal nor uniform constitute sufficient grounds for believing that the hierarchical relations between men and women are socially constructed. But even those feminists who insist most strenuously that women have always been subordinate, and that the roots of this subordination are to be found in the division of reproductive labour, argue that this does not mean that women must remain subordinate. In *The Dialectic of Sex,* Shulamith Firestone argued that women's subordination, stemming from nature's unequal allotment of reproductive tasks, was universal. But, in her words, "to grant that the sexual balance of power is biologically based is not to lose our case. We are no longer just animals. And the Kingdom of Nature does not reign absolute" (1970, 10).

It is difficult to avoid concluding that the sexual division of reproductive labour has made it possible, though not necessary, for men in many different kinds of societies to dominate and control women and their children. Indeed, the organization of contemporary Canadian society ensures that women who bear children will be at economic, political, and social disadvantage compared to the men of their social class, ethnic group, and age. But as this discussion of the sexual division of reproductive labour indicates, this hierarchy is not our natural inheritance, but rather is socially and historically constructed in ways that need to be explored in each situation.

I am persuaded, however, that if we are to understand the subordination of women historically and cross-culturally, and understand why women have not resisted that subordination in great numbers throughout history, we must take into account the sexual division of reproductive labour. It has meant that most women have been dependent upon men for at least part of their adult lives, and that men have had more freedom—more time and energy—to consolidate their power over women. This question of the origins of the gender hierarchy and the role of the sexual division of labour is, I believe, necessary for understanding the broadest sweep of human history (back to its unrecorded beginnings), and why and how this history is so pervasively and variously shaped by gender hierarchies. But Firestone's vision that women's liberation would arrive with the development of test-tube babies (and therefore the end of the reproductive division of labour between men and women) appears naive, at best, and never found favour among feminists (1970, 238).

Apart from simple methods of artificial insemination that permit women without male partners or with infertile male partners to conceive, much of the development of new reproductive technologies has been criticized by feminists (Mosoff 1993; Overall 1993). Their research demonstrates that these technologies are primarily under the control of men, that women have highly unequal access to them depending on their social class and sexual orientation, and that these technologies are linked to forms of genetic engineering and systems of control that provoke prophecies of new forms of fascism rather than women's liberation. Sexual hierarchies are no longer dependent upon a division of reproductive labour but are thoroughly implicated with the complex relations of power that animate contemporary society. Indeed, new reproductive technologies develop *within* the context of those relations of power and threaten to serve and consolidate them (Burfoot 1999). (See Box 1-3.)

Feminist theories are not just about explaining sexual hierarchies. They also aim to understand how and why women resist their subordinate status. This discussion requires a brief diversion into the more general question of how those in power retain—and eventually may lose—their power. This question hinges on the ability of the dominant to convince the dominated that the power relations between them are legitimate, even natural.

Legitimating Power, Challenging Power Just as the kings of the Middle Ages and the aristocrats who lived off the court propagated the idea of the divine right of kings, so many men have insisted that their power is naturally or divinely ordained. A fairly new strategy undertaken by some men, including men in political elites, has been to deny that men have more power or resources than women. The result is similar, however, serving to consolidate the status quo: dominant groups do not willingly give up their prerogatives. About this much, at least, the historical record is clear. There may be a bit of cross-dressing: Friedrich Engels Sr owned factories; yet his son co-authored *The Communist Manifesto* with Karl Marx. Struggles for the abolition of slavery included white men and white women (though not many slave owners). There is evidence of some cross-class solidarity in feminist movements. Some men have allied themselves with feminist struggles, even in the early part of the twentieth century when it was a far less popular cause. Yet such exceptions serve to throw into relief that which is usually taken for granted: that the ideas developed, believed, and perpetrated by dominant groups legitimate their power. These ideas explain the relations of power and the distribution of resources in the society in ways that make them appear eminently reasonable and correct, not just to those whose interests they protect, but to those who are oppressed and exploited by them.

BOX 1-3	Reproductive Technology

Reproductive theory has changed little over time, and its language continues to mediate people and their procreativity. The two main issues, the value of gender and the control of procreation, persist throughout a considerable history of human reproductive thought....

By the early twentieth century, generalized philosophical discussions of human reproduction were replaced almost entirely by a dominant discourse of science and medicine.... Within new reproductive technologies women's breeding capacities are emphasized over experiences and rights of maternity. Embryos are separated from the pregnant woman and become the subject of public property disputes. Men gain reproductive options that increase their chances of genetic continuity. In addition to gender bias exist concerns with the general fragmentation and control of humanity. Also, the site and purpose of reproduction have radically shifted, and genetics has become a determinant of human relations and human value....

Perhaps one of the most extreme forms of denigration of female reproductivity occurs with sex selection within societies where a male preference dominates. Selection issues for both men and women arise with the advent of genetic engineering and screening. Other forms of fragmentation, particularly in women's procreativity, are evident in the new reproductive technologies, especially in vitro fertilization (IVF), egg donation, embryo freezing, and transfer and surrogacy arrangements. For the first time, women experience a level of reproductive uncertainty similar to that of men. In the past women were always certain how their gametes were used in reproduction, and who their children were, whereas men were not. Presently, with IVF and egg and embryo donation, women's genetic contributions in reproduction are as mobile as men's, and new formations of family result....

The new language of reproduction itself can be seen to deny and fragment women's procreativity; women's abilities to control scientific discourse remain limited. This brave new world of reproductive and genetic replication can be compared with Orwellian-like predictions of technological development generally and the implications for reproduction in particular.

Source: Annette Burfoot. "Theories of Reproduction—Ancient to Contemporary." In Annette Burfoot, ed. *Encyclopedia of Reproductive Technologies*, 1999. Republished with permission of Westview Press, permission conveyed through Copyright Clearance Center, Inc.

There is nothing necessarily conspiratorial about this. We all develop explanations for what we are doing that try to make sense of our behaviour and to justify our actions. But we do not all have the same opportunity to disseminate our ideas, to persuade others, and to pass laws that help produce the outcomes we wish.

The ideas of the dominant class or the elites are accepted, in large part, because they appear to describe everyday reality. Those in power *are* more articulate by the very standards that they are in a position to create, define, and enforce; they do have more formal education; and they do own most of the wealth. Dominant groups, then, tend to have a monopoly not just on societal resources and the means to attain and retain them, but also on the development and dissemination of ideas.

Challenges to dominant ideas do not come out of the air; they make their entrance onto the world stage with groups of people whose life activities and relationships are changing in ways that bring their needs and desires into conflict with the dominant social practices and ideas of the time (Williams 1981). All this happens in a most uneven sort of way. The power to effect change is highly variable; laws need to be enforced, not just made. The language encountered from the past and the meaning given to words must be renegotiated (Williams 1976). What is key here is that challenges to established authority and power occur, and in this process great transformations can be wrought.

Michel Foucault's understanding of power "as diffuse and subtle, circulating within and around social relations" has been enormously influential within feminism since it implies the "possibility of resistance and subversion" (Hird 2002, 24; Foucault 1982). This conception of power draws attention to how women resist oppression within intimate social relationships as well as more collectively in the public arena.

Women's Resistance, Women's Movements

Anna Yeatman elaborates three different ways that feminists have articulated their resistance to patriarchal power (1997). While these are not mutually exclusive, feminists have cast women as victims of men's power, as in need of protection from arbitrary power, and as having the capacity to empower themselves. Portraying women as victims—of domestic violence, for example—mobilizes sympathy, outrage, and calls for punishment of their abusers. Victimized women are seen as powerless—and perhaps virtuous—in contrast to powerful men, portrayed as aggressive and cruel. Power is a one-way street in this analysis, and male and female are reinvented as discrete categories. But if the goal is to empower women, what happens to female "virtue" once it is delinked from their powerlessness? Historically, many revolutionary movements simply turn the tables when they gain control of the state. Linking virtue with powerlessness doesn't hold out much hope for a different kind of future.

Seeing women as victims is often linked with the call for protection for women. Because dominant institutions—the state, the economy, the family—have been dominated by men, created in their image, with their needs and imperatives in mind, the call for equality for women appears to suggest special treatment. The call for maternity leave, for example, suggests that women, by virtue of their difference, require legislation to ensure job security. Feminist demands on the state—while couched in the language of equality—often meet the response that they are making extraordinary demands.

Finally, Yeatman sees resistance as capacity, women remaking the world in ways that empower and suit them. It's hard to articulate this as a set of demands because the thinking here is no longer reactive. It involves decentring the status quo so that women's needs and desires are articulated on their own terms, rather than as a reaction to the way things are. Given that human life can only continue if women give birth to children, why should the needs of pregnant women be seen as "special" or marginal? What do things look like if we start, for example, with reproductive activities and the care of children as central to life?

Exploring how and why women resist deprivation and oppression has intrigued feminist scholars from different theoretical and disciplinary perspectives. The next chapter explores how feminist theories developed within social movements, especially women's movements, as an integral part of their protests against the existing order. From these movements, feminist theories first made their way into the academy through both direct and circuitous means. I would argue their continuing presence in university curricula and politics depends upon their maintaining interconnections with emancipatory social movements.

Women's movements are explicitly political—that is, they aim to change social hierarchies, law, policies, and distribution of resources. In so doing, they constitute theoretical challenges to the relations of domination and subordination between men and women. An important aspect of feminist theories has been to seek explanations for women's subordination, the ways in which their subordination is maintained, and the ways in which they have tried to resist the consequences of their inferior status. This question of resistance is of great importance. For feminist theories themselves are products, manifestations, and tools of that resistance.

Chapter 2 provides an interpretation of the contemporary women's movement from the late 1960s, that is, what is referred to as the second wave. I aim to show that books like *Gendering* could not have been written before the 1970s because the questions had not been raised, the analysis not developed, the issues not publicly acknowledged. Certainly women in many locations engaged on many fronts including national and community organizations during the preceding decades to further their quest for equality and to improve their lives and the lives of children. Many of these women had come of age during feminism's first wave, and they worked in organizations like the Canadian Federation of University Women, the YWCA, and the National Council of Women, in political parties and trade unions. Black Canadian women combated racism from their arrival in Canada with the Underground Railroad, and as the legal slaves of Canadians. They formed literacy groups, started schools, and worked through churches (Shadd 1994; Bristow 1994; Brand 1994; Williams 1997). While some of these activities have been documented, much more await researchers eager to discover the lives of their foremothers.

My criteria for selecting the women's movement as an event, and for locating its origin in the late 1960s, has to do with the level of public mobilization during those years. In the course of the following decades not only did people look at each other and their society differently, but relationships, policies, perceptions, and public and private discourse changed, in almost every respect. These changes were neither straightforward nor linear; they produced new contradictions and dilemmas; and they certainly, in retrospect, represent histories of unintended consequences that were unanticipated by those who initiated them. But from this period on, whatever people *thought* about gender, gender relations, and gender inequality, these questions were up for discussion. No forum was too public or too intimate to preclude them.

My construction of this event is intended to demarcate a transition. As historical sociologist Philip Abrams (1982, 195) put it, "events are defined not by any measure of detail, specificity or concreteness within the chronology of happenings but by their significance as markers of transition." If we date the women's movement in Canada from the late 1960s, it becomes possible to speak about "before" and "after" on virtually every topic that has been raised by feminists. That does not mean that everything changed in the way that the participants and supporters of the movement intended. But there was a sea change, or so the next chapter aims to demonstrate.

More than 30 years have passed since the beginning of the mass mobilization of feminism's second wave. The past decade has been characterized as post-feminist by some, the third wave by others.[2] I consider which aspects of the women's movement continue, what has changed, how issues have developed, been critiqued or abandoned, and I hope readers will bring their own observations and analysis to these discussions. The present is very hard to capture—impossible actually. We can all bring our acute powers of observation and our own experience to the task.

NOTES

1. In *Eve and the New Jerusalem*, Barbara Taylor (1983, xv—xvi) provides persuasive evidence that earlier Owenite socialists had called for a "multi-faceted offensive against all forms of social hierarchy, including sexual hierarchy." Marxists replaced this, she argues, with "a dogmatic insistence on the primacy of class-based issues, a demand for sexual unity in the face of a common class enemy, and a vague promise of improved status for women 'after the revolution.'"

2. See the interesting collection of papers, poems and essays, "Young women, feminists, activists, grrrls," *Canadian Woman Studies/les cahiers de la femme* 20/21 (4/1), Winter-Spring 2001.

chapter two

The Women's Movement(s)

If feminism was a person she might repeat Mark Twain's comment upon reading his obituary in a newspaper: "rumours of my death," he wrote, "have been greatly exaggerated." During the 1990s, books and articles appeared arguing that if feminism was not dead, it should be. "The mainstream media, owned largely by wealthy white men, eagerly perpetuates this myth," Cindy Wiggins, Senior Researcher of the Canadian Labour Congress, declared. "In June 1998, *Time Magazine* declared feminism dead [while] *Newsweek* called feminism the great experiment that failed" (2003, 2). Some writers divided feminists into the "good" feminists (who wanted the vote) and the "bad" feminists who kept things going much too long (Sommers 1994; Fillion 1995; Laframboise 1996). Equality between the sexes had been won, they claimed, and young women had turned away from the political struggles of their mothers and grandmothers.

In a special issue of *Canadian Woman Studies*, "*Young women, feminists, activists, grrrls,*" Candis Steenbergen responded to these accusations asserting that the relationship between feminism and young women was "Alive and Well and Still Kicking" (2001). Twenty-five years earlier feminists responded to a cover story in *Weekend Magazine* entitled "Beyond Sisterhood," proclaiming that the women's movement was dead. A large wreath of the sort that is placed on tombstones graced the magazine cover (Dewar 1977).

Part of the media's frustration with this movement, mushrooming as it did everywhere, was that they never seemed to be able to find it or its leaders. If this was a frustration for the media, there were clear advantages for organizing strategies. Individuals could be packaged, presented to the public, and dismissed; the amorphous and multi-faceted organizing of women in all walks of life and of all political persuasions resisted such packaging, stardom, and dismissal. The only feminist media stars were

American imports, such as Gloria Steinem, Betty Friedan, and Kate Millett, or Australian Germaine Greer. Women in Canada did not declare themselves, nor were they declared, speakers for the whole movement.

Any consideration of the women's movement must deal with the range and scale of the counter-revolution or backlash that the movement has unleashed, including reports of its demise. There is a complex and ongoing history of women's resistance and the resistance to their resistance. As a result, any evaluation of the goals and strategies adopted by women's movement activists is very difficult. At times success in a particular area—abortion rights or daycare, for example—seems imminent, only to be replaced by profound defeat and remobilization. Canadian law professor Sheila McIntyre's recent assessment of the history of sexual offence law applies to many of the issues that feminists have taken up in the past 35 years: "[our] efforts to expose, challenge, and eliminate direct, indirect, and systemic inequality," she wrote, "have not only been consistently resisted by police, lawyers, judges and juries, but have consistently generated backlash against those responsible and/or supportive of such egalitarian change" (2001, 72). We must remember, however, that this "backlash" has been generated by the remarkable feminist struggles that occurred during the last decades of the twentieth century.

A second important consideration that has affected feminist organizing here and throughout the world is the globalization of the capitalist economic system through structural adjustment programs in the Southern hemisphere, and economic austerity in the North (See chapter 7). Through this process many feminist "successes" have been dismantled by the state, and for most feminists the "neo-liberal" pro-market world-view that informs this global restructuring appears antithetical to their commitments and goals (Cohen et al. 2002, 6; Bashevkin 2002).

This chapter begins by looking at the conditions that help to explain the rise of the women's movement that began in Canada in the late 1960s. How was it possible for all the social movements of the 1960s, but in particular the women's movement, to go so unheralded—by the media and social scientists alike—in the preceding decades (Adamson, Brisken, and McPhail 1988; Black 1993, 151; Morris 1980; Phillips 1991, 763)? How can we explain women's collective resistance in this time and place?

BACKGROUND TO THE WOMEN'S MOVEMENT

The 1950s appeared to be a conforming and, in many ways, complacent decade in Canada and, indeed, in the other Western capitalist countries. Post-war affluence and the expansion of capitalist enterprises and educational opportunities seemed to converge in an ideology of prosperity and conformity. In the United States, well-known sociologist Daniel Bell wrote a book called *The End of Ideology* (1960) in which he suggested that the days of causes, struggles, and revolutions were over. More than anything else, he argued, youth, working people, and racial and ethnic minorities aspired to share in the good life of middle-class affluence and security. Those already partaking in this good life—prominent among them university-employed social scientists like Bell—agreed that slowly, but inexorably, middle-class living standards, values, and lifestyle were spreading throughout society. The vehicle for this development was not the cries of anguish and concerted action of people in social movements, but the spirit of progress itself, propelling American society to fulfill its special destiny (1960, 35).

Textbooks on the family set out a model of companionate marriage, with men pursuing solid careers and women making apple pie and raising solid little children (Cheal 1991; Parsons 1959; Seeley, Sim, and Loosley 1956). Unions would be content to negotiate on economic issues—every man's salary should be enough to support him and his wife and children. If there were some people still left out of the "good life," it was only a matter of time until the benefits of rational economic production and business-as-usual democracy spread slowly and painlessly throughout the country. No more stirring slogans, no more idealistic youth. With the communist dream revealed as a living nightmare in Stalin's Soviet Union, and German and Italian fascism defeated, America settled down to enjoy its eternal and unchanging place in the sun.

Canada appeared a pale but loyal imitation of the American Dream. There was less wealth but, as the closest neighbour of the United States, sharing the much-vaunted longest undefended border in the world, the standard of living would continue to rise just as surely as more American-made television sets brought more American-made programs into happy Canadian homes.

If social scientists made their living according to the quality of their predictions, most would have lost their jobs during the subsequent decade. With the advantages of hindsight, the subterranean events that eluded educated middle-class observers in the 1950s become visible. To understand the development of the women's movement in Canada, we need to look at two distantly related events: first, the growth of the double day of labour for women coupled with the decline of the marriage contract and, second, the rise of the movements for social and economic justice.

The Double Day of Labour and the Decline of the Marriage Contract

A young woman went to university in the 1950s and 60s, so it was said, to catch a man, thus earning her degree—an MRS. At Queen's University in Kingston, this idea was captured in the welcoming ceremony for co-eds: the women carried candles with a ribbon; the ribbon was said to be in the colours of the faculty of their future (and still unmet) husband. In retrospect, Queen's alumna Priscilla Galloway explained that she had married at 19, while still in the middle of her undergraduate work, because in those post-war days "marriage held the illusion of security" (1987, 109).

The social contract between men and women, a contract codified in law, stipulated that men would share their wages with their wives in exchange for housekeeping, cooking, sex, and full-time care for their children. Canadian law held, for example, that if a man moved to another city, and his wife did not accompany him, she could be charged with desertion. Nor could a wife charge her husband with rape: her wedding vows signed her on to his sexual agenda once and for all. By the mid 1950s this contract was eroding on several fronts.

In *The Hearts of Men: American Dreams and the Flight from Commitment* (1983), Barbara Ehrenreich makes the controversial but persuasive argument that men of the upper managerial ranks were the first to tire of their role as breadwinner, mostly absentee-father, and faithful husband. The magazine *Playboy* founded in 1953 recommended that men should pursue affluence in order to share their wealth with a series of beautiful women, rather than a permanent and boring wife with her boring and demanding children. *Playboy*'s first feature article was a "no-holds-barred attack on 'the whole concept of alimony' and, secondarily, on money-hungry women in general, entitled 'Miss Gold-Digger of 1953'" (43).

But there was a more longstanding problem with the contract: most men had never earned enough to support their wives and children. Most women married to working-class men not only did the domestic labour and childcare, they also supplemented wages in a variety of ways: taking in boarders, laundry, and other people's children, doing piecework distributed from factories, and exchanging services with friends and neighbours (Bradbury 1979; Cohen 1988). Nearly all black women in Canada worked full-time, many of them as live-in domestic workers (Brand 1994, 175). Yet the prevailing belief that a "good" man earned a family wage was applied to everyone, especially in the three decades after World War II when post-war affluence provided the conditions for the white unionized working class to approximate this model. Meg Luxton and June Corman's study confirmed that among Hamilton steelworkers the man-as-breadwinner model was "widely accepted as a cultural ideal, confirming their sense of themselves as part of a cultural mainstream" (2001, 12). During this period all husbands were judged (by others and often themselves) by those standards: a good man did not "send his wife out to work." One steelworker's wife told these researchers in 1984, "I was working before we got married and I liked my job but he really felt his wife should be at home. He kept saying that's what a real marriage is—the man at work and the wife at home—so I'm at home" (2001, 133). More liberal-minded men might "let" their wives go to work—provided that they not let things "slip" at home.

Understanding how this racialized and class-anchored belief held such sway when there were so many households to which it did not apply requires an analysis of the post-war discourse on the "good life," as well as older discourses on family wage, male entitlement, and female "nature." What is believed to be "true" involves not just what is said, but also what is not said. Contemporary theorists read the "silences" of dominant discourses, for example, how they parade as natural and universal, thus disguising their racialized and class assumptions (see chapter 1, page 16). In this case, the economic contributions of women were not referred to in a straightforward way. Far from indicating her accomplishments, a wife's waged work constituted evidence of her husband's inadequacy: her contributions referred directly or obliquely to that which her husband did not do. To preserve the male image women were said to work for "extras" no matter how significant these were to her family's well-being. Even in 1990 a waitress, married to a farmer, told me "I *only* have to earn enough for our food [my emphasis]."

By the beginning of the 1960s, real wages were declining for many working men, and wives could no longer stretch the wages to cover all their families' expenses. As Armstrong and Armstrong demonstrate, "the requirements of households for cash income tended to increase faster than did the real wages of the men in them." There were several reasons for this: "Lengthening education, expanding services and changing ideologies made children more expensive. Taxes, mortgages, heating and transportation costs grew much more rapidly than those related to goods women could still produce in the home placing further stress on household budgets" (1988, 160–61). At the same time, more jobs were opening in the expanding service sectors, and more and more women added full-time waged work to their domestic responsibilities. Even then, the notion that women worked for "extras," continued to legitimate lower wages for women, perpetuated the idea of women's marginal economic contributions to their households, and assumed that women would continue to do the bulk of household work and childcare. Even today when I ask my first-year students, by a show of hands, who does the domestic labour in their house, about two-thirds indicate that their mothers do most of the major chores even when they have jobs themselves.

From the 1960s women began calling this division of labour into question motivated by the pressures involved in women being mothers first—"working mothers"—at the same time that they were doing full-time waged work. The percentage of married women working for wages outside the home has been rising steadily as have the rates for women with small children. Women began to pressure men for "help" at home and governments for new policies on childcare, maternity leave, and wages. The struggles that ensued at the household level were sufficiently intense and numerous that women's double day of work moved dramatically from what C. Wright Mills called *private trouble*—a personal problem for individuals to sort out quietly—to *public issue*—a societal dilemma requiring changes in laws and policies (1959, 8–11). The new ideas articulated through such struggles—public daycare, equal pay for work of equal value, shared parenting and household work, and control over reproduction, as well as a critique of the devastating consequences of economic dependence for many women—all shaped and found expression within the women's movements of the 1970s.

More than 30 years later despite active lobbying, Canada has no national daycare policy, and only 10 percent of children under 12 are in regulated daycare programs (Wiggins 2003, 9). Although governments and the public continue to believe in collective responsibility for education for children from five years old, debate continues about who is responsible for the care of younger children, and for older children beyond school hours. Underlying the continued reluctance to publicly fund daycare is the belief that mothers are—or should be—at home and simultaneously in the work force (Marchand and Runyan 2000, 15).

Social scientists did not anticipate the societal changes involved in the rise of the women's double day of labour and the decline of the marriage contract. Nor did they predict the event—often referred to now simply as "the Sixties"—that provided a catalyst and context for the rise of the women's movements (Adamson, Brisken, and McPhail 1988, 38–42; Kostash 1980; Mitchell 1971). For our purposes, we focus on the movements for social and economic justice that characterized that decade and beyond.

The Social Movements of the 1960s

Movements such as the civil rights movement, the student movement, the new left, the resurgence of the old left, the anti-nuclear and peace movement, the black power movement, and the anti–Vietnam War movement (which brought many American draft resisters and their wives and lovers to Canada) shared a rhetoric calling for economic and social justice. These movements, separately and together, exploded two related myths: that everyone was getting better off, and that getting better off was all anybody wanted.

There were many differences among the members of these overlapping movements: the scions of affluent families looking for more meaning than that provided by replicating their parents' lifestyle in suburbia; African Americans seeking to overturn the de facto segregation that had existed in the South since the Civil War and determined to blast their way out of geographic and economic ghettos; young men unwilling to accept the draft if it meant fighting and dying in a war in Vietnam; women determined to stop the proliferation of weapons of destruction (Adamson, Brisken, and McPhail 1988; Macpherson 1994).

The gap between the rhetoric of the male-dominated social movements and the way many women perceived their own treatment as activists *within* these movements provided, by many accounts, a significant catalyst for the women's movement (Bernstein et al. 1972; Burstyn 1990; Evans 1979; Mitchell 1971). By the late 1960s, there was a visible, active, and growing women's movement—first called the women's liberation movement—in all of the Western industrialized countries, including Canada.

During the same period, the numbers of younger feminist radicals multiplied as college-educated women began to recognize the huge gap between the rhetoric of equality that had underwritten their education and the choices (or lack of choices, more properly put) that awaited them upon graduation. Although they did not realize it at the time, they owed their right to an education and access to professions to those feminists who had struggled for these rights during the latter decades of the nineteenth and first two decades of the twentieth centuries. But first wave feminists—many without formal education or economic inde-pendence—had, for the most part, left the family untouched by systematic critique. Women needed men economically to support them and their children; men were the only meal tick-et in town, and marriage the only socially acceptable way to acquire one. The bequest of first wave feminists to later generations of women was the right to a higher education, the possibility of economic independence, and some of the rights of citizenship (see chapter 5).

During subsequent decades, when women came forward to make their claims, they dis-covered deeper obstacles: the double day of labour, economic dependence, and exclusion from political decision making. Women with college degrees were expected to marry and be interesting companions for their husbands and full-time mothers for their children. Those women who did pursue a career were expected to forego marriage and children (Hamilton 2002), but even so they found their careers blocked in whichever area of work they had chosen (Gillett 1981; LaMarsh 1968; Parr 1987). The Honourable Judy LaMarsh, the only female cabinet minister in Prime Minister Lester Pearson's government, explained what finally drove her from politics:

> Scandal is the first weapon, the most continuous one, and the last weapon used against a woman anywhere, and particularly one of political prominence. I have had repeated to me by friends, families and foes the most horrendous stories of my personal life. I have been accused of the full spectrum of sensual impropriety—funny had it not been so malicious. Perhaps the curiosity is natural, but it was so intensified in my case that it became a cardinal factor in my decision to retire. (1968, 304)

The origins of discontent in women from all walks of life might have been noticeable in the late 1950s and early 1960s to a particularly astute observer. But who notices little rip-ples until they become enormous waves? Then people say, retrospectively, "Yes I remember feeling like this." For when I look back to high school in the 1950s, there were no signs that my friends or acquaintances were developing the skills, insight, or predispositions for life in the social movements of the next decade (Cebarotov 1995; Strong-Boag 1995). One of my friends, who was a great athlete, lamented that she had not been born a boy, but neither she nor I imagined a social movement that would insist on equal athletic opportunities for girls. More than that, when she grew up she realized she was a lesbian; it turned out that you did not have to be a man to love a woman. This we would have to learn for ourselves. In the 1950s, lesbian lives were closeted, and their histories yet to be written.

That was 1959. A short decade later, thousands and thousands of girls-cum-women like ourselves had been swept up in the women's movement. Together we created a movement that uncovered, explored, critiqued, and attempted to transform the hierarchical relations between men and women in every aspect of social life.

The Women's Movements

Throughout the twentieth century, women in organizations like the University Women's Clubs, the YWCA, the Business and Professional Women's Club, the Fédération Nationale Saint-Jean-Baptiste, and the National Council of Women submitted briefs to governments calling for reforms to improve the lives of women at home and in the work force as well as to claim women's equal rights as citizens (Black 1993; Lavigne, Pinard, and Stoddart 1979). Indeed it is such activity at federal, provincial, and local levels—together with the work of other influential groups like the Voice of Women, founded in 1960 to oppose nuclear weapons proliferation—that provides the grounds for the argument that there has been a women's movement throughout this century (Macpherson 1994; Morris 1980; Williamson and Gorham 1989; Tastsoglou and Welton 2003, 115–20). This pressure, given voice and influence by two remarkable women—Laura Sabia, then president of the Canadian Federation of University Women and the Honourable Judy LaMarsh, then Secretary of State—culminated in Prime Minister Pearson's reluctant decision to strike the Royal Commission on the Status of Women (LaMarsh 1968; Morris 1980). Sabia had helped mobilize representatives of 32 women's organizations who formed, in 1966, the Committee on the Equality of Women in Canada. She told Pearson that, if he did not strike a commission, she would bring a million women to demonstrate on Parliament Hill, although she later admitted that she doubted if she could have rallied six women for such a protest (Morris 1980, 15).

The hearings of the royal commission took place over the next two and a half years. During that period, there was something of a sea change in Canadian life. In 1967, the press—everywhere but in Quebec—ridiculed setting up the commission (Morris 1982, 210; Newman 1969). Whatever could such a commission be about? The *Ottawa Journal* editorialized:

> By all means let the girls gather facts and opinions about women's rights in Canada and see how they can be strengthened where they need it. Bosh! But we suggest to them for their own good, of course, that they do it in the same way that they have advanced their cause in recent years—quietly, sneakily and with such charming effectiveness as to make men wonder why they feel they need a royal commission. (quoted in Morris 1980, 27)

Angela Burke Kerrigan, public relations director for the commission, reported that "attitudes changed like day and night over a two-year period. At the beginning you couldn't even talk sensibly to people. The changes occurred because consciousness-raising was going on everywhere for men as well as women" (quoted in Morris 1982, 224).

The commission collected briefs from women across the country in every walk of life, documented their circumstances, and submitted its report complete with 167 recommendations for reform. The commission and its recommendations can primarily be seen as a reincarnation in Canada of liberal feminism (Kowaluk 1972), although, as we shall see, it was liberal feminism with a potentially radical future (Eisenstein 1981; Phillips 1991). In their report, tabled in 1970, the royal commissioners noted that in Canada there were not only equal rights feminists but "local units of the Women's Liberation Movement in 16 cities from Vancouver to Halifax." These units were made up of "increasingly diversified groups of women that try to improve their collective lot as well as to combat discrimination....Some of them are not merely reformist but revolutionary in their aims, seeking radical changes in the economic system as well as in the institution of marriage and the nuclear family" (*Report* 1970, 2).

In Canada this radical movement was heralded by a short manifesto written by women in one of the many radical groups of the 1960s. This particular group had broken away from the Student Union for Peace Action (SUPA). The manifesto "Sisters, Brothers, Lovers...Listen...," written in the fall of 1967, argued that male comrades put "women in SUPA in two categories or roles—the workers and the wives." This, the authors pointed out, "is a situation not unlike that of the dominant society—'behind every successful man is a successful woman.' While their real women are being women by earning money, cooking and housecleaning, their radical partners can be political and creative, write, think and ooze charisma" (Bernstein et al. 1972, 38).

The issuing of such manifestos, whether in written or verbal form, occasioned discussion, debate, breakaways, and splits in virtually all of the social movements of the late 1960s and 1970s. The outcomes were varied: some women sided with those men who argued that feminism was a "bourgeois" issue that should not concern real radicals; some stayed to try and change these original groups; others left these organizations and began autonomous organizing within the women's liberation movement; still others left to begin consciousness-raising groups, the hallmark of early radical feminist organizing. Like the equal rights feminists that sparked the royal commission and its aftermath, all these newer feminist radicals—identified by the commission as part of the women's liberation movement—developed analyses and strategies to transform Canadian society.

From the beginning, the women's movement in Canada was never a single organization, and much of it was never organized in the more traditional sense. First, there was an early—and never completely discrete—division between equal rights feminists and feminist radicals (Black 1993). Second, even in the first wave of feminism (after a short initial period of unity), there were separate equal rights movements in English Canada and francophone Quebec. While first wave francophone Quebeckers tried to accommodate the teachings of the Roman Catholic Church with regard to women's proper roles in society (Hamilton 1995; Lavigne, Pinard, and Stoddart 1979), many Québécoises in the second wave intertwined feminism and the struggle for an independent Quebec (Dumont 1992). Third, from the early 1970s there were—particularly in the United States but also in Canada—acrimonious and public struggles between women based on sexual orientation (Vancouver Women's Caucus 1972). Lesbians wanted full acknowledgment of their numbers and indispensability to the movement and of the specific oppression that they faced. Some feminists, mostly heterosexuals, fought this, ostensibly on grounds that this issue would endanger the respectability of the movement and the chances for success of other campaigns. The implicit and explicit homophobia behind such fears fuelled dissension (Weir 1987). Fourth, Aboriginal women, black women, and women in various cultural groups had formed organizations to serve their members, gain state support for services, and fight discrimination. Increasingly, women of colour revealed publicly the racist practices and assumptions that came cloaked in the language of universalism and sisterhood (Srivastava 1996; Adamson, Brisken, and McPhail 1988; Agnew 1996; Brand 1984, 42; Chunn 1995; Das Gupta 1999; Robertson 1995; Vickers, Rankin, and Appelle 1993, 305–19).

FORWARDING FEMINIST AGENDAS

During the 1970s and beyond, feminists disagreed not only on the explanations for women's inequality, oppression, and subordination, but also on the means to transform their situation. We will begin by looking at the most visible strategy feminists have employed, namely lobbying efforts and direct action.

Lobbying and Direct Action

The century-old struggle for women's legal equality was taken up on a vastly greater scale following the publication of the *Report of the Royal Commission on the Status of Women.* Many feminists believed that the commission's report with its recommendations would be shelved unless they actively intervened. Following the examples of women in the first wave of feminism who had organized the National Council of Women in 1893, and the more recent example of women in Quebec who had formed the Fédération des femmes du Québec (1966), they organized new lobby groups at the provincial and national levels. The National Action Committee on the Status of Women (NAC), created in 1972 to pressure government to bring the laws into conformity with the royal commission's recommendations, is an umbrella group that brings together women's organizations and groups from across the country. Its goal was equality of opportunity for women in all sectors of Canadian society, an apparently quintessentially liberal agenda. Radical and socialist feminists put less stock in the ameliorative effects of legal equality and devoted less time to lobbying. They often criticized liberal feminists for emphasizing these activities, which radicals saw as reformist at best, and more likely co-optive (Findlay 1987; Kowaluk 1972).

However, as Zillah Eisenstein argued in *The Radical Future of Liberal Feminism* (1981), if equality of opportunity were genuinely extended to women, it would require deep structural changes in society. In Canada this became clear as NAC moved far beyond its original mandate and lobbied, for example, against free trade and the Charlottetown Accord and for issues ranging from reproductive freedom and daycare to the repeal of racist legislation (Cohen et al. 2002; Vickers, Rankin, and Appelle 1993). From the beginning there were feminists of all persuasions involved in NAC. Some of them put much effort into encouraging NAC to take more radical positions on questions of the economy, racism, national status for Quebec, and self-determination for First Nations people. By the mid 1980s women of colour and Aboriginal women were challenging white feminists, and the struggle within NAC was "public, vocal and instructive." In response, as former president Joan Grant-Cummings reported, NAC adopted an "anti-racist feminism that had a major impact on its international work and its understanding of capitalist restructuring" (1998, 7).

Alongside NAC, lobbying groups on particular issues, including abortion, daycare, violence against women, and constitutional equality, have conducted wide-ranging campaigns with members of Parliament and the public (Adamson, Brisken, and McPhail 1988; Kome 1983; McIntyre 1994).

Many feminist successes of the 1970s and 1980s were cut short. During the 1990s, draconian government cutbacks to social services, women's centres, and welfare brought tremendous increases to the numbers of desperately poor women and children. Their circumstances make the rhetoric of equality and the "guarantees" of the Charter of Rights and Freedoms appear as a cruel joke, and the grassroots women's movement turned to direct action to demand that liberal democratic legal institutions "honour women's equality" (Beavers et al. 2000, 3). In the fall of 2000, Canadian women joined women from 164 countries in a World March of Women that culminated in a protest at the United Nations on October 17. Preceding this date women representing nearly 400 groups protested across Canada and many came to Parliament Hill to participate in a lobby.

Their manifesto took up a familiar feminist analysis: "eliminating violence against women" requires change not only in the criminal law system "but also in social security policies, housing, equal pay, and the eradication of racism." The manifesto did not stop at easy rhetoric, making 68 demands grouped around eight themes (Canadian Women's March Committee 2000, 21–23), and 13 immediate demands (see Box 2-1). Although Prime Minister Chrétien met with the March Committee, members expressed disappointment "that he failed to demonstrate an understanding of why the fulfillment of these demands was necessary for the well-being of women in Canada" (2000a, 3). But the diversity of participants at this march (and many other protests in the first years of the twenty-first century)—including "trade unionists, youth, the women's movement, peasant and indigenous peoples movements, the peace, social justice and environmental movements—is unprecedented and represents a strength in linkages and solidarity once only dreamt about" (Wiggins 2003, 1).

| BOX 2-1 | **"It's Time for Change!"** |

Social and economic inequality places women in situations where they are more vulnerable to abuse, be it sexual harassment in the workplace, violence in the home, or sexual abuse in private and public institutions. This is why the Canadian Women's March Committee has identified no less than 68 demands in "It's Time for Change!"

In preparation for the Canadian Women's March on Parliament Hill in Ottawa on October 15th, and the National Women's Lobby on October 17th, we have identified 13 immediate demands for which we expect a response from the federal government by October 2000. We are demanding that the federal government take immediate steps to eliminate poverty and violence against women. We call on the government to make changes that will truly advance women's equality rights.

The Feminist Dozen

Thirteen Immediate Demands to the Federal Government to End Poverty and Violence Against Women

1. Restore federal funding to health care and enforce the rules against the privatization of our health care system.

2. Spend an additional 1 percent of the budget on social housing.

3. Set up the promised national child-care fund, starting with an immediate contribution of $2 billion.

4. Increase Old Age Security payments to provide older women with a decent standard of living.

5. Use the surplus from the Employment Insurance Fund to increase benefits, provide longer payments periods, and improve access, as well as improve maternity and family benefits.

6. Support women's organizing for equality and democracy by:

   (a) allocating $50 million to front-line, independent, feminist, women-controlled groups committed to ending violence against women, such as women's centres, rape crisis centers, and women's shelters;

   (b) recognizing and funding the three autonomous national Aboriginal women's organizations to ensure full participation in all significant public policy decisions as well as provide adequate funding to Aboriginal women's services, including shelters, in all rural, remote, and urban Aboriginal communities;

   (c) funding a national meeting of lesbians to discuss and prioritize areas for legislative and public policy reform;

   (d) providing $30 million in core funding for equality-seeking women's organizations, which represents only $2.00 for every woman and girl child in Canada—*our Fair Share.*

7. Fund consultations with a wide range of women's equality-seeking organizations prior to all legislative reform of relevance to women's security and equality rights, beginning with the Criminal Code, and ensure access for women from marginalized communities.

8. Implement progressive immigration reform to: provide domestic workers with full immigration status on arrival; abolish the "head tax" on all immigrants; include persecution on the basis of gender and sexual orientation as grounds for claiming refugee status.

9. Contribute to the elimination of poverty around the world by: supporting the cancellation of the debts of the 53 poorest countries; increasing Canada's international development aid to 0.7 percent of the Gross National Product.

10. Adopt national standards which guarantee the right to welfare for everyone in need and ban workfare.

11. Recognize the ongoing exclusion of women with disabilities from economic, political, and social life and take the essential first step of ensuring and funding full access for women with disabilities to all consultations on issues of relevance to women.

12. Establish a national system of grants based on need, not merit, to enable access to post-secondary education and reduce student debt.

13. Adopt proactive pay equity legislation.

Source: Excerpted from "It's Time for Change: Demands to the Federal Government to End Poverty and Violence Against Women," published by the Canadian Women's March Committee (2000).

Making public demands on government through lobbying and other forms of direct action constitutes a major, and perhaps the most visible feminist strategy for transforming society. But feminists have proceeded on many fronts including consciousness-raising groups, women's centres, women's and feminist anti-racist caucuses, women's cultural and business initiatives, and feminism in the academy.

Consciousness Raising: The Personal Is Political

Apparently borrowed from Mao Tse-Tung's early organizing strategy that encouraged peasants in the practice of "speaking bitterness," consciousness-raising (CR) groups began among feminists in a few large American cities. The idea spread quickly, and in the early 1970s hundreds of such groups met weekly in Canada. The groups were small, perhaps eight to fifteen participants, but the atmosphere was often electrifying as women shared experiences and feelings formerly considered too personal, shameful, or guilt provoking to discuss. Women talked about husbands, children, mothers, fathers, sex and sexuality, about double standards of sexuality, sexual harassment, rape, isolation, and full-time motherhood (Adamson 1995; Adamson, Brisken, and McPhail 1988; Bose 1972). In some ways, CR groups were confessional; but the response was more often anger than guilt, and the answer was not penance but personal exoneration and social change. In other ways, CR groups were similar to group therapy; but while individuals altered their lives, the problems were defined as collective and systemic.

While women from a range of political persuasions and social and economic backgrounds participated in consciousness-raising groups, such groups tended to be the flagship of radical feminism and were often critiqued, even spurned, by other feminists for focusing upon individual solutions to collective problems (Mitchell 1971). But consciousness raising spoke to the ways in which oppressive conditions become internalized; CR groups provided the occasion for women to recognize, reinterpret, and change. With the support of their sisters and a revamped consciousness, women changed their living arrangements, their priorities, their identities, their career goals, and their jobs. Beyond this, the phrase consciousness raising slipped into everyday language, and the analysis and strategy of making the personal political informed feminist organizing more generally. As Stephanie Austin, one of the founders of a collective working with teenaged girls called Partnerships on Women's Educational Realities (POWER), recalled, "the women's movement used consciousness-raising as a tool not only for women's empowerment and emancipation personally but also politically." The POWER collective draws on the experiences from CR "to give young women a chance to become empowered and to come together to effect change in their communities" (2001, 132).

Consciousness raising signalled that the power relations that animated personal life would no longer be accepted as private and therefore outside the purview of open discussion and public policy (Young 1990, 120–21), and this understanding informs feminist work in every area of life.

Women's Centres: From Private Trouble to Public Issue

During the 1970s, women in all parts of the country began establishing women's centres to respond to the growing numbers of women coming forward to declare their private trouble as public issue. Feminists view such centres not simply as service centres but as places where women can connect with the women's movement and join forces with those already seeking social and political change. Such women seek birth control and health information, legal advice, feminist therapy, and referrals to doctors who would perform abortions. Centres offer battered women counselling and help leaving abusive husbands. Before this, women abused by their husbands met exhortations from social workers and psychiatrists to remain at home, examine how *they* were provoking the violence, and alter their own behavior.

Although these new centres offered feminist strategies to their clients, they were nonetheless criticized as too service oriented, and for losing sight of critical explanations for why women found themselves in need in the first place. Given the staggering workloads, the need to find immediate solutions for each woman could easily become the *raison d'être* for the centres. During the 1970s, the federal government began funding such services, and there were dire predictions that this would give traditional social service administrators the power to call the shots within the once-autonomous women's centres. Navigating such waters required creative funding and strategies.

Paralleling and sometimes succeeding the all-purpose women's centre were those organizations set up to respond to particular issues and demands—shelters for battered women, rape crisis centres—and organizations set up by and to serve particular populations of women such as immigrant women, domestic workers, specified ethnic groups, and women with disabilities.

Over time, the workers in government-funded centres found themselves faced with all the problems of traditional social service work: low pay, burnout, and too few resources to serve the need (Agnew 1996, 135; Walker 1990). Such problems continue, intensely aggravated by the cutbacks of debt-ridden governments who often included women's centres among their first targets. There is little question, however, that women's centres are multifaceted, respond to deep and immediate needs, accumulate and publicize the evidence of women's subordination and victimization, and engage in political organizing to transform these conditions (George 2000).

Women's Caucuses: Autonomy and Integration

Women often had organized separately within trade unions and political parties, but most often this was done in the broader interests of the main organization. Women traditionally did "women's work": fundraising, support services, and office work. The usefulness of such women's caucuses to the organization was often considerable, but it was usually invisible or acknowledged in perfunctory—"thanks to the ladies"—remarks at conventions. Feminist-inspired women's caucuses had grander goals. They organized for two main reasons: to pressure for gender equity in leadership positions and to press for the inclusion of their demands on the main agenda. Liberal and socialist feminists pursued this strategy of autonomy and integration most often and systematically (Briskin 1993). Their goal was to change the organization, to make it inclusive of the demands and needs of women. Most women's caucuses met resistance, sometimes short-lived, often prolonged, from men and women. Their impact on parties and unions has often been stunning, but the results are varied and specific (Maroney 1987; Leah 1999). For example, three women have headed two of Canada's three main political parties at the federal level. Women's caucuses had more to do with the election of Audrey McLaughlin and Alexa McDonough as leaders of the NDP than Kim Campbell as leader of the Progressive Conservatives (and Canada's first female prime minister), but it is difficult to imagine the election of any of them without the preceding decades of feminist organizing. Especially from the 1990s women's caucuses have been active in the international arena at virtually all of the major conferences of the United Nations and in many other venues (Steinstra 2000a, 2000b).

Women's caucuses exist now in many professional associations, and their initiatives encourage women to serve in leadership positions and change the priorities and practices of the main organizations. Charges that universities create "chilly climates" for women have been taken up by women's caucuses in the Canadian Association of University Teachers and in discipline-based organizations like the Canadian Political Science Association and the Canadian Sociology and Anthropology Association.

Women's Business and Cultural Initiatives

During the 1970s and beyond, feminists began small businesses and collectives, including book, magazine, and newspaper publishing, art galleries, pottery guilds, and stores. The motivations were various. Publishing ventures aimed to bring the ideas of the women's movement to a broader public, to publish work that would likely have been rejected by the gatekeepers of mainstream—"malestream"—publications, to encourage women to write from their own experience, and to provide more amenable working conditions for women. Some hoped to—and did—make a living through such ventures. More often, they were collectively run and did not produce enough for salaries beyond one or two paid editors. As early as 1970, Toronto women founded the Canadian Women's Educational Press (now the Women's Press) to publish the papers and manifestos of the women's movement as well as feminist-informed studies, fiction, and poetry. By publishing their own material, such companies, along with magazines like *Fireweed*, *Herizons*, and *La vie en rose*, and news-papers like *Broadside*, avoided the gatekeepers of existing publications. Birth control activists founded the Montreal Health Press in the early 1970s and have sold millions of copies of their booklets on sexual assault, sexually transmitted diseases, and menopause. Art galleries like Powerhouse in Montreal attempted to confront the old question, Why are there no great women artists? Even when women had the time and resources to paint or sculpt, they seldom had the gallery space or the networks to convert their artistic creations into public showings. Moreover, those in a position to judge what is "great art" are still overwhelmingly male.

Women also started businesses with the primary aim of supporting themselves under conditions more of their own choosing (Dickie 1993). For some this meant not having to work for or with men (Nash 1995). For others, it meant providing goods and services that were tailored to their own community and that invested profits back in that community (Mackenzie 1986). Women started credit unions as the evidence mounted that banks heavily discriminated against women: women with husbands protested the fact that loans were granted only with their spouses' signature; women without husbands were outraged that they could not establish credit ratings.

Many of these entrepreneurial women were seeking financial independence from men. But they also had the effect of forcing policy changes in mainstream institutions. If banks wanted women's business, if publishing houses wanted the profits from the feminist-inspired book boom, if galleries wanted to show the work that was getting rave reviews and stirring controversy, they had to re-examine their attitudes and practices. Meanwhile women working in mainstream institutions—including universities—pres-sured for change from within.

The move to self-employment itself cannot be idealized, however. Most women who opened their own business during the 1990s did so because of the decline in paid employment opportunities. The largest number and the fastest growing group of self-employed women are in the lowest paid group of the self-employed, those with an average annual income of about $13 000 a year (Jackson 2003, 10).

Feminism in the Academy

There are many accounts of how women's studies began to develop within universities (Tancred and Dagenais 2001, 191–211; Eichler 1992; Hamilton 1985; Strong-Boag 1983). At the most general level, we must start with the women's movements, where feminists first began to raise the questions that turned the "natural" world into socially constructed sets of relationships. Feminists began writing articles, starting small newspapers, and editing anthologies. The titles of some of these publications provide a clue to their contents: in the United States *Sisterhood Is Powerful*; in Canada *Women Unite!* and *Mother Was Not a Person*. Books like Kate Millett's *Sexual Politics* and Shulamith Firestone's *The Dialectic of Sex* were best sellers.

Feminists began enrolling in the university, determined to study the situation of women in a more systematic way. Others were already in the university, and their presence was reflected in a variety of ways: new kinds of thesis topics ("You want to study *what*?" was the response of scandalized, perplexed, and threatened professors); demands for new kinds of courses ("But we already have women's studies—isn't it like home economics?"); and a growing critique of the sexist assumptions that ran through traditional disciplines and normal professorial banter. A few feminists already teaching in the university initiated the first courses on women. Like every workplace, kitchen, and bar in the country, so could every classroom become a potential battleground—in this case between professors and their feminist students and among students themselves. What was up for debate was the long and glorious tradition of Western androcentric knowledge.

The debate escalated as feminist students graduated and began applying for and sometimes securing positions within the university. From this somewhat strengthened position, and in concert with a new generation of students, the struggle for changes to curricula, for new courses and programs, and for the hiring of more feminist scholars proceeded. One can now say that women's studies is well established in the margins of academe. At some universities, it is possible to major in women's studies at the undergraduate and sometimes the graduate levels. Many departments in the social sciences and the humanities and many professional schools, particularly faculties of law, offer feminist courses taught by feminist teachers; a small number of departments in the physical sciences, particularly biology, have moved in that direction. There is a Canadian Women's Studies Association that meets at the Congress of the Humanities and Social Sciences every year. The Canadian Research Institute for the Advancement of Women, founded in 1975, brings together academics and policy makers to hold conferences and publish working papers (Vickers, Rankin, and Appelle 1993, 237). Feminists started several journals to ensure that their work would be disseminated: *The Canadian Newsletter of Research on Women* (1972, later *Resources for Feminist Research*), *Atlantis* (1975), and *Canadian Woman Studies* (1980), all of which are still publishing. Posters of upcoming events on every university campus speak to the traffic in feminist scholars and activists. Most of all, there is a feminist literature that is growing at such a dizzying rate that it has become impossible to be familiar with all the new titles, let alone read them. At the same time, the feminist challenge to androcentric scholarship has barely touched the established curricula and the teaching practices of most of the professoriate. The debate between feminist and mainstream scholars continues to rage, and there is a great deal at stake (see Box 2-2).

| BOX 2-2 | **"What Role Can Academia Play in the Feminist Movement?"** |

The following is an excerpt from an interview between editors of *Canadian Woman Studies/les cahiers de la femme* and members of the Toronto-based Wench Collective (2001).

Afshan Ali: Academia is vital to the feminist movement in that it can be a place where feminism reflects on itself, refuels itself and arms itself. As such, academia gains its value from how effectively it is, or can be, used by the feminist movement. The more esoteric academia becomes, the more useless it is to the feminist activist community.

Debbie Pachecho: Academia can play a crucial role within the feminist movement. I guess I'm a little biased because I'm such a theory junkie. It helps me to organize and better understand the world around me and how I might function as an activist within it. However, it also works the other way around. Academic theory does not just explain or inform the social and activist goals and practices, but practical experience also informs theory. The potential danger of academia and theory is if it remains detached and divided from the practical, namely grassroots feminisms. Also, for academia to play a progressive role within feminist activism, the hierarchy between theory and practice must be dismantled and the line between the two must be reconceptualized and materialized as a border, where people and ideas are welcome to flow, rather than an impenetrable divide. (Idealistic, huh?)

Fatima Mechtab: I think that before academia can reach a mass group of women the structure of it has to change. Formal education contains barriers (language, cultural, and economic) and academic feminism is biased towards middle-class white women who have the freedom to disagree and critique their surroundings. The concept and the importance of knowledge must change. What is important and valuable and to whom? Whom does it speak to and whom does it ignore?

Joanna Pawelkiewicz: Ideally, academia should be a resource for activists. A place to do some critical thinking, a place to interrogate why certain institutions/constructs exist. Academia should complement *not* replace grassroots activism.

Michelle Maloney Leonard: Academics produce some kickin' theory, which influences and structures a lot of grassroots movements. It can make a space available for young women to be exposed to ideas about radical resistance and change.

Mary Roufael: Important role of reflecting on different aspects of the moment itself and how it can move forward to meet present and future needs.

Rebecca Saxon: I think that it has an important influence on a lot of young feminists. My feminist and political ideas have changed and developed because of my women's studies classes. But I think that academia needs to be taken into consideration not only when writing and studying feminist theory in the classroom but also in feminist organizations.

Ruthana Lee: Academia can have the role of providing a very nuanced and extended analysis of social issues and providing a space for re-thinking and challenging the dominant (read: white patriarchal, heterosexist) social order. It can't solve all of feminism's challenges—in fact, I think it's one *of* feminism's big challenges: how can academic feminist theories be transformed and translated to be more accessible? How can academic theories be applied to everyday realities and experiences and attend to social change at a material (rather than a discursive or ideological) level? Sometimes it seems like the gulf between progressive academia and the "real world" is so huge you need to sprout wings to get from one to the other.

Rylee Crawford: I think academia performs a function for the feminist movement by reaching into hegemony and spreading the words of feminists in "acceptable language and form." A sort of transforming from within. Feminist law, for example, can influence those who might otherwise dismiss the feminist movement as too radical for them to pay serious attention. But this would be most effective if feminist courses were manda-

tory in all disciplines, and not just there for those of us who are interested enough to choose women's studies. The dangers of feminist academia are many—elitism, classism, white racism, ableism. So academia in general (and not just in women's studies or feminist courses) needs to seek a more inclusive outlook to those who can't, won't, or don't approximate the white, able, straight, wealthy western European male archetype.

Tara Atluri: Women's studies classes were the first safe spaces in which I encountered women who were proud to call themselves feminists. Educational institutions can be valuable resources for activities, which is ultimately the most productive role I see them playing in the women's movement. Unfortunately, one cannot even begin to envision this until issues of access are addressed. How can we even talk about the good that academia could bring to the women's movement, when the majority of women cannot afford to attend post-secondary education? Furthermore, women of colour and immigrant women do many of the underpaid jobs on university campuses.

If tuition continues to be unaffordable and universities continue to engage in unfair, racist labour practices and canon formation the gap between the women's movement and the academy will be huge.

At Queen's University in 1984, law professor Sheila McIntyre wrote a memo to her colleagues that eventually won front-page space in Canada's daily newspapers (1995). She described her experiences with both colleagues and students in unequivocal terms: harassment, misogyny, and plain lack of good will. Nine years later, Somer Brodribb authored a chilly climate report for her political studies colleagues at the University of Victoria. The report, because of the hostile responses it provoked, earned front-page coverage not only in local papers but in the *Globe and Mail*. A radical feminist analysis is reflected in the unequivocal stance of these reports: men have the power, and they use it to create and sustain the subordination of women; men have to be forced to change.

Going public brings risky consequences for individuals, and Aboriginal women and women of colour who publish their accounts of racism and sexism in the academy know this especially well. What propels them to take the risk is their commitment to other women, and their desire to make a difference. As Patricia Monture-Angus wrote, "at least those coming along will have the opportunity through the sharing of these stories to not be blind-sided by tenure events such as the one I survived" (2003, 34). Her account and those of others describe several aspects of their experience: lack of mentorship; an exclusionary environment; and colleagues with an overwhelming sense of entitlement who give a clear message: we belong, you don't. While teaching provides "the chance to build positive identities" among minority students who have not found their way of life valued in the academy (Monture-Angus 2003, 47), some students, as Joanne St. Lewis writes, "come with the sole intention of stripping me of any expertise or credibility." With those students she is "prepared to battle it out to the end...whether in aggressive dialogue or in civility" (2003, 86). More overarching than their own difficult experiences is their discovery that the university as an institution resists the inclusion of alternative ways of knowing and refuses to confront its own racist practices and assumptions (Monture-Angus 2003; Razack 2003; Bernard 2003; St. Lewis 2003).

My conversations with women's studies students at several Canadian universities in the past few years reveal both their excitement at the challenges as well as the continuing skepticism they face from other students and from their families: Why would you do a degree in Women's Studies? What are you going to do with it? These students give thoughtful answers ranging from future employment opportunities through involvement in women's centres and political movements to their own intellectual development. But as they point out, students in other disciplines are not subject to such a barrage of questions which reflect not only curiosity but also hostility and misogyny.

We have looked briefly at some of the major ways in which second wave feminists have chosen to forward their agendas. The discussion of feminist theories in the last chapter makes it clear, however, that there were many—often competing—proposals for changing society. Furthermore, we should realize that the process for understanding what should be done is indeed that, a process. Only in retrospect can we compose a list of the various goals pursued by feminists in the past 35 years. We are in the midst of a transition, and today's issues may be the next decade's assumptions, or they may have been bypassed, transformed, or defeated, temporarily or not.

DEVELOPING ANALYSIS

Feminists of every persuasion and from every location analyze the relations of power in a society and seek to transform them. From the perspective of the first years of the twenty-first century, we may take a snapshot of the range of interpretations and consequent demands made by feminists from different theoretical and social locations.

The Campaign(s) for Equal Rights

To encapsulate briefly: liberal, or equal rights, feminists worked for a society of equal opportunity for men and women. They sought to complete the agenda of the first women's movement, and they directed their attention primarily to the public sphere, as had the women in the first wave of feminism. They wanted access to the professions as well as to the political arena, and support for women in the home. They urged reform of all laws that either explicitly or implicitly discriminated against women or had differing consequences for men and women. The recommendations of the *Report of the Royal Commission on the Status of Women* were grouped in the following areas: women in the economy; education; women and the family; taxation and childcare allowances; poverty; participation of women in public life; immigration and citizenship; criminal law and women offenders; and a plan for action (1970, 395–418). Equal rights feminists primarily saw before them a legislative agenda coupled with education to change attitudes (O'Neil and Sutherland 1997).

Between 1980 and 1982 feminists mounted an extraordinary campaign to ensure that sex equality rights were written into the proposal for the Charter of Rights and Freedoms (Kome 1983). In the succeeding years feminists have acted collectively as litigators, moving beyond notions of formal equality to present arguments that would have Charter jurisprudence serve "as a force for societal transformation" (Baines forthcoming, 83). "Much of the credit for persuading the Court to adopt a substantive equality analysis," according to feminist constitutional expert Beverley Baines, "belongs to the Women's Legal Education and Action Fund (LEAF)." LEAF is a national non-profit organization that participates in litigation that promotes equality for women and educates the public about the significance of this litigation (Baines forthcoming, 87; Razack 1991). Some of the most important litigation concerns the social relationships of marriage and family and emerges from the radical and socialist feminist analysis of the family.

The Family: Site of Women's Oppression

From the late1960s, feminists argued that the key to women's situation—which they now labelled oppression or subordination—lay in the private sphere of the family and the links between this private sphere and the public sphere. As the feminists who wrote the "Sisters, Lovers..." manifesto argued, as long as women's primary role was to look after men, women would be subordinate to men in all aspects of society (Bernstein et al. 1972). Shulamith Firestone articulated the position of many feminist radicals when she wrote, "the family is neither private nor a refuge, but is directly connected to—is even the cause of—the ills of the larger society which the individual is no longer able to confront" (1970, 254).

The feminist analysis of the family included women's unpaid service to men in the home; their primary responsibility for 24-hour childcare; the double day of labour; their confinement to underpaid job ghettos in the labour force; and their exclusion from better-paying jobs—those known as "nontraditional" (that is, those that were always the prerogative of men), from the professions, and from managerial and leadership roles in all sectors of the paid work force, often on the grounds that good jobs had to go to men because they supported families.

Today the pressure on women to take responsibility for domestic labour and childcare remains, although many households do negotiate a more equitable division of labour. But with the cutbacks to support services, with most mothers in the workplace, and with many jobs requiring well over a 40-hour week, families face a big problem: there is no one to look after the daily needs of adults or to care for children (Hochschild 1990). In Janine Brodie's words, the "phallocentric and patriarchal underpinnings" of the "new order" place "women simultaneously in the workforce and in the home." While this double placing has been an aspect of many women's lives since the rise of capitalism, it now plays out in the lives of most women. Hence Brodie argues that this "fundamental contradiction" has produced "a formula for a crisis in social reproduction" (1994, 57–58).

It is ironic that feminists have stood accused by right-wing groups, like REAL Women (Dubinsky 1985), of failing to value women's contributions to their families. A more accurate reading, historically speaking, would be that feminists insisted that housework and childcare were indeed *work* (see chapter 5). Socialist feminists developed a sophisticated analysis that tried to demonstrate that capitalism itself was fundamentally indebted to and propelled by the unpaid labour of women in the home. Women not only reproduced and raised the next generation of workers but also, on a daily basis, provided the necessities of life, relaxation, and sex to the present generation—their husbands (Luxton 1980; Armstrong and Armstrong 1994). What feminists objected to was that all this labour was done by women for men, that it was invisible and undervalued, and that it was unpaid, thereby leaving women in a situation of economic dependence, with all the dire consequences that it was now clear such dependence entailed.

Love and Romance Given the feminist analysis of marriage and family, they needed to explain why women co-operated apparently so easily in perpetuating these institutions. In the early 1970s they focused on the ideology of romance, love, and marriage for its success in disguising the realities of family life, and for ensuring that women would interpret their discontent and their abuse as products of their own shortcomings. How could one explain the apparent anomaly that while few young women wanted marriages like their parents, almost all young women wanted to marry? The explanation seemed to hinge on the phrase "falling in love." In a society that ostracized young women who became pregnant out of wedlock, denied the unmarried (and, indeed, the married) access to birth control, and described the children of unmarried women as "illegitimate," there seemed to be only one response to falling in love—particularly when one became as old as 22 or 23: get married. So went the words of the popular hit of the 1950s, sung by the soon-to-be-divorced couple Debbie Reynolds and Eddie Fisher:

> Love and Marriage; love and marriage; Go together like a horse and carriage; Dad was told by Mother; You can't have one without the other.

The Needs of Children Once women were married, another set of ideas—which political leaders and others had taken up enthusiastically after World War II to push women out of their wartime jobs—came into play. Children, it was declared, required a full-time mother in the home in order to grow up to be happy, productive citizens. When women "had to" work for wages outside the home, they did so in the face of the message that this was harmful to their children. Not only did governments close childcare centres that had been created to facilitate women's wartime waged work (Pierson 1986; Prentice 1995), but their resistance to daycare was interpreted as in the best interests of children. Feminists called all this into dispute. Children, it was argued, suffered along with their mothers when confined to the isolated nuclear family (Cameron and Pike 1972; Killian 1972). Children were far too important to be segregated all day with their captive moms; children should be the responsibility of the society as a whole, of women and men. Based on their understanding of the needs of children and women, feminists initiated the movement for universal state-supported childcare.

At the same time feminists began wondering whether remaining at home all day with small children was any life for an adult human being. In my consciousness-raising group I discovered that I was not the only young mother who felt guilty and anxious about my unhappiness with full-time motherhood: this came as an amazing relief. As Melody Killian wrote in 1969:

> Most working girls happily assume that they will work only until their first baby arrives. Often I see pregnant girls at work whose expectations are so high and so happy. At first it feels good to be away from a job that was probably poorly paid and dreary. But then, somehow, everybody forgets about her. Lonely and bored in her apartment with her baby, she senses that the rest of the world is going on without her. She begins to wonder why it is that she is not happy. Something is wrong, but she is not sure what it is. (1972, 90)

In the words of Betty Friedan (1963), this was "the problem that has no name," with its symptoms of depression and even madness. Psychiatrists and physicians who offered women Valium to help them accept the injunction that to be good mothers they should have no life of their own came under feminist fire (Chesler 1972). And on the basis of historical and cross-cultural comparisons, feminists argued that the idealized nuclear family was an anomaly, a destructive location for children and an oppressive site for women. Briefly put, the ideologies of love and romance, as well as that speaking to the "real" needs of children, were re-interpreted as part of the arsenal that kept women subordinate and oppressed within the family.

Gendered Socialization Feminists did not explain young women's predilection for marriage and full-time motherhood through these mystifying sets of ideas alone. They argued that girls, from the earliest ages, were educated for marriage, boys for the labour market. Boys were to grow up and be something; girls were to grow up and marry boys who did something. Feminists became critics of every aspect of child rearing and education, from the identification of pink with baby girls and blue with baby boys, through early childhood years when girls were given dolls and boys trucks, to all aspects of the curriculum in public and high schools. In Quebec, the campaign to get little Yvette of the school readers out of the kitchen and onto the hockey rink, and little Guy to take his turn in the kitchen was propelled onto the front pages of newspapers—and into the centre of the 1980 referendum on sovereignty association—when René Lévesque's nationalist minister of state, Lise Payette, called the wife of the leader of the Opposition an "Yvette" (Hamilton 1995).

Marriage as Heterosexist Lesbian feminists were also in the forefront of a thoroughgoing critique of marriage, the family, and what Adrienne Rich (1980) first called "compulsory heterosexuality." This analysis owed a good deal to the foregoing analysis of the family as the site of women's oppression and was obviously predicated upon the demand for an end to all discrimination based on sexual orientation. Rich argued that by making heterosexual marriage the only legal site for long-term intimate relationships, for socially and legally sanctioned sexual activity, for the conceiving, bearing, and rearing of children, and the only means through which a woman might be guaranteed support for herself and her children, men had secured their power over women, their control over children and motherhood, their sexual access to women, and their right to lifelong personal service.

Such an analysis helped underwrite many of the demands for abolishing, altering, and reforming the myriad laws and customs pertaining to marriage, family, children, education, and work, both paid and unpaid. In one way or another, this perspective provided the legitimacy for such diverse demands as custody rights for lesbian mothers, access to reproductive technology for lesbian couples and single women, and the end to the privileging of heterosexual partnerships—whether this be through employment benefits, the family reunification guidelines of immigration policies, or in public demonstrations of affection. More fundamentally, the argument that marriage, as currently practised, was a power relationship between a man and a woman buttressed by law, custom, attitudes, and force pointed to the necessity of transforming the whole system rather than attempting a piecemeal program of social reform.

The royal commissioners had argued that women should have the choice to work in the waged labour force or to be full-time homemakers. But radical and socialist feminists pointed to women's economic, sexual, and emotional dependence upon men, and the costs, at every level, of choosing the latter option. Like Engels nearly a century earlier, they targeted marriage as a property relationship in which women gave men the rights to their bodies, their reproductive capacities, their sexuality, and their labour. This critique of the family posed perhaps the greatest challenge—and threat—of this wave of feminism. The family appeared to many to be the bedrock of society. How could feminists argue that it needed to be transformed, even abolished?

Critiques of Feminist Analysis of the Family

Some women of colour have critiqued a central tenet of second wave feminist thought that the family was the primary site for the creation and sustaining of women's oppression. First, they pointed out that in a racist society the family is often a site of support and resistance for women, men, and children of colour (Dua 1999). Second, far from being a captive of family, black women in Canada and those in many impoverished countries have had to leave their own children to look after those of affluent white Canadians.

Enakshi Dua (1999) pointed out that feminists had missed how the dominant rhetoric extolling the virtues of the nuclear family helped demarcate valuable white citizens from those racialized "others" who were forbidden by the state from marrying and having children. For example, legislatures passed laws denying Chinese men the right to bring their wives to Canada while the media denigrated the same men for not living in nuclear families. Caribbean women had to be single and childless to qualify to come to Canada as domestics, and were denied entry for any other purpose. Through such policies people of colour were characterized as threatening to the good order and whiteness of the developing Canadian nation. Bringing these policies to the foreground exposed as falsely universalistic those feminist theories which focus on the nuclear family as the site of women's oppression. Feminist theories had ignored how the idealization of this family form not only perpetuated gender oppression but also sustained racism by delineating those qualifying as good Canadians from those who did not.

Women with disabilities have pointed out that much current feminist analysis cannot simply be extended to them (Doucette 1989). For example, family looks different if you live in an institution. Abusive practices identified by feminists as family-sited are common occurrences in many group homes and residences for those needing assistance with daily life. Some women with disabilities also argue that the literature on women as sex objects means nothing to women who have often been defined—because of disability—as asexual. Yet, at the same time, disabled persons are particularly vulnerable targets of sexual assault, violence, and theft.

The critique of the assumptions of universality and normality resonates with the arguments of poor women, older women, lesbian women, minority women, indeed all women as we reconsider what is "normal." But the disabled women's movement is also specific, with specific critiques and demands. For example, Judith Mosoff has explained why women with disabilities tend to reject new reproductive technologies, especially prenatal testing, more categorically than do many other feminists. She points out that although "these tests purport only to provide additional information to women about [their] pregnancy, certain diagnoses lead almost inevitably to the termination of the pregnancy." Disabled people argue that "this reflects a value judgment on their own lives as 'not worth living,' thereby exacerbating the existing discrimination" against them (Mosoff 1993, 114).

Feminists have pointed out how mothers are perceived to be responsible for their children's health and character. With the pressure to undergo prenatal tests and to act on the results, however, "mothers can be blamed for the ways that their children turn out at an earlier point than ever before" (ibid., 121; see also Lippman 1989). How dare a woman knowingly produce a disabled child? Disability activists situate this kind of thinking within the attitudes that made possible the scientific and medical backing for "the most horrific modern program of eugenics, the Nazi program of racial hygiene" (Mosoff 1993, 115). As the Canadian Disability Rights Council has argued, embracing eugenics also shifts attention from environmental causes of disability and from the role of poverty, as reflected in poor maternal nutrition and health care, as a major cause of infant disability.

Let us look more closely at some major interrelated issues that emerged from feminist analysis of the family. Significant change in the relations between the sexes would occur, feminists argued, only if they were all addressed as part and parcel of the relations of domination and subordination between the sexes. Two central aspects of the feminist critique of family and marriage need elaboration: sexuality and reproductive rights, and violence against women.

Sexuality and Reproductive Rights In Canada, the first national campaign waged by feminist radicals was for free abortion on demand. As one group in Quebec put it, "Nous aurons les enfants que nous voulons." In 1970, women organized a cross-country caravan, destination the Parliament buildings in Ottawa, where they chained themselves to the seats in the visitors' gallery (Kostash 1980, 175–78). But the struggle for abortion was only the most dramatic aspect of a thoroughgoing reassessment of reproductive rights and female sexuality. Feminists demanded access to birth control for all women, married or not. It is hard to imagine at this point, with easy access to a variety of contraceptives, and with the AIDS epidemic making the advertisement of condoms such an everyday event, that birth control was ever a radical demand. But unmarried women were expected to eschew sexual intercourse until marriage. The penalties for premarital sexual activity were lost reputations and the alternatives of shotgun marriages or adoption if pregnancy should result. In radical feminist terms, women's sexuality passed from the guardianship (ownership) of their fathers to their husbands without interruption. Hence came the critique not just of marriage but of the Christian marriage ceremony—"Who gives this woman to be married?" asks the priest or minister. "I do," answers the father.

Feminists exposed the double standard of sexuality through which men were applauded for "sowing their wild oats" and women divided into "whores" (more recently "sluts") and "virgins." Critics insisted that women's sexual pleasure be a goal in itself, and some raised the argument that men were not necessarily the best sexual partners for women. The first years of the critique of sexuality elaborated upon the "pleasure" side of the sexuality debate. The 1960s movement of sexual liberation, often called "free love," influenced this discussion. The emphasis was upon women actively pursuing sexual pleasure unencumbered by marriage—that is, by economic or sexual dependence upon men. The message in articles with titles such as "The Myth of the Vaginal Orgasm" was that patriarchal ideology and practices in various forms, including Freudian psychoanalysis, conspired to deny women access to pleasure from their own bodies (Koedt 1973). As long as women's sexual experiences were contained by genital encounters of the marital kind, so the new critique went, so long would women's sexuality be in the service of men's sexual pleasure and power. As one 1970 statement put it, "Society has conditioned women to be pleasure givers rather than pleasure seekers or receivers." The group went on to declare, "We feel that until women themselves determine their own code of sexuality based not, as in the past, upon the code of males or society, our myths will not be exposed and our fears will not be eradicated" (Gill et al. 1972, 169).

Given the emphasis feminists gave the importance of women's sexuality and their own pleasure, it might seem strange that during the 1990s some writers and commentators charged that feminists were against men, against pleasure, and against sex (Kostash 1996). Katie Roiphe captured the tone of the critique in her 1993 title *The Morning After: Sex, Fear and Feminism*. Some young women who may identify themselves as third wave feminists also suggest that their feminist foremothers are consumed with the problems rather than the joy and creativity of sexuality. How feminists gained this reputation after proclaiming women's right to sexual pleasure unencumbered by the double standard may be explained by a shocking "discovery" during the mid 1970s: the systemic nature of male violence against women—rape and battery, then incest and sexual harassment. You may search the *Report* of the Royal Commission and feminist publications such as *Sisterhood Is Powerful* and *Women Unite!* from the early 1970s and find virtually nothing on this topic (Bégin 1992).

If, in the first years of the 1970s, women's right to abortion symbolized feminist hopes for sexual emancipation, by the middle of that decade the focus on the danger of rape came as a grim message that sexual emancipation involved more than becoming active players in the sexual encounter. In 1975 Susan Brownmiller's *Against Our Will* was a best seller and, two years later in Canada, Lorenne Clark and Debra Lewis's *Rape: The Price of Coercive Sexuality* hit the bookstores. More than internalized oppression and fear of economic destitution brought women to the sexual encounter aiming to please men, not themselves, authors like these argued. Whether in war, in back streets and alleys, or in marriage beds, men had the strength and physical resources to rape women, resources backed in practice—if not always in theory—by law. In this way we learned that rape had been considered a crime only when one man raped another man's wife or daughter. For a woman could not charge her husband with rape; at her marriage ceremony, when she was "given away," she said "Yes" once and for all.

During the same period, it became clear that rape was not the only method of violence wreaked on women by their husbands. Indeed, the mounting public evidence that the family was a place in which men wielded power and, with impunity, vented their rage and anger against women began to make the radical feminist arguments about the family and oppression increasingly plausible to growing numbers of women. My experience at the New Woman Centre in Montreal was repeated across the country. In 1975 two researchers at the centre began a research project on battered women. There was much skepticism—including my own—about whether this was a problem that feminists should take up. Was this not a question of rare individual pathology? But the day the newspapers first reported the project, the phone began to ring, and it never stopped.

What was new about the feminist analysis was not that women might be the object of violent attack or rape. Indeed, mothers had long warned their daughters about the dangers of being out on the streets alone at night, or of travelling in the wrong circles. The emphasis, however, had been on women behaving themselves, not wearing provocative clothing, not going out alone, and remaining sexually inactive until after marriage. In other words, women were responsible for keeping men in line and for not putting themselves in jeopardy. Feminists challenged this allocation of blame. Israeli Prime Minister Golda Meir seemed to capture the new mood when she stated that it was men, not women, who should be subject to a curfew. More than this, what was new was the realization, made public by the stories of many women, that women were in danger in their own families from their husbands. The sheer empirical evidence for this violence helped extend the analysis that the family was a site—many said the primary site—for the oppression of women. There were disagreements about the explanations for male violence against women, particularly about which factors were more important.

Socialist feminists looked to the exploitative nature of capitalism and the history of women as private property, and tended to articulate the contradictions within the realm of sexuality that gave rise to pleasure and danger (Vance 1986; Burstyn 1985). From this perspective historian Karen Dubinsky "examined the stories of 400 Ontario women who, between the years 1880 and 1929, brought their complaints of unwanted, physically coerced sex to the police." Over half of the women "left the courtroom empty-handed, their stories disbelieved, their intimate lives subject to the hostile gaze of the all-male cast of police, jury, judge, and court reporters." Dubinsky understands why "many feminists believe that sex holds only danger for women and that the secret of patriarchy is sexual coercion." But she shies away from this position, "reluctant to retreat from sexuality as a place of strength, liberation, and pleasure for women." Still the question for her remains: "Why is male rage turned so often against women" (1993, 2–3). Radical feminists, many of them working in the shelter movement looked to patriarchy, and focused on the systemic consequences of men's power over women.

So overwhelming did the incidence of male violence appear that radical feminist interpretations veered close to genetic or biological explanations. The logical extension of such explanations suggested that men should be removed from child rearing, and that women should remove themselves from work or relationships with men. One feminist joke that expressed this attitude was, "If we know enough to put one man on the moon, why can't we put them all there?"

Negotiating their way through this interpretive thicket, other feminists cast about for explanations powerful enough to account for the full slate of male and female behaviours and interactions without lapsing into biological reductionism. The problem, they posited, was not men and women but masculinity and femininity. Their diagnosis came from various appropriations and developments of psychoanalysis. Not only the bad behaviours of brutal men but the range of characteristics of good men—real men—found themselves under the microscope. From infancy, boy children were taught to be in control, to hide signs of vulnerability, and to repress all those characteristics defined as "sissy-like"—that is, girl-like. This monumental task of repression meant that they would project all these despised characteristics onto those who were supposed to carry them, namely girls and women. More than attitudes needed changing, but the problem was not genetic: the diagnosis was misogyny, and this woman-hating permeated the practices and institutions of the whole society.

Regardless of their analysis feminists argue that their immediate responses to women who are battered—shelters, counselling, and helping them to relocate—were only intended as short term. As transition house activist Pauline Funston put it recently: "feminist frontline workers saw our responsibility to the women who use our transition houses as being one of revolutionary practice for political change" (2000, 41). By 2002 women had organized 470 shelters for women (*Assessing Violence Against Women: Federal/Provincial-Territorial Ministers Responsible for the Status of Women* cited in Wiggins 2003, 13) who admitted over 90 000 women and children each year (based on 1997–98 statistics cited in Miller and Du Mont 2000, 116–17). Yet, many women still face serious obstacles to seeking and finding support especially if they are not yet citizens and/or do not speak English or French (Agnew 1996, 194–223; Bannerji 1999), and workers and clients alike report racist practices and attitudes within the shelters (Srivastava 1996). Feminists insist that the systemic relationships of inequality between the sexes must be transformed into those of equality and reciprocity at all levels of society in order to stop the violence. In the meantime "short-term" measures continue and are themselves under siege in the current climate of government cutbacks.

Violence and Homelessness   The deep cutbacks to social welfare payments, women's centres, and indeed all social services have contributed to a huge increase in the number of homeless people living in Canada. Yet these numbers still do not capture the extent of the tragedy: ironically, women in shelters for battered women are not included in the statistics on homelessness; nor are those who stay in abusive relationships because they have nowhere to go. As Miller and Du Mont report, "a frightening 50 percent of shelters report that the shelter was being used more often as a temporary escape rather than as a new beginning" (2000, 117). Such women have no home—no place where they can be safe and where they may safely raise their children. Yet so far public policy makers have been immune to the demand that these women be included in the statistics which would inform any strategy for combating homelessness (115–22).

From Revolution to Reform

Many of the issues raised by radical and socialist feminists were lifted, during the succeeding decade, from their overall analysis and taken up more generally by feminists, civil libertarians, legal reformers, social workers, social scientists, and police administrators. This helps explain why any particular reform did not have—from the point of view of a radical or socialist feminist agenda—the desired effect. Let us take three examples.

1. *Free abortion on demand* The Royal Commission on the Status of Women recommended "that the Criminal Code be amended to permit abortion by a qualified medical prac-

titioner on the sole request of any woman who has been pregnant for 12 weeks or less" and "for more than 12 weeks if the doctor is convinced that the continuation of the pregnancy would endanger the physical or mental health of the woman, or if there is a substantial risk that if the child were born, it would be greatly handicapped, either mentally or physically" (1970, 286–87). In 1988, after two decades of concerted feminist activity, the Supreme Court of Canada struck down section 251 of the Criminal Code, a federal law restricting the conditions under which abortions might be performed. At the moment, abortion is simply a medical procedure like any other. Whether women have access to the procedure, however, is determined by where they live and by their access to receptive medical resources. Doctors and hospitals are not obliged to perform abortions, unlike other procedures, and in many places there are no clinics. Thus, the feminist goal of free abortion on demand has proved elusive. Moreover, the right to abortion was part of the campaign for reproductive rights. The goal was not simply the recognition that women have the right *not* to have a child, but also that they should have access to what they need to raise a child. Favourable conditions for raising children still do not exist for many women: Canada lacks a national daycare policy; the meagre social programs once in existence have been cut back; there is upwards of 9 percent "official" unemployment; the poverty rate for women alone with children continues to soar; when they do have a job, women make, on average, 70 percent of what men make (Philp 1995); and the effects of pregnancy and childcare on jobs and career are punitive. None of this means that the decriminalization of abortion should not be hailed as a feminist victory, or that access to abortion is irrelevant for women's lives. But, as with the granting of suffrage in 1918, the winning of a single issue does not impinge greatly on the overall relations of power between men and women, or the distribution of resources between them.

2. *Sexual double standard* In many ways feminists were successful in challenging the sexual double standard, and women's right to a sexual life outside of traditional marriage and family. But once again things did not work out as we had imagined. Let us take the important example of single mothers. As late as the 1960s pregnant single women faced two choices: marriage or placing their babies for adoption. Families sent their "girls" away to maternity homes, and told stories of summer vacations and visits to grandmothers. Today single women do choose to keep their babies, and some of the old prejudice about "illegitimacy" has gone. If a woman has a decent and secure job she may well benefit from the feminist-inspired changes that have occurred. But during the past decade two new discourses (very old ones, actually) along with old punitive practices have been woven together. Conservative family values and free-market neo-liberalism have together enabled the writing of a new script, namely that children are the sole responsibility of their parents—or more correctly put, of their mothers and any man with whom their mother has a relationship, and any form of dependence on welfare must be eradicated. While feminists "argue that the single mother should have the right to live independently and, therefore, be free to opt out of the nuclear family and still retain access to a full range of social benefits and entitlements that enable her to escape poverty and provide for her children," new social assistance policy leaves her "with essentially two options...attaching themselves to a man...or mandatory work in exchange for welfare" (Vosko 2002, 165–6).

3. *Wife battery* In the 20 years since wife beating was targeted by feminists, there has been a general shift in attitude. Police departments are enjoined to take domestic dis-

putes more seriously; social workers in mainstream agencies refer women who have been battered to shelters rather than sending them home with the promise of marital counselling; governments have funded shelters; politicians no longer laugh publicly when the issue is addressed. No feminist could fail to appreciate these changes. Yet, as Gillian Walker (1990) has demonstrated, when wife battery became one of a list of social problems, it was lifted, without ceremony, from the feminist analysis of male domination and women's subordination, from the analysis of the family as a site for creating and sustaining women's oppression, and from an understanding of the formation of masculine and feminine subjectivities. Instead, the problem of family violence is now widely perceived within a revamped functionalist perspective: the dysfunctional family, the violent male, and the female as victim. The social intervention that occurs—when it occurs—creates two new social actors: the criminalized male (the batterer) and the social welfare client (the female victim). Little or nothing is done for the woman—now victim—who lacks the skills or education to support herself or her children; little is done to provide young men in school with the information, skills, and understanding to become men for whom it would be inconceivable to have their way through violence (Currie 1989; Walker 1990).

Feminists raised many of the issues that, stripped of their radical context, gained wide support in succeeding decades. Many of the issues raised by feminist radicals were subsequently taken on and supported by liberal feminists and even by mainstream politicians. In this process, particular issues were isolated and lifted from an analysis of oppressive family structures (including the relationship between women's economic dependence upon men and their subordination to men) and redrafted as issues of formal equality and individual rights.

The struggle for same-sex marriage is an example, however, of how formal equality rights seem to have worked in the intended manner. Charter arguments persuaded the Canadian Supreme Court to extend "spousal" recognition to same-sex partners not on the grounds of sex equality but by adding sexual orientation as "analogous to the enumerated grounds" (Baines forthcoming, 99). From a feminist perspective marriage still harbours many practices and policies which serve to subordinate women. Yet, at the same time, the right of same-sex couples to marry carries a dramatic challenge to the whole history of legal discrimination, social ostracism, and exclusion that continues to plague the lives of lesbians and gays. The responses to gay marriage from The Vatican and some other church leaders, some Canadian politicians, and a declining number of so-called ordinary Canadians, reveal the deep-seated homophobia that continues to permeate social relationships. That the prime minister could be threatened with "burning in hell" for eternity by an Alberta bishop if he makes same-sex marriage legal, and that this story could earn front-page coverage in the *Globe and Mail* may make us shake our heads (Lunman 2003, 1), but the real anguish for gay and lesbian Catholics should not go unremarked. Nor should the long and persistent struggle of gays and lesbians to make Canadian society and all its institutions more inclusive.

From this formal equality perspective gays and lesbians have engaged in successful Charter litigation for spousal rights and the right to marry. While most gays and lesbians welcome this development (indeed many are ecstatic that their relationships will finally be recognized legally), some point out that marriage as an institution benefits some and not others. Gary Kinsman offers an incisive critique not only of the "normalizing" process involved, but also of the ways in which the state can now extend its practices to those in gay marriage. For example, just as single mothers can be denied social assistance because there is a "man in the house," so may gays and lesbians be denied assistance if their partners have an income (Kinsman 2001, 231–34).

As we have seen, the women's movement has directed much of its energy towards pressuring the federal government–in other words, the Canadian state–to change laws and initiate policy. But many Québécois feminists and Aboriginal women have taken quite a different stance towards this state.

CHALLENGES WITHIN/FOR FEMINISM

Feminism and Nationalism: The Women's Movement in Quebec

A strong and influential wing of the feminist movement in Quebec linked women's equality to the nationalist struggle for the independence of Quebec. While English-Canadian feminists were enjoining the Canadian state to change laws, make laws, create new policy, and fund services, many Québécois feminists wanted powers transferred from the federal to the provincial government. They did not recognize the legitimacy of the Canadian state, so it made little sense to join with English-Canadian feminists in campaigns that were directed towards federal action (De Sève 1992; Dumont 1992). More than that, feminist *indépendantistes* pointed out that English-Canadian feminists were thoroughly entangled in, and privileged by, their dominant national status. Not to put too fine a point on it, they were the *maudits anglais*.

From the beginning of the second wave in Canada, sisterhood was as likely to be fractious as powerful. For when the sisters belonged to different hierarchically related nations, it meant that they could not always act in unison. Certainly, most English-Canadian feminists did not become supporters of the nationalist struggle, nor did most of them see why the Québécoises would not lend their support to the organizations described as national in character, the *National* Action Committee, for example. The Fédération des femmes du Québec (FFQ), the umbrella organization for liberal feminism that predated NAC by six years, did join NAC from 1972 until 1981 and again from 1984 to 1989. Both its withdrawals centred on constitutional disagreements: the FFQ supported the Meech Lake Accord; NAC did not. The FFQ was against the Charlottetown Accord, and although NAC was also against it, many of its member organizations were not. The bottom line was that English-Canadian feminists saw the federal government as potentially more responsive to their demands than were the diverse provincial governments. Furthermore, most failed to understand the fundamental objections of the Québécoises to the Canadian state and their passionate desire for sovereignty. In Quebec, radical and socialist feminists, while they were likely to be *indépendantistes*, put much less stock in the power or will of *any* state to take on board their demands, not unlike their counterparts in English Canada. Thus, struggles within Quebec among liberal, radical, and socialist feminists tended to parallel those elsewhere in Canada.

Women and Self-determination: The Aboriginal Challenge

In 1956, Mary Two-Axe Early, a Mohawk woman from Kahnawake, raised the issue of discrimination towards Indian women before the Standing Committee on Indian Affairs and

Northern Development (SCIAND). As an Indian woman who had "married out"—that is, married a non-Indian—she had lost her legal status as an Indian under the Indian Act, her band membership, and her right to transmit legal status and band membership to her children (Weaver 1993). Fourteen years later, the Royal Commission on the Status of Women recommended that the offending section of the Indian Act (12(b)) be repealed. In 1985, following a concerted struggle by the Native Council of Canada, Indian Rights for Indian Women, and NAC, and legal challenges by Jeannette Corbière Lavell and Yvonne Bedard to the Supreme Court of Canada (they lost) and Sandra Lovelace before the International Covenant on Political and Civil Rights (she won), this section was removed from the Indian Act. The successor legislation, Bill C-31, sustained gender inequality, however, by establishing the second-generation cut-off rule. Nearly 30 years after her original public statement, Two-Axe Early appeared again before SCIAND to protest that the grandchildren of a woman who "married out"—unlike the grandchildren of a man—would not be eligible for reinstatement or band registration.

This struggle represents a long-term and successful joint endeavour by mainstream feminist organizations and (primarily) Indian women who had lost their status through marrying non-status men. On its surface, section 12(b) appeared as a straightforward patriarchal law. But as Aboriginal women and men have argued, the Indian Act was also a racist and imperialist piece of legislation that was imposed upon the indigenous peoples in ways that distorted their internal relations, structured their subordination to non-Aboriginal peoples, and threatened their extinction (Monture-Angus 1995). In recent years, Aboriginal women's major call has been for self-determination for their peoples and an end to the tragic results of colonization, imperialism, and what many consider the importation of Western practices of male domination. As with Québécois feminists, they argue that people who do not support their demands—feminists or not—are part of the oppressive relationships and structures that have brutalized and destroyed their peoples. The complicated nature of relationships of subordination and domination are here revealed: Aboriginal women direct their admonitions to French and English alike, to the Canadian state as well as to the government of Quebec, and to the nationalist aspirations of the Québécois that do not take account of Aboriginal prior claims.

No wonder, then, that the approach of Aboriginal women to the Canadian state differs sharply from that of English-Canadian feminists, and their approach to the government of Quebec differs from that of the Québécoises. In both cases, Aboriginal women and men look to self-determination for their peoples as their primary strategy and hope for the future. Furthermore, the radical feminist critique of family also left many Aboriginal women cold: "Our lives and our communities," said Theresa Tate, "include men and our children and we can't leave them behind" (Cowan 1993, 23; see also Castellano and Hill 1995). Just as socialist feminists have tended to focus upon the exploitative relations of capitalism to explain male brutality, so have Aboriginal women looked to the long history of Western imperialism and the dispossession of Aboriginal peoples from their land. They argue that Aboriginal men learned the advantages of patriarchy from their conquerors and that, in the context of the deprivation and state-initiated violence of their lives, they vented their frustration and rage on women, children and on themselves.

To the extent that there is a shared critique of patriarchal relations, there is some meeting ground for Aboriginal and non-Aboriginal feminists. Folk singer Buffy Sainte-Marie put it this way: "Native men get the same message as colonial men. Some men in the Indian movement have not wanted to hand the microphone to me and never wanted to give credit to women....In not getting the credit sometimes our older and younger sisters don't get the encouragement of having role models" (1993, 31). But a more sustained meeting ground will have to be on different terrain. While "some Aboriginal women have turned to the feminist or women's movement to seek solace (and solution) in the common oppression of women," Patricia Monture-Angus writes that for her such a turn does not provide "a full solution....[I]t is not solely through my gender that I perceive the world, it is my culture (and/or race) that precedes my gender" (1995, 177).

The problem of and for feminism is serious in this context: is such a meeting ground possible? Feminist critiques of capitalism, imperialism, and the state gain breadth, focus, and passion when reinterpreted from the location of Aboriginal women. Who controls land and development, and in whose interests? Who makes and enforces the criminal law, which sends Aboriginal peoples to prison out of all proportion to their numbers in the general population? In whose interests has the environment been rendered close to uninhabitable for plants, animals, and human beings? For many Aboriginal women, these must be feminist questions, or they will continue, largely, not to identify their own struggles as feminist. Until now, as Monture-Angus writes, "the women's movement has never taken as its *central* and long-term goal, the eradication of the legal oppression that is specific to Aboriginal women" (1995, 175).

Third Wave Feminism? Post-feminism? Anti-feminism?

In the past decade several popular books and many journalists have adopted the term "post-feminism." Post-feminist suggests that feminist struggles are over; those that deserved to be won have been won, and the rest have been rightfully abandoned. Other books and commentators blame feminism for destroying the relations between men and women and for making life—well—less fun (Fillion 1995; Kostash 1996; Laframboise 1996; Roiphe 1993). "Those who have received the most public attention," according to Candis Steenbergen, "contend that the women's movement advanced a single, antiquated vison of what constitutes 'good' feminism, and 'good' feminist sex through the promotion of women's victimization and men's inherent legacy" (2001, 8).

But Steenbergen argues that in declaring feminism dead, "the popular press targeted the wrong group of women." For contesting both post-feminism and anti-feminism is a "generation of young women actively addressing the complexities of women's everyday experiences and the personal and structural relations affecting them" (2001, 8–9). Most of these women "have not lined the bookstore shelves with mass-market bestsellers, [or] done the talk-show circuit....Instead, their voices appear in independently-produced zines, in book reviews hidden in the backs of journals, on walls and across public advertisements [and] in non-mainstream publications...." (2001, 9).

CONCLUSION

The second wave of feminism was remarkable in many ways: the sheer numbers of women who shaped its ever-expanding agenda; the links that were drawn between aspects of life once considered discrete—economic life and the family, private and public, work and home, love and brutality; the interconnections between the feminist movement and movements for lesbian and gay liberation, peace, and ecology, and against racism; its development as women's studies within the academy; and, from the vantage point of 1990, its

longevity. Indeed, of all the social movements of the 1960s, the women's movement, however diversified it became, however its strategies were adapted to new circumstances, continued to grow in countries throughout the world.

While many assert that the agenda of the women's movement of the 1970s largely was
set by middle-class, white, educated women, this has been overstated, with the effect of
rendering invisible the struggles of working-class women within labour unions and political parties (Luxton and Corman, 2001; Maroney 1987). Similarly, during the 1980s, as
Vijay Agnew documented in her study of community groups in Toronto, "consciousness of
gender oppression provided a language for conceptualizing and asserting equal rights for
women of other races and classes" (1996, 26). Many women claim the term feminist, and
in this sense we can say that the movement is far larger and more diversely located than
ever before. Aboriginal women, women of colour, women with disabilities, lesbians, immigrants, and refugees have often pursued a similar strategy with regard to the women's
movement as have feminists with regard to mainstream institutions: one of autonomy and
integration (Briskin 1999). In this process they seek to change existing feminist organizations—NAC, FFQ, women's presses and magazines, and women's studies programs—in
two major ways. They insist on equity in the policy-making and leadership positions of
these groups, and they struggle to ensure that these organizations embrace their perspectives, practices, and goals. Certainly feminism—in its theoretical and organizational manifestations—is contested territory. This promotes the prevailing assumption, much propagated in the media, that the movement has become splintered and fragmented.

Two points should be made to qualify this idea that a once-unified women's movement
has now self-destructed. First of all, in Canada at least, the movement was never one.
Second, for the media's descriptors like splintered and fragmented, we may wish to substitute terms like diversified, multifaceted, and enriched. Certainly, the women's movement
appears as a fluid and open-ended event; those who have tried to draw boundaries or act as
gatekeepers have been persuasively challenged.

Many of the issues initially raised by liberal, socialist, and radical feminists have been
taken up, elaborated upon, or challenged by women who insist that gender is only one—
and sometimes not the most important—aspect of their oppression and exploitation.
Socialist feminists, as we have seen, have always considered the intersection of class and
gender; women of colour focus on racism; disabled women on disability; many
Québécoises on national subordination; Aboriginal women on self-determination. In the
past decade young women have identified themselves as part of the "third wave" while others have declared that we now live in a "post-feminist world." All this has brought many
feminists to new perspectives that do not rank one form of oppression over others, that
always insist upon historically specific and local analysis, and that direct attention away
from causes or origins to complex interrelationships (White 1993).

This chapter has provided some interpretations of the questions, issues, and perspectives feminists in different and overlapping locations have raised in the past 35 years. The
focus has been the women's movement in Canada. But, as we noted, feminists diverge
widely in their relationships with, their assessment of, and the demands that they make of
the Canadian state. Chapters 3 and 4 elaborate on some of these feminist critiques of the
Canadian state.

The Canadian State:
Feminist Perspectives

As the last chapter suggested, feminist challenges to the Canadian state have come from many social locations and political perspectives. Gendering the history of the Aboriginal–European encounter, the formation of the Canadian state, the negotiations that shaped Confederation and the period thereafter, reveals specific and complex relations of domination and subordination between men and women. These gendering processes shape and are shaped by, among other aspects, class, regional disparities, national hierarchies, and racism. Chapters 3 and 4 explore feminist challenges to the state in terms of their theoretical alignments and their political goals.

Feminists have expanded upon various existing theories of the state: liberal pluralism, neo-Marxism, and anti-racist theories of colonialism and imperialism. They have also developed theories that include analyses of law, social policy, and state practices and that seek to demonstrate that the state is *patriarchal*; that is, that the state incorporates and sustains a system of male domination as an intrinsic, however variously expressed, aspect of its mandate and functioning. But, as many feminists have argued, this notion of a patriarchal state cannot be taken as a given or as self-explanatory, but must be demonstrated in any particular context. Nor can the state's patriarchalism be singled out over its role in supporting the interests of capital or creating and sustaining systemic racism. Most of the recent emphasis focuses upon the intersection of sexual, racialized, and class hierarchies in state formation, practices, and priorities. In chapter 4 we turn to the anti-racist and nationalist challenges to the legitimacy of the Canadian state that have been issued by Aboriginal women, by women of colour, and by feminists in Quebec. This chapter explores feminist challenges that draw upon, extend, and alter liberal pluralist and neo-Marxist theories of the state.

In the 1970s feminists clearly identified the state as a locus for patriarchal control, seen so evidently, for example, in the surveillance of women who received social welfare. "Is there a man in the house?" welfare officers inquired. Cupboards could be searched, neighbours interrogated, and an affirmative answer meant no welfare. What was a man for, after all, but to look after a woman and her children? Under feminist protest this policy was terminated but it was resuscitated in 1995 as part of the Ontario Conservatives assault on single mothers (Little 1998, 187). Four women successfully challenged the policy arguing (with the support of the Women's Legal Education and Action Fund) that it violated Charter equality rights, and in 2002 the Ontario appellate court determined that this law not only discriminated because it overwhelmingly affected women, "but also because it reinforced the stereotype that women living with men must be financially dependent" upon them (Baines forthcoming, 114).[1]

Nor, as women discovered in the 1970s could they receive welfare and go to university. A co-worker at the New Woman Centre earned a law degree; her three children covered for her when the welfare worker came round. We applauded her creative and gutsy children—and in 1976 we went into action to convince the newly elected Parti Québécois government to change the rules. It did, as did other provincial governments, but once again Ontario Conservatives told single mothers they could choose: university or welfare, and that still stands.

While the state seemed almost irremediable to some second wave feminists in the 1970s, most feminists envisioned the liberal democratic state as a major instrument for facilitating sexual equality and social justice. In the context of a federal government "guided by a philosophy of 'social liberalism plus,'" captured in Prime Minister Trudeau's phrase "the Just Society," "activists had the sense that more was possible" (Mahon 1999, 255). During the 1970s, as we saw in chapter 2, feminists lobbied the state with some success not only for changes in legislation but also, along with activists in other social movements, for the rights of all citizens for a greater share in societal resources.

Since the 1980s, however, "as the state [abandoned] 'social' for 'neo' liberalism" (Mahon 1999, 255), feminists found themselves fighting to "hold the line" as one program after another was dismantled or eroded. The paradox for feminists was clear: the state that they found congenitally patriarchal was, it seemed, necessary for their transformative agenda. As Marjorie Cohen et al. declared, "for the past 150 years feminists have understood that the whole point of public policy was to counter the market's failures and to bring about social goals that could not be fulfilled" through the market (2002, 6). And now this state seemed intent, in Canada as elsewhere, on "dismantling itself [at least] in terms of redistributive policies" (Albo and Jenson 1997, 216). Ironically, in the dominant discourse, as Marianne Marchand and Anne Sisson Runyan observed, the "patriarchal" state itself became "typically 'feminized' in relation to the more robust market by being represented as a drag on the global economy that must be subordinated and minimized" (2000, 14).

In this scenario, the state saves itself from contempt "by strengthening its capacity to regulate in favour of the priorities of the market"(Albo and Jenson 1997, 216), and by forcing state institutions, whether hospitals or schools, to mirror the practices of the market. Presto! You are transformed from patients and students to clients and consumers who must be managed efficiently, and who must pay for services. (No wonder some students believe that high fees should bring them good marks.)

This snapshot of the present gets us somewhat ahead of ourselves. We need to look more systematically at feminist approaches to the Canadian state in order to see what might be strategically and politically useful today.

LIBERAL PLURALISM AND THE STATE

The earliest and most sustained feminist challenge to the Canadian state drew upon and extended a liberal pluralist understanding of the state. From the 1800s through to the present day, feminists have demanded that the state include women as full and equal citizens (Bacchi 1983; Errington 1993; Strong-Boag 1986). At first this appeared a reasonably simple proposal that required only the political will. Women should be granted the vote, the right to higher education, the right to hold property, and admission to the professions. For liberal feminists, the state was essentially neutral and could *in principle* extend the rights of citizenship to all.

This assumption regarding the state's neutrality has underwritten the dominant—that is, liberal—historical and political interpretations of Canada's past and present (Bakker and Scott 1997, 294–5). The notion of neutrality went hand-in-hand with the idea that the state should facilitate the development of trade and commerce, the growing strength of the bourgeoisie that had emancipated itself from feudal and aristocratic fetters, and the expansion of enlightened and progressive European societies (Whitaker 1977, 31). From this point of view, European explorers discovered Canada, developed relations with the Indians through offering the exchange of guns and trinkets for furs, fought the Indians and defeated them when their co-operation was not forthcoming or when they refused to accept the authority of the newcomers, and paved the way for the founding of Quebec and other colonies. In the battle for Canada between French and English, the latter won fair and square on the battlefield, a victory that was subsequently confirmed by treaty. From the point of view of traditional English-Canadian historiography, the battle of the Plains of Abraham in 1759 legitimized English rule over New France and, in the process, provided the basis for the eventual assimilation of Aboriginal peoples.

One hundred years later, the Fathers of Confederation met to forge political and economic links between the various colonies that made up British North America. Sobered by the states' rights rationale for the Civil War in the United States—when the southern states had seceded in protest against the federal law banning slavery—Canadian politicians sought to avoid a similar challenge to the legitimacy of the state they were creating. Canadian school children have been taught how the powers of the provinces were carefully delineated and all residual powers vested with the federal government.

Those who provide such an interpretation of Canada's past would not deny that there have been times when the state used force against sections of its own population: during the wars against the Indians and the Métis; quelling the Rebellions in Lower and Upper Canada; against workers in the 1919 Winnipeg General Strike; with use of the War Measures Act in 1970 in Quebec; in the armed attack on Kanesatake in 1990; and more recently during the protests at meetings of the World Trade Organization in Vancouver, Quebec City, and Montreal. Liberal pluralism, however, accepts that the state has a legitimate monopoly on the use of violence for the purpose of maintaining—in the words of the British North America Act, the original constitution of Canada—"peace, order and good government." Those in power who order the deployment of force may be chastised for errors in political judgment, for using excess force, or for failure to compromise, but this does not change the overall rules of the governing game.

This kind of account provides a backdrop for the politics of liberal pluralism. Canada is a country made up of people of diverse origins: the Aboriginal peoples, the French, the English, and subsequent waves of immigrants. All levels of government are constituted by, and beholden to, different groupings of people who may lobby for their own interests. In such accounts, governments are power brokers; if they make enough people unhappy, they will be defeated in the next election (Albo and Jenson 1989, 181). In response to unpopular laws and policies, new lobby groups may mobilize and, depending on their strength, their demands will be gradually incorporated.

Liberal pluralist theory accepts that society is stratified but argues that equality of opportunity mitigates this unequal distribution of resources and ensures that the most able and motivated will rise to the top. As we saw earlier, John Porter's *The Vertical Mosaic* was the first major study of stratification in Canada. Porter demonstrated that social mobility occurred largely *within* well-organized strata based on country of origin and educational attainment of parents. Descendants of charter groups from England and Scotland not only occupied the majority of influential and well-paid positions, but were able, through a variety of well-honed strategies—private schools, clubs, camps, and other forms of networking—to carve out similar places for their children (1965, 293–95). Similarly, those dispossessed by the white colonizers, capitalists, and politicians passed on a legacy of poverty, ill-health, low life expectancy, high infant mortality, and marginal employment to their children. Those who arrived from non-English-speaking countries with little or no capital were able to accumulate little for their children, who tended to fill the same kinds of jobs as did their parents. Even with education, the sons of immigrants from these countries were less likely than sons of British charter members to attain the pinnacles of economic or political power.

Porter did not abandon the belief that a liberal democracy could produce equality of opportunity, and he argued for a system of education, open to all, in which the most able, rather than the most privileged, would rise to the top. Such a meritocracy would require a comprehensive system of income redistribution so that the most academically inclined children of all segments of the population could pursue a higher education. Whether such a meritocracy is possible in a liberal democracy has not been put to the test in Canada. The cost of university education rose significantly, especially during the 1990s, leading to a declining proportion of university students from low-income backgrounds (Bouchard and Zhao 2000; Marron 2003)[2] and the growing spectre of professional schools filled with rich kids. During the same period, as Statistics Canada has revealed, the rich became richer and the poor became poorer (Schofield 2001) as a result of state taxation policies and the erosion of social welfare (Bakker 1996). A 2003 poll found that "65 percent of parents believe rising tuition and living costs are putting post-secondary education out of reach for their children" (Scotia Bank 2003).

LIBERAL FEMINISM AND THE STATE

The predominant stream of feminist politics fits—although, some have argued, very uneasily—within the politics of liberal pluralism. We are going to explore the liberal feminist perspective on the state by looking at three feminist campaigns: for suffrage, for inclusion in the federal cabinet, and for pay equity.

The Meaning of Suffrage

The main goal of liberal feminism from the time of Mary Wollstonecraft, through the first wave of feminism that culminated in the vote, to the lobby that produced the Royal Commission on the Status of Women and beyond, has been equality of opportunity. Although liberal feminists increasingly have recognized the obstacles to achieving this ideal, they argue that society, as constituted, can accommodate equality of opportunity for women and men. Through education and political lobbying archaic laws and attitudes can be changed, allowing women to achieve all levels of political, economic, and social power.

Like the first wave's struggle for the vote and women's right to a higher education, the lobbying efforts of groups like the National Action Committee on the Status of Women and the work of feminists within government bureaucracies have been predicated—at least until the late 1980s—on the fundamental idea that women can achieve equality in this society. From their perspective, the liberal democratic state exists beyond the interests of any particular group, yet is capable of shifting and responding to newly organized constituencies.

The history of universal suffrage is often invoked as evidence for this conception: in the beginning no one had the right to vote; gradually, so the story goes, men of property, followed by most men, and finally most women were granted suffrage.[3] Suffrage was key to the liberal feminist agenda, for it represented citizenship. A liberal democratic state rests upon the right of citizens to choose their government. As long as women were excluded from this right, the very notion of equality between the sexes remained moot. In Canada, female suffrage for all British subjects was conceded at the federal level and in all provinces except Quebec between 1916 and 1922. It had been a long struggle: "The campaign had taken some 60 years to win....[T]housands of women and hundreds of organizations had been involved in the fight for political rights" (Prentice et al. 1988, 209).

Does this success constitute evidence for the validity of liberal pluralist theory? Many historians argue that the granting of suffrage changed much less than feminists had imagined and their opponents had feared. Rather than proving the reforming potential of the liberal state, the granting of suffrage, they argue, illustrates the limits of liberalism. Other feminists (Bacchi 1983, 47–49), not necessarily in disagreement with this judgment, insist that we must evaluate the victory in the context of those times. As Ann Snitow has put it, "at a time when criticism of women's separate family role was still unthinkable, imagining a place outside the family where such a role would make no difference was—for a time— a most radical act" (1990, 26).[4] If the demand for the vote was, at one point, "a most radical act," and since that struggle was successful, we can see the grounds on which some would argue that liberal democracies can encompass gender equality. Yet there was an underside to the struggle for suffrage and to the reasons why it was granted that puts in a different light feminists of the time and the politicians who represented the state.

For there was a racist and francophobic dimension to the struggle for suffrage that reveals the divisions among women and raises questions about the state, as neutral arbiter, moving towards representing a new consensus of gender equality. Some English-speaking, middle-class suffragists engaged in racist and ethnocentric arguments that pitted women like themselves against immigrant men and women from non-English-speaking countries. Arguing that hearth, home, and nation needed protection from the foreign multitudes, they appealed to the male electorate and politicians to grant them suffrage in return for safe votes from like-minded women. As Isobel Graham of the Manitoba Political Equality League wrote in 1913: "Are we Western farmers so cultured, so steadfast, so loyal, so philanthropic that we can bear dilution by the ignorance, low idealism, and religious perversity of the average foreigner?...Keep aback the foreigner. Give us good, sound British stock—women already British, already civilized, already subjected to both earth and heaven for conduct" (quoted in Bacchi 1983, 52–53). For its part, the federal government first granted suffrage in 1917 to women nurses serving in the First World War, and later that year "extended the franchise to wives, widows, mothers, sisters and daughters of those, alive or deceased, who had served or were serving in the Canadian or British military or naval forces" (Prentice et al. 1988, 207–8). This selective franchise was calculated to shore up support for the re-election of Robert Borden's Union government and its mandate for conscription. The Conscription Crisis—like the war itself—had divided the country and the women's movement. In Quebec the war was unpopular: why sacrifice the lives of young Quebeckers for a war among foreign powers, an ocean away? For them Great Britain was scarcely the "mother country." Feminist pacifists also opposed the war on principle.

The federal government's Wartime Election Act selectively enfranchising women drew both praise and outrage from suffrage advocates. Those who "in the wartime context, believed in the superiority of the Anglo-Saxon race and saw the vote as a way of reshaping society according to their values," welcomed the federal initiative (Prentice et al. 1988, 208). Opponents insisted that "valid change could only be achieved when all women acquired equal political rights with men" (ibid.). This history of the federal suffrage reveals that the so-called neutral state had its own agenda, and politicians in power their own reasons for granting suffrage. They had committed the country to a war that was unpopular with a large segment of the population; selective female franchise was a small price to pay for electoral victory.

Yet within four years of the Armistice, women's franchise had been extended at the federal level to all women who were British subjects. Among those not included were Asian women who along with their men were not eligible to become British subjects, and Aboriginal men and women who remained disenfranchised under the terms of the Indian Act until 1960 (Prentice et al. 1996, 235). After decades of struggle, did (most) women win? Or did politicians decide that women's franchise, despite all the extravagant claims made for and against it in previous decades, posed little threat to the status quo? Certainly what appeared as a radical demand in the first decades of the century quickly became incorporated into the ongoing electoral process. Indeed, extending the vote to women broadened the state's claim to legitimacy, since governments in power can claim victory in a free election in which almost all adults have the right to vote. Today even anti-feminists do not argue that women should not have the vote (Eisenstein 1981). Does this history sustain or challenge the liberal feminist perspective?

The Promise of Equality of Opportunity

Fifty years after the granting of suffrage, the Royal Commission on the Status of Women declared that equality of opportunity between the sexes was still elusive in Canadian society (see, for example, *Report* 1970, 12, 90–91, 97). The statistics seemed to speak for themselves. There were few women in Canadian parliaments, and there had never been more than one in cabinet. Corporate boardrooms were free of women. Indeed, when one of the major Canadian banks was challenged by the Honourable Marc Lalonde in 1976 to appoint a women to its board, the bank's president replied that there were no qualified women (Newman 1976), although after a significant public outcry he found one.

Thirty years after the tabling of the *Report* of the royal commission, and as many years of concerted feminist mobilization, we may ask the question again—What about equality of opportunity between women and men?[5] Since liberal democratic feminist theory locates decision-making power within government, it is germane to see how women have fared in their representation in federal cabinets, especially since successive federal governments have espoused the goal of equality between the sexes. Until 1957, there had never been a woman in the federal cabinet, and until 1972 no prime minister appointed more than one woman to cabinet. While Prime Minister Jean Chrétien appointed more women than his predecessors, women still comprised only 25 percent of his last cabinet, and when Liberal MP (and chair of the Liberal Women's Caucus) Carolyn Bennett expressed her disappointment publicly, Chrétien gave her a "harsh dressing down" at a caucus meeting (Clark 2002, A1). Bennett, a medical doctor, had told reporters that the image of nine men (and only one woman) among the new members of cabinet "sent the wrong message to Canadian women because the new group was dominated by 'white male faces'" (quoted in Clark 2002, A1).

Women's gains in party politics more generally have been marginal (O'Neil and Sutherland 1997). Women won 2 percent of the seats in the 1972 election, 13 percent in 1988 (Trimble 1995, 100), and 21 percent in 2000 (Library of Parliament 2003). The success rate of women candidates is about half that of male candidates. This does not mean necessarily that voters are less likely to vote for women. Rather, political parties have been more willing to nominate women in ridings that they expect to lose (Bashevkin 1993). In the provincial and territorial legislatures, women represent, on average, 20 percent of the membership, from a low of 11 percent in Nova Scotia to a high of 30 percent in British Columbia (Campbell 1998).

Linda Trimble has shown that women are better represented on city councils and other elected offices at the municipal level, and that their numbers are rising. She takes issue with those who have argued that this is because there is less power at the local level and that what happens there is less important. She suggests that "politics at the city level—'politics where we live,' is...more tangible, more immediate, and more rewarding than political action at the federal and provincial levels" (1995, 110). One aspect of the federal state's withdrawal from social spending, however, was the replacement of targeted payments to the provinces with block funding arrangements that "transfer smaller and declining [amounts] to the provinces and territories with few strings attached" (Mahon 1999, 160; Albo and Jenson 1997, 216). As the Ontario Coalition for Better Child Care observed: "fiscal problems have been passed onto the provinces which in turn will pass them onto the municipalities who will dump them onto service providers and users" (quoted in Mahon 1999, 161). In this context, one wonders if the sense of satisfaction for city councillors may be declining, and if women's 'preference' for participation at the local level may have more to do with family responsibilities. How many women can imagine spending much of their time in Ottawa or a provincial capital?

Pay Equity and the Limits of Liberal Feminism

We may catch another glimpse of the liberal equality of opportunity perspective in action by looking at another feminist demand first raised in the early 1970s. When feminists first looked at the remuneration for men's and women's work, they assumed that men's work required more skill and education, and they emphasized the importance of sexist barriers to professional schools and skilled trades. But subsequently the penny dropped: the jobs that women did were paid less not because they required less education and skill but because they were done by women (Gaskell 1986). (And, it was said, any woman could do these things; it came with the biological territory, and required little skill or training.) As a result of this insight, feminists began developing a set of policies that Ann Snitow has described as "humble and earthshaking,...this little brown mouse of a liberal reform"—policies that come under the rubric of the feminist slogan "Equal pay for work of equal value" (1990, 41).

The main strategy for implementing this demand has been the struggle for pay equity legislation. Such legislation was introduced at the federal level to cover workplaces under its jurisdiction, and in Quebec, Manitoba (in the public sector), and Ontario for firms with more than 100 employees (Burt 1993, 224). The legislation requires places of employment to develop job evaluation plans that compare, along a variety of dimensions, jobs usually done by men with those usually done by women. When such a plan is constructed and implemented conscientiously, the result is salary increases for those doing traditionally female jobs (Armstrong, Cornish and Millar 2003, 163).

Such legislation was a clear improvement on earlier provincial and federal laws that applied only to identical or substantially similar work and could only be mobilized by an individual seeking redress (Burt 1993, 220–21). That legislation, mobilized by the earlier slogan "equal pay for equal work," "implied that pay inequality was a minor and individual problem for a few female employees who were discriminated against by a few misguided employers...and suggested that the widespread practice of paying women low wages was justified and necessary, a matter of women's productivity or women's choices" (Armstrong and Armstrong 1990a, 31–32).

In some ways, the newer formulation of equal pay for work of equal value is also informed by liberal pluralist theory. Feminists inside and outside government pressured public policy makers to enact laws that oblige employers to implement such plans. The working assumption behind such a strategy can still be a neutral state, open to assessing and resolving conflicting demands. In this case, the numbers of women in the workplace mean that they are in a position, as never before, to have their demands for equality at work mandated.

But it is striking that pay equity legislation also involves a departure from the liberal idea of the free and open marketplace, as corporate and business leaders have lamented. Their opposition clearly is not based only on philosophical grounds. The prospect of paying women salaries equivalent to those paid to men doing work of equal value provokes heated opposition, particularly from the owners of small businesses with narrow profit margins. The viability of small enterprises often rests on the low wages paid to women and visible minorities. But large corporations, employing huge numbers of women in clerical positions, also resist pay equity legislation. Such legislation challenges the liberal notion that society is made up of discrete individuals in competition with each other. When liberal feminists argue for legislation that would alter the conditions of work for most women, the inadequacy of traditional liberal theory for understanding and attaining liberal feminist goals becomes apparent.

Rather than arguing that the best woman or man should get the jobs at the top, or that any woman should have an equal opportunity with every man to do nontraditional jobs, pay equity targets women as a group and allows what could be called sex action suits. This analysis declares women as a sex to be disadvantaged in the waged marketplace, not because they are less hard working, less intelligent, less motivated, less educated, less needy, less skilled, but because they are women. Pay equity legislation is motivated by an analysis that declares that women's work is undervalued compared to men's simply because women do it. Such legislation relies on an analysis of power relations that rests uncomfortably, if at all, within liberal pluralist political theory.

It is true that invoking the state to correct such inequities suggests that another part of liberal pluralist theory is retained: that the state is neutral arbiter and, if lobbied effectively, can be part of the solution. Yet so-called liberal reforms like pay equity challenge the liberal conception of society and state. For Ann Snitow, this "little brown mouse of a liberal reform" has potentially subversive consequences that contribute to the destabilization of gender hierarchies throughout the society. Comparable worth "erodes the economic advantages to employers of consistently undervaluing women's work and channelling women into stigmatized work ghettos where pay is always lower....[C]omparable worth undermines the idea that all work has a natural gender." More than this, "a woman earning [decent] money is an independent woman. She can change the family; she can consider leaving it" (1990, 42–43).

But pay equity settlements have had a tortuous road, running into great resistance (Armstrong, Cornish, and Miller 2003). In June 2003, for example, the Supreme Court "rung Bell Canada's bell in a marathon pay-equity dispute" that went back 13 years. Bell had refused to abide by the ruling of the Human Rights Commission. But the Supreme Court ruling does not assure that the thousands of telephone operators, most of whom have been laid off, died, or left the company, will receive the retroactive pay that is owed them (Makin 2003, A8). In the neo-liberal climate pay equity legislation is seen as special pleading rather than an attempt to redress systemic inequalities, and provincial governments have moved to take the teeth out of the process or abolish it altogether (Evans and Wekerle 1997, 23; Findlay 1997, 326). More seriously, the growing conversion of full-time permanent jobs to part-time, temporary, and contracts effects an end run around pay equity legislation. Bell now contracts out to other companies many of the services the women used to provide (Makin 2003, A8). From 1989 to 2001, the proportion of women in full-time permanent employment as employees or self-employed dropped from 66 to 62 percent, and the drop was even greater for men: from 81 to 73 percent (Jackson 2003, 2).[6] This comparison supports Pat Armstrong's contention that women aren't catching up, men are "harmonizing down" (1996).

Liberal pluralist theory has proven inadequate for understanding and redressing the hierarchy between men and women in society. Most feminists would agree this theory rests on the assumption that most people can compete for the most rewarded and influential positions, and that superior ability and drive will win out. Not only do these assumptions ignore (colossal) head starts provided by privileged class, ethnic, and racialized positions, as John Porter first signalled, but they also obscure the power relations and gendered division of labour that structure familial relations.

Put simply, women cannot compete—even with men of their social class—in a free and open marketplace because that marketplace is predicated on the reproductive labour and childcare done by women somewhere else. Not only do women continue to do the lion's share of domestic labour and childcare, but also the work they do draws lower wages than men's work. No wonder, for many women, the right to work for pay has been a mixed blessing, thus provoking the title of Andrew Jackson's paper: "Is Work Working for Women?"

Make no mistake: most women must work to support themselves and their families. But the obstacles remain steep. The Royal Commission on the Status of Women's proposal for universally accessible, quality childcare was taken up by three different federal governments in 1984, 1987, and 1993 "but each failed to deliver," and the 1995 budget dashed "any hope that a breakthrough was imminent" (Mahon 1999, 260). Hundreds of thousands of young children whose mothers work for pay have no regulated daycare space (Kholsa in Michalos 2000, 271; Ferguson 2002). Mothers and fathers must perform high-wire juggling acts to ensure the daily well-being of their children but mothers still receive most of the blame when things go wrong at home, and feel most of the guilt for not "being there" all the time. A 1995 poll found that half of the female and nearly two-thirds of the male respondents agreed or strongly agreed that "pre-school children will suffer if both parents are employed." One might hope that what people really mean by this response is that conditions for working parents and their children must be improved. Yet another item in the same poll indicates that 46 percent of the respondents believe that "a job is all right, but what most women really want is a home and children" (Ghalam 1997, 6). Even if this is so—and is it?—most women cannot manage this *without* a job. In the absence of high-quality, affordable, and accessible daycare "part-time work or work at irregular hours often becomes the only means for reconciling employment and childcare in a context where few can afford to 'choose' between them" (Mahon 1999, 261).

Those of us who believed that "the politics of reform that had emerged from the 1960s to shape the social movements of the 1970s and 1980s" would develop into a "larger project of transformation" (Findlay 1997, 325) are forced to acknowledge that the trajectory has been quite in the other direction. A major clue that the state had abandoned any pretence that public policy should improve the lives of poor women, for example, may be found paradoxically enough in an all-party resolution in the House of Commons in 1989 to eliminate poverty among Canadian children by 2000. Ending child poverty is clearly an admirable goal, and many Canadians wonder how it is possible to have so many poor children in an affluent society. But those of us watching on the sidelines wondered—as I hope you will too: how on earth do you end child poverty without transforming the conditions that keep their mothers poor?

In the neo-liberal environment of the late 1980s many progressive people supported the shift from poverty to child poverty as the only politically possible option. For them the results have been monumentally disappointing. In an excellent research paper Wanda Wiegers concluded that "the major policy solutions advanced to date have not substantially reduced the incidence or depth of child poverty nor substantially addressed the costs of child rearing or the systemic causes of women's poverty" (2002, vi–vii). By 2001, more than 1 000 000 children—an increase of about 28 percent since the 1989 resolution—lived in households with incomes below Statistics Canada's low-income cutoff. What the shift to child poverty did foster was a state-sponsored discourse which blames women for their poverty, and mothers for their children's destitution. The social relationships that produce women's poverty—"the socially assigned responsibility for caring labour, a lack of affordable, accessible and high quality child care, and discriminatory or exclusionary conditions within the labour market"—are magically erased and replaced with a construction of adult recipients of social assistance as "deviant or unnatural" (Wiegers 2002, viii).

A report that Prime Minister Chrétien delivered to the United Nations in the fall of 2001 documented that it took "75.4 weeks of work—the equivalent of 1.5 full-time jobs at an average wage to cover basic expenses for the Canadian family each year." Try as they like, most single mothers cannot provide decent housing and regular meals, and with the result that homelessness and food banks mark their lives. The million families headed by women earn the lowest annual household income of any family type (McClelland 2001). In her recommendations Wiegers urges women's groups to "adopt a strategic vision that...promotes a shift in state discourse from a focus on pity and blame to one of social justice and respect," and to support existing efforts "within women's anti-racist and anti-poverty activism" (2002, viii).

In the past three decades feminists struggled to expand the scope of liberalism in ways consonant with these recommendations. But while Marxist and socialist feminists supported liberal feminist reform agendas, they were never sanguine about the possibilities of the state becoming a force for social equality and social justice. They argued that feminism must explain and transform the conditions and potential for all women and men, and in so doing they engaged in useful adaptations of Marxist political economy.

NEO-MARXISM AND THE STATE

John Porter's analysis of Canadian society as a vertical mosaic was both welcomed and challenged by Marxist scholars. They argued that Porter had accurately described a society in which rewards were differentially distributed according to ethnic and class background but that his explanation bypassed a crucial relation between those who owned capital and those who only owned their labour power. Wallace Clement (1975) and others agreed that the owners and managers of capital were largely members of the English and Scottish ethnic groups, but it was their ownership of capital that was crucial in sustaining and expanding their power and in excluding others. Their special and multifaceted links with the Canadian state were key to this strategy. In the eyes of neo-Marxists, the building of the Canadian state was not so much the work of enterprising business leaders, clever politicians, and industrious colonizers. Rather, it was the story of the state mobilizing the resources, through three successive National Policy regimes, to build an infrastructure that would make possible the easy movement of resources and people in the interests of accumulating profits. Central to this story was the seizure of Aboriginal lands, the use of military and police to quell revolt, the creation of disciplined work forces (by making agricultural land scarce and expensive, and importing skilled workers who did not have to be paid at the going rate), together with raising and deploying capital (including taxes) (Teeple 1972; Albo and Jenson 1997, 225; Brodie 1997, 249–50). Reg Whitaker called these developments "private enterprise at public expense" (1977, 43).

In *The Communist Manifesto*, Marx and Engels declared that "in the modern representative State," the bourgeoisie had "at last...conquered for itself...exclusive political sway." The role of the state, henceforth, was to manage "the common affairs of the whole bourgeoisie" (1969 [1848], 110–11). However, the growing power of the state in the succeeding century led theorists to develop more complex understandings of the relationship between economic and political power. Canadian Marxists argued that capitalists did not all have the same interests. Some made money from exporting resources; others through indigenous manufacturing and industry. The state had to be in a position to mediate conflicts and also to accommodate any strenuous popular movements. These ideas were encapsulated in the phrase the "relative autonomy of the state." If the state were to protect the long-term interests of capital while continuing to elicit consent from the governed, there had to be room to negotiate (Panitch 1977, 3).

Feminist Political Economy

Socialist feminists found the neo-Marxist analysis of political economy and the notion of the relative autonomy of the state useful in explaining their involvement in struggles to pressure the state into changing laws or making new policies, including legislation like pay equity. Unlike liberal feminists, but like neo-Marxists, they held that the state is not neutral. However, unlike neo-Marxists, but like radical feminists, they argued that the state did not simply have a special relationship with capital: it also incorporated, created, and sustained patriarchal relations within its own networks and throughout the society. Moreover, largely in response to feminists, "the political economy is now defined to include households and communities, as well as formal economies, the social relations of gender as well as paid and unpaid work" (Armstrong 2001, viii).

The socialist feminist conception of the state ensures that the state is seldom treated as an ally, and then only for strategic purposes. Since the state has the capacity to respond to the demands of popular movements—and indeed at times must respond in order to maintain its legitimacy—it followed that strategies aimed at transformation of policies and practices could have desirable results. At the same time, this analysis—and the resulting experience of feminist activists—indicated that the state would work to ensure that any resulting legislation was as narrow and inexpensive as possible. Socialist feminists realized also that the struggle for such legislation might also benefit from the divisions within capital. Some large international corporations might be able to incorporate such legislation without cost, while smaller businesses might depend for survival on employing cheaper female labour. While feminists capitalize on divide-and-rule strategies, the state tries to formulate a new accommodation that does not aggravate those who own and control big capital and that defuses the popular movements that campaigned for the new policies.

This is why Marxist feminists Pat and Hugh Armstrong argue that the Ontario pay equity legislation *could* "legitimize women's right to better pay and transform the definitions of skill, effort, responsibility and working conditions while challenging established, hierarchical ways of organizing work" (1990a, 30). But the conditions for such success do not rest on the existence of the new legislation itself but on foiling the attempt of the state and capital to pacify the organizers and their supporters. Under the new regime of neo-liberalism this understanding of the state resonates with feminists from many perspectives, and informs feminist postmodernism as well as central currents of feminist activism. We are going to look at how feminist political economy has been developed to study two areas: the health care system and Canadian regionalism.

Health Care

In a concerted attempt to "save" the Canadian health care system from the market, sociologist and activist Pat Armstrong, along with many collaborators, has engaged in a sustained research agenda from a feminist political economy perspective. She starts by noting that although reports on health reform say little about women, they "provide about 80 percent of the paid and unpaid care and constitute a majority of those receiving care" (2001, 122). A feminist political economy considers the integration of politics, the economy, and family through the social relationships of power that animate and connect them, and through this lens, these researchers have studied all aspects of the health care system. Armstrong and her collaborators have informed policy makers and the general population about the ways in which the forces of the global market have made inroads into Canada's public health care system; the consequences for health care workers, and for paid and unpaid caregivers in the home; and the various and inequitable impacts for diverse groups in the population.

Until the 1970s health care was delivered primarily by non-profit concerns. At that point, corporations, "running out of places to invest" looked to the public sector, first in the United States, and by the end of the 1980s in Canada as "the unopened oyster." By 1999 they were demanding that the World Trade Organization (WTO) grant foreign companies the right to deliver health, education, and transportation services. These corporations know, as do federal and provincial governments, that the health care system is "Canada's best loved social program," so they offer to make the system better through rationalization, cutting costs, transforming permanent jobs into contracts, and "just-in-time" work forces (don't come to work unless we call you) (2001, 126). There are many consequences to the corporate approach, but consider these two—the first in the hospital setting, the second in the family and community.

By applying the principles of mass production to the work of care-giving, consultants break down each task into small components and measure how long each takes. This strategy (Taylorism) has been seriously critiqued in the industrial setting, partly for taking the human mind out of the work; this is particularly egregious when the work *is* other people. Indeed, nurses have repeatedly identified "caring [as] one aspect of the job that [is] impossible to measure in this way." Helping someone get better involves communication and education; warmth and humour; in short, discretionary time. And that's what's gone. Patients suffer but so do nurses. By 1997 "days lost per nurse because of illness and disability...[were] more than double for all full-time workers" (McDonough 2001, 211), and many nurses have left the profession they loved because they can no longer feel satisfaction in their work.

Once these rationalization schemes, informed as they are by the principle that "if you can't measure it you can't manage it," are put in place, health care work forces are reduced, patient days in hospital are cut back, and people are sent home earlier and earlier to recover. But this process involved a major deception of the public. While governments cut back on institutional care in order to cut costs, they sold this project politically by insisting that community and family care was better, and that this was where resources would flow. And this second step never happened. In Ontario, for example, after hospital restructuring, those discharged from hospital were only entitled to 2.6 hours a day of home care regardless of their illness or their home conditions. As Pat Armstrong notes, women's support in the household is taken for granted. Moreover, a patient was only entitled to these few hours when there was no "capable caregiver" in the home even if that caregiver worked outside the home (Armstrong 2001, 137).

As you see from this brief account, a feminist political economy of health care takes an approach that is "global and capitalist, as well as local and familial" (Armstrong 2001, 140), and reveals how all the processes and relationships not only carry gendered messages and consequences, but, in fact, are made possible by women's (invisible) work (see Box 3-1). But the deleterious effects of this women's conscription into home care-giving takes its toll on their health and well-being, and indeed on all those who care for family members with little or no support.

| BOX 3-1 | A Feminist Political Economy of Luck |

Recently my sister Susan, physically incapacitated from multiple sclerosis, spent several weeks in hospital in Maple Ridge, British Columbia following complications resulting from a bedsore at the base of her spine. No one knew whether her immune system, damaged from MS and many rounds of antibiotics, could handle this latest assault. In hospital, I began to realize that other patients thought Susan was "lucky." Lucky is a word that neither Susan—nor those who know her—choose to describe her situation. Forced onto permanent disability from her position as sociology professor at Concordia University, she has not walked for years, nor been able to turn herself over in bed. What constituted her "luck," as described by her fellow patients? As I pondered this later, I decided it turned on two events: the quality of contemporary care in Canada today and Canada's Live-in Caregiver Program.

Susan's fellow patients were recovering from serious illnesses. The nurses and other hospital workers appeared to be trying their best but there just weren't enough of them. One day, when a nurse gave a sweet elderly woman a sponge bath, her first in several days, she was immensely grateful. Clearly, the nurse had to squeeze time from her monitored schedule to be able to offer such a treat. I remembered my mother who stayed many times in this hospital reporting that she received amazing care in the intensive care unit, but that on the regular ward she was on her own, dependent for nearly everything (including edible food) on family. Getting looked after in hospital has become a luxury, and this is the first element that created the appearance of Susan's luck, for she did receive

excellent care. Today most patients are unlucky, not just to be there, but in the lack of care they receive.

That she did receive quality care may be traced to Canada's Live-in Caregiver Program that feminists, anti-racists, human rights activists, and others rightly deplore (see chapters 4, 111, and 5, 132 and 137). Under this scheme individuals from third-world countries gain admission to Canada provided they "live in" with their employers for three years, at which time they become eligible to apply for citizenship. Several years earlier, Lina came to look after Susan. For nearly 20 years she had been a teacher in the Philippines; life was difficult, and not getting any better. Borrowing money from her principal, she applied to the Live-in Caregiver Program and came to Canada. When her first job proved too demanding, she came to work for Susan.

By the time of the hospital stay, Lina had become a Canadian citizen; she continued to live with Susan, and to seek other work as well. Susan had sponsored Lina's niece, Lhen, who was undertaking most of her daily care.

When Susan went to hospital, so did Lina and Lhen. They took turns, together spending 12-hour days in hospital with Susan's weekend caregiver taking over on Saturdays. This was the second element of Susan's luck. In hospital, as at home, she received excellent care and support, friendship and laughter, from women who had come half-way round the world seeking a better life. From the vantage point of her fellow patients, Susan looked "lucky."

Now they are all back home. Susan's physiotherapist recommended new equipment in order to take pressure off her wound that has taken a year to "almost" heal. Perhaps this is the third element in her "luck." Her work-related insurance plan paid for the Rolls Royce of wheelchairs, an installed lift system (good for her and her caregivers), and a mattress with constant airflow.

As a feminist political economist I learn many things from Susan's story: the importance of creating a health care system so that patients like Susan do not look "lucky"; the necessity of retaining a live-in caregiver program that attracts those who want to come to Canada but removes all the current discriminatory and demeaning conditions

attached; the importance of expanding the public health care system so that those without work-related insurance plans receive what they need.

But this is not the whole story. Susan decided that her house should belong to her and to Lina; she sponsored another niece who hopes at the end of three years to bring her husband and children. Lina organizes the household; makes a beautiful garden; sends money home; looks after Susan. From their two worlds—of the seriously disabled and of third-world poverty—they have created new relationships of friendship and family.

Regionalism in Canada

The concept of region has most often been used to delineate geographical areas: the prairies from the mountains; the coastal areas from inland regions; certainly the North from everywhere else. Canadian political economy looks at these spatial considerations in the context of capitalist development and the role of the state in "the political creation of regions" (Brodie 1989, 156).

Maritimers with long political memories, and those aided by a new generation of Maritime historians, view the Canadian Confederation with skepticism (Buckner 1990). From their perspective, the political act of confederation helped wealthy investors create a nation *a mari usque ad mare*—from sea to sea—by removing impediments to the movement of people and resources from the Maritimes to Central Canada. Nor was the political expansion of the Canadian state into the West greeted with universal accord, certainly not by the Métis and their leader Louis Riel, acknowledged as a hero of his people by the Canadian Parliament 100 years after his execution (Saint Onge 1985; Sprague 1980). In Janine Brodie's words, Canada's First National Policy (FNP) "forged an east-west economy, leaving in its wake, an industrialized and diversified centre, a deindustrialized east, and a primary-exporting western hinterland" (1997, 252). Among other events, the Great Depression "dealt the final blow" to the FNP, but it was not until the last months of World War II that a new growth plan—the Second National Policy (SNP)—was unveiled that provided for the development of social welfare programs; Keynesian-inspired fiscal and monetary policies; and a commitment to a liberalized international trading regime, especially with the United States (Brodie 1997, 253). This plan supported a period of prosperity, but not for all. Ontario prospered most, and various regional development policies tried to reduce the gap between rich and poor regions of the country. But global restructuring interfered with these modest attempts to redistribute wealth regionally.

By the1970s, Ontario and Quebec saw countless manufacturing jobs move to low-wage countries, and unemployment and inflation remained high. By 1980 the economy fell into the deepest recession since the 1930s. Increasingly a neo-Conservative critique that blamed the crisis on government spending, especially social welfare programs, gained ascendancy. The Third National Policy that was developed in the past 15 years included hemispheric economic integration (NAFTA), market-driven development (even in health care as seen above), reducing the role of the state, and privatization (Brodie 1997, 255). The big question becomes: but with all this, do we still have a country? Just as the neo-liberal order mandates every man, woman, and child for herself, so it would seem the future of every region of the country will depend on its own ability to carve a niche for itself in the new economic order (Brodie 1997, 258).

In most of the literature on regional disparity in Canada, women are invisible—whether the focus is upon federal–provincial conferences, tariffs and transportation policy, or social movements. The relatively recent feminist literature has taken up this challenge, and several broad considerations seem clear. First, women develop survival strategies for themselves and their families that are thoroughly attentive to the changing conditions created by regional disparities. The belief that women are economically dependent upon men, and that men are obligated to support wives and families does not sustain families where unemployment is high or employment seasonal, where men are thrown out of work because of mine and factory closures, or even where men may make a living wage. Pat Connelly and Martha MacDonald's (1986) research in Nova Scotia fishing communities reveals that women worked permanently in the fish plants (until the collapse of the industry), made childcare arrangements, and encouraged their husbands to "help" with cooking and housework. Changing conditions and capitalization of the fishing industry meant that men's wages could not be stretched to cover basic familial needs.

In her study of Nova Scotia's offshore fishery, Marion Binkley explains how the industrialization of the fishery eroded earlier gender complementarity within the household. "Historically, fishing families exercised a strict gender division of labour. Men caught and gutted the fish, while women and children processed the fish on shore" (1995, 50). When men still catch fish, they now do so on company-owned and operated vessels, and women process the fish in industrialized plants. But the wives of offshore fishers were less likely to work in the plants than were the wives of fish plant employees because of the difficulty of providing care for children during their husbands' long absences. Offshore fishing is also dangerous work, and the division of labour includes an emotional division: "fishers trivialize the risks they take, their wives characterize their lives as being full of uncertainty and fear that their husbands may return maimed or not return at all" (ibid., 154). Such complete dependence of wives upon husbands aggravates tensions and expectations. As one fisher told an interviewer, "When I come up over the dock, she better have the car turned around, the driver's door open, the trunk open and be sitting on the passenger's side waiting for me....My car not being there really spites me....I just hate waiting to go home. I only have forty-eight hours" (quoted in ibid., 58).

With the collapse of the offshore fishery, tens of thousands of men and women have lost their livelihood at the same time that the federal government has been slashing assistance programs. Women and men stitch together survival strategies that draw upon social welfare, part-time and poorly remunerated work, work in the informal economy, exchanges of goods and services with friends and neighbours, and intensified household work to make ends meet, as Suzanne Mackenzie (1986) also found in Trail and Nelson, BC and Kingston, Ontario.

In the decades since the 1930s, many farming families have sold their farms, overwhelmed by debt and the impossibility of competing with large agribusiness. In 1973 Canadians learned that farm wives could also lose their right to any share in their farms at the time of a marriage breakdown. Irene Murdoch's marriage ended in 1968 after a violent incident in which her husband broke her jaw. She took her case for a share of the family ranch to the Supreme Court of Canada and lost. The court argued that Murdoch's work—which included "haying, raking, swathing, mowing, driving trucks and tractors and teams, quietening horses, taking cattle back and forth to the reserve, dehorning, vaccinating, branding"—was only the work "of any ranch wife" (quoted in Prentice et al. 1996, 439–40). Such work did not give her a claim in partnership.[7] The assumption that women are economically dependent upon men, and in return provide "a labour of love," including sexual access, underwrites such a decision.

Regional inequalities have fuelled social movements that identify Central Canada as the enemy and have buttressed other movements that target the power of capitalists (who have been concentrated in Central Canada). Women and men from across Canada founded the predecessor of the New Democratic Party, the Co-operative Commonwealth Federation (CCF), but the greatest support for its program, the socialist Regina Manifesto, was from the Depression-racked Prairies. Women's participation in such movements, once as hidden as their work in the household, has been brought to light through autobiographies, feminist research, and a new generation of social historians who look behind official institutional histories (Finkel 1993; Sangster 1989).

From a feminist perspective, we might speculate that regional differences and inequalities affect and bind women more than men. Their primary responsibility for children and home has tied them more tightly into local conditions and encouraged them to make the best from what they find there (Conrad 1986). From this vantage point they have organized as feminists in groups across the country. In her study of Bay Saint George Women's Council in Newfoundland, Glynnis George found that the council's politics were "directed towards the state and the way state power is exercised in its locality." Through their work these feminists seek to eliminate gender inequality and promote the "democratization of power" (2000, 224). They intend to make life possible and better in the face of poverty, marginalization, and the destruction of the fisheries. Some of their activism garners widespread support. But when they turn to issues like violence against women, others accuse them of creating cleavages in communities that are struggling to survive economically.

Historically men have been more mobile. Those with capital to invest not only move to the centres of capital, but may travel the world to make the deals upon which profits depend. Young working-class men have been likely to "go down the road" looking for employment elsewhere; married men commute to seasonal and permanent employment in those locations where capital investment in natural resources and mines provides work (Bray 1991).

When women and children accompany husbands and fathers who have found jobs in new locations, it has often been to the resource towns built north of the main line of settlement across the country. Such towns have been built because capitalists and planners wanted to attract and keep a stable work force. The reasoning was that men accompanied by, and responsible for, women and children were more likely than single men to stay (Luxton 1980). Such towns have been described as "no place for a woman" (Kreps 1979).

As Phyllis Bray, a wife in a resource town for ten years, demonstrated, company towns provided no paid employment for women. The towns were designed with little concern for women looking after young children in small detached houses through long, hard winters and with no resources to create a life for themselves. Yet women still raised families and started churches, libraries, volunteer groups, and more recently (and with much community opposition) resources like shelters for women escaping abusive husbands (Bray 1989; 1993). The towns that women developed became home for many of them, and when company closures destroy the possibility of making a living—as they have across the country— women have worked hard to attract new industry and to provide new ways of sustaining life (Mackenzie 1987).

Arguing that women are more tied to particular (regional) locations is not meant to obliterate the long history of female migration to Canada and across Canada, nor to overlook those women who broke with gendered expectations by migrating alone and taking up many of the activities believed to be the province of menfolk (Errington 1995; Barber 1985; Parr 1990; Roberts 1979). Just as the phrase "migrants and their families" was a code for "male migrants and their wives and children" at least until the 1970s in international migration literature, so it was in the Canadian literature. As Monica Boyd and Elizabeth Grieco have recently pointed out, feminists began questioning "the near-invisibility of women as migrants, their presumed passivity in the migration process, and their assumed place in the home" (2003, 1), and the result is a much more complex set of research questions about the circumstances under which women do and do not migrate.

Whether women migrate as wives and daughters or on their own they have created regions, stretched the constraints posed by location, and been active in those movements that sought to redress poverty, devastation, unemployment, high infant and childhood mortality rates—indeed, the whole spectrum of conditions that are exacerbated by regional inequalities.

Just as Marxists and neo-Marxists have tried to specify and demonstrate that the state is deeply implicated in protecting capital and enhancing the interests of those who own and control capital, feminists have been exploring the ways in which the state may be seen to embody and produce patriarchal relations between men and women as an intrinsic part of its mandate. But before considering this question more specifically, we need to look at the broader feminist insight that, whatever the role of the state, the relations of domination and subordination between men and women are constituted in society more generally. In pursuing this idea, socialist feminists have drawn on the ideas of neo-Marxists on the relationship between the state and what has been called "civil society."

State and Society

In the neo-Marxist conception, the state is not a set of institutions with discrete functions but rather a dense network of relations that feminist sociologist Dorothy Smith captured with the concept *relations of ruling*. Relations of ruling identify "a complex of organized practices, including government, law, business and financial management, professional organization, and educational institutions as well as the discourses in texts that interpenetrate the multiple sites of power." This concept brings "into view the intersection of the institutions organizing and regulating society with their gender subtext and their basis in a gender division of labour" (1987, 3). So, for example, the relations of ruling within the health care system inform the relations nurses have with their patients as well as the actions of a woman juggling paid work with care for children and a sick husband. The relations of ruling inform your experience at university including burgeoning classes, the shift from essays to multiple-choice exams, increasing fees, whether you need to work to pay your way, whether you were part of Ontario's double cohort.

What falls outside the relations of ruling (or outside the state broadly conceived)—which does not mean that it is impervious to its influences—has been called *civil society* (Swift 1999): familial and household relationships, labour unions, churches, voluntary associations, and political parties. Whether and how a concern or demand within civil society over values, meanings, priorities, and precedence is taken up within the state is highly variable and complex. The history of how any concern moves from "private trouble" to "public issue" will not only depend on the numbers of people with the private trouble but also upon who they are. Do they belong to a powerful class, group, or sector? Do those who are powerful see them as credible? Do they articulate the concern in a language and form that resonate with others? Does it become incorporated within dominant forms of discourse? A feminist analysis reveals that the private troubles of women have had a rocky history in attempting to become part of the dialogues and debates through which state policies are reconsidered (Walker 1990).

If we conceptualize the relations between state and civil society as continuous and multifaceted, we can see that the power relations within civil society will provide some with more access than others to having their interests taken up by the state. So it is not just that women have been part of the "private" world, but that within the whole realm of civil society—family, church, labour unions, and political parties—they have, for the most part, been subordinate to men. Long before issues might become part of state dialogues, then, the concerns raised by women in their families, in the women's auxiliaries of churches and political parties, and within labour unions, have been effectively marginalized and silenced.

Consider the derisive reaction that greeted women during the movements for suffrage, during the hearings of the Royal Commission on the Status of Women, and later when the first parliamentary report on wife battering was tabled on 12 May 1982. Monique Bégin, then sitting as a front-bencher in the Liberal government, remembered the "appalling" response: "a number of male M.P.s laughed nervously and made silly comments and vulgar jokes" (1997, 22).[8] This was not just (nervous) laughter at the actual content of women's demands, but also a reaction to any articulation of their demands in the public sphere. We might imagine Canadian society as a broad panoply of stage settings—women around breakfast tables with men and children, at church meetings, at party nomination meetings. Here in the varied and elaborate settings of civil society we can see the thousands of jokes that greet women's ideas, particularly when they constitute challenges to authority. Such ridicule, sometimes backed up by physical force, constrains women from taking even their own feelings and demands seriously. When enough women dared to be the objects of male humour, all the small private jokes broke through into public ridicule and laughter in the House of Commons, in the heart, we might say, of the state. We knew that something had changed when those laughing men themselves became the target of scorn and public censure.

Here we may see why many feminists have challenged the liberal pluralist notion that governments should play a limited role in society. In particular, such a conception of government is predicated upon the division of society into private and public life, with liberal theorists arguing that governments should only intervene in public life. Radical and socialist feminists, in particular, have challenged this understanding of state and society. First, they argue that the interconnections between public and private life are dense and thorough. Second, they maintain that the state not only intrudes in the so-called private sphere but that it helps create its boundaries and the relations that inform family and household. Third, they insist that the theory that the state should not intrude in private life has provided a rationale for sustaining the economic dependence of women upon men, and has provided a virtual licence for the more powerful members of households to physically and emotionally abuse the less powerful.

It is not difficult to find support for these claims. Feminists in Canada, for example, have waged a 35-year struggle for the right of a woman to choose to terminate a pregnancy (Brodie 1992). That the state had laws that not only prohibited abortion but also forbade contraception makes a mockery of the liberal notion that the division between public and private life is clear and that the state does not intervene in private life. During the same years, however, feminists have waged just as vociferous a campaign to insist that the rape of a married woman by her husband was indeed rape and should be against the law, and that the battering of women by their intimates should be prosecuted, as are assaults by strangers. Here the rationale of the law had to be challenged: a man's home, feminists argued, should not be his castle.

The state's role in legitimating marriage provides shifting sets of advantages and disadvantages for men and women, the married and the unmarried, and for heterosexuals, lesbians, and gays; this history alone defies any analysis that claims the absence of the state from so-called private life. What feminists have argued, then, is that not only is the state patriarchal but so is the liberal conception of the relationship between government and governed, based, as it is, on a presumed natural division between public and private life.

By looking at Canadian society in terms of the relations between state and civil society, we can see why feminists direct their attention to both the hierarchical relations within civil society and the structure, relations, personnel, and discourses of the state. Unless the subordination of women within civil society is challenged, it is unthinkable that sufficient numbers of women would be in a position to engage in the public discourse that leads to transformation of the relations, policies, and legislation of the state. Yet this is not a one-way street. To the extent that state policies enhance the possibility of women's economic independence, they help women challenge their unequal place in their personal lives as well.

A PATRIARCHAL STATE?

The argument that the Canadian state is a patriarchal state has been made from a number of feminist perspectives. Taken together, the case is persuasive. Men (the "Fathers of Confederation") negotiated the Canadian state. The existence of the participating colonies was predicated upon, but did not acknowledge, the invisible labour of women in households and on farms (Errington 1996). Since Confederation, the vast majority of those with formal power in all aspects of state relations—from members of Parliament to primary school principals—have been men. The legislation of the state—from family law to criminal law—has been gendered in ways that disadvantage women politically, socially, and economically. Not only have those with influence been predominantly male, but they respond to the world in ways that protect the interests of men throughout the society, and ruling-class men in particular. Finally, male–female hierarchies inform the society in which the state is located in all its relations.

To describe the Canadian state as patriarchal, however, is not to identify a monolithic or unchanging structure or set of relations. The complex relations between state and civil society have been uncovered by long periods of feminist activism. When women disrupt the relations of civil society and challenge their subordinate locations in that realm, those disruptions are felt within the relations of the state. The reaction of governments and state bureaucracies has been to re-establish their legitimacy with the population by appointing women, sometimes even feminists, to higher office and by undertaking policy review and legislative changes. Writing from her experience as director of the Women's Program at the Department of Secretary of State during the 1970s, Susan Findlay wrote that "when the state is more vulnerable to women's demands, feminists [within the state] can play a more active role in the development of state proposals to promote women's equality...by taking advantage of the state's need for legitimation" (1987, 48). It is clear, however, that in Canada the process of incremental reform is neither linear nor even; and "the reforms that emerge from these periods are not necessarily permanent" (ibid., 48). How transitory such gains may be became glaringly apparent from the 1980s when federal and provincial governments began retreating "from initiatives to promote women's equality" (Findlay 1999, 133). Someone must have enjoyed this retreat because it continues.

Even feminist reforms that did not involve state expenditure have often had unintended negative consequences. Reforms to family law that were intended to place women on an equal footing with men at the time of marital dissolution, have been designed and implemented in ways that disadvantage some women even more than in the earlier legislation. Unlike men, women and their children are overwhelmingly poorer after separation and divorce. Mary Morton (1988) has argued that this is because the new legislation has been predicated on the fallacious assumption that men and women are equal *now*. When judges treat divorcing couples as a pair of equals, dividing marital property but giving women no right to a share of their husbands' future earnings, they ignore the overwhelming evidence that women who have spent years looking after their children are in no position to maintain the marital standard of living (Chunn 1995, 196–99). Divorced men—usually the non-custodial parent—are, by contrast, more likely to be better off financially after divorce.

Treating men and women as if they were equal now does not produce equitable outcomes, as many of the briefs prepared over the years by The National Association of Women and the Law demonstrate. The Association's concern that proposed changes to child custody and access provisions (Bill C-22) of the Divorce Act would put women who had been abused by their husbands at risk, along with their children, resulted in modifications to the bill. But drawing on evidence from Australia and the United Kingdom, Susan Boyd argues that the Divorce Act, at minimum, requires a preamble which acknowledges "the prevalence of violence against women and children" as well as women's ongoing role as the major caregivers in the family. Without this, the revised legislation "continues the growing trend in the field of custody reform debates to render this area of law gender-blind" (2003).

Equality, feminist legal scholars now argue, has been predicated within liberal theory on notions of sameness. But women and men are not the same, either biologically or sociologically. In particular, women's monopoly on childbearing and their subsequent responsibility for those children do not figure in liberal understandings of equality.

In 1979 the Supreme Court ruled that denying pregnancy benefits did not constitute sex discrimination. Here the problem of equating equality with sameness comes clearly into focus: the rights of men were used as the yardstick for all human rights. (If he can't get pregnant, she can't get maternity leave.) The Charter helped the Supreme Court figure this out (as did LEAF who intervened in this case and many others), and in 1989 the Court used Section 15 to reverse its earlier decision (Baines forthcoming, 103). Later the same year the Court declared "that every difference in treatment between individuals under the law will not necessarily result in inequality and, as well, that identical treatment may frequently produce serious inequality" (quoted in Baines forthcoming, 86). Since then the Court has declared that the purpose of Section 15 is "to prevent the violation of essential human dignity and freedom through the imposition of disadvantage, stereotyping, or political or social prejudice, and to promote a society in which all persons enjoy equality recognition" (quoted in Baines forthcoming, 86).

"Charter jurisprudence," Beverley Baines concludes, "has been relatively successful in naming male privilege and/or leading to legislative changes that benefit women in the area of athletics, reproduction, crime, family and employment." Using the Charter the Supreme Court has forced the state to abandon some patriarchal legislation but has failed to provide rulings when "women required positive action to alleviate their situations" (forthcoming, 117).

The case that the state is patriarchal does not rest on any particular legislation or set of practices. But rather, to recall the argument in chapter 1, in order to make a world for themselves women have had to challenge "the way things are," that good old comfortable status quo. As a result, in the context of the dominant order, the normative order, the legal order women appear as—variously—a special interest group, special pleaders, victims, whiners, man-hating, child-hating—sometimes worst of all—feminists. An early feminist slogan—if a man could get pregnant, abortion would be a sacrament—comes back to me as I write these words. At the same time, listen for the contempt in the voice of politicians who talk about "special interest groups," and ask yourself how it is, for example, that women have to plot long and hard to find the "right time" to have a baby.

From the early 1970s, feminists argued sex equality required that all members of society had to take responsibility for childcare. That meant tax-supported 24-hour childcare centres. A feminist peace poster of the mid 1970s challenged the state's funding priorities: "What if there was child care for every child and the military had to have bake sales to buy their bombers." Feminists argued that a state with unlimited resources for the military and for war and few if any resources for childcare earned the designation patriarchal.

Making the claim that the Canadian state is patriarchal does not eliminate the need for an historically specific analysis that attends both to changes over time and differences across space. In the next chapter, the focus is upon how the patriarchal assumptions, policies, and laws of the Canadian state are manifested and experienced by the Aboriginal peoples, by Quebec francophones, and by those disadvantaged by racism. In those discussions, a further debate about the Canadian state is raised: What are the historical and contemporary grounds for arguing that this state is not only patriarchal but racist? From this vantage point, we may look at the ways in which patriarchal, racist, and class interests are intertwined in different social and political locations.

NOTES

1. Falkiner v. Ontario (Ministry of Community and Social Services, Income Maintenance Branch), [2002] O.J. No. 17771, online: QL(OJ).

2. From 1990/91 to 1999/2000, undergraduate tuition fees rose by an average of 9.6 percent per year. However, beginning this decade, the rate of increase of tuition fees has slowed to an annual average of 4.9 percent (Statistics Canada, August 12, 2003).

3. In British North America, some women of property appear to have voted in some elections, particularly in Lower Canada. There were debates about the legality of women's suffrage and, in the end, specific legislation was required to ban women from voting (Prentice et al. 1996, 98–99; Riddell 1928).

4. See also DuBois (1978). She argues that it was women's involvement in the suffrage movement as historical and collective agents, "far more than the eventual enfranchisement of women, that created the basis for new social relations between men and women" (201).

5. Alex C. Michalos evaluated federal policies designed to create gender equality since the Royal Commission using 29 indicators. After detailed quantitative analysis he concluded that there is "more evidence of improvement than of deterioration in the status of women." But he added that this "is not a particularly robust conclusion, not as positive as I would have preferred nor as negative as I feared it might be" (2000, 275).

6. Andrew Jackson, Senior Economist for the Canadian Labour Congress, derived his data from Statistics Canada's Labour Force Survey Historical Review CD-ROM 2002.

7. The lump-sum maintenance payment that Murdoch was finally granted in 1973 was not on the grounds of the economic partnership of the marriage but rather on the grounds that women were entitled to support during marriage and appropriate maintenance after break-up in return for domestic duties and sexual availability during the marriage. The Murdoch case helped fuel the feminist struggle, which resulted in legislation in most provinces recognizing that domestic and other economic activities, usually done by women, made it possible for wage earners to acquire money and property (Prentice et al. 1988, 398–99).

8. Monique Bégin served as Secretary to the Royal Commission on the Status of Women. Later she was appointed to the cabinet of Pierre Trudeau as Minister of Health and Welfare. From this location she is credited with saving universal accessible medicare in the 1970s.

chapter four

Challenging the State:
Self-determination,
Nationalism, and Anti-racism

On the front page of the *Globe and Mail* on 14 October 1988, there was a story head-lined "New map diminishes Canada":

> Canada's sprawling place in world cartography is cut dramatically in a new world map issued by the National Geographic Society. And at the unveiling of the new map yesterday, society officials were only slightly apologetic that it shows a distinctly wizened true north strong and free. The problem, they said, is that Canadians have been living a geographical lie. The sweeping expanse of pink on most maps that has reassured generations of Canadians about their place in the world gives the country about 2 and a half times the credit it is due. The new National Geographic map uses a projection designed to remedy much of the distortion that is inevitable when a sphere is portrayed on a flat piece of paper....Instead of being 158 per cent larger than it would be on a globe of the same scale..., Canada shrinks to 21 per cent larger. (Mackenzie 1988)

> (Reprinted with permission from the *Globe and Mail*)

Map making, as the inventor of the new projection, Arthur Robinson, commented, is "pretty much an artistic process rather than a scientific process." Maps are representations, symbols, just as words are symbols, and as such they communicate and distort simultaneously.

The Aboriginal peoples living on that land represented by the "sweeping expanse of pink" point to another distortion inherent in the depiction of "Canada." In public protests and negotiations, many Aboriginal people have made it clear that they do not acknowledge the legitimacy of the Canadian state. This state, they argue, was formed by conquest, broken promises, and expansion by force and trickery. European laws instituted a regime of private property that excluded the original inhabitants from access to the land and use of its resources (Abele 1997; Green 2003). In Joyce Green's words: "Colonialism initiated by imperialism, forms the foundation of Project Canada.

Colonization is not only about the physical occupation of someone else's land but also about the appropriation of others' political authority, cultural self determination, economic capacity, and strategic location" (2003, 52).

Since the mid 1960s, a growing number of people of French descent in Quebec have also provoked a renewed challenge to the legitimacy of the Canadian state for failing to accommodate the aspirations of the French nation in North America. In the second of two referenda on the question of independence from Canada, held on 30 October 1995, the vote in Quebec between those favouring secession and those against ended in a dead heat, with the "no" side unable to claim more than a truce. To complicate this picture, the Cree of Quebec acknowledged that the Québécois had a right to secede from Confederation but no right to the vast proportion of the land occupied by Aboriginal peoples. The Cree asserted that they would continue to negotiate with the government of Canada for self-determination, regardless of the outcome of the referendum.

This chapter continues the discussion of feminist challenges to the Canadian state by looking specifically at the Aboriginal struggle for self-determination, the Québécois quest for independence, and the continuing struggles by those disadvantaged by racism to transform the policies and practices of the Canadian state. There are three main themes to the discussions that follow from the discussions in the previous chapter. First, the formation of the Canadian state was based on and is sustained by fundamental inequalities. These inequalities are not incidental features of a society that in all other respects is fair-minded and just. Second, all of these structured inequalities are informed by patriarchal assumptions and laws, but we can only understand how this is so through specific historical and sociological analysis. Third, the patriarchal state has different ramifications for women of different social classes, in different civil societies, and for those who are advantaged or disadvantaged through racist assumptions and practices.

COLONIZATION AND DISPOSSESSION: THE CANADIAN STATE AND THE ABORIGINAL PEOPLES

The Aboriginal peoples of Canada[1] lived in the territory that is Canada for thousands of years before the arrival of the French or the English. Their claims that the Canadian state does not represent them and that, by deception and force, they were deprived of the use of the land on which they had lived have been made eloquently and often in the law courts, through the media, in political protests of many kinds, and in forums like the International Court of Justice (Abele and Stasiulis 1989; Tennant 1990).

In mounting their challenge to the legitimacy of the Canadian state, Aboriginal peoples have faced overwhelming obstacles. They share a history of dispossession of land, disenfranchisement, resettlement on reservations, and programs and policies such as residential schooling designed to promote their assimilation as subordinate members of the mainstream culture and the developing Canadian nation.

"No people in Canada [have] been so reduced materially and discursively as Aboriginals, or so compromised politically" (Million 2000, 99). A stunning array of evidence—from census data on life span, health, incarceration rates, and infant and maternal mortality to ethnographic and anthropological studies that detail how a way of life was destroyed—has been brought to bear on the case that there is a third world within Canada's borders. In 1995, 40 percent of Registered Indians lived in families that were at or below Statistics Canada's low-income cutoff (LICO). Four times more Aboriginal persons in major Western cities live in poverty than other Canadians. The poverty rate in 1995 for off-reserve Aboriginal peoples, 15 years and over, was 42.7 percent for women and 35.1 percent for men, over double the rates for other Canadian men and women. These figures, as the National Council of Welfare notes, would be higher if they included reserve populations (2002, 144).

Aboriginal peoples are not one people, but many, each with a long history before European contact and a particular history of contact with Europeans. As Frances Abele cautions, "It is as difficult to generalize about First Nations as it is to generalize about the diverse nations of the United Kingdom and Europe" (1997, 120). Without a common language, culture, and—most importantly—territory, Aboriginal political struggles with the Canadian state have generally been isolated and fragmented, spread out over thousands of miles. At the same time, the ongoing struggle at the local level for individual and community survival has been monumental and exhausting.

Yet from these diverse locations, a shared Aboriginal response has been in the making for at least the past three decades. The increasingly unified demand to have their territory returned and for sovereignty over that territory was forced dramatically onto the Canadian political agenda in the summer of 1990 at Kanesatake when "an attempt by the Mohawk to stop a municipal golf course from being constructed on land they believed to be theirs led to an armed stand-off and one death."[2] Clearly Aboriginal peoples have found ways of demonstrating that excluding them from negotiations that affect their lives and the viability of their communities will have crucial repercussions for the political future of the country. In the aftermath of Kanesatake (and the solidarity blockade at Kahnawake), the federal government struck the Royal Commission on Aboriginal Peoples that, after wide consultation with Aboriginal peoples, developed a mandate to study "virtually every feature of the institutional relationships between Aboriginal and non-Aboriginal Canadians" (Abele 1997, 127).

We can examine the precontact histories of Aboriginal peoples and the history of the Aboriginal–European encounter by asking some feminist questions. First, what was the precontact history of gender relations in the diverse Aboriginal societies? There were great differences across these societies in the relations between men and women, the status of women, the sexual division of labour, and the roles of men and women in decision making. Yet most of the anthropological evidence, including the earliest oral histories provided by elders, depicts societies organized on relatively communitarian and egalitarian lines. "In small hunting and gathering bands, where decision-making was often communal, women do seem to have shared power with men. In the Iroquois and Huron agricultural communities, matrons (the leading women in charge of the longhouses) appear to have had great authority in all realms of life." Among some northwestern and western peoples, on the other hand, "high class women could be chieftain...but many women were relatively powerless" (Prentice et al. 1996, 29; Mitchell and Franklin 1984). Noted North American anthropologist Bruce Trigger determined that "in North American Indian societies, decision making depended upon a slow process of achieving consensus" (1991, 1214). There is evidence that, in many of these societies, women were by no means excluded from that process (Van Kirk 1987).

In an attempt to seek "a positive vision of Native womanhood" through studying cultural symbols and listening to the oral histories of many elders, Kim Anderson was mindful of how "our losses and our need to reclaim our original ways can lead us down the dangerous path of romanticizing, generalizing, or essentializing our heritage and traditions" (2000, 34). She found that Native women had "not been equally valued, placed or conceptualized in their various societies." But at the same time, her conclusions resonated with those of Laguna Pueblo/Sioux writer, Paula Allen Gunn. Allen Gunn concluded that although "the tribes see women variously...they do not question the value of femininity. Sometimes they see women as fearful, sometimes peaceful, sometimes omnipotent and omniscient, but [never] as mindless, helpless, simple or oppressed" (cited in Anderson 2000, 36).

Given these informed interpretations, what was the impact of the arrival, settling, and consolidation of power of Europeans upon the relations of power between the sexes within European and Native societies? Again, this is a question that reaches back to the first contact and continues today. Several points, briefly put, will help frame the discussion. Roman Catholic missionaries came to the New World in the seventeenth century to Christianize the "heathens." Their belief that the unconverted faced eternal damnation in a fiery hell helps to explain why some missionaries were willing to face martyrdom in pursuit of saving souls. Successful conversion, the missionaries came to believe, had to involve a transformation of the Aboriginal way of life and a reconfiguring of Native relationships. In their work with the Huron and Montagnais, for example, the missionaries were struck by women's freedom and autonomy, especially in regards to sexual practices and marital relationships. The missionaries urged men to bring their wives under control and to practise sexual monogamy to ensure that their wives bore only their children. In anthropologist Karen Anderson's assessment, in no more than three decades "many women had...been subdued, rendered docile and obedient" (1991, 4).

An extensive anthropological literature reveals that hunter and gatherer societies are likely to have more egalitarian relations between the sexes than are sedentary agricultural societies (including the feudal societies that predated capitalism in Western Europe and England) or capitalist societies (Gough 1973). As power becomes more centralized and as state structures replace household structures as locations for decision making, men gain the advantage and women are increasingly excluded. Certainly there was some centralized decision making in some Aboriginal societies, and women seemed to have played a less direct role than men in such decisions. But this centralization pales in comparison to postcontact history when power over people and resources was wrested away from Aboriginal communities and replaced by the interventions of white male administrators from the Department of Indian Affairs. In this process, women were more excluded and disadvantaged than men because the laws and policies that structured access to resources were thoroughly informed by the patriarchal practices and beliefs of the white conquerors (Stevenson 1999).

During the nineteenth century the policy of collecting Indians on reservations began in earnest. Marlene Brant Castellano has summarized the devastating effects of this policy, particularly on Indian men in the migratory groups "whose education from infancy was directed to preparing them to assume the roles of hunter, warrior, [and] visionary." Ojibwa women, under conditions of deepening hardship, retained much of their traditional role caring for children, processing and preparing food and other necessities, and adding "colour and beauty to the daily round of subsistence work through the creation of handicrafts" (1989, 48). From another vantage point, Emma LaRocque has written that while "colonization has taken its toll on all Native peoples...perhaps it has taken its greatest toll on women" who suffer from sexism as well as racism. "Racism and sexism found in the colonial process have served to dramatically undermine the place and value of women in Aboriginal cultures, leaving us vulnerable both within and outside our communities" (1996, 11).

The reservations policy of the Canadian state was intended to be temporary. The longer term strategy was assimilation—also known as cultural genocide—and forced residential schooling became a key method for achieving this goal. Noted author Jeannette Armstrong identified residential schools in Canada as "the single most devastating factor in the breakdown of our society." In this process, which continued for over 100 years, Aboriginal children "were seized from their homes and forcibly placed in sterile, military-like, hostile institutions [where they were] raised in racist hostility and dispassion" (1996, x). Anthropologist Jo-Anne Fiske explains that in Canada, as elsewhere, "colonial curricula ignore, contradict, and deny the students' culture; their language is forbidden and their daily life is structured according to the foreign moral precepts of the colonisers" (1996a, 168).

From the 1940s Aboriginal people protested the existence of the residential school system both because the system threatened their cultural survival and political sovereignty, and because the education was so inadequate. But another charge against the schools—the existence of widespread physical, psychological, and sexual abuse—found its way onto the public agenda only in the mid 1980s after most of these institutions had closed.[3] An intense campaign to demand redress forced the federal government in 1998 to create a $350 million Healing Fund while the four Christian denominations—Roman Catholic, Anglican, United, and Presbyterian—joined the apology. The court cases continue. Given the "seemingly endless array of...abuse endured by First Nations children across several generations at the hands of their guardians" Dian Million sought to explain both the 100-year silence and the timing of the campaign that broke the silence (2000, 92).

There are several considerations. During the previous decade Aboriginal women began organizing to redress their historic subordination by the Canadian state and by their own bands. In this context they had raised issues of gender relations, family, abuse, healing, and mental health (Million 2000, 98). Second, as we noted earlier, relations of domination and subordination inform all aspects of civil society, and it is within civil society that shifts in power relations occur that make possible the naming of previously invisible practices. From the early 1970s, feminists began bringing to light the "ordinary" violence including child sexual abuse that exists within families, churches, orphanages, and other institutionalized settings. Within this context, the stories that adult survivors of residential schools began to tell could be heard—and believed—by a very broad public. Celia Haig-Brown's ethnography based on the individual narratives of adults who had attended residential schools served as a catalyst for opening the public discussion (1988; Million 2000, 98–102).

The conquerors' intention—to produce assimilated individuals living in patriarchal nuclear families—was a spectacular failure as the ongoing Aboriginal struggles for self-determination reveal. Several researchers have pointed to the unintended consequences of the residential schooling system in developing political leadership among male graduates. In her research on the Lejac Residential School in central British Columbia, Jo-Anne Fiske documented that the Oblate priests who operated the school "considered the matrilineal kinship system of the Carrier...to be a degraded state, the outcome of 'looseness of morals and absence of social restraint.'" The Oblate schools emphasized moral instruction and, for girls, domestic skills. Seldom did students have more than two hours a week of academic studies. The girls resisted their teachers' impositions more subtly than the boys, and more girls than boys completed grade 8, and later went on to secondary classes (1996a, 174). Nor did the girls take away the intended messages of female docility and obedience. Later in their life Carrier women revealed their "strength and perseverance [assuming] leadership roles in their communities" and drawing in part upon political skills learned at school (Miller and Chuchryk 1996, 7).

In general, the white Western patriarchal notion that men look after (and we have seen the underside of the meaning of "looking after") women means that when Western, developed nations "come to the aid" of undeveloped nations, the resources—from job-training programs to discretion over distribution of material resources—are channelled through male leaders and targeted for men (Fiske 1991; Hale 1988; McFarland 1988; Mosse 1993). With Aboriginal men coming to hold most of the leadership roles in post-colonial organizations, the negotiations that have taken place between the First Nations and the representatives of the Canadian state could be described as racialized sessions of a boys' club (Fiske 1996a).

In the past 30 years, Native women have begun organizing against the ways in which the patriarchal practices of white society have affected their status within their own society (Silman 1987). This has meant challenging not only the Canadian state but also male Indian leadership. These women argue that many male Indian leaders identify their community's interests with their own interests. Women are excluded from decision making, have fewer resources than men, and have become subordinate to men in ways unimaginable in precontact days. The inequality between Indian men and women was specifically written into law by the Canadian state during the 1880s with the Indian Act. This specifically patriarchal aspect of the Indian Act was also an enabling measure for a racist policy.

The Indian Act was a racist piece of legislation in a very precise meaning of the word racist. First, the category Indian was created, and the people of disparate societies who lived in the provinces and territories of Canada were so labelled. In creating a category Indian, another category, non-Indian, had to be created. The decision about who is in what category becomes entirely arbitrary, since the creation of the categories themselves was an arbitrary act. The underlying assumption for this argument is that there is no meaningful biological category called race that has consequences for reproductive or political life; there is, rather, one race—that is, the human race. What divides people are social practices, including laws that create such categories. Such laws can be called racist because they assume that people can be divided into such categories in ways that matter. Racism then serves to divide people both by categorizing them and by consolidating the hierarchical arrangements that originally motivated the categorizations.

The Indian Act clearly served to divide people. It divided people arbitrarily into racial categories—Indian and non-Indian—and then mandated different treatment, different obligations and responsibilities, and differential access to resources to each group. In so doing, arbitrary differences between people were encoded into law, while all differences among those placed in each category were made invisible. So it was that many people who considered themselves members of Aboriginal societies and whose parents, brothers, sisters, and cousins may have been categorized as Aboriginal were deemed non-Indian. The means for implementing this racist categorization was propelled by a thoroughly patriarchal idea: that societal membership of women and children is determined and legitimated by their husbands and fathers.

The Indian Act incorporated the Western patriarchal law that children are the children of their mother's husband.[4] A non-Indian woman who married an Indian man became an Indian, as did her children. An Indian woman who married a non-Indian man became a non-Indian, as did her children. The law was made retroactive, and the business of registering Indians was based on an attempt to determine whether a person's father, not mother, was an Indian. Given that the law was made more than 200 years after the first contact (including sexual contact) between Europeans and Aboriginals, the attempt to figure out who was and who was not Indian would be the subject of satire if it had not had such far-reaching and tragic consequences.[5] A non-Indian could include a person with two Aboriginal parents as well as all those with no Aboriginal ancestors.

The Indian Act proved useful for the Canadian state. The categorizations that it created and perpetuated pitted members of Aboriginal societies against each other: men against women, sisters against sisters, those who had married Indians against those who had married non-Indians. In the last two decades, some Aboriginal women have struggled successfully against the racism and patriarchalism of the Indian Act, in particular section 12(1)(b). Their struggle was motivated by the poverty and destitution of their societies, their exclusion from decision making within those societies, their analysis that male leaders, husbands, and fathers were misusing their power and resources, and, most dramatically, by the forced evictions from Indian reservations of women, along with their children, who had married non-Indians.

Martin Cannon has analyzed this exclusion as discrimination at the intersection of race and gender (1995, 38). This specific discrimination was accomplished by treating sex and race as separate categories, rather than as inseparable dimensions of power, identity, and ascription that inform the relationships among individuals. This categorization made possible and sustained legislation and social policy based on an original fiction: that women—and only women—were divisible. They could be *either* Indian (by marrying an Indian) or women (by marrying a non-Indian), but not both. Indian women's struggle for reinclusion was a struggle against discrimination that made them unequal to Native men, who did not lose status when they married out, and to non-Native women, who gained Indian status by marrying an Indian. In another sense, we could say that it was a struggle for recognition as Indian women.

Just as the Indian Act divided and categorized people, so has the resistance by those seeking to sustain the exclusion of women who married out. In the 1970s, status Indian organizations such as the National Indian Brotherhood feared that any tampering with the Indian Act would aid the Canadian government's attempts to eradicate the special citizenship rights accorded to Indians by the act. More recently, the struggle by Indian women has been resisted in the name of collective rights. In a brief to the Standing Committee on Indian Women and the Indian Act, the Assembly of First Nations (AFN) argued that "as Indian people, we cannot afford to deal with individual rights overriding collective rights" (quoted in Cannon 1995, 98). First Nations leadership uses this argument, for example, to block attempts by Aboriginal women to use the Charter of Rights (and thus the Canadian state) to settle what the AFN perceives as internal disputes.

The assumption implicit in the position of the AFN is that Indian women struggle for equality as women, while the status Indian groups struggle for the collective rights of Indian people. But it must be remembered that the Indian Act first separated Indian women from the collective. This forcible separation has made possible their treatment as individual women whose struggles are now seen to threaten the collective. What the AFN fails to recognize is that the Assembly itself is an outcome of imposed systems of Indian Act governance. The AFN mobilized against the Charter in the name of culture and tradition that predated colonialism. Yet it was their history as a colonized people that produced not only the partitioned and subordinate status of Indian women but also political organizations like the AFN itself, which were no more part of traditional culture or politics than was the discriminatory treatment of women (ibid., 103).

In contrast to the position of the AFN, the Native Women's Association of Canada (NWAC) has supported the application of the Charter to the First Nations. NWAC representatives argue that Native culture and tradition have been transformed by the history of colonialism, a history that lodged official power in the hands of the mainly male leaders of postcolonial Native organizations. Thus, without the Charter, Native women would be unable to resist the discriminatory actions of band councils, or any future form of self-government (Stacey-Moore 1993; see also Cannon 1995, 92–93).

Some Aboriginal women state categorically that they share neither NWAC's position nor what they perceive as a feminist preoccupation with equality. For such women, equality promises something different from—and less than—the kinds of relations between men and women in their precontact societies. Skonaganleh:ra, a Mohawk woman, explains: "I don't want equality. I want to go back to where women, in aboriginal communities, were complete, where they were beautiful, where they were treated as more than equal—where man was helper and woman was the centre of that environment, that community" (Osennontion and Skonaganleh:ra 1989, 15).

Some insist that Aboriginal societies were animated by a "communitarian" notion of responsibility rather than egalitarianism (Prentice et al. 1988, 40; see also Turpel 1993, 180), and that therefore native women should not seek the protection of the Canadian Charter of Rights and Freedoms. But history is a resource that can be mobilized to serve various contemporary positions. Emma LaRocque cautions that as women we must be

> circumspect in our recall of tradition...[T]here are indications of male violence and sexism in some Aboriginal societies prior to European contact and certainly after contact. But, at the same time, culture is not immutable, and tradition cannot be expected to be always of value or relevant in our times. As Native women, we are faced with very difficult and painful choices, but, nonetheless, we are challenged to change, create and embrace "traditions" consistent with contemporary and international human rights standards. (1996, 14)

John Borrows argues that "while colonialism may be at the root of our learned disrespect for women, we can not blame colonialism for our informed actions today" (1994, 46). Indeed, "status and gendered hierarchies, along with patriarchal prerogative, have been institutionalized and internalized" within Native communities (Cannon 1995, 105).

Aboriginal women's struggle for full participation in their own communities and within Canada and Quebec, for the sharing of decision making, and for access to resources for themselves and their children is complex and multifaceted. Their struggle for self-determination for their communities has had to include the struggle for full recognition *within* their communities. The concept of equality does not have easy applicability in those societies with no concept of individual economic rights. Importantly, however, native women's associations have not invoked the concept of sex equality but rather used "the position of Indian motherhood...as a supportable and powerful metaphor and material fact of their organization. In their narratives, Indian, Métis and Inuit women positioned their selves as the foundation of healthy families and communities rather than as 'feminists' demanding equal rights" (Million 2000, 99). As women and mothers—nurturers and healers—they needed to share power and resources with men in order to restore their communities (Fiske 1996a). Still, they are portrayed by the dominant organizations as spoilers, individuals who put themselves before their communities—from which they are excluded.

This analysis of the history and contemporary circumstances of the Aboriginal peoples reveals their rationale for challenging the legitimacy of the Canadian state. The colonization of this country by Europeans and the subsequent formation and expansion of the Canadian state wreaked havoc, by accident and design, on the peoples who had lived here for hundreds of years. The call of Aboriginal peoples for self-determination today is based not only on the legal claim to land never relinquished, but also upon the evidence of the past century that the Canadian state does not represent their interests as collectivities or individuals. For women of Aboriginal societies, the struggle for self-determination is painfully complicated by the splits in their own communities between men and women. Many Aboriginal women insist that this struggle will not be successful unless they first restore the position and status that they enjoyed before their communities were decimated by the advent of the Europeans and before their men were persuaded by the privileges of male domination. As Sandra Lovelace Sappier said, "We could get Indian self-government but we have to work together and be equal" (quoted in Silman 1987, 245).

The formation of the Canadian state was negotiated as if there were no Aboriginal peoples in the country. Their struggle for self-determination stems in large measure from their invisibility in the resulting confederation. But the Canadian Confederation also consolidated another systemic inequality between peoples—the French and the English—that produced another and, to date, more politically successful challenge to the legitimacy of the Canadian state.

QUEBEC AND CANADA: "DEUX NATIONS"

The Québécois challenge to the legitimacy of the Canadian state rests upon the existence of a conquered people with a common language and shared culture living in a particular territory. But the remarkable success of this challenge owes a great deal to the constitutional map drawing that provided them with a state of their own—the province of Quebec—within Canada. Although there are many conflicting and complex interpretations of this history, my intention is to provide a basis for understanding the relations between English and French in Canada as a relationship between nations. Such an interpretation contributes to an understanding of nationalism in Quebec and underpins the social movements for sovereignty-association or for a separate state.

By the Treaty of Paris in 1763, New France was ceded to Britain. Because most members of the elite in New France had strong ties with France based on patronage from the Crown, trading alliances, and familial networks, they left the ceded territory and returned to France. Approximately 60 000 people of French origin, most of them living within the modified feudal structure of the seigneurial system, were left in the colony. Men, women, and children lived and worked within family-based households, dependent upon each other's labour. The priests and nuns of the Catholic Church ran the hospitals and schools, but their numbers were sparse and, as with most European peasant populations, the church's influence on the daily life of the people was minimal. After France ceded Quebec to Britain, British traders and settlers moved to Montreal and, with their capital and contacts, soon dominated in trade and business (Guindon 1988; Hamilton 1988).

English economic domination was paralleled by attempts to ensure political domination. This was attempted by redrawing political boundaries three times—in 1791, 1840, and 1867. The Constitutional Act of 1791 created the division between Upper and Lower Canada, which gave the English, then the minority in the colony, control within Upper Canada. In the late 1830s, rebellions against the aristocratic elites dominating politics roused much of the population in Lower Canada against English rule and their domination of the economy. The resolution of the rebellions of 1837–38 was to render the French a minority by creating a joint legislature of the Canadas, Canada East and Canada West. By this time, the United Empire Loyalists and their descendants had swelled the English to majority status within Canada. Thirty years later, the Canadian Confederation ensured that the French would remain a minority in the new country. Nevertheless, the French were powerful enough to oppose the unitary state favoured by their English counterparts, thus securing a federal-provincial system. Given that this meant Quebec would henceforth be one province among several English provinces, there was much hostility in Quebec for the new confederation.

Confederation created a federal state and (eventually) ten provinces and carefully delineated the division of powers between them. Provincial prerogatives over crucial areas such as education and social welfare mean that many of the assumptions and laws that deal with the relations between men and women vary from province to province. These differences are particularly notable between Quebec, where the French Civil Code prevails, and the other provinces, which follow British common law. The British North America Act continued the process through which Quebec became the (only) geopolitical location for the French nation in Canada and at the same time ensured its subordinate status.

For 100 years after Confederation, the Catholic Church provided the institutional framework for the survival of "la langue, la foi, et la famille." The church was in the position to do this because of the remarkable mobilization campaign engineered by Bishop Bourget in the 1840s to bring church people, disaffected with postrevolutionary, "godless" French society, to the more hospitable New World. By the time of Confederation, the church had defeated almost all of its internal enemies who were seeking secular institutions. It had developed the entire infrastructure of schools, hospitals, and social welfare that persisted in Quebec until the Quiet Revolution of the 1960s (Fahmy-Eid and Laurin-Frenette 1986). These institutions provided work for men and women; in 1930, one in ten francophone adults was a priest or a nun.

Sociologist Hubert Guindon has argued that the underlying political contract of Confederation was between English-speaking capitalists and the Catholic Church of Quebec. This arrangement was facilitated by another provision of Confederation: the protection of Protestant institutions within Quebec. This provision effectively preserved English as the language of business and helped to ensure that English capitalists would own and manage the corporate structure with its links to the rest of Canada, the United States, and Britain. The French would run a small provincial government—small because so many of the functions that were handled by governments in the rest of the country were organized in Quebec by the church. French politicians and bureaucrats who wanted to work in the federal area had to work in English (Beattie 1975; Guindon 1988). The relationship between the provincial government and the Catholic Church in

Quebec from the time of Confederation was, with dramatic exceptions, symbiotic. The men of the church and state shared the same faith, came from the same families, and were educated in the same schools. From the vantage point of a largely francophobic English Canada, this meant that Quebec society was reactionary, an economic back-water, and the people slavish followers of church dogma, superstitious, and unwilling to accommodate modern ideas.

That women did not win provincial suffrage in Quebec until 1940, two decades after most of the other provinces, contributed to this belief. Yet a more nuanced reading is required if we are to explain the Quiet Revolution of the 1960s and the enormous suc-cess of second wave feminism in Quebec. Is there another reading of this history that helps to explain the massive acceptance of feminism in the 1970s in Quebec?

A popular idea, with origins in the 1920s, suggested that the French defeat on the Plains of Abraham had been avenged by women who were willing to devote themselves to bearing and raising large families. In this way, the English—who desired nothing more than the extinction of the French—were outwitted. This idea was encapsulated in the phrase *la revanche des berceaux* (the revenge of the cradle). Such an idea was powerful in Quebec, capturing both the nationalist anxiety about French-Catholic survival and male anxiety about women breaking out of their maternal role. This idea was invoked during the struggles not only against suffrage but against all of women's claims to civil and political equality in Quebec (Stoddart 1973; 1981; Trofimenkoff 1977).

But were women the docile baby makers and saint-like mothers that politicians and bishops venerated and English Canadians scorned? And if so, how was it possible that women in Quebec abandoned this role with such apparent ease? First, it is important to realize that the veneration of mothers by the Catholic Church in Quebec was not simply rhetoric adopted to keep women in their place. As early as 1866, Abbé Laflèche wrote that the raising of children was the work of the mother and the priest. How different this is from Protestant formulations, which stress that the father is the head of the household. It is true that the mother was to obey her priest, but given that this was not a daily consultation (as it might be with a husband on the premises), in theory, at least, this arrangement left her with a good deal of discretion within the home. Furthermore, there is ethnographic evi-dence to support the church's claim that the mother was the centre of the family and that her influence over the daily life of her children was paramount. I would speculate also that because the Catholic Church treated the wife/husband relationship as a secular rather than a holy relationship until well into the 1940s, Quebec women's subordination to their hus-bands lacked much of the ideological and psychological resonance of that of their Protestant sisters. When the power of the church collapsed in the 1960s, women accepted the idea of equality between the sexes with astonishing rapidity and pragmatism.

Feminist historian Marie Lavigne launched a second challenge to the conventional his-tory of women (1986). In path-breaking work, she showed that only a minority of women in Quebec had had very large families. Many women remained celibate—both in convents and in lay society—and many more had small families. Why then, Lavigne asks, did every-one believe that all women had huge families? Her answer has a simple resonance: because most people *came* from large families. There were many more people with several broth-ers and sisters than there were people with one or two, or none at all. Her research suggests that many women did not follow church teachings, and that many married women must have practised birth control despite the church's prohibition.

A third note of caution comes from historians who have researched the history of nuns in Quebec. Feminists have tended to view nuns as obstacles to women's emancipation. First, it was assumed that nuns were simply servants of the church, with little opportunity or desire to take initiative or wield influence. Second, in Quebec, it was nuns who did much of the nursing, teaching, charity, club, and church work that in English Canada was being taken up by lay women. Thus, ambitious middle-class women in Quebec found less scope for activities outside the family or the convent than did their sisters in the rest of Canada.

Feminist historian Marta Danylewycz challenged both these ideas (1987). She pointed to evidence that laywomen and nuns co-operated in many instances. In addition, she argued that traditional interpretations overlooked the range of opportunities open to nuns in a society where the entire infrastructure was organized by the church. Nuns ran hospitals, schools, orphanages, and charities. Indeed, it is now clear that many women entered convents not simply because their religious beliefs were strong but because the work open to a nun provided desirable alternatives to life as a wife and mother.

With the collapse of the church in Quebec, thousands of nuns and priests left their religious vocations to do similar work in newly secularized institutions. Young women no longer looked to the church for work but, like their aunts and older cousins, they did not automatically opt for marriage and motherhood either. Many women of all social classes continued to choose a single life, or to combine one or two children with paid labour. Women flocked into existing feminist organizations in massive numbers and also started new ones (Bégin 1992; deSève 1992; Dumont 1992).

From the late 1960s, many women linked their feminist demands with nationalist aspirations. They argued that their goals of equality with men would mean little in a society informed by hierarchical relations between the English and the French. As long as the language of work—particularly managerial and professional work—was English, and as long as priorities regarding health care, immigration, and cultural life were determined in Ottawa, women and men in Quebec were destined to subordinate national status. Feminists flocked into the pro-independence Parti Québécois (PQ), helped the party enunciate an ideology of sexual equality, and developed social policies to match. In terms of many feminist demands, Quebec was ahead of the rest of the country and remained so. Not surprisingly, many Québécoises did not join the campaigns by feminists in the rest of the country for section 28 of the Charter of Rights and later against the Meech Lake Accord for the omission of a guarantee of sex equality (deSève 1997). While feminist nationalists understood the rationale for these campaigns, they argued that transforming the patriarchal relations of their society also meant emancipating Quebec from its subordinate national status and that the Canadian state did not represent them either as women or as Québécoises (Dumont 1995). This was a double challenge to the legitimacy of the Canadian state.

At the same time, both history and contemporary politics indicate that struggles to ensure that feminist demands are an intrinsic part of the nationalist agenda require vigilance (Dumont 1995; Lamoureux 1987; Maroney 1992; Green 2001, 104). For example, feminists viewed the continuing nationalist pronatalist response to the plummeting birth rate with great suspicion. These policies aim to encourage women to have more children and resonate with the powerful ideology that women bore many children to ensure national survival (Hamilton 1995; Green 2001, 15). Only in 1997 did the state acknowledge the ineffectiveness of its pronatalist policies, and moved instead to consolidate family support policies (albeit continuing to articulate anxiety about the low birth rate) (Krull 2003).

Through the 1990s, the Parti Québécois tried to sustain nationalist momentum by continuing to assert that the government should actively work to maximize new economic opportunities; protect social safety nets as much as possible; and promote social solidarity (Salée and Coleman 1997, 267). Despite the increase in poverty, unemployment, and social exclusion, many progressives supported the government and its strategy of negotiating with business, labour, and community groups in order to develop a "social economy," (Mendell quoted in Salée 2003, 31). As Quebec began grappling with a neo-liberal globalizing agenda, however, these policies, along with many others, faced erosion.

In 1999 the poverty rate for all persons in Quebec—at 19.5 percent—was above the national average along with Manitoba and Newfoundland and Labrador (National Council of Welfare Reports 2002, 31). These negative outcomes helped to destabilize the nationalist dream which rested on the development of a consensus that a "modern, politically sovereign, economically self reliant, and French-speaking nation" could be achieved in Quebec (Salée and Coleman 1997, 270). In the face of the victory of the countervailing view that "market-grounded 'realities' justify the dismantling of the social welfare state as well as policies designed to support a strong national economy" (ibid., 271), this consensus had unravelled, and the Parti Québécois was defeated by the Liberals in 2001.

By then, feminists had moved from skepticism about the state's commitment to sexual equality to outright confrontation. The Fédération des Femmes du Québec (FFQ) along with other advocacy groups, had unceasingly "confronted the government...on a host of social and economic policy changes" (Salée 2003, 40) for their negative impacts on poorer segments of the population, and women in particular. The proposal for the World's Women's March 2000 (which we discussed in chapter 2), in fact, originated in Quebec with the FFQ.

In its present institutional incarnation, the feminist partners have called off the marriage between nationalism and feminism—a marriage which feminists never thought was made in heaven. They have discovered, as have feminists elsewhere, that the state cannot be relied upon to further the goals of social movements unless those movements continue to mobilize support from substantial sectors of the population (Guindon 1988, 164).

This does not mean, however, that feminists support Jean Charest's federalist Liberals who are staking out a full-scale neo-liberal agenda. In August 2003 the Liberals even put Quebec's daycare system on the chopping block, ironically a system, despite its limitations, extolled as a model by childcare advocates across Canada (Ferguson 2002; Krull 2003). In August 2003, 17 women's groups along with the labour movement and community groups not only protested this retreat from universality and accessibility, but argued for extending hours for parents who work shifts and adding places for special needs children (CBC Radio).

While many feminists embraced the nationalist-feminist partnership during the 1970s and 1980s, there was never unanimity among feminists for the independence option. At a large conference of feminists in 1992, delegates refused to take a position on the constitutional referendum because they could not reach unanimity (Cauchon 1992). Non-white women, in particular, fear a nationalist agenda predicated upon notions of "'Québécois pure laine' (or of French descent)" (Smart 1997, 16; Hamilton 1995). Even for many long-time feminist nationalists, the 1995 referendum campaign proved disappointing for its lack of attention to women's emancipatory goals and its failure to address the diversity of the society. There was little acknowledgement from the leadership of the "yes" side that Quebec itself is a multicultural society, riddled with racism towards non-whites and immigrants. Nor did the sovereigntist leaders display much understanding of the aspirations of Aboriginal peoples for self-determination (Salée and Coleman 1997, 276–78). As Daniel Salée and William Coleman have written, "if public discourse claims that being Québécois applies to everyone residing in Quebec, in reality access to Québécois culture is restricted to those who were born into it" (1997, 278).

Within women's literary debates in Quebec, as well as in their fiction, however, there are complex, empathetic, and controversial understandings about questions of identity, entitlement, and belonging. Many writers affirm that Quebec society is not about essentialism, lineage, or exclusions that rest on the naturalized claims of others to belong. Using notions of cultural hybridity and multiple identities, they are creating autobiographical and fictional persona more in keeping with the changing composition of the population. During the 1990s, according to Mary Jean Green, "a sustained vision of a multicultural Montreal" emerged (2001, 137), although in the writings of immigrant women, there were, as yet, few "affirmations of a complex multi-ethnic identity that also asserts itself as thoroughly Québécois" (2001, 153). What women writers in Quebec share, whether immigrants or not, according to Green "is the project of giving voice to silenced women of previous generations whom they see as essential to the construction of a woman's identity that can only be fully understood in relationship to the past" (2001, 154).

This process of deconstructing Canada and looking behind appearances has uncovered the systemic inequalities between Aboriginal peoples and the rest of the population, and between French and English. The struggles to dismantle these inequalities produced demands for self-determination and independence, respectively. Central to the early development of the Canadian state was the dispossession of the Aboriginal peoples from their land and the subordination of the French nation to the English. Subsequently, in the period since Confederation, more people from all over the world have immigrated to Canada. The history of immigration provides an opportunity to review John Porter's research to see if Canada remains a vertical mosaic with people from England and Scotland occupying the lion's share of elite positions as well as the more favourable positions throughout the stratification system.

Porter's research revealed, in particular, the presence of economic stratification based on racialization, with Aboriginal peoples and those from the African diaspora the most clearly disadvantaged economically, socially, and politically. Although pre-Confederation Canada had only a short period of legalized slavery, black people who lived here from the eighteenth century, and whose numbers were swelled by United Empire Loyalists and by those escaping slavery on the Underground Railroad, were confronted by as exclusionary a regime as that existing in the segregated South of the United States (Winks 1971; Clairmont and McGill 1999). Their treatment, and the treatment accorded later generations of non-white immigrants, together with postcontact European-Aboriginal history, provides evidence that the Canadian state—that is, the networks involved in the "relations of ruling"—engages in racialized policies and practices. In the process the state racializes its citizens, immigrants, and those seeking entry in ways that advantage some and disadvantage others. This is by no means a linear process that keeps getting more—or less—equitable, but rather a more complicated and shifting set of processes and relations. To take an important contemporary example, the reaction in Canada to the events of September 11 not only resurrected earlier racist discourses but invented new ones as scapegoats and potential "enemies" were sought among Canada's citizens, landed immigrants, and potential refugees (Thobani 2002, Nadeau 2002).

THE VERTICAL MOSAIC: ETHNICITY AND RACISM

Porter's analysis has been subjected to a number of important criticisms. *The Vertical Mosaic* did not address the particular situation of women but rather assumed that, for the most part, their location in the stratification system was a function of their fathers' and then husbands' position. Nonetheless, women's role as primary caretakers of children meant that their work as mothers and wives was shaped by the amount of income their husbands earned and were prepared to devote to family/household survival. Familial resources are not necessarily shared equally among members, nor decisions jointly made.

Like the liberal pluralist equality of opportunity perspective, Porter's analysis concentrated on individuals rather than on the structured networks of hierarchical relations in which their lives were embedded. Nonetheless, two important findings from Porter's research remain viable, even if explanations for the findings have shifted. First, in an otherwise unfavourable assessment of Porter's work, sociologist Robert Brym concludes that "ethnic inequalities at the elite level appear to be considerably greater than at the mass level" (Brym with Fox 1989, 112). Members of the elite have been able to reproduce ethnic privilege both by preparing their own children with the particular skills required, and by acting as gatekeepers to those not similarly positioned. Ann Duffy has noted the importance of the role of upper-class women in reproducing the elite (Duffy 1986).[6] In Bonnie Fox's words, "Maintaining power requires that money be transformed into 'social capital'—the kin and friendship networks, and the social events and institutions that maintain such relationships—and...the people largely responsible for this 'social capital' are women" (1989, 138–39).

While men of British descent—with the active help of their mothers and wives—continue to be overrepresented in the elite (Nakhaie 1997), access to elite positions has become more open. As well, according to Vic Satzewich and Lloyd Wong, at non-elite levels while "patterns of inequality between ethnic and racialized groups still exist...those patterns are complicated [especially by] class, gender and generational inequalities...within particular groups [which may] arguably be just as large and as socially significant...as inequalities between groups" (2003, 364).

There is statistical evidence then, based on income, occupation, and other dimensions, that access to elite levels is becoming more open. Patterns of racialized inequality are loosening up somewhat both in the sense that members of groups historically disadvantaged through racism have become, through their strenuous efforts, more economically and socially mobile. Evidence also suggests that class and gender hierarchies are present within these groups as in others (rich and poor white people, rich and poor white women, fairly rich and poor black women, etc.).

This evidence cannot be overdrawn, however, as the rest of this chapter argues. More especially, the dominant ethos represented in everyday conversation continues to define whites as insiders and non-whites as outsiders. Consider as a mundane but telling example the question that non-white people are asked in so "many different contexts [and] in so many different ways" (Marshall 1999, 185): "But where are you really from?" Hazelle Palmer (1997) borrowed this question as a title to her "collection of thoughts by women of colour on their forced battle to fit into the supposedly welcoming Canadian mosaic" (Marshall 1999, 185). "You should know," sociology professor Sherene Razack informed her audience parenthetically "that it doesn't matter where you were born because you are slotted into the category of immigrant if your skin is not White" (2003, 58). A young woman I know very well indeed, my daughter in fact, born and raised in Canada, had answered or ducked the question more often than she cared to remember and, at 30, began casting about for creative answers. "Why man," she now responds to unsuspecting questioners in a finely honed Jamaican accent (she has been a perfect mime since childhood): "why I was born on a beaut-i-ful island. Yes I was born on the beaut-i-ful island of Mont-re-al." My heart skipped a beat from pride and delight, and how I laughed. I bet this answer sticks in the mind, which is, of course, why I asked Susan for permission to repeat her story.

While the question—where do you come from?—could be asked naively, even benignly, the question vaunts a racist pedigree that continues to be fostered through state policies (see chapter 7 for immigration policies), shifting discursive regimes, and social interactions at every level. While sociologists find that racialized inequalities—as judged by income and occupation—may be loosening up, the experience of non-white people, at whatever professional level they reach, reveals the insider/outsider dichotomies to which this question—where do you *really* come from—gives voice.

Consider the experience of Sunera Thobani, a professor in Women's Studies at the University of British Columbia, who presented a keynote address on 1 October 2001 at a Woman and Resistances Conference in Ottawa, one month after the September 11 attacks (2002). Thobani described her speech as an anti-war speech, aimed to mobilize feminists against President Bush's "war on terrorism" and more especially against the war on Afghanistan. In the strongest terms she urged Canadians not to join in this attack, and as part of her argumentation she provided a harsh and informed critique of American foreign policy. In response, the Canadian media did not simply critique her views (which she shared with many others, including many influential commentators); they attacked *her*. How dare an immigrant woman of colour voice her objections to US policy in so open and critical a manner? How could that woman launch an attack on us and our way of life? One study showed that over a period of six days, in six newspapers, a total of 119 items focused on Sunera Thobani (Nadeau 2002).

My point here is simple: Thobani earned a doctoral degree in Canada and teaches at a good Canadian university, thus representing the "more open" access to professional positions that sociologists have documented. But her experience continues to be marked by a racialized insider/outsider discourse that white people, similarly placed, do not have to contend with.

The history of immigration to Canada is riddled with shifting assumptions about who is a desirable immigrant and who is not. These decisions reflect the requirements of capital and state for labour. Some peoples were deemed useful for certain kinds of labour that those already in the country refused to do, but they were not desirable as permanent citizens. A head tax on every Chinese immigrant, for example, made it virtually impossible for women to accompany the men who built the railroad. Later, when the need for such labour declined, a federal law was passed prohibiting Chinese immigration, which was repealed only in 1947.

Gender continues to be a "complicating" factor in any analysis, and until recently sociologists have solved this problem by studying only men (Fox 1989). Clearly, however, the social and economic mobility experienced by successive waves of immigrants owes much to the labour of women, as wives, mothers, household managers, and waged workers (Williams 1997, 73). Explaining the lower rates of mobility for women involves looking at both the gendered hierarchies in Canadian society and the particular nature of the "multiple patriarchies" that men and women bring with them as part of their cultural and gendered identities (Grewal and Kaplan 1994, 34), and at how the second is played out in the context of the first. Because women who migrate are treated by the laws structuring immigration as appendages of men, the state puts few, if any, resources at the disposal of women[7] (Burnet 1986; Gannagé 1986; Knocke and Ng 1999).

The power of men in their households is thereby intensified, and the possibilities for women are highly constrained, as two examples—on wife abuse and access to services—will indicate.[8] First, "women who do not speak English and who are victims of wife abuse [face] particularly poignant circumstances," as Vijay Agnew documents in her fine study of women's community organizations in Toronto. "They work in poorly paid jobs that require long difficult hours, which reinforces their dependence on their spouses. Their lack of English isolates them...and they may be unaware of legislation regarding wife abuse and the social services available to them" (1996, 199). Even if they are aware, "a woman will experience strong feelings of guilt and betrayal if she has to call the police in order to stop the violence. The community [may] condemn the woman who called the police or went to court, if the man had been previously jailed or tortured in his country of origin. She, then, will be accused of using a repressive institution to inflict more pain on 'the poor man' so to speak" (Pinedo and Santinoli quoted in Agnew 1996, 202), or of confirming the racist beliefs of white Canadians. "But such reasoning," in Agnew's words, "asks the abused woman to bear the brunt of gender violence so that other members of the community are not exposed to racial oppression" (Agnew 1996, 194–223; Bannerji 1999).

Family class immigration policies must bear the brunt of immigrant women's double jeopardy. Each family may only have one principal applicant who is almost always the husband/father, and he becomes the sponsor—the one responsible for the others. For several years (it used to be ten but has been reduced recently to three), other members cannot apply for social welfare nor are they eligible for English-language and other forms of training. Unless she is willing to charge an abusive husband with an offence (which carries its own risks of community ostracism or retaliation from him), she cannot leave him to live independently (Thobani 1999).

A second example involves the discovery by immigrant women who were not entitled to become permanent residents (some of them because of disability) that, under the Ontario provincial health insurance scheme, they were denied coverage for basic medical services such as prenatal care, pediatric visits for children, and treatment of ongoing disabilities. They appealed the decision unsuccessfully despite the intervention of LEAF, the DisAbled Women's Network Canada, and the Ontario Council of Immigrants who argued that this scheme discriminated on the basis of immigration status and disability. The provincial appellate court ruled in 2001 that, although the scheme distinguished between permanent and non-permanent residency, it did not violate Charter equality rights. Hence, in the words of Beverley Baines, "some immigrants in Ontario, including pregnant women and women with disabilities, will continue to lack basic medical care" (forthcoming, 112).

When Canada needs the labour of women—because those already here choose not to do it, as with live-in domestic labour—the conditions of entry change depending upon the class and racial biases of those seeking help and making policy. In 1919, the goal was to attract "the best class of household worker" rather than "unqualified women from British mill and factory, who in addition to their lack of training for domestic service, bring with them only too often, serious mental and moral disabilities...[and who] end up, alas! too frequently, in our jails, hospitals, and asylums" (quoted in Barber 1985, 114).

Although there have been successive policy changes regarding foreign domestic workers, Rina Cohen argues that the latest version—the Live-in Caregiver Program (LCP), enacted in April 1992—is "the most intrusive program created by the state's immigration authorities" (1994, 86). If we want to understand why there has been "a gradual regression in both citizenship and labour rights for foreign domestics throughout the twentieth century," Cohen continues, we must look at changes in the racial composition of domestic labourers (ibid.).

One way of approaching the entire history of who is welcome in Canada, and under what circumstances, is by examining the changing dominant understandings of who belongs here and who is "other." This categorization can be described as racist (always cross-cut by gendered and sexist assumptions), in the sense that racism creates the shifting categories of hierarchically arranged races. We examined the ways in which racist assumptions informed the making of the Indian Act. Throughout much of this century, the failure of the French to conform to English norms was explained by deep-seated cultural, psychological, and even biological differences. Former Prime Minister John Diefenbaker once referred to the "three great Canadian races—the English, the French and Everyone Else." The non-English-speaking immigrants who came to Canada in great numbers in the early decades of the century—Ukrainians, Italians, Mennonites—were perceived in many quarters as "dangerous foreigners" who even with time could scarcely be assimilated, let alone accommodated within an English-speaking Dominion (Avery 1979). Prime Minister Mackenzie King saw Jews as members of another species and turned them away from Canada when they tried to escape Nazi Germany (Abella 1982).

During the last decades of the twentieth century, the idea of race tends to be reserved to distinguish superficial physical differences, notably skin pigmentation. Whiteness now includes, by common usage, all shades of pale and many people of darker hues, once not seen as white. Yet race clearly still matters. Consider Robert Brym's conclusion to his discussion of Porter's work on ethnicity and stratification: "a substantial body of research demonstrates that, with important exceptions—consisting mainly of racial minorities—ethnicity does not strongly influence status or income attainment" (Brym with Fox 1989, 113). Here "racial minorities" appears as a self-evident category, a kind of subset of ethnicity. I am arguing that racial minorities are neither: who gets included in the category racial minority is historically specific, and race is not a subset of ethnicity. Racism is more properly identified as a system of power relations that rationalizes and normalizes differential treatment at the institutional and personal level. We have already examined how this has worked historically to create hierarchies of power and resources between the descendants of Europeans and Aboriginals. The other glaring and continuing example of institutionalized racism in Canada resides in the historical and contemporary treatment of those now identified as African Canadian. That the racial hierarchy between white and black is not about ethnicity—which could be described as residing in shared culture and language—may easily be seen. The black population of Canada is part of the African diaspora that was initiated by European slave traders three centuries ago and includes immigrants and refugees from many African countries, the Caribbean, and indeed from throughout the world, who have been arriving ever since.

Black people have been in Canada for centuries, and English or French is the first language for most (Brand 1991). Yet they are disproportionately represented in low-paying jobs and face a tangled web of practices that exclude them from promotion, housing, and decent treatment on the street. They cannot be described as "exceptions to the general rule" (Brym with Fox 1989, 110) whereby succeeding waves of different ethnic groups achieve proportionate distribution in the stratification system: they do not constitute an ethnic group, and indeed differ, at times substantially, on how to deal with racism in Canada (Williams 1997).

The social relations of racism have pervaded the country's history from its inception, creating sustained and shifting categories of "otherness"—those defined for all practical purposes as outside the Canadian polity. As Abele and Stasiulus conclude, "The picture of racism that emerges is that of an immensely supple, variable, and seemingly intractable 'common sense,' socially and politically constructed within a range of important locations—education, social services, private corporations, trade unions, and the mass media" (1989, 266).

The process of racialization rationalizes the creation and sustaining of social and economic inequalities. But it is a mistake to think that racializing the other is dependent upon these hierarchies. The history of anti-Semitism in Europe, for example, was nourished by envy for the perceived political and economic success of some Jewish people and the political opportunity presented for scapegoating such a people for the ills of the society. Political philosopher Hannah Arendt provides a complex analysis of the process through which what she called social anti-Semitism became racism during the first half of the twentieth century:

> It was Hitler who...knew how to use the hierarchical principle of racism, how to exploit the anti-semitic assertion of the existence of a "worst" people in order properly to organize the "best" and all the conquered and oppressed in between, how to generalize [their] superiority complex...so that each people, with the necessary exception of the Jews, could look down upon one that was even worse off than itself. (1951, 121)

Nikki Gershbain and Aviva Rubin write that "although at this moment in Canada the light skin of many Jews grants us a relative degree of privilege, when this no longer serves the purposes of the state, our access to it may simply be revoked" (1994, 58). The complexity of the history of Jews in Western civilization provides important theoretical understandings about racism and graphic illustration of my major point that race is socially and historically constructed. "Racism," asserts Arendt, "may indeed carry out the doom of the Western world and, for that matter, the whole of human civilization....For no matter what learned scientists may say, race is, politically speaking, not the beginning of humanity but its end, not the origin of peoples but their decay, not the natural birth of man but his unnatural death" (1951, 37).

The systemic and shifting inequalities between Aboriginal and non-Aboriginal peoples, between English Canada and French Quebec, and between those privileged and victimized by racism have motivated demands for more equal methods of distribution of resources, more equitable representation in the forums of power, and even for secession from Canada. Women have challenged the Canadian state to intervene and transform the gender hierarchies that inform the relations of state and economy and civil society at the same time as they have participated in movements for self-determination, sovereignty, and regional equity, and for an end to the racist practices rooted in the history of the country.

Taken together, we can argue that the promise of equal opportunity for all is more honoured in the breach than in the observance. People live their lives within the intertwined networks of capitalist, national, gendered, and racist relations. Individuals may achieve social and economic mobility. Overall, the contemporary political/economic system provides high rewards for a very few, moderate rewards for a middle range of managers and professionals, decent wages for a (declining) industrial working class, low wages for many (including most women in the expanding service sector), unemployment and underemployment for a growing number, and bare subsistence payments for those unable to enter the work force because of age, disability, or responsibility for childcare or the care of dependent adults (National Council of Welfare 2002). This means that significant changes to people's lives can only come through transformed economic and political relations.

CONCLUSION

If Canada is to survive, national policies that legitimize its power must be pursued. But those national policies must include rather than thwart the aspirations of the Aboriginal peoples for self-government, the people of Quebec for sovereignty, and the visible minorities for full citizenship. Across all these divisions run the jagged and shifting hierarchies between men and women. Women have been part of general social movements and have created, more than once, their own autonomous movements. Whether feminists can unite around common interests for equality, and whether they use whatever power they have to work together to erode rather than buttress the inequalities of nation, ethnicity, region, and gender are open questions.

In very different ways, global restructuring and the "hollowing out" of the federal and provincial states are transforming the conditions through which social movements for self-determination, nationalism, and anti-racism pursue their goals. As Joanne Green writes, "at the precise moment in Canadian history when citizenship seems most inclusive, authentic, and emancipatory, the content and capacity of citizenship is being challenged by a neoliberal ideology that provides the cultural logic for globalization" (2003, 56). Green is not glorifying the present: the constitutional recognition of "existing Aboriginal and treaty rights (section 35 of the Constitution Act of 1982)," for example, has been interpreted paternalistically so that the sovereignty of the Canadian state remains intact. Nor have Aboriginal leaders been included as equal members in constitutional negotiations. But the movement to more inclusive decision making has, in fits and starts, been underway. Paradoxically, the Canadian state, author of the colonization of the Aboriginal peoples, has shown signs of having the capacity (if not the will) to renegotiate those historical relations of inclusion and exclusion.

But this process becomes aborted with the ceding of state power to international treaties (NAFTA and others) regulated by bodies with no claim to democratic membership or processes. As Marjorie Cohen and others have warned: "The sweeping limitations on governmental powers that are found in the trade agreements are enforced by dispute panels whose procedures are entirely confidential. No citizens or organizations have access to the process, although what is at stake is nothing less than the capacity of our national governments to maintain laws, often for the public's protection" (2002, 9). "Neither federalism nor the state itself are immune to neoliberal demands for the imperative of economic rationalism, even at the cost of fracturing federal processes, constitutional obligations, citizenship capacity, or sociopolitical coherence" (Green 2003, 57).

Aboriginal people in Canada as elsewhere have in the past decades pursued their struggles through the United Nations, and have joined with other groups protesting the agenda of the World Trade Organization. Organizing globally becomes increasingly necessary as power shifts from the national to the international level. An Indigenous Peoples conference held in conjunction with the anti-globalization protests in Quebec City in 2001 aimed to develop a "network of resistance" to the decision of governments in the Americas to "establish a new commercial policy...in violation of the Aboriginal rights, titles and treaties of the hemisphere's Indigenous peoples" (quoted in Green 2003, 72, fn. 2).

In the discussion on Quebec, we also saw how the decisions of the government to reverse direction both in terms of actively intervening in the economy and working towards relations of equality has eroded support for nationalism among progressive sectors of the population including feminists. If Quebec is going to be a state just like the others—which is to say a non-interventionist state that cedes power to the marketplace—then the passionate arguments for an independent state may ring hollow.

In the struggles against racism the state has also played an ambivalent and paradoxical role. Founded and sustained on systemic inequalities, the state, nonetheless, has become a site for struggles for equality, particularly through the Charter of Rights and Freedoms. At times sufficient pressure has been mounted to change immigration policies, to provide newcomers with support in establishing themselves in Canada, to pass employment equity and pay equity legislation, and to fight racism in schools and in the police. These struggles—against and within the inner sanctums of the state—represent the promise of democracy. But during economic restructuring the state traded in commitment to equality policies and practices for a strategy of deficit and tax reduction in order to attract capital and gain the support of wealthier sectors of the population. At the same time the state strengthens its policing and "security apparatuses" in the name of protecting law-abiding Canadians (those who have historic entitlement and resources) from those who seek entry (the increasing numbers of those who seek a better life). In chapter 7 we discuss more thoroughly how economic restructuring, the decline of the "welfare" state and the intensifying of the "security" state disadvantages women disproportionately throughout the world.

In the next chapter we look at the whole area of work—in families, labour force, and communities—which is informed by all of the social hierarchies that have been discussed so far. Work-related issues rank high on feminist agendas and have involved challenges to the state to change laws, remake public policy, and open private and public institutions to women.

NOTES

1. Shifting terminology results from the process whereby those living on this land prior to the arrival of the Europeans were named *Indian* by the newcomers, and the response of the first occupants—over time—to name themselves. Wotherspoon and Satzewich provide the following summary: "Aboriginal peoples refer collectively to status Indians, non-status Indian, Metis and Inuit people in Canada....First Nations tends to refer to groups of status Indian origin: groups who are the first occupants of the lands that now make up Canada. Status, or registered Indian people are those who are defined as Indians by virtue of the Indian Act" (1993, xv). The use of the term *indigenous peoples* is increasingly common, especially in the growing collective movements of indigenous peoples worldwide.

2. See Christine Welsh's evocative film, "Keepers of the Fire" (1992). In this film she talks with the elders about the events at Kanesatake, and why they were willing to risk so much in that struggle.

3. In 1931 there were 44 Roman Catholic (RC), 21 Church of England (CE), 13 United Church (UC), and 2 Presbyterian (PR) schools. These proportions among the denominations were constant throughout the history of the system. http://www.irsr-rqpi.gc.ca/english/maps.html

4. Prior to contact, Aboriginal societies had determined the membership in their tribes by a variety of principles of descent, marriage, residence, and adoption. Most tribes followed a bilateral method, tracing descent through both the mother's and father's lineage. Most of the rest of the tribes were matrilineal, with patrilineal descent much less common (Weaver 1993, 95).

5. In her research on the fur trade in the early Canadian West, Sylvia Van Kirk has examined "the remarkably wide extent of intermarriage between incoming traders and Indian women, especially among the Cree, the Ojibwa and the Chipewyan." These relationships—known as marriage *à la façon du pays*—were key to the generally harmonious relationships between Indians and Europeans in the Canadian West until the early nineteenth century. It was primarily Anglican missionaries, arriving in 1820 under the auspices of the Hudson's Bay Company, who began roundly denouncing such unions as "immoral and debased" (1986, 64). Van Kirk concludes that "this attack upon fur trade custom had a detrimental effect upon the position of native women" and together with the arrival of British women served to augment racial prejudice and class distinctions (ibid., 64).

6. For an excellent historical treatment of how upper-class women contribute to the reproduction of class, see Katherine McKenna's biography of Anne Murray Powell (1994).

7. See the excellent articles in the *Canadian Woman Studies* special issue, "Immigrant and Refugee Women" 19(3) Fall, 1999.

8. The Canadian government's recent decision to cut back on English-language training increases resettlement problems for all immigrants and refugees from non-English-speaking countries. While this is usually seen as a problem only for employment, Macthoura Nou, a Cambodian refugee, recounts how the doctors did not understand when she tried to tell them about the respiratory problems of her infant son. "I just tell him that my baby cry and stop breathing. [The doctor] told me, 'Don't worry, your baby won't die from crying.' He did not understand me and my baby died." Nou now helps other Cambodian women get English-language training in Winnipeg (Lett 1995, B3).

chapter five

Challenging the Sexual Division of Labour: Family, Employment, and Community

In many ways the feminist challenges to the sexual division of labour in all areas of society have been successful. Most people no longer believe that women should be excluded from certain kinds of work, or that men are incapable of caring for children or doing housework. Yet the restructuring of economy, political life, and family that would be necessary to support these changes in practice have proved elusive.

Consider an interesting article entitled "Breadwinner now likely to be a woman" in the *Globe and Mail* on 15 September 2000. The opening line begs for your skills at deconstruction: "Never before have Canadian women looked more like men...as they picked up briefcases and donned suits...." The norm against which women are being measured here is the upper middle-class male executive—a small subset of all men, and it suggests that clothes really do make the (gendered) person. While this is an article sympathetic to working mothers, the only woman featured is Patricia Croft who "embodies the new generation of corporate working mothers juggling a high-powered salary with the never-ending travails of raising three kids, aged 17, 13 and 9. 'It's all about tradeoffs,' Ms. Croft said. Having a nanny is absolutely essential" (Philp 2000, A3).

If this is the media face of feminism, no wonder many women feel betrayed. Most cannot afford nannies, or even decent daycare, and some of them are nannies, mainly from Third World countries. Are feminist goals only useful for those who make it into the upper echelons of the corporate world? Indeed, an ironic charge against feminists has been circulating for some years now. Feminists, some say, have denigrated the work that women do in the home; they have belittled the contribution of wives and mothers to children and to society more generally. Feminists have encouraged women to become like men. The quintessential feminist-inspired woman, as pictured above, abandons her children and husband on a daily basis, picks up her leather briefcase and heads out to the corporate world dressed in a professional suit (Pierson 1995, 1). Resting on her conscience, say her detractors, should be the overwhelming problems besetting modern society: the collapse of the family, rampant juvenile delinquency and crime, the degeneration of morals.

Feminists deal with these charges in different ways—confronting them, ignoring them, ridiculing them—but, like crazy glue, the charges are sticky. They surely contribute to the oft-repeated sentence, "I am not a feminist, *but....*" They not only feed active hostility to feminism but create confusion and distress among many who long to see the relations between the sexes transformed.

In this chapter I consider feminist perspectives on work, paid and unpaid, in the family, in the labour force and in the community. My method will be both historical and theoretical. First, I note the main issues that feminists have raised over the past century about women, work, and children. Second, I discuss the main theoretical questions that contemporary feminists have asked about these same issues. In this process, feminists—particularly feminist historians—have revisited the past, raised new questions, and produced new interpretations on women and work. Feminists from different theoretical perspectives— liberal, Marxist, radical, cultural, lesbian, anti-racist, poststructural—have looked at these issues through their different lenses, and this will also guide the discussion.

What I believe will become clear in the course of this discussion is just how immensely complex feminist considerations of the sexual division of labour have been. For this is a huge topic that encompasses—from some perspectives at least—almost all of social life. In this chapter, I hope not so much to put the charges against feminists to rest, but rather to show how and where they misrepresent the focus of much feminist discussion and also how it is that the charges can still stick.

FIRST WAVE FEMINISTS

From the late nineteenth century until the end of World War I, feminists took up the question of women and work in several ways. First, and perhaps best known, were the struggles women undertook for admission to higher education and entrance into the professions. Equally important, for many decades, were responses feminists developed to problems facing women who worked for wages: the conditions and hours of work, wage levels, and safety travelling to and from work. A third set of concerns was how women would care for their children when they were at work. Fourth were the problems of sexual morality that, many observers argued, faced working women, especially young women. Finally, many first wave feminists insisted that women's special nature and interests suited them for particular kinds of volunteer work in the broader society. Let us look more closely at these five issues, the context in which they were formulated, and some contemporary feminist reflections upon them.

Admission and Accessibility

Many of the women who fought for the right to attend university and enter the professions were no more willing than many young women today to call themselves feminist. They wanted to get on with their lives; many of them experienced a "calling" to a particular profession—the ministry, medicine, teaching, or law. During the early decades of the century, when two-thirds of the population living in Canada were regular churchgoers, young women often framed their aspirations for themselves and their society in religious terms. Whether these women adopted the label feminist or not, their struggles allied them with those whose avowed political purpose was to create equality between men and women in the public sphere.

Even when women tried to legitimate their goals in religious rather than secular terms, they often faced astringent opposition (Brouwer 1990). In the Fédération Nationale Saint-Jean-Baptiste (FNSJB), founded in 1907, Catholic feminists in Quebec tried to negotiate a path that the church would recognize as legitimate. Given that the church not only opposed suffrage, but officially opposed women's access to the professions and higher education as well, this was ultimately a doomed struggle (Lavigne, Pinard, and Stoddart 1979, 86). In 1909, for example, the Archbishop of Montreal censored an article on compulsory education written by journalist Françoise (Robertine Barry) for the Fédération. Barry wrote to FNSJB president Marie Gérin-Lajoie protesting the acceptance of such censorship:

> I recognize that, for the Federation to triumph, you need the force of the clergy, all-powerful in our country. Sacrifice your burnt offerings to them. I only hope that they will not ask you for yet greater sacrifices such as...giving up women's suffrage. In the meantime, I pity you, because in sacrificing me you go against the sense of integrity, loyalty, and justice which I have always admired in you, since, as you avowed yourself, you saw nothing reprehensible in what I wrote. (quoted in ibid., 79–80)

God, it seems, had not intended women to become professionals, an argument currently made in more specific, but still blunt and vociferous, terms by Pope John Paul as rationale for excluding women from the priesthood of the Catholic Church.

Closely allied with the religious argument were various biological arguments that many male doctors used to insist that their field (and most others) should be restricted to those of their own sex. In 1892 *The Canadian Practitioner* printed a report of a lecture given by Sir James Crichton-Browne, MD, to the Medical Society of London in which he "traced out several bodily differences between the sexes...[in particular]...differences in the brain." The doctor cited evidence that "the specific gravity of the grey matter in every lobe of the brain in the female was lower," and the consequences of this for female "victims of higher education" were horrendous: tuberculosis, chorea, mental malfunction, and "gastric disorder now so common that it might receive a distinctive appellation and be called anorexia scholastica" (257–59).

Such attitudes were not universal. Two years earlier, the editors of *The Canada Medical Record* had defended women's place in medical school after women at the Women's Medical College in Kingston had met with a "cold shoulder" from male students:

> We cannot view with any satisfaction the tendency of the women of this age to shirk their manifest and divine destiny; but, in spite of all this and the many physical disabilities under which the female doctor must labor, there will be female doctors. As long as women labor under the delusion that it is an easy way to earn a living, it would be unjust and ungenerous for us to throw any obstacles in their path. We may as well welcome them to our ranks, and let the fittest survive the struggle. (119)

Canada's first female doctors graduated in the United Kingdom and the United States, having been refused entrance to universities in this country. By the last decades of the nineteenth century, several Canadian medical schools were accepting women, to mixed receptions from faculty and students (Prentice et al. 1988; Strong-Boag 1979). Only in 1918 did

McGill University accept its first female medical students. Jessie Boyd Scriver of the class of 1922 recalls the university's opposition:

> We knew that repeatedly through the years, McGill had refused to consider admitting women to the Faculty of Medicine. It will be remembered that in 1888 Grace Ritchie appealed unsuccessfully for the admission of women to Medicine and that our renowned Maude Abbott was also denied entrance to the Faculty—but both received their medical degrees from Bishop's University in the early 1880s. (Years later [1910] when Dr. Abbott was recognized as a worldwide authority on congenital cardiac abnormalities, McGill bestowed on her an M.D. degree *honoris causa*). (1984, 5)

Like students at other universities, Scriver and her classmates found most faculty and students helpful, or at least tolerant. But some male students suggested that they drop out of school rather than face a dissecting class "which would be very distasteful to young ladies of our upbringing" (1984, 6). Women were not supposed to know how bodies worked, or even what they looked like.[1]

Women and Waged Work

It is always easier to see the hypocrisies of another age. But it is hard to imagine how those people opposed to the entrance of women into the professions conducted their campaigns for so long and with such righteous indignation when all around them women were working for appallingly low wages and long hours in factories, sweatshops, and in middle- and upper-class homes. Middle-class feminists took up some of the causes of their working-class sisters, but in ways that revealed their class biases (Klein and Roberts 1974, 214–18; Strong-Boag 1976). Working-class men sometimes defended working women in the union movement, but in ways that betrayed their patriarchal assumptions. Working-class women took up their own cause in private and sometimes in public venues. It is not surprising then that there were different and often competing understandings of what the problems were, and what the solutions might be.

Responses to the plight of women in the work force were debated in both suffrage and labour organizations. One such response was the idea of protective legislation. Generally speaking, suffragists were more concerned about the ways in which such legislation would be used to further exclude women from gainful employment, while trade unionists "viewed any protection against sweated conditions, no matter how it was won, as a desperately needed reform" (Ramkhalawansingh 1974, 301). Male unionists demanded a "family wage" for working men, which would enable men to be the sole supporter of their families. Working women—when we hear their voices—demanded equal wages and access to work. They participated in work stoppages as strikers or members of the families of strikers (Klein and Roberts 1974; Sangster 1979; White 1993). The Ontario Commission on Unemployment of 1916 seemed surprised to find that "generally speaking women wage-earners are not convinced that the principle of higher pay to men as bread-winners works out justly" (cited in Ramkhalawansingh 1974, 269). We will deal with these concerns in turn, but it is worthwhile noting that all these responses were formulated in a society that had not yet come to terms with the full consequences of industrial capitalism. Nostalgia for an idealized rural life, where men and women worked side by side in the clean country air for themselves and their children, fuelled the discussions about the outrages of waged work for women.

Public concern about the conditions of work for women led most provinces to hold Commissions of Inquiry into women's wages, hours of labour, and working conditions in industrial occupations. The resulting protective legislation took several forms: exclusion of women from those occupations defined as most dangerous to their health or reproductive potential; a limit to the hours that women and children could work; and laws setting minimum wages for women working in the new industries. In addition, the federal government amended the Criminal Code in 1920 to provide penalties for male employers who tried to take sexual advantage of "previously chaste" female employees under 21 (Burt 1993, 217–18). Middle-class social reformers, including some feminists, argued that these new laws addressed the worst abuses of the capitalist order.

The list of worst abuses, as formulated by these reformers, did not generally include the pitiful wages for the large numbers of women who worked as domestics (Errington 1993; Leslie 1974). Neither did they include unequal wages for men and women or wages that were insufficient for women to support their children. Rather, the underlying concern was "protecting women's reproductive functions and…keeping young working girls pure for marriage" (Burt 1993, 218). As the Nova Scotia Commission put it, "If we are to have a healthy virile race, it is of primary importance to preserve the homes and conserve the health, morals and efficiency" of women (quoted in ibid., 217). Single girls should remain virgins and support themselves when necessary. But most were to marry and stay home, supported by their husbands. As the Minimum Wage Board in Ontario declared, the minimum wage should be "the least sum upon which a working woman can be expected to support herself" (quoted in Ramkhalawansingh 1974, 299; see also Burt 1993, 217–19; McCallum 1986, 126; Prentice et al. 1988, 126). Even this view was not widely shared. For example, employers stressed in the Report of Labour Conditions in British Columbia that "women were not expected to have to live on their salaries and, therefore, women's wages had nothing to do with any notion of a living wage" (Creese 1988, 125). As Frederick Gibson opined in his history of Queen's University, single women at home "found in a salary of $624.00 a year a welcome supplement" (1983, 98). Such a notion was long-lived—Gibson wrote this in the 1980s. As Ruth Pierson notes in her study of unemployment insurance debates during the Depression, "It was principally as non-mothers that women and their labour-market interests qualified for the attention of trade union spokesmen, socialists, and eventually liberals" (1990, 83).

Men, on the other hand, were said to need what came to be called a family wage, and this was one of the major grounds on which the labour movement demanded higher wages for its members. In precapitalist society, a wage was most often a supplement to the support people gleaned for themselves from the land (Clark 1982 [1919]). The idea that individuals would actually have to support themselves with a wage was a long time coming, and wages very often didn't (and still don't) reflect that reality. As life on the land gave way to wage labour, men and women—married and single alike—sought waged work, although married women were more likely to take intermittent, part-time jobs. Since anything less than employment for all adult members left many working-class households destitute, this meant that there were many desperately poor families (Bradbury 1993). The demand for a family wage was intended to ensure that only one adult in the family had to work for wages. Not surprisingly, that one adult was assumed to be the father/husband (Pierson 1990).

When the voices of women working for wages are heard, it is usually to demand higher wages and better working conditions for themselves. If the voices of working women in the written records are few, they had other ways of clarifying their preferences for some work over others. In overwhelming numbers they voted with their feet, deserting positions as servants in the homes of others and opting for work elsewhere. Work as a servant in a nineteenth-century household was physically arduous, with hours often limited only by the number in a day and a night. Servants were constantly on call. Employers used the presence and behaviour of their servants to mark their own status and respectability, and so monitored this behaviour on and off the job (seldom off—many advertisements indicated that a free Sunday afternoon was all that might be expected). With no possibility of a social or domestic life of their own, servants were often on the move (Errington 1996; Leslie 1974).

Middle-class reformers loudly lamented the dearth of servants, complaining that they had trouble finding a "good woman" to assist in their households. They insisted that domestic work was much more suitable an employment for women than any of the alternatives (Barber 1985). Domestic work was what women did naturally (how interesting, then, that the complaints about the work habits of domestic servants went on endlessly). Such work was safe, appropriate, and provided good apprenticeships for later lives as wives and mothers. It is no small wonder that protective legislation was never instituted with regard to domestic service. From our vantage point, middle-class feminists appear caught in a conflict of interest. Ostensibly concerned about working conditions for women, they seldom turned the spotlight on the working environments in their own homes. Rather, they joined in recruitment efforts abroad to find replacements for recalcitrant Canadian "girls." Great Britain was the preferred recruiting ground for English-Canadian households that could afford servants. Not only would British women share language and culture but also, in time, they would take their own place as wives and mothers in the expanding Canadian nation (thereby, of course, keeping the "servant problem" alive) (Bacchi 1983, 95–96).

Those who struggled for the family wage shared the assumption that work for women should be a stopgap measure until marriage and motherhood. The growing union movement developed aspects of Marxist analysis and rhetoric indicting capitalist employers who, for a pittance, would squeeze every last ounce of labour power from every member of the family. The struggle of union members meshed with some of the concerns of middle-class reformers that family life in working-class sections of the burgeoning cities was all but impossible. With fathers, mothers, and older children all in the factories for long hours, younger children and babies went undernourished and neglected. Children reared in such households lacked not only physical care but moral guidance, and threatened to swell Canada's delinquent and criminal populations. The family wage was meant to remedy all this. Providing a working man with a decent wage enabled him to support his wife and children. With a mother at home to care for her children, the runaway social problems that endangered the very social fabric of the new nation would be brought under control. The key to well brought-up children and future good citizens was a wife/mother in the home.

Certainly working-class women had much to gain from decent wages for their husbands and the fathers of their children. But like protective legislation, the family wage was also intended to keep them out of the paid work force, certainly out of those occupations that commanded better wages. Furthermore, the family wage remained an elusive goal for most male income earners, and an illegitimate demand for women, even those who were the sole supporters of their children.

Mothers, Children, and Work

In Canada's preindustrial and precapitalist settings, women cared for children, raised crops and tended animals, made clothes and soap, and preserved food, all at home (Errington 1996). During the nineteenth and early twentieth centuries, the physical separation of home and work, the separation of most men and women from the land, and the growing dependence on wages produced a crisis for women that continues to this day. As Margaret Little observed: "economic dislocation dissolved many families. The number of widowed, deserted, and unwed mothers increased as did the accounts of neglected and delinquent children" (1998, 2).

Almost everyone, including most first wave feminists, who left any sort of record of these times seemed to agree that women's special mission was to care for children, husband, and home. Some feminists countered this prevailing ideology when they struggled for women's access to education and the professions. But most of them seemed to concur that women who chose careers must also choose singledom. The radicalism in this view was the insistence that remaining unmarried to pursue a career was not unnatural.

There were various efforts by social reformers to provide childcare for very poor women. The East End Day Nursery in Toronto and the Jost Mission in Halifax not only provided care for children but acted as employment bureaus for women, though often for the most menial and poorly paid jobs. A report in *Saturday Night* commended the arrangement whereby women could leave their children at a crèche during the day: "These nurslings of poverty cannot be expected to behave like little ladies and gentlemen and we cannot blame private families for objecting to their washerwoman or seamstress bringing their offspring along" (quoted in Klein and Roberts 1974, 211; Simmons 1991).

Activist Flora Macdonald Denison was a vocal critic of such crèches and the society that forced women to use them. She repeatedly pointed out that not all women had men to depend upon: "The women who were worst off were those mothers who had to be out in a labour force that did not recognize their right to be there and that therefore provided them with little or no support or protection" (Gorham 1979, 65). She became a radical critic of the privatized family, arguing for more communal and democratic arrangements.

Women, Work, and Sexuality

Denison's was a minority view. Most working-class unionists and middle-class reformers agreed that waged work for women threatened the physical and moral well-being of their children. They also shared another perception: waged work put women themselves in the way of moral dangers. How was the sexual purity of women to be preserved once they entered the dangerous and tempting fray of the working world? Again, nostalgia for what was believed to be the wholesome rural life pervaded discussion and solutions. Middle-class reformers claimed that domestic service offered a negotiated way through the thicket. Such service provided wages for women in environments that were supposedly morally safe.

The testimony of working women provides a different story. As Karen Dubinsky (1993) has noted in her study of turn-of-the-century Northern Ontario, "rural live-in domestic servants found themselves in a position of extreme vulnerability" and were subject to a range of abuse from employers, including sexual assault, life-threatening violence, and an array of daily, small humiliations. Clearly domestic service was not excluded from public discussion about women's safety and morality because such work actually provided safe havens. Although we may understand why families and households did not come under scrutiny from those in influential positions in the union and reform movements, we may still ask why many such people mounted vitriolic attacks on alternative and morally less dangerous workplaces.

Perhaps it was because women who worked in factories had more freedom than those in domestic service to engage in their own liaisons, create their own fun, and decide how to spend their discretionary time (Barber 1985, 105). For many in the middle class, unattached young women working for wages became a symbol of a society in potential decay. Women, it seemed, could not be trusted to preserve their own sexual purity, nor could the men about them be trusted to provide pristine guardianship. Whether naive, weak-minded, or lascivious, women needed others to tell them what to do. Paradoxically, while many proclaimed that women's natural proclivities were for wiving and mothering, they remained anxious that women, especially young women, left to their own devices, might choose otherwise. The concern that vulnerable young women would engage in sexual intimacies or, worse, in prostitution informed the debates, laws, and regulations about their engagement in waged work. Carolyn Strange has noted, for example, that the *Report* of the 1889 Royal Commission on the Relations of Labour and Capital only discussed women workers in sections of the text devoted to the moral implications of urban industrialization (1995, 33–34; see also Valverde 1991, 20). Many middle-class feminists, far from being the upholders either of women's natural virtue or of their right to their own sexual lives, shared these concerns (Strange 1995, 22–23). Unsupervised women—both those with, and in need of, a livelihood—would meet unsuitable men, might even marry them.

Canada's immigration policies have long represented an unholy amalgam of pragmatic needs for labour and explicitly racist practices. As we noted earlier, political and economic leaders were willing, on occasion, to admit those who didn't qualify as "white" to fill particular labour shortages, but they did not admit their families. Such policies, as it turned out, had unintended consequences. Racist employment and immigration practices did not prevent men and women from forming relationships across shifting "racial" lines. "White" working women were presented as vulnerable to a shifting parade of "foreign," racialized men from Italy, China, East India, or, in the case of middle-class women, any man from the working class. Carol Bacchi (1983) has written about the racist attitudes of English-Canadian suffragists, concerned that pure white women would fall for the empty promises of untrustworthy, non-British men. Once again, domestic service was presented as protection from mixed gender and racial working environments, and from the dangerous freedom waged work presented for women during their leisure hours. Yet the clear and present dangers for those women "in service"—black women, immigrant women, and poor women generally—went unremarked, providing robust protection for affluent men to prey on vulnerable women working in their households.

Women, Community, and Society

Whether out of pragmatism or sincerity, most feminists argued that women should be in the wider world because that world desperately needed the special skills and predispositions that they had carefully honed for generations in the home. Just as certain kinds of waged work were more suitable for women, so were particular venues in the social and political sector. The world needed cleaning up, and women were cleaners par excellence. Capitalism needed a human face and nurturing hands and heart. Women should provide them. Men needed taming; they required persuasion to abandon boyish wickedness and become men. Certainly husbands and fathers needed the law to ensure that they shared their hard-won wages with their wives and children and treated them kindly in the process.

There were many women's groups at the turn of the century that concerned themselves with "social housekeeping." The Woman's Christian Temperance Union (WCTU), founded in the late nineteenth century, was the largest and most effective nationally organized women's reform association of its time. It fought for prohibition of the sale and consumption of alcohol, which temperance advocates identified as a primary curse of family life: "it turns men into demons, and makes women an easy target of lust" (quoted in Mitchinson 1979, 154). As this quote makes clear, the culprits were men and the victims women and children. During the course of its long struggle, the WCTU supported other social reforms, including suffrage. Far from rejecting dominant views of women, members argued "that what made them different from men and what made them the centre of domestic life necessitated their involvement in temporal society" (Mitchinson 1979, 166; see also Cook 1995; Valverde 1991, 58–61).

The WCTU was a Protestant organization, and temperance was never as significant an issue in Catholic Quebec. Still, the Fédération Nationale Saint-Jean-Baptiste (FNSJB) espoused the platform of the Anti-Alcohol League in 1910, believing that women had "a unique capacity for moral regeneration" (Lavigne, Pinard, and Stoddart 1979, 77). In Montreal, where the infant mortality rate was one of the highest in North America, the FNSJB distributed milk to poor families and set up programs to aid mothers during and after childbirth. It also campaigned against prostitution. After the First World War, the FNSJB increasingly succumbed to the conservative influence of Catholic social doctrine, even withdrawing from the suffrage movement. Nonetheless, the organization continued to work with other lay women and nuns to help parents care for their children. The orphanages run by nuns accepted not only children with no parents or those of single mothers, but very often the children of those too poor to feed and care for their young (Bradbury 1993, 209).

In Ontario, as elsewhere, middle-class reformers, including those in the National Council of Women, lobbied hard, and ultimately successfully for state support for widows with young children. "Promoting a maternal ideology that purported the moral superiority of Protestant Euro-Canadian women, this select group of women established themselves as rescuers, reformers, and even experts" (Little 1998, 5). Margaret Little's excellent study of the struggle for Mother's Allowance from its inception in 1920 explores both the concern for the plight of children as well as the consuming interest in distinguishing between their deserving and undeserving mothers.[2] Widows should not be held responsible for their situation (unless they exhibited signs of unworthiness) "whereas deserted women were considered morally dubious and unwed mothers (who were expected to give up their children for adoption), were flatly unacceptable" (27). Ontario was the fifth Canadian province to introduce Mother's Allowance, following the four western provinces. All the plans were highly restrictive, but none more so than Ontario which disallowed mothers with only one child until 1935. The rationale for this exclusion? Mothers with one child could become live-in domestic servants. But the real motivation was clearly to save taxpayers money (Little 1998, 30).

This examination of feminist responses to women and work in the late nineteenth and early twentieth centuries provides little ammunition for those who argue that feminists have devalued the work that women traditionally do. Yet many first wave feminists did seek to expand women's terrain to include higher education, professional work, social reform, and community and social service. While most feminists agreed with dominant views that women were especially suited to caring for others, they argued that such caring needed to be exercised not only within the home but in the larger society.

SECOND WAVE FEMINISTS

First wave feminists tended to focus upon legal barriers to entry to professions and to share dominant societal views about the greater suitability of domestic employments for working-class women. Today, feminists from virtually all perspectives share an assumption that access to education, training, and all forms of paid work should not be denied because of gender. Such a simple-sounding goal has proved elusive, and a good deal of feminist theorizing and research has helped explain why that has been so. In the past few decades, the emphasis has been on elucidating and undermining systemic barriers, and revealing and transforming discourses on work that are explicitly and subtly gendered, sexualized, and racialized. Liberal feminists continue to focus upon the barriers to equality of opportunity in the workplace, although they have had to shift the boundaries of liberalism considerably in their quest. Socialist feminists focus on the intersection of capitalist and patriarchal relations in shaping women's super-exploitation in paid work, their primary responsibility for domestic labour, and the resulting double day of labour. Lesbian feminists have led the way in confronting the heterosexist practices that exclude them completely from some lines of work, as well as the images of femininity that subtly and not so subtly shape women's working lives. Feminists using the techniques of poststructural analysis have revisited the categories into which work has been divided to reveal how apparently neutral categories are infused with gendered language and assumptions.

So much had changed as a result of the victories won by first wave feminists and by the entry of so many women into the paid labour force. The formal barriers to higher education were down, and by the late 1960s women made up over one-third of undergraduate student populations. At the graduate level, there had been a gradual increase in female enrolment since 1955. Nonetheless, when the Royal Commission on the Status of Women issued its report in 1970, the figure had still not equalled the 1920 high when 25 percent of graduate students were women. Two world wars had revealed that women could do virtually every job, although support for them to do so in peacetime was slight. Women's relative strength in the labour market had grown as first single women, then married women with no children or with grown children, and finally during the 1970s the majority of women with young children began working for pay. Overwhelmingly, however, they were doing "women's work" for low wages and in poor working conditions.

How, then, have the issues about women, work, and children been formulated in the past two decades? I am going to deal with these issues under the same categories as in the first part of this chapter: admission and entrance, women and waged work, work and children, work and sexuality, and women and community. The categories themselves have to undergo quite a metamorphosis in order to accommodate the discussion. This in itself serves as some kind of barometer for the continuities and changes in the lives of women during the twentieth century.

During the following discussion, try to keep in mind the question posed at the beginning of this chapter: just when and how did feminists come to be charged with devaluing the work women do in the home? How the quintessential feminist, as portrayed in the media, became the career woman so vilified by anti-feminists is a mystery that requires investigation (Dubinsky 1985).

Admission and Entrance

Early second wave feminists were a rather ungrateful lot, although their ingratitude was primarily a function of ignorance. Like others, they knew little of the struggles of their predecessors for entrance into university and the professions. But even when they did, many tended to perceive those struggles as narrowly middle class, even elitist. Socialist and radical feminists spurned political mobilizations around these issues, even when many of them individually took an academic and professional route. Their long-term agenda was revolutionary, nothing short of the replacement of capitalist patriarchy with feminist socialism. Their immediate focus was upon working-class women both because they were the majority and because it seemed that they had more to gain and less to lose from revolutionary change than their middle-class counterparts.

Socialist feminist interest in the wages and conditions of working-class women coincided with that of many more mainstream feminists. One of the common goals of the struggle was to break down the gendered segregation in the non-professional sectors of the labour force. Such an interest resonated with women across the country, no longer willing to be confined to low-paying job ghettos.

In the period since women won admission to universities and to the professions, the huge area of white-collar jobs had opened up. Women made up the majority of office employees in the corporate and state sectors. Men had once done such jobs, which had paid better and carried more prestige than blue-collar jobs. But once women dominated such positions, wages in the white-collar ghettos were surpassed by the wages of the best male blue-collar jobs. Women all over the country began looking outside these sectors for work. *Nontraditional* became the label for those jobs from which women had been excluded and to which they now—individually, and collectively as part of feminist campaigns—demanded entry.

Protective legislation, the family wage, explicit policies of craft and industrial unions, and sugar-coated and blatant misogyny had kept women out of many jobs in all but the wartime decades of the twentieth century. In the early 1970s, many feminists began to focus on women's exclusion from these jobs. It was abundantly clear that many women needed to make more money: women who were supporting themselves and often their children too, whether out of choice, the desertion of their husbands, or their decision to leave an abusive marriage; women married to men who did not make the much-vaunted family wage; and women who were finding the courage and support to live openly as lesbians, and hence without the desire or expectation of male financial support. No longer was it just the exceptional woman who wanted waged work. Many women turned a critical eye on their economic dependence on men and determined that they—or at least their daughters—would be self-supporting. In this quest, they broadened their horizons and began looking at every kind of paid work.

If a primary rationale for women's exclusion from higher education and professions had been the unsuitability of their bodies for intellectual work, the argument that women did not belong in the better-paid jobs of the working class rested also on the inadequacy of their bodies, this time their physical weakness. When this argument wore thin, challenged by women capable of the most arduous physical work (Sugiman 1994) and by the fact that many of these jobs patently did not require great physical strength, secondary defences were produced. Men in dangerous occupations—primarily in war but also in mines and mills—needed to trust their comrades, the argument went. The presence of women interrupted male bonding. Moreover, what self-respecting man would be willing to look to a woman for protection? Male bonding, as some of the women first hired for jobs in such environments discovered, had a lot to do with objectifying and disparaging women (Gray 1987; Sugiman 1994). Some women described their experience with metaphors drawn from combat; others spoke of adjusting, becoming "one of the boys."

The idea that work should not be defined by gender has been taken up by women in the workplace and, notably, within and through their unions. Their success is visible in many areas of public policy and the law, employment practices and attitudes (Maroney 1987; Sugiman 1994). Pamela Sugiman has documented the major role played by a core group of women in the United Auto Workers in the late 1960s to break down sex-segregated workplaces. "Their struggle was momentous. They played a key role in amending the Human Rights Code in the province of Ontario [to include sex as a prohibited ground of discrimination] which in turn, eliminated all sex-based language from union contracts" (1994, 167). Yet those shop floors and mines that have not been shut down due to restructuring of the Canadian economy still have a predominantly male work force. When women are hired, they are also first fired.

The struggle to integrate nontraditional jobs continues. In September 1999 a Supreme Court of Canada decision restored a BC woman's "dream of being a firefighter."[3] Nearly five years earlier 33-year old Tawney Meiorin had lost her job when she failed one of four new government fitness tests.[4] The nine justices ruled unanimously that "the test standards—based primarily on a sample of the aerobic capacity of elite male firefighters" (Makin 1999, A1–2)—"was not neutral but discriminatory" (Baines forthcoming). Nor was there "credible evidence" to show that this capacity was necessary to perform the job satisfactorily. Feminist lawyers hailed the ruling as "a major blow to the sort of systemic discrimination that has impeded women trying to move into jobs traditionally monopolized by men." It was a long struggle for Tawney Meiorin: "Sometimes I really wanted to give up....But now I'm really glad I kept at it" (Makin 1999, A1–2; Baines forthcoming).

Employment equity legislation has been a major legal instrument devised for ensuring that women, visible minorities, Aboriginal peoples, and persons with disabilities are hired in those occupational categories—nontraditional, professional, and managerial—where they have been underrepresented. Those employers covered by such legislation are required to show how they plan to achieve equity goals. The guiding principle is that each occupational category should have numbers from each of the target groups that are proportionate to their numbers in the qualified population. Proponents of such legislation rested their case on the evidence that members of target groups face systemic discrimination in the work force, and that, left to their own devices, employers would not pursue equity goals.

But the very conscious and unconscious prejudices that exclude these groups (and we must note that three of the target groups are made up of women and men) come into play when people try to enforce such legislation. While some people use employment equity legislation in their struggle for inclusion, others, often in the name of individual rights, oppose any attempt to regulate employment practices.

The legislation designed to rectify women's systemic underrepresentation in the work force has been used to denigrate women who do get jobs: "You only have this job because you are a woman" has become a familiar line. In the universities, the question has been posed in terms of equity versus excellence. We are happy to hire women, many say, but more importantly we must always hire the best candidate. Such a statement carries with it several assumptions: "we" always know who the best candidate is; "we" ourselves are free from any prejudice against the designated groups; there is a yardstick that will objectively measure "best"; and, most fundamentally, "best" is an objective quality (Moghissi 1994). When a member of a designated group or groups is hired in a field dominated by white, able-bodied men—complete with all the credentials that confirm competence—s/he faces an ongoing charge, spoken and unspoken: "You only have the job because of your ascribed characteristics." Such assumptions create "chilly climates." Few would dispute that this is a step up from "frozen out," but in its numerous manifestations it can erode confidence in one's own competence and make life miserable and uncomfortable and careers impossible to pursue (Monture-Okanee 1995; Young and Majury 1995). Assumptions that candidates from targeted groups could not really be qualified have fuelled a backlash against women in previously male-dominated fields, especially those that have traditionally been better paid and associated with higher social status.

Although Ontario's employment equity legislation called for employers to determine their own measures and goals to remove discrimination on the basis of sex, race, and disability and to make reasonable progress towards achieving this goal, the election strategy of Mike Harris's Conservatives in 1995 portrayed the legislation as a quota system. Some observers regarded such a stance as election-year manipulation: "If we call it quotas—and promise to get rid of it—they will vote for us" (quoted in Burr 1995). The Conservatives did call it quotas; they did win; and they did "abolish" the legislation (Findlay 1999, 140). "Activists challenged the constitutionality of repealing this law, arguing that it violated women's sex equality rights."[5] In this case, in Beverley Baines' words, "the Charter abjectly failed women" with the provincial appellate court ruling that even though governments have enacted anti-discrimination laws to redress women's economic inequalities, the Charter does not obligate a government to enact other positive measures to achieve economic equality for women (forthcoming).

While women can no longer legally be excluded from work if they are or are perceived to be heterosexual, lesbians and gays have had a tough struggle fighting legally sanctioned discrimination. As mentioned in chapter 2, the Supreme Court has accepted sexual orientation as analogous to the other prohibited grounds of discrimination as enumerated in Section 15 of the Canadian Charter of Rights and Freedoms. But as James Robertson has noted, "the difficulty with relying solely on the Charter is that it applies only to governmental action...[and the process]...is costly, time-consuming and entails an adversarial approach" (1995, 3). As a result, lesbian and gay activists have pushed for inclusion of sexual orientation in human rights legislation because this arena provides the possibility of swifter administrative action and broader remedies. By 2003, human rights acts and codes in all jurisdictions except Prince Edward Island included sexual orientation as a prohibited ground of discrimination.

When the Ontario Court of Appeal ruled that the Canadian Human Rights Act was discriminatory because it did not protect gay men and lesbians from discrimination based on their sexual orientation, the federal government indicated in August 1992 that this ruling would be applied throughout Canada. Two months later, the Canadian Armed Forces admitted—after making an out-of-court settlement with former Air Force lieutenant Michelle Douglas—that its policy against hiring or promoting homosexuals was unconstitutional and announced the end of this restriction (Bindman 1992; Robertson 1995). Twenty-eight-year old Douglas, who had joined the military in 1986 after having graduated at the top of her basic training class, had been stripped of her "top secret" security clearance and released from the military in 1989 because of "admitted homosexual activity" (Bindman 1990; 1992). She welcomed the settlement in these terms: "This is not only a great day for me, but it's a win for all gays and lesbians in Canada and in the Canadian Armed Forces" (quoted in Bindman 1992).

Another example of long public struggle by gays and lesbians is for ordination as ministers and priests. In 1988, the United Church of Canada finally granted lesbians and gays the formal right to be called to the ministry. The decision provided stark evidence of the degree of homophobia in society. Five years later, the first congregation publicly accepted a gay man as minister (Todd 1993). Whole congregations withdrew from the church rather than accept the majority ruling; newspaper reports were filled with the most virulently hateful quotations and letters from those intent on continuing the exclusive practices. Yet in the context of Canadian society, the United Church has been at the forefront in terms of the ordination of women as well as gays and lesbians.

Women and Waged Work

At first, the move to desegregate the labour force and ensure that women had access to better-paying jobs seemed straightforward enough. But some cross-cultural observers were quick to notice a problem created by the assumption that men's jobs paid more because they demanded more skill, more experience, more training. Such critics argued that the move to open nontraditional jobs to women was underwritten by the same assumption that rationalized unequal pay scales in the first place: that the work men did deserved higher pay. What if work traditionally done by women was badly paid not because it demanded fewer skills, but because women did it? Suppose it was the sex of the job incumbents that endowed the work with low or high status and corresponding pay, rather than the other way round (Gaskell 1986)? As Graham Lowe discovered in his studies on the transformation of clerical work throughout the twentieth century, previous researchers have missed "the rather obvious point that the increasing recruitment of women as low-priced administrative functionaries largely accounted for declining average clerical salaries" (1987, 163). This insight about "the persistence and magnitude of the male-female earnings gap and the continued problem of the occupational segregation of women" (Chaykowski and Powell 1999, S20) provided the motivation for the development of pay equity.

Like employment equity, pay equity legislation represents a contemporary outcome of feminist historical, sociological, and legal research into the relations of power that have shaped salaries and conditions of work throughout the labour force. It reflects, as well, the political mobilization needed to translate these interpretations into legislation. The notion that skill itself was socially and historically constructed in space and time was breathtaking.

This analysis went beyond exposing the obstacles to equality of opportunity by calling into question the legitimacy of the opportunity ladders themselves. Pay equity legislation helped to erode the commonplace notion that people are paid what they deserve. Under this legislation, jobs done primarily by women are compared—in terms of skill, effort, responsibility, and working conditions—with those jobs done primarily by men. As Pat Armstrong, Mary Cornish, and Elizabeth Millar, all experts in different aspects of the pay equity process, have observed, however, the "new emphasis on market forces and deregulation [made] pay equity difficult to implement in the face of mounting resistance" (2003, 181).

Overall, pay equity represents the tip of the critical iceberg. The critiques of women's work in capitalist society have come from many sources: anthropological, historical, and sociological analysis of women's work in different modes of production; Aboriginal women and men; and feminist critics of imperialism and racism. For the purposes of the discussion at hand, I draw on these literatures to address one overriding question: what do they tell us about hierarchies of work in Canadian society? Such critiques go beyond those offered as rationales for pay equity to consider the underlying historical, political, and cultural explanations for the exploitation of working-class women and for the gendered and racialized organization of work.

Hierarchies of Work: Women and Unions Socialist feminists argued that women's lower wages relative to those of men resulted in large part from the disproportionately small numbers of women in unions, and on their subordinate place within them. Many became active in organizing initiatives as feminists and as workers. Their writing provides an excellent source of material on the challenges and obstacles faced by wage-earning women. During the 1970s, women organized unions in banks, offices, nursing, and teaching, as well as caucuses within virtually all of the existing industrial and public sector unions and provincial and federal labour organizations. These struggles confirmed and furthered feminist theorizing on the state (Briskin 1999; Briskin and McDermott 1993; Warskett 1988) and provided new evidence of the unwillingness of many male unionists and union leaders to alter their practices to include concerns raised by women. Feminist initiatives brought out the particular hardships women face when they want to organize, hardships occasioned by their domestic and maternal obligations. Such difficulties provided graphic illustration of the lengths to which many working women would go to win better pay and working conditions as well as leadership roles within unions.

That labour unions are underwritten by ideals of social and economic justice, that they have deployed a rhetoric about the dignity of work and all human beings, and that they are engaged in ongoing struggles with representatives of capital and the state all help explain why, at times, women have been more successful in their struggle for union recognition than they have been in either capitalist (private) enterprise or the institutions of the state. For women, this has proved something of a pyrrhic victory as labour unions have been denuded of numbers and power both by the movement of capital to more fertile ground in impoverished Third World countries and by the draconian steps of the state to reduce debt. Unions have been forced into defensive positions, and in the process many of the potential gains made by women were unrealized, especially in the public sectors where women predominate. Unionization does narrow the male-female wage gap considerably, however. A 1994 analysis revealed that "while the difference in average income between males and females among non-unionized workers was $17 243, the difference among unionized workers was only $11 082" (Chaykowski and Powell 1999, S16).

Aboriginal Women and Work In their quest to understand women's oppression in capitalist society, feminist scholars, particularly during the past 25 years, cast a comparative eye on precapitalist society and non-Western societies. They asked big questions. Do all societies have a gendered division of labour? Is such a division always hierarchically organized? Is it possible to transform the patriarchal division of labour in capitalist society? Feminist anthropologists and many Aboriginal women have argued that women in pre-contact societies in the territory now organized by the Canadian state lived in egalitarian, or communitarian, relationships with men and indeed wielded much of the influence and power (Anderson 1988; Fiske 1991; Leacock 1986; Monture-Angus 1995; Turpel 1993). The white conquerors not only destroyed the economic base of Native society as they progressively removed Aboriginal peoples from the land, but they also engaged in political and ideological assault on the status of women. Mary Ellen Turpel explains:

> The traditional teachings by our Cree Elders instruct us that Cree women are at the centre of the Circle of Life....It is women who give birth both in the physical and spiritual sense to the social, political and cultural life of the community. It is upon women that the focus of the community has historically been placed and it was, not surprisingly, against women that a history of legislative discrimination was directed by the Canadian state. (1993, 180)

Women's and men's work alike was undercut and often eliminated as Native peoples were dispossessed from the land and separated from their livelihood. In this process, the work that women do in Aboriginal societies has come more and more to resemble the domestic labour that feminists identified as women's lot in capitalist society. Just as the idea of working-class women as full-time homemakers was a kind of cruel parody of this practice in more affluent households, so it is in Aboriginal communities. Under conditions of extreme poverty, ill health, and demoralization, Aboriginal women struggle to keep their communities together and to raise their children. When they move to cities to look for paid employment, they are considered primarily for jobs in poorly paid service occupations (Peters 1987). Many Aboriginal women have created jobs in friendship, social, and health centres to serve their urban communities. Those who have acquired the formal training and education that provide the credentials for better-paying work often remain open and passionate critics of the system that they enter and of the consequences of European conquest for women's lives, both on and off reserves (Horn 1991; Monture-Angus 1995; Turpel 1993). They point to evidence that, despite the unspeakable hardships, women have remained central to the organization of families and households (Peters 1987). They argue that non-Aboriginal feminists have been too universalistic in their analysis of women's childbearing and raising activities, and that such activities were not only accorded the highest value in precontact Native societies but, despite all that has happened, continued to be highly valued.[6] Such interpretations highlight the importance of providing historically specific analyses of the work that women do as mothers and members of households.

Racism, Immigration, and Work The women descended from those who first lived on this land remain, for the most part, in the lowest-paid jobs. In addition, Aboriginal women do most of the unpaid domestic work in their households, and under the most poverty-stricken conditions that exist in this country. The historical legacy of racism as an integral aspect of the practices and rationale for capitalism and imperialism has also shaped work and working conditions for those who have immigrated here since contact. When people came, from where, and how they have been racialized all contribute to the creation of work hierarchies and how people are distributed within them (Henry et al. 2000). Consider the population of Canada variously labelled and self-identified as negro, coloured, of colour, black, Afro-Caribbean, and African Canadian. Some are the descendants of those who arrived in British North America as United Empire Loyalists or fleeing slavery during the century between the American Revolution and the Civil War. Others arrived during the 1950s and 1960s to attend Canadian universities and stayed. Others—women only—have come as domestic servants under conditions closely akin to indentured labour. Only a racist society would categorize all these people together. Only a racist society would provide the conditions for strategies of resistance based on "racial" characteristics.

But to refuse an analysis of race would render invisible the gendered and racialized hierarchies of work in Canada. Such hierarchies have been created by legal and de facto discrimination, by carefully crafted immigration policies and practices, and by personal and institutional prejudice. The late Rosemary Brown, who served as Director of the Ontario Human Rights Commission and earlier in British Columbia as an elected member of the provincial legislature, recorded her astonishment at the racism that she encountered when she arrived from Jamaica to study at McGill in 1950. The university moved her to a single room in residence "because the College had been unable to find a roommate to share the double with me....I was stunned!" (1989, 24). Finding work in Montreal that summer was a "nightmare." After graduating, she and her husband moved to Vancouver. Jobs were plentiful, but "the unwritten rule seemed to be that, aside from entertainment, the special jobs open to [blacks] were domestic work for women and portering on the trains for men." Brown was "determined to find the one person in the whole city of Vancouver who would look beyond the colour of my skin and would hire me solely on the basis of my competence as a typist and my Bachelor of Arts degree from McGill" (ibid., 46).

Sedef Arat-Koc provides a critical analysis of the racist immigration law whereby women from the Caribbean were granted entry into Canada for the sole purpose of relieving the shortage of live-in domestic servants in affluent Canadian households. Such a policy only attracts people because of the abysmal conditions of work in the Caribbean—a legacy of slavery, colonialism, and foreign ownership of resources. Live-in domestics have only minimal legal safeguards, and those few a result of concerted struggle. Few can scrape together the resources or have the time to prepare for different work. The catch-22 is that if they do find other work, they may find themselves ineligible to stay in the country. Yet domestic work is valuable and necessary. What requires transformation are the conditions of work and the role of the state in creating second-class citizens.[7]

Like Aboriginal women, some African Canadian women have criticized the explicit and implicit universalism of some feminist analyses of the family, women, and domestic labour. They have argued that the family has also provided a site of resistance to racism. Furthermore, they point out that most black women have always had to engage in (poorly) paid work: historically, the "luxury" of remaining home with children while a husband brought home a paycheque has seldom been available to black women (Brand 1984; 1991).

Other feminist scholars have written about the working conditions of non-English-speaking women who immigrate to Canada as part of families that both the Canadian state and their husbands see as male-headed (Arnopoulos 1979; Gannagé 1986; Iacovetta 1992;

1995). The assumptions about such women are many, the consequences predictable. These assumptions provide the rationale for public policy that not only meets the immediate demands of employers but also works to ensure that immigrant women who do not speak English or French have little or no occupational mobility. In such ways, particular kinds of work become identified with certain racialized groups of women and particular ethnic groups. Even when women from certain designated countries arrive in Canada with specialized training—for example, as nurses—they are often denied employment on the grounds that they lack training in the Canadian system.

Women, Children, and Domestic Labour

The insight that women's work was devalued *because* women did it dovetailed with the analysis feminists were beginning to produce on activities women did in the home: mothering, housework, cooking—all the "never done," invisible, and unpaid work. The deeply engrained belief that women's activities in the home were natural, demanding no special skills outside of genetic endowments, and that the work that they did for wages was simply an extension of this kind of gendered inheritance, helped legitimate the low wages and value accorded to that which women did. Clearly a full-scale reassessment and renaming of everything women did was required. In a society where only paid work was valued, it became crucial to begin by naming women's activities.[8] Thus, childcare through housework, cooking, feeding and caring for husbands, to sex itself was recognized, in Meg Luxton's words, as "more than a labour of love" (1980)— *domestic labour*, as socialist feminists termed it.[9]

But if this was work, and it was undervalued and unpaid, what should be done? The popular 1970s feminist children's record "Free to Be" by Marlo Thomas expressed the views of many: "If there's housework to do, do it *together*." As recent research into household division of labour indicates, this proved rather more difficult than the upbeat lyrics of the song made it sound. Women were easy to convince; they had more difficulty persuading their partners. Struggles in individual households over the division of labour picked up steam through the 1970s, and most evidence suggests that they continue. That women married to men who financially supported the household would do the lion's share of housework had seemed almost axiomatic. But as many studies show, this unequal division persists even when women are employed full-time (Haddad and Lam 1988; Nakhaie 2002).

Not all feminists shared the view that domestic labour and childcare should be a joint responsibility. Some radical feminists argued that men—at least in their present incarnation—were not to be trusted around children. They argued for women-only households and communities where children could be raised in safety. Socialist feminists argued that sharing work in the household, however admirable, was not a sufficient solution. Domestic labour should be socialized: co-operative households and communes, communal kitchens and childcare provisions were all needed to ensure that labour was social and not privatized, recognized and not invisible. They engaged in hefty debates about the relationship between domestic labour and capitalism. Was such labour productive in the sense that it produced surplus value and hence profits? Was capitalism itself dependent upon the unpaid household labour of women. Many argued that women could not be liberated in a capitalist society.[10]

Some feminists argued that women should be paid wages for housework, an idea that germinated with some women who remained, or wished to remain, home with their children. Most feminists were, to say the least, leery of this plan. Would it not simply confirm the gendered division of labour in its present hierarchical and oppressive structure? Social "wages" of any sort—for example, family allowance or mothers' allowance—have been notoriously low. Would not wages for housework simply sustain, even strengthen, the status quo where the alternatives for most women were to be economically dependent on men or very poor (or both)?

In the excitement of the huge insight that women worked in the home, worked hard at tasks crucial for the well-being of their husbands, children, and society, and for capitalism in particular, some rather disparate activities appeared to get lumped together. Children did mean work, but that wasn't all they meant. Many felt that the pleasures of raising children were eclipsed in the new discourse. Similarly, sex for many might indeed function as an exchange for housework and personal care, but the appeal of such an analysis for most young people was less than overwhelming. But I would argue that feminists, even in the heyday of the exciting new insights, never reduced intimate and nurturing relationships to work. Rather, they exposed the ideological mystifications that enveloped any consideration of women's contributions to men and children. But they have been interpreted as having so reduced these relationships, and we might want to keep this in mind in trying to understand the resonance of the charges against feminists.

Feminists were countering what some called the rhetoric of the pedestal, and many men and women resented this. Women's contributions were very valuable, conservative critics of feminism argued, far too valuable to be debased by the designation work. Women were born being able to do things that required patience, dexterity, and docility, whether that activity was changing a diaper, typing, caring for others as teachers, nurses, and mothers, or working long hours in a sweatshop, and they didn't really need monetary reward. Indeed, monetary reward would almost be insulting, an argument that was made when teachers and nurses began to organize for better salaries. Women did most of these activities out of love, and that came naturally too.

Unlike most first wave feminists, feminists in the 1970s challenged such assumptions and arguments. All the activities that women did—both in the economy and in the home—constituted work. That women did this work for little or no money wasn't because these activities did not require skill and training, or because women didn't need or want to be paid properly. Women did this work because they were oppressed in the household and exploited in the economy. The beneficiaries, whether as husbands or capitalists, were men. Yet changing this situation was no easy matter, primarily because this involved rethinking the care of children.

Essentially, children and work appear together in the feminist discourse of the past quarter century in two interrelated ways. First, as noted earlier, feminists insisted that, whatever else bearing and rearing children might be, in this society, the activities constituted work. Second, they drew attention, as had never been done before, to the fundamental incompatibility between reproductive labour and childcare, on the one hand, and paid work on the other, as well as to the profound consequences of this incompatibility.

At one level, it seems almost a truism that children mean work. Yet everyday expressions give away the extent to which this work still goes unacknowledged. "She's looking after the kids" does imply some responsibility, however casual. But we also hear, "she's at home with the kids" or "she's just at home with the kids," conjuring up the inherent passivity, innocuousness, and even triviality of time thus spent. As was suggested earlier, it is feminists to whom such views are often attributed. The irony is that it was feminists who first confronted such attitudes, arguing that childcare is indeed work, work that is integral to sustaining any society. In their arguments to this effect, socialist feminists drew upon and elaborated a famous passage from Friedrich Engels' book *The Origin of the Family, Private Property and the State*:

> According to the materialist conception, the determining factor in history is, in the last resort, the production and reproduction of immediate life. But this itself is of a twofold character. On the one hand, the production of the means of subsistence, of food, clothing and shelter and the tools requisite therefore; on the other, the production of human beings themselves, the propagation of the species. (1948 [1884], 5–6)

By only following up on production, Marxists had effectively eliminated from their analysis, strategies, and policies the work that most women do (Burstyn 1983). Mary O'Brien (1981) employed a Marxist materialist mode of analysis to argue that reproductive labour was not just labour *in name* (as in the expression "she's in labour") but also in reality and in its consequences. Harriet Rosenberg (1987) used the word *motherwork* to indicate the intrinsic connection between children and the creation of work.

At the same time as they countered popular notions that anyone—provided the anyone was of the female persuasion—could bring up children, feminists also had to engage and counter a parallel discourse about the needs of children. While it seemed that any woman worthy of the name should be able to mother, children also required full-time home care by their mothers if they were to grow up to be good citizens and well-adjusted adults. In support of this view, post–World War II childcare experts drew upon the wartime observations of psychologist John Bowlby. Bowlby reported that babies in orphanages who were left in their cribs all day did not develop normal attachments to other human beings. Those who were picked up for feedings did not demonstrate these symptoms of deprivation. Dr Spock, most famous of the childcare experts, warned mothers in his best-selling book, *Baby and Child Care*, that although the children of mothers who had to work usually turned out normally, some grew up "neglected and maladjusted" (1957, 563). Spock had to make a big leap from Bowlby's important observations to the assertion that babies needed full-time mothering in the home. After feminists aimed their logical, practical, empirical, and critical objections at the assumptions inherent in such judgments, Spock's 1985 message was rather different. "Both parents have an equal right to a career if they want one, it seems to me, and an equal obligation to share in the care of their children, with or without the help of others" (37).

One of the major practical and political objections feminists made to the insistence that children needed full-time mothers in the home was that such a notion was predicated on the idea of the family wage, more especially on the economic dependence of mothers upon fathers. Such an assumption, many argued, was heterosexist, class-blind, overlooked the consequences of the absence of a male breadwinner in many households, and assumed all women's availability, suitability, and desire for life as a 24-hour-a-day custodian and caregiver.

Here we may properly turn to the second overarching theme of the feminist discussions on children and work. Feminists argued that many women need and/or want to work for pay. But, as feminists began to reveal through historical and cross-cultural studies, by creating forums in which women could speak, and through mass political mobilizations, there was a fundamental incompatibility in Canada and other industrial capitalist societies between having children and working in the labour force. The problem was simple: at one point or another it faces every woman who is a mother and leaves the household to "go to" work. What to do with the children?

Feminists led the way in transforming every woman's private trouble into a public policy issue. If the organization of society could not take pregnancy and parenting into account, then workplaces and households alike required reorganizing. Feminists developed strategies that ranged from blueprints for new feminist socialist utopias, through lesbian communities, communes, housing co-operatives, and other forms of egalitarian spaces and households within capitalist patriarchal societies, to reforms intended to enhance equality of opportunity for women in the paid labour force.

The 1970 *Report of the Royal Commission on the Status of Women* called for daycare and maternity leave. Yet, the extent to which children are held to be the responsibilities of their parents may be seen in the continuing controversies about the necessity and viability of state-supported daycare as well as in the continuing comparisons between parental care in the home and daycare. During World War II, when the state wanted women to work in industries related to and supportive of the war effort, objections to daycare were quickly overruled. As soon as the armistice was declared, the daycares were closed, not without protest from the women who used them. Historian Ruth Pierson has documented that women worked because they needed the money, and because they worked they needed daycare. The government of Canada portrayed women as working because of their patriotism; once the war was over, they happily returned home to their natural destiny. Today "natural destiny" isn't "in" as a public statement, but neither, on the other hand, is daycare (Pal 1993).

In 1993, former Supreme Court Justice Bertha Wilson chaired a study for the Canadian Bar Association, which documented what she called the systemic biases against women in the profession of law. The suitability of future partners for law firms is determined within a legal culture that has been shaped by men, for men, and "is predicated on historical work patterns that assume that lawyers do not have significant family responsibilities" (quoted in Gibb-Clark and Fine 1993, A10).

First wave feminists, even the most utopian among them, never foresaw the day when a report with such findings would see the light of day (even in the 1990s it encountered more heat than light). Women who did become professionals tended not to marry or have children, and such a choice, painful as it might have been, seemed unavoidable. In 1920, Agnes Macphail, the first woman to win a seat in the House of Commons, found that "most of the members made me painfully conscious of my sex." While she "did not shrink from the responsibility that she had accepted, taking it so seriously that she rejected several marriage proposals, in order to continue her work, she was sensitive over being a 'spinster' in an era when marriage was highly valued, and took pains to announce the marriage offers publicly" (Prentice et al. 1988, 279–80). Such choices do not just belong to history. One woman, hired at a Canadian university in the late 1970s, asked about its maternity policy. "Our faculty don't get pregnant," replied the personnel officer. In her study of female lawyers in the early 1990s Fiona Kay found that not only did many women postpone pregnancy until their careers were established but "others decided not to have children at all" (1997, 209).

Work norms in the law firms reflected the life situation of an ambitious, physically healthy man who could work all hours, including weekends. That schedule was (supposedly) facilitated by a wife at home, caring for him and for his children. The work norms assumed that there were no conflicts between parenting and work in the labour force. One of Kay's respondents provided this assessment: "The general issue is that in order to advance, make sure that you don't have children....Although it is certain that the male associates will become partners, I honestly believe that women who choose to have a family will become permanent associates (1997, 213).

Feminists critiques of capitalist society draw attention to the absurdity of an economic system that makes no provision for the exigencies of human reproduction and childhood dependence. They confront the patriarchal relations and assumptions that leave women responsible for the care of their children without providing the resources or the opportunities to garner the necessities of life.

This analysis of women, work, and children would lead to the conclusion that women can either have children or they can support their children, but not both at the same time. Yet in 1999, 61 percent of mothers with children three and under were part of the work force (Statistics Canada as reported in Philp 2000). Their strategies are various and are shaped by many factors broadly related to the economic resources they can deploy, the number of adults who play an active parenting role in their children's lives, and the age, health, and behaviours of their children. Some affluent families seek live-in caregivers to facilitate their working lives. Most of the time, the women they hire receive low wages for long hours of work. Because native-born Canadian women refuse such conditions, they hire women from Third World countries. Sedef Arat-Koc points out a consequence of these decisions: "As a relationship between female employers and workers, domestic service emphasizes, most clearly, the class, racial/ethnic and citizenship differences among women at the expense of their gender unity" (1989, 52). The wages and conditions of work of domestic workers reflect, more generally, the low value society places on the care of children. Daycare workers, most of them non-unionized, earn low wages for exhausting and demanding work for which they often have formal training and much experience (Teghtsoonian 1997).

In light of the lack of daycare and after-school programs, many women seek employment that is as compatible as possible with their children's school schedules. For some, that is part-time work. Such a strategy provides less income, and usually means that a person will not be considered for on-the-job training or promotion. Jobs, not careers, usually result from part-time employment. As Duffy and Pupo argue in *Part-Time Paradox*, such work is "acceptable to women because it is frequently what is available to them and because there have been few structural accommodations to women's participation in the public sphere" (1992, 104). In 1998 nearly 70 percent of all part-time workers were women. Fifteen percent of them—and only a negligible number of men—cited child care as their reason (Chaykowski and Powell 1999, S12), differences as Chaykowski and Powell note, reflecting "the fact that women continue to take on the role of primary care-provider." "Part-time work offers fewer non-wage benefits and little prospects for an occupational pension." As a result, such work will not "help mothers who are trying to achieve financial independence in the long run" (1999, S21).

Some corporations describe part-time work for women who seek to combine careers with motherhood as the "mommy track." It goes without saying that this innovation—captured by Duffy and Pupo as "off the main track" (1992, 116)—will not contribute to equality of opportunity with men unless there is an equally well-worn "daddy track." (See Box 5-1.)

BOX 5-1	Women, Work, Daycare, and Mixed Messages

In recent years we have seen two very different stories about women who want to mother full-time. The first story is about married women who leave well-paying jobs to stay home with their children. The women are portrayed sympathetically, sometimes with a subtext aimed at feminists, announcing "we told you so: 'THIS' is what women *really* want" (and clearly some do, at least for a while) (Eldridge 2002). The other story is about welfare mothers depicted as "on-the-take" from the system. Their children, it would seem, do not need them at home full-time. They have been hounded off the welfare roles, and forced to take any job available—minimum wage or worse. These mothers are prime candidates for "workfare," a once discredited system of forced labour, which has been rehabilitated in the current right-wing political climate.

How might we explain this differential valuing? Women who have good earning power and who have partners with good salaries are valued if they don't work for pay, while women alone with little earning power are humiliated if they care for their own children at home. Perhaps the women who choose not to work are valued for not "competing" with men and for confirming traditional beliefs about the proper role for women. Women on welfare, on the other hand, are forced to do the jobs that others don't want to do and will not accept. Underneath all this are older versions of deserving and undeserving women, good mothers and bad mothers. Does this sound far-fetched?

Consider this: the wage gap between men and women—still "downright depressing" in Alex Michalos's words—has narrowed somewhat in the past 30 years (2000, 246). When Richard Chaykowski and Lisa Powell broke the 1994 population data down into five quintiles, however, they made a startling discovery. "Relative to men, a larger share of the aggregate income of women workers is held by women in the single middle quintile, a larger share of the aggregate income of women workers is held by women in the lowest quintile and a much smaller share of the aggregate income of women workers is held by women in the highest quintile" (1999, S16). Moreover, "among females the population shares in each quintile decrease as one progresses from lowest to highest quintile while the opposite pattern holds for males" (1999, S16). In other words, the overall figures on the gendered wage gap disguise the fact that women are concentrated at the bottom and middle, and men are concentrated at the middle and the top.

What would it take to close this gap? Essentially, a decent federal child-care policy with national standards. Canada appeared on the brink of having such a policy in 1986 when the Liberal government's Task Force on Child Care recommended a fully funded childcare system but successive governments, first Conservative, then Liberal, retreated from this (Teghtsoonian 1997, 114–15). In the debates about daycare, mothers in the work force are pitted against mothers at home. Many Canadians argue that infants and small children should be the (sole) responsibility of their parents. This ideology manages to obscure some fundamental realities about contemporary society. Bureaucratic organizations, consecrated to profit and efficiency, leave considerations of pregnancy, babies, children, and families in the hands of individuals, and this mostly turns out to mean mothers. Capitalism honours profits. All other considerations about human life are left out.

For this reason during the past 200 years, men and women fought for publicly funded education, health care, infrastructure, and the list goes on. The welfare state developed from the realization that people die on the streets and in their homes without a so-called "safety net." Many of these "victories" are now being eroded. But in Canada, a line was already drawn in the sand, and on the wrong side of that line stood publicly funded daycare. Even in Quebec, which stands out from the rest of the country in providing parents day-

care at a modest daily cost, thousands of children are on waiting lists. More generally, according to Liberal MP John Godfrey, who chairs the National Children's Agenda Caucus, Canada is "'moving backwards' thanks to developments in Ontario and British Columbia" (quoted in Ferguson 2002, 60). Only 10 percent of Canada's 2.8 million children under six are in regulated care (Ferguson 2002, 58).

Left unaltered, these attitudes and policies about daycare and parental responsibility will sustain economic inequalities between men and women into the foreseeable future despite women's increasing educational achievements, and leave many children in makeshift childcare arrangements. Mothers who earn well are encouraged to stay home and poor mothers—especially those on their own—are forced into paid work.

Most women working for wages try to "find the right time" to have a child in a world that does not provide one (Currie 1988). After the birth they choose the most acceptable option and then hope for the best. Hoping for the best under such circumstances increases the anxiety, stress, health problems, and fatigue inherent in the double day of labour. Nor do women receive accolades for carrying on. Rather, middle-class social reformers and the media have interpreted their options in ways that blame them for real or perceived negative consequences of their efforts to cope with the contradictions of mothering in a patriarchal capitalist system. School dropouts and students with high absentee records are often older children who have been kept home from school to look after preschool siblings whose mothers "neglect" them by working for wages. Latch-key children—inevitable figures in Canadian society for more than a century—are children whose mothers work for wages outside the home and who therefore have to look after themselves after school or when they are sick. Of course, fathers also leave the home to work for wages, but in their case they are not deemed neglectful for doing so. Rather they are considered inadequate fathers if they *don't* earn a family wage, and this, of course, creates its own distress.

Women, Sexuality, and Work

Women's presence on terrain once conceded as male has revealed that first wave feminist warnings about the dangers of the workplace—which they conceived as problems for women's sexual morality—were prescient. The dangers, it turned out, were real enough, but the analysis and solutions have been radically reconceived. Working women coined a new term—*sexual harassment*—and it became part of everyday speech. Sexual harassment refers to unwanted behaviours that (primarily) men direct towards women who are their employees, co-workers, fellow students, or simply those with whom they share space, for a moment, on a city street. The term has been used to capture a range of behaviours from a sexist joke to a bum pat to a suggestion that a woman's job or promotion might be linked to her willingness to have sex with the boss. As the stories from working women proliferated, women stopped silently blaming themselves for unwanted sexual and sexist behaviour. Once such behaviours became grievable under harassment policies, the privileges and prerogatives of men in working environments were converted into misdemeanours and crimes.

Contemporary feminists shift the burden of responsibility for such workplace dangers from women to men. Thus, if the workplace or classroom is deemed morally dangerous for women, the call would not be to exclude them; rather, the onus would be on those who create the dangers to change their behaviours. For contemporary feminists, the problems reside in unequal power relations between men and women and among women. The dangers for women at work produce demands for new laws, new practices, and consciousness raising.

Such a shift in perspective was part of the larger feminist critique of the double standard of sexual behaviour. Here most contemporary feminists part company with their predecessors whose overwhelming concern was with women's respectability, defined largely in terms of their sexual behaviour. Most contemporary feminists believe that a woman's sexuality is hers alone to express, regulate, or enjoy. Sexual dangers may lurk at work, but so does the possibility of meeting friends and lovers, the sorts of opportunities that created hand-wringing among early twentieth century social reformers, including feminists.

Before we shake our heads at our old-fashioned predecessors, we might want to look at a topic with which they were greatly concerned and which, some argue, creates similar concerns today for the same reasons: the prostitution question. Perhaps this question elicits more division among feminists today than any other work-related issue. Is prostitution simply another form of work, as some women working as prostitutes have argued? Should feminists simply be concerned with ensuring standards of pay and safety as in other gainful employment? Is the present-day feminist refusal to grant prostitution legitimacy as a job category a continuation of the moralistic concerns of their first wave predecessors (Bell 1987)? Or is prostitution a continuing legacy of a patriarchal society in which men are permitted to use (and abuse) women's bodies for pay? Philosopher Christine Overall answers "yes" to this last question in the conclusion of her incisive analysis of prostitution in a capitalist patriarchal society, arguing that patriarchy creates "both the male needs themselves and the ways in which women fill them, construct[s] the buying of sexual services as a benefit for men, and make[s] the reversibility of sex services implausible and sexual equality in the trade unattainable" (1992, 724).

Would emancipated women who have fair options ever choose prostitution as a career? Perhaps, some say, it is almost impossible to answer such a question in a society with such a long and dishonourable history of dealing with women's sexuality. It stretches credulity for most feminists to imagine a world where contracts between equals over the buying and selling of sexual services could have as much or as little meaning as buying and selling labour power for the purposes of building a house. Yet that response smacks of condescension to some women working as prostitutes in the here and now. They point out that, despite the evidence, presented earlier in this chapter, of the exploitation, oppression, and racism informing so many working practices in contemporary society, no one suggests that people should abstain from working until we reach a utopia.

In a recent article, Kathleen Shellrude, a Women's Studies student at the University of Winnipeg, argued that "the denial of sexual labour in 'normal' jobs makes problematic and stigmatizes the 'sex industry'"(2001, 41). "Although I have never sold sex *per se*," she explains, "I have sold the *possibility* of sex, and have used my sexuality and my body to make money, drinks, and other things that were to my advantage." Using her experience as a server in the restaurant industry, she provides several examples that deal with how she tries to please management (the pimps, in her words), the kitchen staff (the cops), and the customers. "When I go to work the kitchen staff say to me 'Hey, good lookin'! Thanks for last night!' Though most certainly I did not go home with them I reply 'No, *thank you*...best night I ever had! [my italics] I know that if I do not play along with this sexual game my food will come out late, burnt, and wrong, and the night will be bad" (2001, 44). "Prostitution wouldn't be so stigmatized," she insists, "if [other] people stopped denying that [they too are] using their sex(uality) to get what they want" (2001, 43–4).

Nearly three decades of feminist discussion has revealed how women historically and in the present are divided into "good" and "bad," depending upon their sexual practices and often upon the nature of their relationships with men. With all the shifting definitions of good and bad that have occurred, woman as prostitute remains almost continually the quintessential bad woman. Feminists might agree that one of the goals of their struggle is to eliminate these dichotomous categories of good and evil. The question some ask is, can this be done while retaining prostitution as a marked category that can never be admitted into the sphere of legitimate work?

This discussion does not conclude that there is a right answer to these questions, but it does serve to illuminate the broader issues surrounding women, work, and sexuality. Discourses of sexuality, feminists have argued, still shape ideas about women and their suitability for different kinds of work. Women have grieved against employers who have fired them or refused them employment or promotion for being too old, too young, too sexy looking, or too straight-laced. The woman dressed for success, as magazines and advertisements caution, has had to change her wardrobe several times in the past decades, depending on where she works. Should she wear a suit tailored like a man's? How should she express her "femininity"? What length should her skirt be? Are pants acceptable? When?

All the ads make one thing clear: women at work should dress to please men, the men who are their bosses, their co-workers, and their clients. Such are the heterosexist assumptions that pervade most work environments. From the 1970s, the women's movement and the movements for gay and lesbian liberation publicly confronted these assumptions and, in the process, revealed the deceptions that lesbians and gays have had to perpetrate to get and keep jobs. Some have argued from the historical evidence that, in the first decades of the twentieth century, women who lived with other women were free from harassment or discrimination because no one thought of them as sexual beings (Faderman 1981). But in the era of sexual liberation, supposedly inaugurated in the 1960s, the willingness to tolerate such invisibility gave way to the desire for openness, on the one hand, and the assurance of unwelcome surveillance, on the other.

As co-workers get to know each other and talk about their personal lives, daily stresses, and ideas, many lesbians report that they are cautious about revealing the names of their partners, let alone discussing their personal lives in any detail, for fear of ostracism, losing their jobs, and jeopardizing references for future jobs. Women who are not out to their colleagues pick up their homophobic comments, dropped casually in conversation, the bonding of "us" versus "them," and resolve to remain closeted. Or not. Either way, their daily work lives and long-term prospects remain informed by discourses of sexuality that divide the normal from the abnormal, and those who belong from those who don't.

This discourse still forms the basis of Canadian legislation on who qualifies as a spouse for whom—though probably not for long. In this area, legislative discrimination against gays and lesbians has been absolute with Canadian law defining "'spouse' uniformly in exclusively heterosexual terms" (Robertson 1995, 8). Because many laws use the term "spouse" to allocate work-related rights, powers, benefits, and responsibilities to partners, lesbians and gays have confronted a deep thicket of exclusionary laws and practices. The relevance of these exclusions for working life helps explain the immense lobbying efforts by lesbians and gays to expand the definition of spouse (Blackburn 1995; Herman 1995). The struggle reveals the permeability of the so-called private-public split. How people are treated in the workplace, even at the level of legislation, has been shaped by their relationships and identities in their households and in their "free" time.

Women, Community, and Society

First wave feminists emphasized that women should be involved in the world beyond their households *because* of their special talents and concerns. Such reasoning has been hotly contested during the past decades. Feminists have tended to argue that women should be everywhere that they want to be. Transforming social institutions, attitudes, and practices so that this would be possible has, as we have seen in this chapter, engaged feminists from all perspectives.

In this final section, I consider some of the work-related organizing that has been about creating (predominantly) women-only spaces—from women's centres and cultural sites and communities to an immense variety of small businesses. The varying perspectives of feminists have influenced where, how, and why they have organized, but the type of organization has also confirmed or challenged the assumptions of the participants. A radical feminist or lesbian separatist analysis motivated some women who organized women-only spaces. But working in women's shelters and rape crisis centres and seeing the consequences of male violence for women's lives also provided the evidence, as some women report, for the correctness of such an analysis. One Vancouver woman wrote to her friends, describing her horrific experience leading support groups for women who had been battered: "I no longer think we live in only cold war conditions. It looks a lot more violent and hateful than that" (personal communication).

Today, virtually every city and town in the country includes organized spaces for women, although harsh government cutbacks have forced many closures. The movement for such centres started in the early 1970s. Feminists saw themselves not only creating space for women to meet and support each other, but also laying the ground for reform and revolution. Increasingly, such centres began responding to the needs of women who came, and feminists opened more specialized centres. There has been continuing pressure for these centres to become more like traditional, bureaucratic organizations. The sheer numbers of women who present themselves for support mean that struggling to help each woman can take the place of more long-term organizing goals. More importantly, given this overwhelming need, such centres have had to seek stable funding from the state. Although organizers struggle to maintain their decision-making autonomy, the pressure to rationalize the organization, produce a hierarchically organized staff that is "accountable," and keep countless records has taken its toll. From the outside, many centres now look like way stations for the destitute run by a staff of poorly paid professionals. Some shelter workers claim that this has been the fate of these centres. However, this picture of co-optation scarcely does justice to the many ways in which women as paid workers and volunteers have negotiated their way through the administrative thickets without abandoning their ways of working or their goals. More serious have been the effects of government cutbacks. Many centres and services throughout the country have been forced to close, and those that remain open come to demand even longer hours from their workers in return for even lower wages.

The motivation for developing women-only work sites has run the range from the pragmatic to the revolutionary. Starting small businesses, for example, has been popular with women for different reasons: lack of employment elsewhere; the inclination to work according to non-hierarchical, collectivist principles; the desire not to have to work with men, which may include women providing safe spaces for themselves and others; the political motivation to provide feminist-inspired services for women facing and resisting abuse or poverty or seeking assistance in altering relationships, work, and life directions more generally; the desire to have more control over one's work life (Dickie 1993).

Some of the small businesses—from artisanal shops to book stores, credit unions, therapeutic services, and retail stores—have been inspired by those often referred to as cultural feminists. Cultural feminists seek to create a world—or as much of a world as possible—that women organize for women, along non-hierarchical lines. Particularly in large cities and towns, such establishments form a network to support alternative lifestyles, household arrangements, and politics. Often such networks include primarily lesbian feminists who have created spatial and social environments in which they may live openly with their partners, friends, acquaintances, and children (Rudy 2001; Nash 1995).

CONCLUSION

Given this overview of feminist questions and challenges to women and work, let us briefly consider the charge that feminists encourage women to turn their backs on children, on nurturing, on caring for others. Some of this resonates. Feminists have led many struggles for women's freedom to choose whether or not to have children. By redefining childcare—whether in the private household, daycare, or school—as work, feminists made it more possible to see having children as a choice, as indeed other forms of work are portrayed. The idea—let alone the reality—that women may choose whether to have children raises anxiety and hostility for different reasons. I cannot discount, as an important factor, the desire and interests of many in maintaining women's subordination and oppression both in households and in economic life more generally.

What about the charge that feminists have ushered in a world in which women are encouraged to model themselves on some version of the corporation man? As some women seek equality with men in the workplace, an equality that feminists espoused, many have chosen or felt forced to undertake the same gruelling work schedule that has been the route for many ambitious men. It is easy to blame the media for promoting images and views with which one is not in sympathy, but this does not mean that such blame is not warranted. For

20 years, the mainstream media followed the feminist story in terms of "the first woman who...." More often than not "the first woman who" was a woman who had made it into the top ranks of a public or private corporation. Equally interesting to the media were stories about the woman who did and had everything: she had a successful job, fabulous kids, and devoted husband; she was an excellent housekeeper and cook; she ran the local branch of the Red Cross and was the kind of person everyone wanted for a neighbour. Of course, she was also "beautiful." "Ordinary" mortal women reading these stories were, at best, disbelieving, and, at worst, provided with another occasion to feel inadequate. Or they could just blame feminists for holding up such unworkable, unrealistic images.

But feminists provide a shifting target. In her *Globe and Mail* column, Margaret Wente charged feminists with failing to appreciate the gains made by some women in reaching the top. In 1994 she took NDP leader Audrey McLaughlin and NAC to task for not cheering for a woman's success just because she was "white, privileged, ruthless, pragmatic, ambitious, unpleasant or (Goddess help us) profit-oriented" (1994, A2). Once, feminists were under attack for only being interested in the issues affecting white, middle-class women. Now that the media identifies the face of organized feminism as NAC—which increasingly focuses upon poverty and racism—feminists are being attacked for the opposite sins that dogged them a decade ago.

This chapter has provided an overview of many of the predominant discussions, debates, organizing initiatives, and issues that feminists have raised in the past century around women and work. There is no end to the story, of course. The current restructuring of the Canadian economy continues to erode the ranks of two sorts of workers: relatively well-paid men organized in industrial unions and the recently developed ranks of state-employed women in better paying jobs from nursing to social work to middle-level administrators. Jamie Swift (1995) demonstrates that, increasingly, two kinds of jobs are being created: highly paid technical jobs and a far greater number of low-paid, casual, now-you-see-them, now-you-don't service jobs. The proliferation of jobs in the latter category helps to explain the continuing erosion in middle-class households, including those who only remain in these ranks because they have two full-time wage earners.

Those men and women who do work full-time face increasingly long workweeks, often for no additional remuneration. The 2001 National Work-Life Conflict Study found that "one in four Canadians now work more than 50 hours a week, compared to one in ten only a decade earlier."[11] As Kathryn May wrote, this is a "far cry from expert predictions barely 30 years ago that Canadians would be working 28 hours a week by 1985." Indeed, hours of work are getting closer to those of "the industrial workers in the mid-19th century whose punishing 12-hour days, six days a week, led to the first wave of work week reforms." The survey found that men and women were working these gruelling schedules whether they had children or not. "You do it to get ahead and a growing number of workers feel they don't have the option of saying no to overtime or taking flexible work arrangements" (2002, 13).

But this is also a gendered process as women respond to these expectations by choosing not to have children, to have fewer children, or to simply opt out of the competition. Given cutbacks in social services, daycare, and the social wage generally, and increasing numbers of low-paid jobs and sole-support mothers, there seems no reason to believe that the contradictions posed for women by the demands of childcare and care of aging parents and disabled family members, on one hand, and waged work, on the other, are abating. Many of the gains achieved through feminist organizing are already being turned back.

Now it seems that many of those new good jobs for women are period pieces, there only during the days before the heavy cutbacks in state spending in every sphere. Autonomous organizations have been replaced by state services paying minimum wage to women who deal with the increasing casualties of an economic restructuring that provides more for the few and less for the many. Those who speak about a "post-feminist" world may be conjuring up a society in which there is no more organizing based on gender inequality, but putting a "post" before feminist will not eradicate the inequalities that feminist organizing continues to address (Brodie 1995).

In this chapter, we have examined women's paid and unpaid work, their interconnections, and the implications and consequences of the current distribution of work. Except for the very wealthy, the kind of paid work to which we have access shapes our standard of living, whether we live in comfort or poverty, and whether our children have access to education. The ways in which that work is organized shapes our influence and control over its conditions and our feelings about ourselves.

How we come to think about ourselves as gendered, what that means for our lives, and how we are presented to ourselves in literature, art, media, advertising, and political and legal discourse constitute the interrelated themes of the next chapter. These themes pervade all feminist-inspired organizing and writing. Chapter 6 looks at these issues of representation and subjectivity in the context of shifting definitions and discourses about gender, sexuality and sexual orientation, race, nationality, age, health, illness, and disability. Feminist questions and practices have helped bring these discourses to consciousness so that they might be critiqued and transformed. The geopolitical context remains Canada, but the topics of representation and subjectivity refer to culture, broadly defined, and these issues, perhaps more than those in the previous chapter, defy any national or geographical boundaries.

NOTES

1. For interpretations of women's role in nursing, midwifery, and community and public health, see Dodd and Gorham (1994).

2. Mothers' Allowance was expanded to include other categories of women including single mothers. In 1997 the Harris government passed Bill 142 which incorporated all groups requiring state assistance under one welfare policy linked to employment. This marked the "end of 77 years of mother's allowance policy in Ontario" (Little 1998, 182).

3. British Columbia (Public Service Employee Relations Committee) v. BCGSEU.

4. She took 49.4 seconds too long to complete a 2.5 kilometre run that had to be completed in 11 minutes (Makin 1999, A2).

5. Ferrel et al. v. Attorney General of Ontario (1999).

6. I am grateful to Margaret Horn for first explaining this to me.

7. For an in-depth analysis of "the significance of citizenship status in mediating the entire matrix of relations pertaining to paid domestic labor on an international scale," see Bakan and Stasiulus (1995). They demonstrate the "pivotal role of private domestic placement agents in negotiating citizenship rights for migrant domestic workers and their employers" (304).

8. Wally Seccombe examines the ways in which some economists have moved to incorporate feminist insights into their models of the household. First, they began to conceive of unpaid work as integral to production as well as consumption. Second, they began to abandon the assumption that family

households were always "income-pooling, work-sharing and joint consumption groups" and to grapple with the evidence that points to "persistent inequalities in labour burden, leisure, property ownership, pension provision and decision-making prerogative—all to the wife's detriment" (1986, 200–1).

9. In 1996 Statistics Canada announced that census questions on unpaid household work, childcare, and care and assistance to seniors would be included in their long questionnaire which is sent to 20 percent of households. The agency noted that the significance of this unpaid work has been recognized for a long time and that Statistics Canada had been working on questions since the late 1970s (*Canadian Social Trends* 1996, 33). Though there is no attribution, it is clearly the feminist movements that initiated this interest.

10. Leah Vosko has provided a recent summary and analysis of all these debates (2002).

11. Linda Duxberry and Chris Higgins undertook this study for Health Canada. They surveyed workers at 100 organizations in the private, public, and non-profit sectors (May 2002, 13).

Representation
and Subjectivity

Imagine my surprise upon reading an article in the *Globe and Mail Report on Business* about the Links for Women Golf School (Sanati 2003, 59). The little pink book provided at the end of the instructional day includes this advice: "Be Silent and Still,"[1] so close to the motto of Canada's first school of nursing: "I See and Am Silent" (Coburn 1974, 140). Nursing students should watch quietly, refrain from offering advice, never contradicting the doctor-gods. Presumably female golfing students in 2003 cannot be expected to know when to talk—and when not to talk—in the presence of the golfing-gods. But doesn't anyone who casually watches a golf tournament on TV notice the lull that descends on a crowd as a golfer tees off? Do women need this advice, and is it offered (in writing) to men?

These golfing schools are not just teaching *any* game, it should be clear. They are preparing women in the corporate world to play the game, which more than any other, will prepare them for high-powered networking. Does it work? Some wonder: "Most guys don't even like golfing with women. They golf with their friends," according to one woman in the course. But Paul Aslop, representing a corporate sponsor, argues that without golf "women are missing a critical business skill." Still he is perplexed to find that the women who enrol in the school "chiefly want to spend more time with their husbands and family" during vacations: "cracking male bastions comes further down the list" (Sanati 2003, 59). This is a small and amusing example of gendering at work and play: the condescension towards women who are told to be quiet (and remember to bring "feminine products" and some money), the presumptions that women will behave as men do in their quest for success, the desire of men to golf with their own kind.

Historically, in Western societies, all forms of work have been deeply gendered; work is implicitly, and more often explicitly, perceived as "women's work" or "men's work" or at the least, more suitable to one sex than the other. More generally, not just work, but most forms of activity and behaviour are similarly gendered. I mean this in two inter-related ways. First, activities and behaviours, in every aspect of social life, are represented verbally and pictorially, as gendered. During World War II, government recruitment posters geared to attracting women were careful to depict conventional femininity. In case the point was lost, one poster showed a mother with a photograph of her daughters who had joined the service, with a caption that read "My girls are the real glamour girls" (Pierson 1986, 142–43). Sixty-five years later, when Dr. Caroline Baillie accepted the Dupont Chair of Engineering Education, Research and Development at Queen's University, the story in *The Kingston Whig-Standard* noted that Dr. Baillie was "in her 30s...had her long dark hair tied back...and was dressed in flowing black pants and a funky white blouse." The message seems clear: one doesn't have to abandon femininity to become an engineer, "a field tra-ditionally dominated by men" (Hammond 2003, 1).

Second, women and men are likely to think of themselves in ways that make some kinds of work, activity, and behaviour more appropriate for them than others simply because of their sex. Old rationales for gendered employment ghettos—women's physical weakness, greater manual dexterity (good for typing), and raging hormones (keep them away from decision making)—are still summoned on occasion. Moreover, as Karen Messing (1987) has documented, keeping women away from equipment for the purposes of protecting their fertility and their fetuses provides new grounds for exclusion. She argues that this rationale is used selectively by employers for their convenience and ignores the effects of exposure for men's fertility.

What we do, how we see ourselves and are portrayed, and who we think we are, are all interconnected. Feminists have explored each of these three aspects of social life, trying to figure out how they are related to each other and how, together, they shape relations of domination and subordination between the sexes. What motivates this analysis is a com-mitment to social change. But, strategically speaking, how do we go about changing soci-ety? Is it more important to expand women's and men's options for the sorts of work they choose? To change the ways in which they are represented? Or is social change well nigh impossible until women and men—that is we ourselves—are changed?

For analytical purposes, we could think of these three questions as reflecting three areas of social life: activity, representation, and subjectivity. The focus of the last chapter was on activity—in particular, work. In this chapter, the focus shifts to the last two parts of this trilogy. First, how are men and women represented in this culture? What are the dominant ways in which men and women are portrayed in the media, in law, in education-al institutions and texts, in virtually any social location? Second, how and in what ways do human infants become men or women in social terms? What does it mean to be a man or woman in this culture? What are the connections between the ways in which people feel themselves to be men or women and come to behave as men or women, and the represen-tations of men and women that they see in their social worlds?

My approach, once again, will be historical and theoretical. Such discussions immerse us in feminist debates about what is more important for women's liberation, how the vari-ous issues are connected, what sort of explanations are most useful for analyzing the rela-tions between men and women, and which strategies are most likely to transform those relations. I am going to start with a dramatic feminist protest in the late 1960s and use the issues it raised to set the terms of the discussion in this chapter. That protest was about the sexual objectification of women, and this has been an enduring theme of feminist activism and scholarship ever since.

On 7 September 1968, the media reported that a group of women had disrupted the Miss America Beauty Pageant in Atlantic City. For many people, this protest, together with reports that some women had publicly burned their bras, not only marked the beginning of the women's movement but also became its lasting symbol. Bra-burning feminists: for many, the words were forever linked despite the fact that no bra had been burned (Brownmiller 1999, 35–41). The image amused, threatened, and outraged. Its meaning was pliable: on the one hand it was used to ridicule—*this* was what women were struggling for? How trivial! How absurd! But, if bra burning and beauty pageant protests were that trivial, why was so much sustained attention given to them? What did it mean when women protested against time-honoured beauty pageants and made the brassiere an optional garment? Why all the ridicule and why all the fuss?

First, the question of ridicule. Among the many and interrelated social movements of the last half of the twentieth century, the women's movement was surely alone in eliciting an early and predominant response of ridicule from the media. Women's protest, whatever it was about, made people chortle. Women could not be taken seriously even when they were rebelling. During the hearings of the Royal Commission on the Status of Women, Peter Newman noted that "most editors seemed to think there was something uproariously funny about the whole idea of women contemplating their navels" (1969, 23). Women's rebellion was ridiculous, and this ridicule helped legitimate continued subordination: this was an early insight that would be taken up more elaborately in later feminist cultural and poststructural analysis.

Second, if women's protests were so ridiculous, why so much attention? For the media, the protests provided great copy and good footage. But the level of interest betrays, I would argue, considerable anxiety. What did it mean to have women refusing the role of beauty queen? What did it mean when women insisted that they did not want to be represented as sexual objects? Taken together with feminist critiques of compulsory motherhood and demands for free abortion and access to contraception, feminists appeared to be pulling the rug out from under the whole social order. Protesting a beauty pageant was a protest against a system that judged men by their intellectual and physical achievements and women by their appearance. It was a protest against a single standard of beauty that measured women against each other and found almost all of them wanting.[2]

More than 30 years later, Dawn Currie's teen-aged respondents revealed that these assessments continue. "You can get a lot of abuse from guys," reported 16-year-old Kelsey. "[T]hey can make fun of you—comment on your chest size or whatever, right, and they'll mean it as a joke, but it hurts. Like it can hurt, you know. A lot of things that are tough about being a girl are about looks" (1999, 234). "The toughest thing about being a girl," confirmed Kelly, also 16, "is that you always have to be concerned about what you look like. [Most] of my friends get into a frame of mind that somebody's always watching. You always have to look good for that person....I gotta look good. I gotta look good" (1999, 231) (see Box 6-1).

When we look back at the protests against beauty pageants, it is possible to tease out many of the substantive and theoretical issues that became important within feminist activism and scholarship. What were the forms, the extent, and the impact of sexual objectification on women's lives? What were the links between representing women as sexual

BOX 6-1   Lisa Simpson vs. Rory Gilmore: Is This the End of Smart Girl Phobia?

Each and every Wednesday night, I eagerly settle in for my favourite television show, *The Gilmore Girls* (no disrespect to Buffy for this displacement, but let's face it, this season Buffy really blows). For a while, I could not put my finger on why I liked *The Gilmore Girls* so much. Was it the quick-witted trash talk? The unlimited array of tall boots? The quirky small town setting that made me weepy for *Northern Exposure* reruns? Well sure. It was all of these delightful things. But it was something else too, something transgressive and feminist and fresh. It was the fact that 17-year-old Rory was a smart girl. But hip smart. Likeable smart. Happenin' smart. And that's not the kind of representation you see everyday. At least not for girls.

Rory's happy-go-lucky charm, low-key good looks, and perpetual dating schedule, combined with her dream of attending Harvard and obsessive interest in books, affirm a possibility that has heretofore been unfathomable. With the exception of a very few isolated examples, for the first time in history, smart girls are cool. Imagine that.

When I was in high school, just the opposite was true. By the late 1980s, my friends and I had all been force-fed a steady diet of smart girl phobia: the popular girls in *Heathers* were bitches without brains; *The Breakfast Club* offered up a hyper-feminine ditz in Molly Ringwald and self destructive sad girl Ally Sheedy, and in *Some Kind of Wonderful*, Leah Thompson (remember her?) was all empty-headed faux refinement. To be a smart girl was to write yourself a one-way ticket to Loserville—population you. So I spent much of the time trying to pretend I wasn't smart. Sure, I secretly studied in my room by night. But by day, I was queen of the smoking area—doing my best to blend in with stoners, drunkards and Jim Morrison worshippers.

Smart girl phobia has continued to grow thanks to countless excessive representations. Velma from *Scooby-Doo* wore geeky glasses and a pleated skirt. She had buckteeth and a potato sack body. And next to ditzy Daphne...well, let's just say intelligence didn't seem too glamorous. Janet Wood from *Three's Company* was the sensible one. The level headed loyal one, like a good Smurf—not exactly an enviable social position. Diane from *Cheers* was the cerebral one—all stiff and starchy, a real cold fish. And Lilith Crane? Forget about it. She made intelligence look about as attractive as an eye infection. Sabrina from *Charlie's Angels* was the smarty-pants bossy one. Bailey from *WKRP in Cincinnati* was the brainy yet timid one. And then, of course, there's Lisa Simpson....

I will confess right now that I think Lisa is the coolest character on *The Simpsons*. She is ironic, miserable, overly sensitive to the plight of the world and smart as a whip. But for all of Lisa's highbrow beauty, she remains a pitiable character. She can't seem to make any real friends. She always ends up alone, crying and beaten down by the dim-witted boobs that surround her. Alas, her smartness is represented as a curse that she would gladly trade for a date with Jimbo Jones or for one piggyback ride from Homer. Homer and Bart's supreme stupidity stand in juxtaposition to Lisa's intelligence. They always win. She always loses. The message is loud and clear: being a smart girl just doesn't pay.

So it's no wonder that *The Gilmore Girls* caught my attention. Rory's intelligence—unlike Lisa's—is enviable. And other such representations have also crept in under our noses to combat smart girl phobia. Willow Rosenberg from *Buffy the Vampire Slayer* was a gawky hacker who could recite Einstein's theory of relatively just as easily as she could stake a vamp. But instead of playing the role of the tragic smart girl, Willow took the geek comments in stride and became a super-sized witch with super-sized brains. And the Powerpuff Girls could constitute their own think tank and still save the world after kindergarten and before bedtime.

All is not lost. Smart girl phobia is transitioning into smart girl chic. There is a new kind of girl out there. Maybe she's a computer whiz. Maybe she's informed and alert and aware of the world around her. Maybe she gets how the media operates. Maybe she stands tall and talks back to boys who itemize her body parts. Maybe she knows that she can be bright and cool at the same time. And maybe she's out there, waiting for better, smarter representations of girlhood to hit the airwaves. Hey, aren't we all?

Source: Shauna Pomerantz, "Lisa Simpson vs. Rory Gilmore." *good girl magazine* 5:15. Pomerantz lives in Vancouver and is completing a PhD in Education.

objects and how women thought about themselves, how they treated others, and how they chose courses of study and work? More succinctly, what were the links between how women were portrayed and who women really were?

The insight that women are expected to present themselves, and be treated, as sexual objects contributed to an exploration of the ways in which women are represented in all aspects of social life. Feminists subjected advertisements, television programming, school textbooks, and pornography to searing critique and often mass protest. They went on to unmask how women were represented in family law, rape law, laws about contraception and abortion, and in the assumptions underwriting the development of reproductive technologies.

The issue of beauty and sexual objectification contributed to exploring issues around women and health. Feminists argued that the cultural standards of beauty demanded that women treat their bodies as enemies to be pummelled and starved into submission. Plastic surgery on parts of the body deemed too big or too small, constant dieting, and other "beauty" techniques that contribute to ill-health have been central feminist concerns.[3]

The question of sexual objectification became elaborated into more general reappraisals of sexuality. Defining women as sexual beings in their own right, criticizing the double standard of sexual behaviour, launching a full-scale critique of "compulsory heterosexuality," debating the meanings and consequences of pornography: all this captured the attention of feminists in many social and theoretical locations. Was sexuality a terrain of danger, pleasure, or both for women? What would it take for women to have the power to define and pursue their own desires?

The feminist analysis that presented women's oppression as intricately wrapped up with their sexual objectification was subsequently challenged, from many quarters, for its apparent claims to universality. Not all women were treated as actual or potential sexual objects, and certainly not in the same ways. Racialized women, women with disability, older women, and lesbians, among others, wrote thoughtful and often stinging rebukes of the assumptions of what they came to call white, middle-class, ageist, and able-ist feminist assumptions.

Let us look back in more detail at the issue of sexual objectification and some of the related questions that this concept helped to mobilize and then at some of the critiques that have been offered of this analysis.

WOMEN AS SEXUAL OBJECTS

Until the late 1960s, beauty contests were a regular feature on university campuses. My 1962 Carleton University Yearbook includes full-page pictures of Frosh Queen, Arts Queen, and Winter Weekend Queen. They received their titles by garnering the highest number of votes in a student plebiscite, after nomination by the specific dance committee. Pictures of all nominees flooded the campus in the days prior to the vote, and the winner was duly crowned at the dance. Only heterosexual couples attended the dance. "Girls" waited for an invitation—no invitation, no dance. Single men and women did not attend, nor did lesbians and gays. Indeed, there were no out lesbians or gays on campus. The dances were exquisitely heterosexual events; for women, attendance was a sign of their acceptability by at least one member of the opposite sex. Election as queen of the dance represented the epitome of more general appreciation.

Working women were also encouraged to participate in beauty contests. During the 1950s and 1960s, the Recreation Association (RA), catering exclusively to federal government employees, sponsored interdepartmental contests for Miss Civil Service. As the contest advertisement for 1952 pointed out, "Your Department has as much chance as the next one. All you need is a good-looking girl. From what we can see...there are a lot of good-looking girls in the Civil Service. And your Department has its quota" (quoted in Gentile 1995). Patrizia Gentile has argued that these beauty contests served at once to legitimate women's growing presence in the civil service and to reinforce almost perfect occupational segregation, hierarchically arranged.[4] The Civil Service Commission's method for keeping women down (and often out) was simple: women were hired as "'stenographers' and 'typewriters' while men became 'general clerks,' who, incidentally, climb the administrative ladder while 'typewriters' could not" (Archibald 1973, 15). There was a place for typewriters to compete, however, and that was at the "Night of the Stars." How well did they represent the "typical government girl"? Winners were "preferably single with no children, heterosexual, well-groomed, tall, thin and 'beautiful' with shiny hair." Their height, weight, and measurements were published in *The RA News* (Gentile 1995, 29–30).

Looking back, it is easy to see why feminists attacked beauty contests.[5] That beauty contests were such an intrinsic aspect of university and working life indicated how pervasive was the system of judging women by their facial features and the shape of their bodies, rather than by academic accomplishments or even athletic prowess. Renowned social activist Joan Newman Kuyek recalled her reaction to winning the beauty queen title at the University of Manitoba in 1962: "I saw the heartbreak in the faces of all the other contestants, and I realized what a horrible thing competition truly is. I was supposed to be happy at the expense of these other young women and I wondered, 'What kind of system is this?'" (Lowe 1995, 14).

Women were to look at; men were to look. But of course women looked too—at each other and at themselves. Every day could be a re-enactment of the beauty contest, as women judged themselves harshly and surveyed other women as potential competitors. A beautiful woman with much male attention was assumed to have it all. Her penalty was often the hostility of other women. Women who saw their own opinions as mattering little, and their own physique as inadequate, assumed that they did not have the power to hurt a more beautiful and popular woman.

In the late 1960s, the beauty pageant appeared to feminist protestors as a straightforward case of men using women as sexual objects. The language varied, but feminists depicted the women who participated as falsely conscious or brainwashed. Deprived of their own desire, they strutted on stage to satisfy the voyeuristic pleasures of men. Underneath the eager-to-please exterior, feminists argued, lay the genuine woman, awaiting emancipation so that she might pursue her own projects and pleasures.

This interpretation may be described as part of the development of radical feminism. Men's power over women was blatant and easy to identify; feminists had to confront such power directly; men had to be prevented from continuing to wield this power over women. Once this happened, women would be free to exercise their own will and develop their own capacities and talents. Women would stop obeying men and begin to please themselves. Clearly this would involve an end to beauty pageants. But such contests were only a symbol of the problem: women dressed to please men; used cosmetics to please men; had sex with men in order to please men; and shaped their bodies in myriad ways to please men.

The radical feminist analysis was far-reaching in its critique, and many of the issues were taken up, disputed, and elaborated upon from other feminist positions. In *Sexual Politics*, an early text of second wave feminism, Kate Millett cast the situation of women—the beautiful and the not-so-beautiful—into sharp relief:

> The continual surveillance in which she is held tends to perpetuate the infantilization of women even in situations such as those of higher education. The female is continually obliged to seek survival or advancement through the approval of males as those who hold power. She may do this either through appeasement or through the exchange of her sexuality for support and status. (1971, 54)

Millett succinctly captured the dilemma of women, thrown into competition with each other on the basis of their appearance. Treated as mindless, deprived of power, set against each other, women internalize the lack of esteem in which they are held and "despise both themselves and each other" (ibid., 55). Millett presents a more complicated picture than some radical feminist positions that suggested that lurking beneath women's outward capitulation to male power was their real self, a self capable of self-love, love for other women, and the capacity for realizing their own projects. In Millett's understanding, *misogyny*—the hatred of women—far from being a prerogative of men, is also lodged deep in women's own psyches.

Novelist Margaret Atwood has created female characters who may be seen in the light of Millett's conceptualization. Atwood's riveting portrayal of Cordelia and Elaine in *Cat's Eye* (1988) resonates with many female readers. Cordelia is everlastingly mean to her vulnerable friend Elaine, catching her off-guard, offering enough reward to sweep her back into her orbit whenever she demonstrates the will to escape:

> "There's dog poop on your shoe," Cordelia says. I look down. "It's only a rotten apple." "It's the same colour though, isn't it?" Cordelia says. (1988, 71)

With so much capacity to influence others, will Cordelia grow up to run a corporation, a university, or a family? No, by mid-life Elaine finds Cordelia living at the Dorothy Lyndwick Rest Home, "a discreet, private loony bin...the sort of place well-off people use for stowing away those members of their families who are not considered fit to run around in public" (ibid., 354). By then, Elaine has realized how she had internalized the contempt that Cordelia had projected: "There is the same shame, the sick feeling in my body, the same knowledge of my own wrongness, awkwardness, weakness; the same wish to be loved; the same loneliness; the same fear. But these are not my own emotions any more. They are Cordelia's; as they always were" (ibid., 419). Elaine and Cordelia were raised in the 1940s and 1950s, growing up to be women in a man's world. In their world of the relatively powerless, they jockeyed for position, humiliated others as a strategy for self-survival, and, at the limits, destroyed the other—emotionally and physically. All this was the stuff of ongoing daily interactions, and remains so. There is now extensive literature on the particular kinds of bullying in which girls engage (Pepler, Craig and Connelly 1999), and apparently girls lead the way in their use of the Internet to wreak havoc with the lives of other girls.[6]

These differences point to a complex conundrum that psychoanalytic feminists have addressed. What are the differences between growing up female and growing up male? How are the relations of domination and subordination lodged in the psyches of the next generation? This is not only the work of men subjecting women to their will, as the radical feminist position tends to suggest; this is also the work of girls and women, the Cordelias and the Elaines. In *The Bonds of Love*, Jessica Benjamin argues that this is *relational* work, that it takes two to tango. The powerful are equally dependent upon the powerless, although their inability to acknowledge this dependence leads to tyranny. Meanwhile, the powerless make a last-ditch attempt to save their egos by identification with the powerful (1988, 85–132). This is what conventional heterosexual romance and marriage has been about. Simone de Beauvoir reckoned that "when woman gives herself completely to her idol, she hopes that he will give her at once possession of herself and of the universe he represents" (1952, 717).

Cordelia's mother cannot affirm her daughter because she has not affirmed herself; she cannot take her daughter's projects seriously because her own life is about facilitating her husband's. Nine-year-old Elaine, from a more unconventional family, is getting the picture from her friends:

> Something is unfolding, being revealed to me. I see that there's a whole world of girls and their doings that has been unknown to me, and that I can be part of without making any effort at all. I don't have to keep up with anyone, run as fast, aim as well, make loud explosive noises, decode messages, die on cue. I don't have to think about whether I've done these things well, as well as a boy. All I have to do is sit on the floor and cut frying pans out of the Eaton's Catalogue with embroidery scissors, and say I've done it badly. Partly this is a relief. (Atwood 1988, 54)

Elaine is learning to be surveyed and found wanting; she is also learning that girls grow up to be women who are inordinately interested in domestic life. In her research on working-class high school students in Vancouver in 1977, sociologist Jane Gaskell confirmed the corollary: boys are not interested in things domestic. As one of her female respondents put it, "I just couldn't picture my husband doing it—cleaning, making beds, making supper. I guess it's picturing my brother and dad." Most of the boys in the study agreed with her: "If I marry my girlfriend, I'd help her out. I don't like doing it. If someone doesn't ask me, I won't do it" (1988, 154–55).[7]

In the 1950s, sociologist Talcott Parsons (1959) had noted that growing up female in America was a tricky business, though he stopped short of thinking that anything should be done about it. Girls had to present themselves as sexy in order to catch a man who would be willing to marry them. Once married, however, they were expected to shun the role of sexual object for a thoroughly domestic existence. Feminists pointed out that it was more complicated than this. Even beauty queens were to present themselves as sexual objects—to be gazed upon—not as sexual subjects with their own desires. Contestants were expected to be virgins; having already had a child, for example, was not just a disqualifier, it was a monumental blot on one's character.[8] So it was with all girls. Be sexy enough to keep boys interested, but never go "all the way." Girls who didn't get that message not only risked becoming pregnant (which was only the girl's fault), they could count on a reputation as "bad girl" and a lifetime sentence of singledom.

Feminists have linked the two symbols—woman as sexual object (always perilously close to whore) and woman as mother (hopefully as close to virgin as possible). Neither type is expected to feel or exhibit her own sexual desires. Although "the image of woman is associated with motherhood and fertility," Jessica Benjamin explains, "the mother is not articulated as a sexual subject, one who actively desires something for herself—quite the contrary. The mother is a desexualized figure" (1988, 88). Many students in my introductory class laugh nervously at the very notion that their fathers, or indeed any man, let alone woman, might have once (hopefully not *now*) seen their mothers as sexy. But sexy for women does not mean having sexual desire. As Benjamin continues, "the sexy woman—an image that intimidates women whether or not they strive to conform to it—is sexy, but as object, not as subject. She expresses not so much *her* desire as her pleasure in being desired." Benjamin confirmed through psychoanalytic analysis the discoveries of early second wave feminists that "neither the power of the mother nor that of the sexy woman can...be described as sexual subject" (ibid., 89).

Being a sexual subject is part and parcel of being a *subject*—that is, the author of one's own life script, one who directs energy into her own projects and not just into facilitating those of others. In her research with teenagers at a Toronto shopping mall in the 1980s, Elaine Batcher found that "whether it is an individual skill like breakdancing, or a group talent in football or basketball, boys are more likely to be found doing things, and girls found cheering them on" (1987, 154). The groups that Batcher observed "centre around boys who like power and girls who like boys" (ibid., 155). One of Gaskell's teenage male respondents expressed it this way: "there's a difference between raising kids and looking after them. The woman might spend more time with the kids, but the father has the authority" (1988, 161). Psychoanalytic feminism explores the links between sexual desire and desirability and these broader questions of autonomy and dependence. What is the relation between the sexual object and sexual subject? What are the processes through which cultural notions of proper femininity and masculinity are internalized and resisted in the course of psychosexual development?

For Benjamin, the enormous social, cultural, and psychic consequences of relations of domination and subordination between the sexes are rooted in the psychosocial construction of gender polarity: one is *either* masculine *or* feminine. This gender polarity goes far beyond individual expressions of masculinity and femininity because it pervades the structuring of both private and public worlds and their separation from each other. The public world is supposed to be governed by notions of *instrumental rationality*—that is, the emphasis is on the most technically efficient means of reaching goals. This helps explain why some female lawyers quit, or at least change jobs: "I left Toronto," one of Fiona Kay's respondents wrote, "because I did not feel it was possible to find a job as a lawyer where

I would not have to 'sell my soul' to the firm....My current job allows me to be a mother and a lawyer, but of course my salary is much lower than [if I] were working for a firm where billable hours was the most important factor" (1997, 210).

Whether in the realm of bureaucracy, public policy, or multinational corporations, the preoccupation with this narrow form of rationality marks the public world as a stereotypical expression of "masculinity."[9] All emotion, love, intimacy, caring, and nurturing are relegated to the private world of family and friendship, where they are marked as the special domain of women. Sociologists Reginald Bibby and Donald Posterski found these gendered differences reflected in their 1992 survey of Canadian teens. Girls placed greater importance on integrity and civility and a higher value on human relationships. *Globe and Mail* columnist Michael Valpy wrote that these findings "limn a society of dominant and subordinate constituencies—with feel-good, physically stronger, bellicose males on top....They suggest that Canadians should think again about all the contemporary rhetoric of gender equality" (1992, 2).[10]

In her research on World War II, Ruth Pierson found that people perceived (appreciatively) that life in the army made men more masculine, but feared that military life threatened women's femininity (1986, 140). Similarly, women who reach beyond the glass ceiling in corporations or government bureaucracies report that they take great care in not presenting themselves as too feminine while at the same time steering clear of any behaviours that might be perceived as masculine. Former Canadian Alliance MP Deborah Grey received some unsolicited advice in the pages of the *Globe and Mail* from Terry Ritcey, owner of a posh Toronto salon: "Her hair is too short [and] very solid, very mannish-looking. It gives her a hard unapproachable look." Ritcey goes on to say that Grey might take her cue from singer Anne Murray, "a perfect example of a woman with a strong masculine-looking face" (Raphael 2001, B3). This is not an easy business.

Just as women's hairstyles and clothes must give the message that their wearers should be taken seriously but that they carry no threat to male authority, women's behaviour must negotiate the thicket between deference and assertiveness. *Globe and Mail* business reporter Kimberly Noble asks: "Ever tried confronting a guy who says something suggestive about your face or your legs or your breasts? The remark will pass unnoticed at a dinner party or in a roomful of people or on the street; if you get angry, however, you can ruin an evening, shock a crowd into embarrassed silence and be labelled as a bitter, aggressive ballbreaker who probably can't get dates" (1991, A18). Rick Salutin, a columnist for the same paper, marvelled

> at the hostility and ridicule [politician Sheila Copps] provokes from other politicians and the media. *Sun* columnist Doug Fisher on "her relentless bloodymindedness"; *Maclean's* Alan Fotheringham on "her rpms turned up too high"; The *Globe's* Jeffrey Simpson saying she's "never seen a microphone into which she could resist shrieking." Why shrieking? Would he use that word about a male MP? Would he even comment on the tendency? What's bugging them?" (1993, C1)

It's a double bind: men must be protected from aggressive—strident, bitchy, shrill—women; but deferential women clearly don't merit success. Sheila Copps has a simple response: "People have said I'm shrill. I'm not shrill. I happen to have a female voice" (quoted in Nolin 2002, 228).

Decisions in the public world are supposed to be made without considerations of emotion, nurturance, or care. This tendency not only promotes the maintenance of male-only spaces—or, at the very least, male-only behaviours—in the lofty confines of major deci-sion making, but also legitimates creating and sustaining a world that fails to take account of the needs, desires, and dreams of most people. The consequences for the private world, as feminists have observed, are no less devastating. There, the relations of domination and subordination between the sexes obscure the knowledge that human beings are interde-pendent. As long as women provide for men without insisting upon acknowledgment, men can have their cake and eat it: they can have their needs met without having to acknowl-edge their dependence on those who meet them. For their part, girls who grow up without receiving recognition for themselves as people whose own desires and projects matter may identify with those who assume that they are—and should be—the centre of their world. Such girls and women consciously or unconsciously say, "I will strive for personhood by identifying with a man who assumes that he is a person, and I will seek visibility (to myself) by furthering his needs and wishes." Such asymmetry in relationships is both prod-uct and cause of relations of domination and subordination.

Listen to conversations about boys, men, and love among girls and women, and you can detect certain themes. There is often an assumption that boys and men are unreliable: they pull you into involvements, and then? Consider David Caravaggio in novelist Michael Ondaatje's *The English Patient*: "He is a man in middle age who has never become accus-tomed to families. All his life he has avoided permanent intimacy. Till this war he has been a better lover than husband. He has been a man who slips away, in the way lovers leave chaos, the way thieves leave reduced houses" (1992, 116). Not that Ondaatje's female char-acters accept men's behaviour without resistance. The English patient himself asks Katherine Clifton, his colleague's wife:

> "What do you hate most?" "A lie. And you?" "Ownership," he says. "When you leave me, for-get me." Her fist swings towards him and hits hard into the bone just below his eye. She dress-es and leaves. (ibid, 152)

What an interesting exchange. Clifton is responding to her lover's lack of commit-ment: "forget this ever happened," he says. "You don't own me." She hits him. But crim-inologists point out that, in fact, it is women, not men who are at risk when they decide to leave relationships. As Rosemary Gartner, Myrna Dawson, and Maria Crawford con-clude: "The predominance of men's rage over separation as a motive in intimate femicides has no obvious counterpart in killings of men." Like others they "see this motive as a reflection of the sexual proprietariness of males towards intimate female partners" (2002, 138). This anger, declares Andrée Côté, Elizabeth Sheehy, and Diana Majury, "is con-structed on outmoded, sexist and misogynist values." Men become angry "because they believe that they have a right to appropriate a woman's sexuality, labour, and love" (2000, 17). (See Box 6-2.)

Writing in 1970, Shulamith Firestone argued that the structure of culture was "saturat-ed with the gender polarity." The male half is termed "all of culture [but] there is a female 'emotional' half" which men must live "on the sly." As a result, "the question that remains for every male is...*how do I get someone to love me without her demanding an equal com-mitment in return*" (127, 137)?

Feminist psychoanalytic approaches provide answers to this question by focusing on the *gendered* nature of psychosexual development and subjectivity. When women are noth-ing more than the objects of men's desire—that is, they are not recognized as full human

BOX 6-2	Confronting Violence

During the early 1970s, feminists "discovered" and documented the troubling stories of the violence many women endured at the hands of those who "loved" them—their boyfriends, partners, and husbands. As the discussions in this text reveal, feminists connected these experiences with women's subordination to men within the family and other patriarchal institutions, and to the construction of hegemonic masculinity. In these accounts, nothing short of dramatic—some said revolutionary—changes in the society could eradicate this violence, thereby empowering women, and transforming the hierarchical relationships between men and women into egalitarian relationships. For many feminists the mutually supportive relationships of capitalism and patriarchy had to go. In the meantime, they developed shelters and other support services for women in immediate need of protection, all the while lobbying governments for more resources, and educating police, judicial officials, and welfare officers who "refused to grant women welfare checks if they were leaving men, even abusive men" (Lakeman 2000, 26).

However difficult it was to gain public support for services—and it was painfully difficult and slow—paled beside the Herculean task of real societal transformation. Instead some violent men are singled out for punishment (often not in time to save lives) and women—in flight from their abusers—become new claimants on social services. The systemic nature of violence, rooted in women's subordination to men, lack of options, economic dependence, and familial responsibilities espe-

cially for children, was, at best, overtaken by a discourse of (male) criminality and (female) victimization (Lakeman 2000; Walker 1990; Snider 1994).

On 6 December 1989 the murder of 14 women at the Ecole Polytechnique in Montreal by a man declaring his hatred of feminists intensified an ongoing debate between those who saw such violence as behavioural manifestations of sick (psychotic) men, and those who saw this event as illustrative of systemic misogyny. As criminologist Anthony Doob wrote in response to the critics of the Statistics Canada Violence Against Women Survey (VAWS) four years later, not only do "the findings of high levels of violence directed at women [disturb] anyone concerned about violence, but [they] also appear to disturb those who would prefer to believe that violence against women is not a problem" (2002, 61; see also Johnson 2002). Yet the evidence is clear. In Ontario between 1974 and 1994, for example, men killed 98 percent of the women killed while women killed only 17 percent of adult males killed (Gartner, Dawson and Crawford 2002, 137).

The primary response to violence against women today comes from a state sponsored law and order agenda that moves to lock up more people for longer. Men who are violent towards women are depicted as "monsters," declared outside the human orbit. This portrayal sidesteps the fact that "monsters," like everyone else, are raised within social relationships, and are creations of human society. At the same time "everyone else" can use the so-called monsters as objects upon which to project their own anger (fear, aggression), thereby "saving" themselves from having to acknowledge their own jagged edges and subterranean fantasies.

The complicated journey to "becoming" a person involves discovering that there are others in the world besides oneself. In the best scenario children experience through their interactions with others that they can be in a relationship without dominating others or being subordinate to them. Young children seek to do their own thing while not alienating the affections of those upon whom they depend. Where the penalty is too high, they may cave into authority; where (m)others behave as doormats they can rule the roost. According to feminist psychoanalyst Jessica Benjamin, in a patriarchal society girls are more likely to resolve this tension ("the paradox of recognition") (1988, 31) by resorting to subordination, by finding a "self" through identifying with a more powerful other, while boys go for domination because acknowledging their dependence and vulnerability is so painful. (Boys don't need help; they certainly don't cry.)

At the extreme when adult men kill intimate partners who desert them, they are often motivated by the rage that comes when they can no longer control what they experience as "theirs" (Gartner et al. 2002, 138). (The ruse is up: all this time I needed you even though I treated you as though you were just an extension of myself and without value in your own right.) In contrast, when a woman murders her partner, she reports a long history of abuse by her husband. In long-time activist Lee Lakeman's words, she waits for an opportunity when he has "fallen into a drunken stupor or...failed to hide a weapon [and she acts] to prevent the next predictable beating or rape" (Lakeman 2000, 26).

Despite this history such women typically earned long prison terms, and in response some feminist activists developed a defence tactic known as the Battered Wife Syndrome (BWS). In accepting this defence, the Supreme Court of Canada argued that insisting that a physical assault must be in process would be "tantamount to sentencing her 'to murder by installment.'" Yet, by invoking a notion of "'psychological paralysis' that prevents her, despite the constant beatings, from terminating the relationship" (Comack 2002, 279), "the BWS offers an account that serves to individualize, medicalize, and depoliticize an abused woman's experiences" (281). In Elizabeth Comack's words, "abused women are transformed into victims—not so much of their abusers but of their own dysfunctional personalities"(281).

Given that men and women kill for different reasons, and women much less frequently, it is understandable why some feminist statements veer towards gendered essentialism. Benjamin's analysis offers to explain why men are more violent than women without attributing it either to their sex (in which case what can be done?) or some explanation that lies outside the social—monsters, aliens, or some group cast outside the boundaries of "human-ness" (1988, 1994).

Understanding the impetus to declare others "not fully human" was taken up by sociologist Zygmunt Bauman in his attempt to "understand human atrocities such as the holocaust." For Bauman this involves the creation of strangers and the "implied threat" they appear to pose to the way things are (and should be). Discriminating against large numbers of people on the basis of some characteristic (race, ethnicity, religion) "requires a discourse which positions a 'them' as representative of everything to which 'we' stand opposed" (cited in Hird 2002, 4). Myra Hird proposes applying this understanding of "stranger creation" to gender in order to explain the "persistence of heterosexual interpersonal violence" (ibid., 5). Boys and men must avoid at all costs appearing to be like girls and women—sissies, wimps, those who would rather run than fight. "What do women want?" some men ask, as though women were from a different (and single) species. And women, for their part, return the favour, shrugging their shoulders, rolling their eyes in conversations about men.

Bauman's explication of how we put the concept "strangers" to use in ordering the social world also sheds light on the brutal murder in Victoria of 14-year-old Reena Virk by her (mainly female) school mates. As Yasmin Jiwani discovered, the media depicted Reena Virk as a girl who didn't "fit in," drawing attention in particular to her weight and height. Just "what she needed to 'fit into' was never explored, nor were the assumptions underlying normative standards of beauty and behaviour for teenage girls" (2002, 449). As a "misfit," she was an acknowledged stranger. In contrast, the media and the justice system not only erased her "racialized identity" but also paid little attention "to the possibility that her death was racially motivated" (ibid., 447) despite considerable evidence. As a racialized girl she was an *unacknowledged* stranger—not just to her attackers but to the media and the justice system—because this could not be taken on board without admitting that racism is not confined to the "acts of organized hate groups" (ibid., 449).

Just as the insistence that men who commit violent acts are psychotic, rather than misogynist (or that their psychosis is mediated through misogyny), so were Virk's murderers portrayed as maladjusted kids (or monsters) rather than those whose behaviours enacted a profoundly racist (and sexist) script. These forms of violence involve the projection of self-hatred and contempt onto the "other"—and that "other" is an ongoing creation of dominant and (still) legitimate public discourse and institutional practices. Holding onto notions of gendered and racialized essentialism will get us nowhere because such notions are deeply implicated in the problem we confront; nor will a refusal to attend to misogyny, racism, or other forms of stranger creation that puts others beyond the reach of our empathy, that is our understanding that others are both like and unlike ourselves.

---

beings in their own right—the way is cleared for their invisibility to others in their life, whether husbands, lovers, boyfriends, or children. If mothers are those who do for you, without thanks, acknowledgment, or any claim on reciprocity, if children learn how to be male or female from those who mother them, if boys grow up believing in their own autonomy and that any sign of dependence is a sign of weakness, then men will seek control at all costs because dependency causes such anxiety and threats to their (imagined) autonomy, and therefore their precarious sense of self.

Control may be wrought by means psychological, emotional, and physical. The 1994 Statistics Canada's survey, *Violence Against Women*, reported that "three in ten women currently or previously married in Canada have experienced at least one incident of physical or sexual violence at the hands of a marital partner" (Rodgers 1994, 1). Over 20 percent of those abused by a marital partner reported that they were assaulted during pregnancy, and 40 percent of these women stated that the abuse began during their pregnancy (ibid., 12).

Since the early 1970s, with the growing realization of the extent of men's violence towards women, feminists have been in the business of developing explanations for these behaviours. All these explanations deal with power, men's power over women. Sometimes the exercise of this power is taken for granted, as in the phrase "men assault women because they can." This has undoubtedly been so. Men are often stronger; they have held control in households and in every area of society; until recently their behaviour was likely to go unnoticed except by the women subjected to their violence, and it was usually unpunished; male power and violence are represented as heroic and exciting in the media. But to say that men *can* use violence does not explain why so many men *do* use violence or, for that matter, why so many more do not and, indeed, may not even be able to imagine themselves doing so. We might want to use an analogy here. All parents are stronger than their children. Many parents do use violence against their children, often or occasionally. But their ability to use violence is not sufficient explanation, for it begs the question, what about all the rest who could but do not?

There has been speculation that violence towards women increases with women's growing assertiveness. From this perspective, the feminist movement has been tagged as contributing to the increase in such violence (Phillips 1995). But, from a feminist psychoanalytic perspective, it is important to understand that the person seeking absolute control cannot bear to acknowledge that the other person is not just an extension of himself. The other person's separateness provides constant reminder of his dependence upon her. He may be the dominant partner, but he needs her, the less powerful, less valued person in the relationship (and in the culture more generally). Dominance is a strategy to avoid acknowledging vulnerability, and violence is one common technique in that never-ending struggle. Never-ending because, since internal vulnerability is the problem, control of the other can never be the solution. When a man murdered 14 women at the Ecole Polytechnique on 6 December 1989, he then turned the gun on himself, as do many men after killing their partners. Eradicating the other is intricately related to eradicating oneself, whether physically, psychologically, or emotionally.

The evidence from the violence against women survey indicates that women may be at risk both when they resist and when they comply. Assault occurs when women leave partners—although it usually does not begin then (Rodgers 1994, 12)—and when they stay quiet and remain with abusive partners. Twenty-two percent of the respondents had never before told anyone that they had been assaulted—not police, doctor, clergy, friends, or family. Ten percent of these women had at some point feared for their life (ibid., 20). Yet the *Globe and Mail* could still provide space in its feature guest column on 10 November 1995 to air the views of a man who believed that the way to eradicate violence against women was for women to "stage a strategic retreat to the ostensible subservience of times past." David Phillips concluded that "as long as there is a rough parity between the sexes, violence and victimhood will be woman's lot" (A22).

I have been discussing the relations of domination and subordination as if they coincided with the relations between men and women. A good deal of feminist writing, including psychoanalytic writing, proceeds in this way. Language promotes unreflexive use of these categories. Common sense observations seem to support them, as does much research into male and female behaviour. What is important to remember, however, is that *in social terms* human beings become gendered *after* they are born. Not only are the classifications of biological sex "fundamentally social productions" (Findlay 1995, 46), but sociological gender has for a long time been recognized as a postnatal development by anthropologists, historians, and certainly by generations of feminists.

There are two considerations for feminists seeking to explain the development of gendered subjectivity. One explores how human beings become social beings who vie for domination or must tolerate subordination. The second focuses on the ways masculinity and femininity are themselves constructed and represented as discrete categories. The behaviour of women in boardrooms may be similar to the behaviour of men. But it may well be perceived differently because of the (perceived) sex of the biological body who is behaving. Similarly, seeking control in relationships may well be seen as masculine, but this doesn't mean that only (biological) men want to control. Research on relationships between men, and between women, whether of love or friendship, reveals that the power dynamics do not always tend towards reciprocity and symmetry. Some lesbians have written bitterly about their experiences of being turned away from shelters for battered women because their assailants were women (Elliot 1991).[11] We seem stuck with a vocabulary and a discourse that equates masculinity with activity and dominance, and femininity with passivity and subordination.

This is part of the conundrum that feminist poststructuralists have taken on energetically and insightfully. Their challenges to the discussions of sexual objectification, representation, and gender attend to the discourses through which assumptions about masculinity and femininity are created and transformed. Feminists working with poststructuralism and deconstruction have argued that the focus of attention should not be the gendered individual per se, but rather the ways in which specific historical discourses produce gender and gendered representations, both explicitly and implicitly. The reference here is not to a gendered individual, but rather to the ways in which representations of gender are part of a continuing production of language. The concept of *subjectivity* speaks to the ways in which individuals are constituted—in myriad continually shifting ways—through discourse. *Gendered subjectivity* refers to the ways in which notions of masculinity and femininity are integral aspects of the production of subjectivity in any discourse.

Such interpretations do not distinguish between subjectivity and representation but rather see them, if you like, as *both* sides of the same coin. Gendered subjectivity is always a representation, never an actual reproduction or reflection. This is because language can never reproduce an already existing reality, but is always engaged with producing interpretations. Those interpretations then become the object for (poststructural) analysis. Representation once referred mainly to visual images—what women see reflected back at them in paintings, films, or advertisements. The concept is now used to refer to visual, literary, documentary, and oral depictions. Nor is the goal to determine what the author or painter or advertising copywriter intend to say. In poststructural analysis the focus is rather on the text or image itself and the interpretations (or readings) of the observer, reader, or person in the audience.

Close attention is paid to the meanings and hidden meanings in the text or image. Representations produce meaning only by suppressing other meanings. In her article on the poetry and fiction of Michael Ondaatje, Lorraine York asks, "Why don't we have a gender criticism of Ondaatje in the nineties?" (1994, 71). She hypothesizes that "feminist critics shied away from Ondaatje because they assumed that there wasn't much to write about" or that they would end up simply cataloguing various "victim positions" of women that appear in his work. While she insists that such indictments of male authors have a place— she approvingly cites Kate Millett's *Sexual Politics* (1971) for its "energizing, astringent effect on women readers and critics who...[henceforth felt] that they had a right to a dissenting voice"—York has a different aim. She seeks to reveal that Ondaatje shows increasing awareness of issues of gender, "especially as they relate to ownership: the poet's ownership of the material, the patriarch's ownership of the female, and the imperialist's ownership of the colonized" (1994, 75). In other words, she demonstrates that gender and gender assumptions infuse Ondaatje's politically complex texts, and not just in those places where he is speaking specifically about victimized women (1994, 76).

Feminists using poststructuralism have shown how to read texts—from foreign policy documents to corporate law to university lectures—as gendered discourses. The old expression "appearances may be deceiving" receives new meaning in the hands of poststructuralists. The previous theoretical positions we have considered present gendered and sexual identities as relatively fixed realities: fluid up to a point, socially constructed in time and place, but nonetheless integral to a person's self, personality, or character. Such theoretical formulations tend to confirm everyday understandings. We assume a correspondence between what we see and hear—that is, how people represent themselves—and who people really are in gendered and sexual terms. The poststructuralist position shifts the focus to the production of gender as a continuing outcome of discourse: hence the special interest in the text.

CRITIQUES OF SEXUAL OBJECTIFICATION

Many women have disputed the link that feminists made between women's oppression and their representation as sexual objects for men's desire. Dominant standards of beauty—as represented in criteria for beauty contests, modelling, advertisements, or film—are narrow, with only a small fraction of women eligible. Nor have standards of beauty become more flexible since early feminist protests. Naomi Wolf reports that, in 1970, the average model weighed 8 percent less than the average American woman; 20 years later, she weighed 23 percent less (Wolf 1990, 184). If real women had measurements proportionate to the ubiquitous Barbie Doll—40–18–32—they would not have enough body fat to menstruate regularly. Older women continue to be represented as desexualized. Racialized women point out that they never met the standards of beauty of the dominant culture. Women with disability have raised the only apparently contradictory situation that they are more likely than able-bodied women to be the objects of sexual assault (Rodgers 1994, 6) yet are unlikely to be perceived as meeting the standards for sexual objects. There are many rich, nuanced, and historically and culturally specific analyses of traditional feminist views of sexual objectification, and we will look at some examples that deal with intersections between sexism and racism, able-ism, ageism, and sexual identities and desires.

Anti-racist Critiques

In 1979, Toronto writer Makeda Silvera took part in a protest with other black women against the Miss Black Ontario Pageant (1985, 69). The protest was ridiculed in the black community newspapers and, as she put it, "we were not given space in our newspapers to articulate our position on the issue." Such pageants were a response to the exclusion of black women from existing competitions. The 1960s slogan "black is beautiful" proved a powerful message of resistance to dominant cultural representations in which whiteness was a necessary, though not sufficient, condition of beauty. But in a patriarchal society, the slogan was parlayed into different meanings for men and women. Men would still gaze; women would be the object of the gaze. Adopting white sexist practices such as beauty competitions sidestepped the different ways in which racism shaped the lives of men and women, compounded the oppression of black women, and perpetuated heterosexism.

A black beauty contest did little to interrupt black–white hierarchies that made white women appear more desirable than black women to men generally. It also extended rather than challenged the treatment of black women as sexual objects that was rooted in its most brutal form in the political economy of slavery in North America. Such contests also had a different impact upon black men than upon white men. In the slavery and post-slavery days in the United States, black men were constructed as hypersexualized and were subjected to savage retribution for the mere charge that they had gazed upon a white woman. White men, on the other hand, raped white and, particularly, black women with legal and social impunity. The messages suggested, then, by a black beauty contest for the (gazing) black man appear complex and contradictory. Did such a contest suggest that black men might gaze on black women—but only black women—with impunity? Did the image of the gazing black man resonate with social constructions of hypersexualization, thus leaving white men—with their history of licensed assault—constructed as normally sexed.

My point is that beauty contests, like other cultural events, carry with them a range of meanings about age, sex, gender, race, and nation. In July 1994, for example, a group of young Filipino Canadian men and women protested in Winnipeg against the Maria Clara beauty contest held by the Knights of Rizal, a Filipino cultural group. The protesters argued that Maria Clara, a fictional character in the work of Jose Rizal, was submissive, and that the contest encouraged young women to model themselves after her. They argued that "Filipina women have always been in the forefront of the struggle for national liberation and they should be celebrated without the kind of stereotyping that is so offensive to young women in Canada today" (Nett 1994, A7).

Black feminists have pointed out that black women had been portrayed as sexual objects, though not as beautiful sexual objects. At the same time, they were denied the other model of appropriate femininity open to white women, that of the good mother. The good mother was the mother who stayed home with her children, looked after by a good husband and father. Long before most white women sought waged work, black women worked, mainly as domestics in the homes of others, to support their families. Maxine Tyne's evocative poetry and stories (1987, 11–12, 68–71; 1990, 69–70, 85–89) capture the dignity of those who worked "in service," the complexity of the social relationships, and the resistance to discrimination, especially when it took the form of hypocrisy and rudeness.

With black men in Canada generally relegated to jobs as porters and janitors (with a few in the entertainment industry) (Williams 1997), the family wage never reflected either reality or ideal for most black families (Brand 1984; 1991; Sadlier 1994). The experiences of black women—raising and supporting families, active in their communities, and struggling against discrimination—not only remained outside dominant representations, but also were not captured by feminist analysis. At the same time, white publishers (including feminist publishers) rejected writing by black women on the grounds that they were unable "to comprehend how the work resonates or illuminates the condition of women of colour" (Silvera 1985, 71).

Aboriginal women offer another critique of the feminist equation of women as sexual object with women's oppression. Beth Brant, an Indian lesbian writer, wants to dispel the prevailing idea "that Indian women are not sexual....It really is a stereotype that we are not, that we just give birth to kids without a process, or that we're only interested in planting corn or something. This really angers me and I think that Indian lesbians are the ones who are going to be talking about sex" (1985, 59). Brant seeks to distinguish the stereotypes of the Indian woman "and all these things that we have been called as squaw" from "a truth that we are poor, that we often have to exist in substandard ways." The writings of Aboriginal women not only challenge dominant representations but also present a range of experiences, images, dreams, and desires that confirm the dilemmas inherent in any attempts to represent woman or Indian woman or Indian lesbian, as though one image would do for all who might be so categorized.

Beth Brant expresses the constraints and possibilities not only of images, but of the language in which she writes. The "language of our enemy," a language with

> new words that do not exist in our own language.
> RAPE, MURDER, TORTURE, SPEECHLESSNESS, INCEST.
> POVERTY, ADDICTION.
> These obscene words that do not appear in our language.

She asks, "If love could be made visible, would it be in the enemy's language?" And answers:

> It is the only weapon I hold: this pen, this tool, this knife, this language. The writer has to know how to tell. It is the weapon I know how to use. (1991, 16–17)

Dis/ability and Objectification

In a train station in London, England I saw a sign: "Disabled Toilet," and underneath an arrow giving direction. The grammatical mistake highlights the problem with everyday language. Until recently, people used the phrase "disabled person," thereby indicating by the positioning of the adjective that a person was being described. Activists for those with disabilities struggled to change the language. I may have a disability but I am not a disabled person. The bigger problem with disabled person is the implication that others are not disabled—hence normal. We have seen in the discussions about racism and sexuality that assumptions of normality are implicated with processes of power and entitlement.

In turning to the writing on "women with disability," I am struck by the impossibility, the distortion, even the deception involved in any attempt to proceed as though one concept would do for all who might be so categorized. Not long ago, while facilitating a panel on women and diversity, I asked a panelist if she had seen a particular television program. "It's been a long time since I've seen any television program," she retorted sharply but with humour in her voice. Kristin is blind; for some public purposes, she calls herself a lesbian with a disability. She tires of raising the question of accessibility at all gatherings, feminist and otherwise, but feels compelled to do so when no one else does. As a result, she represents herself often, and may be perceived, as a "one-issue candidate." In any case, other people will categorize her as "woman with disability," along with women who—for reasons ranging from conditions attendant at birth through impairment suffered in accidents or from abuse to effects of chronic and progressive illnesses—may not be able to walk, talk, or read. If anything unites all these women, it is not their disabilities as such but rather their treatment by a society that disadvantages them and their collective resistance to that treatment (Russell 1989). In her study of people with multiple sclerosis, Susan Russell (1989) delineated the route from "Disability to Handicap." As a person who could not walk she defined herself as having a disability. But stairs, heavy doors, and students who were impatient with someone lecturing from a wheel chair handicapped her: these handicaps are social productions.

Kristin's sharp retort to me, following my casual assumption about seeing, breaks with dominant representations of women with disability as "victim," as "needy," as "grateful," or even as "quiet and nice." My reaction—of embarrassment, some enjoyment that others were laughing at my expense, and admiration—resembled the "click" made famous in early issues of *Ms.* magazine to describe any moment when the penny dropped, when one had a consciousness-raising moment related to one's treatment as a woman. This time I was the one who had the click, certainly, and it resulted from this very public transformation in my perspective. My language had betrayed my assumption about what was natural and shared, and this assumption was shattered by Kristin's response.

Francine Odette has critiqued the feminist assumption that "identifies women's alienation from themselves and their bodies" with "the objectification of the female body" (1992, 42). Growing up with a physical disability may take one out of the running altogether as someone who elicits attention as an attractive person. The problem, Odette explains, is not sexual objectification but exclusion from the possibility of the appreciative gaze. Recently, I saw a young woman with long blond hair who was modelling a sweater in an advertising brochure. She was sitting in a wheelchair. The presence of this (rare) image clearly resulted from the pressure for inclusion of those with disabilities in the range of images presented by TV programming, advertising, school textbooks, everywhere. This is surely a victory. In this culture, most girls spend considerable time on their appearance: they care about how they are perceived, whether they fit in, whether they look cool. As Odette notes, "for young girls with disabilities, the invisibility of our lives becomes reinforced by the fact that popular advertising suggests the 'normal' body is that which is desirable" (ibid., 42).

Feminists with disabilities critique the socially constructed notions not only of "the body beautiful" but also, in Odette's words "the notion of the 'body perfect'" (ibid., 42–43). Such challenges reveal the ways in which the lives, experiences, and fears of women with disabilities are similar to the lives of all women[12] and also how an attention to "differentness" extends the previous feminist cultural critiques. For example, although Odette raises an issue from the particular perspective of women with disabilities, the issue bears on the lives of all those who require medical consultations. While "the way in which women's bodies are portrayed as commodities in the media may not be a reality for many women labelled 'disabled,'...our bodies become objectified for the purposes of domination...as part of the medical process" (ibid., 42). In hospitals, people's bodies are often used as a teaching tool as though they were detached from the thinking, feeling, meaning-creating human beings seeking control over what happens to them.

Age and Sexual Objectification

Second wave feminists who launched the critiques of sexual objectification and the unreachable standards that represented female beauty and sexiness were mostly in their twenties and thirties. They tended to share the presumptions of their peers expressed in the 1960s slogan "You can't trust anyone over thirty." Only members of a society seriously denying the process of aging could develop a slogan that propelled one into the arena of the bad guys for no better reason than the onset of one's thirty-first year on earth. But as second wave feminists inevitably crossed the line into their thirties, they began critiquing the partiality of their earlier formulations. In this process, growing old(er) was not only reclaimed as a universal human process, but the gendered consequences of aging became an important focus for feminist analysis and activism (Carpenter 1996).

In this process, one of the great taken-for-granted assumptions of cultural life was subjected to scrutiny and was rejected: namely, that women could be beautiful and sexy only when young, while men could gain in sexual power and attractiveness their whole life through. Canadians had a very public example of this truism: in 1971 Prime Minister Pierre Trudeau, aged 51, married Margaret Sinclair, a woman 29 years his junior. Everyone—including Sinclair's father, a one-time cabinet minister in Lester Pearson's government—expressed great pleasure upon this occasion. But what if a woman in public life—or any woman, for that matter—had married a man almost young enough to be her grandson? Such an act would evoke more than social ridicule; it would be almost against nature: a man marrying a woman *old enough to be his mother*? Indeed, as Judy LaMarsh reported in her autobiography, just travelling with a younger man on cabinet business— "although I was always careful never to travel with just one young man"—became the subject of media scrutiny and was reflected in articles teeming with rumour and innuendo (1968, 304). That she was targeted for travelling with younger men during the same period in which Trudeau contracted his marriage illustrates the gendered story of love, sex, and age in the 1960s and beyond. Why did the eye rolling and tongue clicking only happen when women were associated with men younger than themselves?

Feminists point to two related explanations. First, the mere suggestion of sexual encounters between older women and younger men may create a generalized anxiety because such relationships threaten the sexual hierarchy. The advantages of age may confound the advantages of sex. In relationships men were supposed to take the initiative, make the important decisions, certainly be the more experienced sexual partner. But when the woman was older, wouldn't *she* know more? Have more experience? Perhaps be less willing to be the subordinate partner? When a man is widowed or divorced, he has traditionally not only been free to remarry, but free to choose from among women who are younger, including the young and never married. But women, enjoined to marry only men older than themselves, have had fewer choices. No longer sexual objects, they are not acceptable as sexual subjects either. Wouldn't she dominate her partner? Would this not be against the laws of god and nature? The perspectives of older women reveal the dense nature of patriarchal relations, practices, and attitudes in all arenas of social life.

Second, women are positioned as sexual objects not sexual subjects, and then only when they are young and beautiful. Older women may be portrayed, but only as mothers, harridans, or caregivers. Relationships between older women and younger men raise the question: can she be old(er) and sexy? Certainly the representations in popular culture provide one answer: a resounding no! The stereotypical explanation held that a younger man interested in an older woman was only after her money.

That older lesbian couples, in particular, escaped public scrutiny in so many communities in the days prior to women's liberation and beyond may be attributed in part to the assumptions discussed above. First, if women were sexual objects (for men's desire), not sexual subjects, then the question of sexuality remained publicly invisible when there was no man present. When Judy LaMarsh travelled with younger women, this was not news. Second, as women aged, any suggestion that they were sexual beings faded commensurately. Recently I asked my mother about Celine and Edith, friends she had in the 1950s:

> "What was the nature of their relationship?" I asked. "Well, they were friends." "Just friends?" "Yes." "Did they live together?" "Yes, for years and years." "How many bedrooms did they have?" "One." "How many beds?" "One."

My point here is not to draw conclusions from my number-of-beds-in-the-house research! There is much evidence that many married couples, for example, sleep in one bed without sharing an explicitly sexual life. But if my mother had known a man and a woman living in a similar arrangement, she might well have assumed that they were more than friends. In a memoir about her relationship with her sister, Karen, and their coming-out stories in the 1980s, Joy McBride writes that Karen "was involved in long-term relationships with women, though I very naively thought she and her 'roommates' just didn't have enough space or money for two beds. (Honestly.)" (1996, 182).

Heterosexism and Sexual Objectification

The story of Celine and Edith draws our attention to one of the central critiques offered by lesbian activists and scholars to feminist analysis of the sexual objectification of women by men. Put simply, the dominant cultural stereotypes—however pervasive—that only young women are beautiful, that women are only sexual objects not sexual subjects, or that women care whether they attract male attention have served to hide more than they reveal. What they hid was the risky, often dangerous lives of women who loved women, of women who dressed to attract women, of women who—not to put too fine a point on it—couldn't have cared less if they attracted male attention except insofar as men might have been decoys for their interest in women. The National Film Board's *Forbidden Love* (Weissman and Fernie 1993) weaves together interviews with lesbians talking about their strategies for living and loving in the decades after World War II with a dramatization of a typical lesbian pulp novel of the period. One woman explained, with evident satisfaction, how dating gay men provided a front, diverting the attention of family and friends from her intimate life. Such creative acts of subterfuge reveal some of the limitations of reading the history of contemporary culture in terms of the sexual objectification of women by men.

Cultural stereotypes are steeped in heterosexist assumptions and, since the dawn of feminism's second wave, lesbians openly challenged much feminist writing for buying into those assumptions even as they aimed to transform them. The cultural stereotypes say little about who appears beautiful, desirable, or sexy to whom or why. Long-time peace activist Kay Macpherson revealed in her autobiography that "for a long time I clung to the conviction that a married woman who had a relationship with another woman wasn't really being 'unfaithful' to her husband" (1994, 148). The culture's heterosexism filtered out any understanding of sex and love that did not fit the preconceived categories. Women and men, the transgendered, lesbians, bisexuals, and heterosexuals, live lives that confound and oppose the stereotypes, and only by understanding this can we understand the origins of the social movements for sexual liberation of the last decades. These social movements not only provide locations from which to wage the right to live and love publicly, but they also occasion a profound questioning of the past. That human beings historically and cross-culturally engaged in a range of sexual practices, heterosexual and homosexual, is not at issue. But when and how do women and men forge identities, create communities, carve out space within hostile environments to find, attract, and live with those of their own sex?

Researchers have used such questions to reread the historical record: diaries, letters between friends, newspaper articles, advertisements, court records, and novels from the classics to pulp fiction. They conducted many interviews, and women have told their own stories (Chenier 1995; Ross 1995; Weissman and Fernie 1993) In this process, many divergent and overlapping paths for exploring "forbidden love," bestowing affection, creating space, and sharing time, households, and beds with other women have been made visible. A rich history of intimate female friendships and long-term coupling challenges conventional history. Lesbians carved out urban spaces such as bars and clubs where liaisons with those similarly minded could be wrought, and they developed a range of signs for ascertaining who might be interested in one's interest in them (Chamberland 1996). All these practices challenged, whether openly or secretly, the dominant order.

Coming-out stories are richly diverse and often funny, at least in retrospect. One woman writes about arriving at the Alberta farm of her Roman Catholic parents and making this announcement at the dinner table: "I've changed my name to Gillean Chase, the name I'll use when I'm published. I've converted to Judaism and I'm a lesbian" (Chase 1996, 62). Often there is relief, as with Joy McBride:

> Before my sister came out to me, I had never met anyone who was out. This isn't surprising, considering how hard I had worked to isolate myself socially. I had grown up with the theory that I was unlovable, and this stuck with me as an adult so strongly that it never occurred to me to think that I might instead be a lesbian—one who had been brought up in a world that hadn't taught me how to recognize or cherish myself. (1996, 183)

Surely no one, at least in contemporary culture, navigates the route from childhood through adolescence to adulthood without experiencing unrequited love; but those who have lived unremittingly as heterosexuals might stop to think how much more complicated this is when there are few, if any, ways of telling whether the object of your affections—or anyone else—even shares your desire for other women, let alone an interest in you. Some things have changed. In the 1950s, girls didn't dance with each other at school dances: we awaited invitations from boys and, when they weren't forthcoming, we remained "wallflowers," a status that brought neither prestige nor fun.

But young people growing up report that high school culture continues to normalize expressions of heterosexual affection, discussion, and ritual, while ostracizing and policing the same activities when performed by lesbians and gays. Indeed, activities like school dances, which were once the prerogative of high school students, are now normal events in primary school. Explicit and public priming for a heterosexual adulthood appears to start earlier and earlier. Becki Ross estimates that "nine-tenths of the 'lesbian population' continue to live in fear of disclosure and the attendant loss of family, friends, jobs and the custody of children" (1995, 9). Of course, it is not just children who come out to their parents. Parents also come out to their children, and sometimes they come out with each other:

> Sharing one's sexual identity with one's mother and sister is the norm if one is heterosexual. This is not the case if one is lesbian and living in St John's, Newfoundland. As far as I know, we are truly unique. We [the writer, her mother, and sister] thus tend to be fairly conspicuous, as the three of us, with or without our respective lovers, enter the gay bar or the bimonthly women's dance. I have heard various kinds of comments, ranging from

"Here comes the cute family" to "Do I have to get your mother's permission to dance with you?" (Yetman and Yetman 1996, 214)

MALE/FEMALE; MASCULINITY/FEMININITY

Discussions in this chapter on representation of women and femininity presuppose, of course, a discourse on men and masculinity, and I want to deal with this more directly now. The assumption in early second wave feminism was that the problem of women's subordination was femininity (its attributes, dress, characteristics), restricted roles, and sexual objectification by men. The corollary was that women should give up feminine trappings—high-heeled shoes, make-up, skirts and dresses—for more sensible attire; they should abandon nurturing for self-actualization; they should train themselves for male-dominated professions and jobs; and they should refuse sexual objectification in favour of asserting their own sexual needs and desires. Although the explicit goal was not so much to become like men, but rather that women should share power and resources equally with men, there was a subtext that suggested that women, not men, had to change. But masculinity—its characteristics, attributes, aims, and hubris—was on the threshold of scrutiny from many quarters.

Radical and cultural feminists began to insist that the problem was not women's activities and characteristics but men's behaviour and psychology. Women should not strive to share the power that men wielded; rather, that power should be dismantled at the psychic and social level. Men have waged war; women have made peace. Men have been systematically violent; women and children have been their victims. Men are sexual predators; women are nurturing and affectionate. In short, women aren't the problem; men are. At a descriptive level, at the level of accumulated evidence, it's a hard case to refute. But satisfactory explanations for these gendered differences in power, behaviour, and experience are harder to come by. This is not only because the generalizations can be shown not to apply to all men or all women.

Almost all feminists and feminisms reject the most obvious explanation—that the problem must be laid at the doorstep of biology. Notice this response in the *New York Times Book Review* from radical feminists Catharine MacKinnon and Andrea Dworkin to the charge that they blame biology: "Biological determinism is the complete antithesis of everything either one of us has written and done for the last quarter-century. We have each explicitly and repeatedly denounced systems of inferiority and superiority based on biology" (1995, 47). If it's not biology, most feminists reason, it must be social. Something has to happen after birth to explain gender differences, to explain how ideas of masculinity and femininity appear most of the time as givens of social life. This understanding is captured in theories that explicate, in a variety of ways, two interrelated concepts—power and social construction. Relations of power inform, indeed saturate, the social relations between the sexes, socialization practices, and especially how such practices are received and internalized as children grow up.

Socialist feminists, especially those engaging with psychoanalytic formulations, launched a critique of the construction of masculinity, arguing that "normal" masculinity was constituted by denial of emotion and by subsequent aggression and violence, underpinned by deep psychic anxiety, self-hatred, and insecurity. In *Beyond Patriarchy*, Michael Kaufman (1987) discusses the masculine trilogy of violence against self, against other men, and against women. Boys growing up in this society must dis-identify with their mothers, their less powerful parent, in favour of identification with their fathers. The consequences are deep-seated, long-lasting, and extensive. Given that women are the only legitimate repository for nurturing, care, emotion, and attention to relationships, boys must repress their emotions, their love, and their feelings of dependence upon others in order not to be like their mothers. The vulnerability boys feel as small and dependent people goes underground; bravado and bullying take its place. But that vulnerability returns to be projected onto those perceived as vulnerable—girls and women. Hence the scorn, the repudiation, what psychoanalyst Ruth Brunswick called "the normal male contempt for women" (1948). The result, according to feminists, is not a good recipe for living in a social world, and it's certainly not been good news for women and children. The boy in the schoolyard who does not demonstrate success in this endeavour is called a sissy. A sissy is a boy who acts like a girl. Here we see early training for misogyny. If boys who act like girls are contemptible, what does this say about girls, the model for this contempt?

Many feminists challenge the view that masculinity is constituted through a set of social and linguistic practices that repeats and consolidates an apparently uncontested division between the sexes. They suggest that we could have a masculinity that was clearly linked with male bodies but did not share in this repudiation of femininity. This would amount to an analytical and objective distinction between sex and gender. Could such a distinction be sustained? Lately, some poststructuralists who have coined the term *queer theory* have been questioning the assumption that male and female bodies are givens, waiting to be filled, as it were, with socially constructed gendered and sexual identities. As Kathleen Pirrie Adams explains:

> By arguing that all gender identity involves the impersonation of an abstract (gender) ideal, and, by continually remarking on the artificiality of the gender norms that organize and regulate sexuality, queer theory has shifted attention away from questions of who is (really) homosexual to questions about how homosexuality is realized and made visible socially, as well as how it runs throughout the culture as a whole—invisibly, inarticulately. (1993, 31)

For queer theorists, pride of analytic place shifts from the text to "notions such as performative identity, gender activism and gender performance" (ibid., 31). Performance draws attention to how we *do* gender as ongoing bodily and linguistic presentation. The concept of performance permits a convergence of the poststructuralist emphasis on discourse with a theorization of the body and therefore of sex and gender. From this perspective, sex and gender are understood as intertwined processes, produced as acts—"on site," as it were, through and with our bodies—and reiterated endlessly. The very reiteration of these acts—these *norms*, in sociological terms—masks their boundary-creating character (Adams 1994). They appear with no history, no rationale; they are "what is." But we are the agents of these reiterations, and by these acts we participate in sustaining and shifting that which the culture permits and forbids. Queer theory draws attention to these reiterations of gender and sexuality—to the social visibility of sexual differences—but sees them as an ongoing happening, always with the possibility of disruption. The disruptions may be more dramatic in some locations than others. Consider Adams' comments on the lesbian bar scene in Toronto:

> Who hasn't seen or been this: girl who arrives, returning weekly with a new sign (cropped, dread-locked, shaved or dyed hair, new boots, cut-offs, pierces, tattoo), leaving weekly with a new inspiration, a new friend, more certainty and more confusion. The bar is an arena of possibility, a public space in which sexual identity is sought and discarded, and so if we describe it simply in terms of what we do there—dance, talk, drink, have sex—we can lose sight of some aspects of what we are doing there. (1993, 30)

Judith Butler has been in the forefront in developing queer theory's reassessment of sexual and gendered identities. She questions what has usually been assumed in other theoretical (including scientific) perspectives, asking exactly what about the body and sex is given, already there? She is not disputing that we have bodies, but rather she asks, just what can we say about those bodies that falls into the "already there" category? She argues that anything we might say about those bodies has already been taken up by socially constituted discourses on gender, sexuality, race, age, and so on. There is no pure discourse through which we can speak about the already given body.

Furthermore, our own sense of who we are—in psychoanalytic terms, our *ego*—is constituted (in part) through our projections of our bodies. But those projections are thoroughly informed by our participation in cultural (including linguistic) practices. The sense, therefore, that we have of being male or being female cannot be partitioned into biological and social compartments. It's not so much that the social infuses the biological, but that the biological can only be thought of and named through the social, namely through discourses, among others, on gender, race, sexuality, health and illness, religion and ethics, and physiology. These discourses, of course, infuse each other: only for the purposes of a list are they separable.

In Freudian discourse, for example, the significance attached to the presence or absence of a penis mobilizes a huge literature on gender, sex, relationships, neuroses, and psychoses. While some feminist appropriators of psychoanalysis have shifted the importance from the penis to the symbol of the penis—the phallus—there remains the connection between male bodies and power (either because of the presence of the penis or the connection between penis and phallus). But what sustains this connection? Butler argues that it is sustained through reiteration of linguistic practices, practices that, because of the reiteration, become *sedimented*, or materialized. But the sedimentation is an illusion to the extent that what sustains it is in fact the reiterations. The reiteration depends on people engaging in repetitious acts; however, the repetitions are never simply repetitions. Everything that has *not* been acknowledged in previous repetitions can always make an appearance in the next; that which is desired but unacknowledged always remains, in whatever partial or distorted sense, as possibility. In this sense, then, the connection between penis and phallus is not signed, sealed, and delivered for eternity, but neither will the connection be severed all at once.

Judith Butler seeks to destabilize the connection. For, as long as the connection between penis and phallus is not questioned, all the questions about power and gendered identities will take their cue from the *assumed* differences between men and women. This is Butler's critique of psychoanalysis in both its Freudian and Lacanian versions, and to make her point she gives her chapter on this topic the provocative title "The Lesbian Phallus" (1993, 57–92). Both versions of psychoanalysis, she asserts, assume that entry into the symbolic order—the social world—is predicated upon already existing, biological, prediscursive differences between the sexes. These theories organize the prediscursive differences hierarchically, with masculine principles constructed as the entry point into the symbolic order. Butler asks why acceptance into this world of meanings should be contingent upon collusion with masculine principles and a dichotomy between masculine and feminine. After all, this hierarchical dichotomy is simply the ongoing product of endless reiterations, including those produced by psychoanalytic theory. Why should the phallus (power) and the penis be assumed to be prediscursively connected and therefore left unquestioned? To put it another way: castration anxiety (the prototypical male problem) and penis envy (the defining characteristic of femininity) would lose their privileged status in psychic and social terms once the connection between power and penis became just one of many (optional) possibilities.

If this sounds unbearably abstract, think for a moment about the underlying messages behind the following oft-heard statements: "All she needs is a man"; "All she needs is a good fuck" (with the implication that only a person with a penis could provide this); "She's a lesbian because she had a bad experience with a man"; "He's gay because he had a suffocating mother"; "Lesbians/feminists hate men"; "He's a wimp, he must be gay"; or "Bisexuals can't commit." One of my (male) students told the following joke: "Why do so many men give their penis a name? Because they don't like to take orders from a stranger." Many feminists have used the word *phallocentric* to describe society or even civilization itself. The connection is to men via the assumed link between power and penis. Butler questions this connection theoretically and socially. In so doing, it becomes increasingly difficult to take the differences between male and female bodies as given. Accounting for, and deposing, male power becomes implicated with challenges to the privileged status accorded to sex/gender differences.

Feminists have been aware of this for a long time. In offering critiques to the first words said upon the arrival of a newborn—"It's a boy!" or "It's a girl!" rather than "It's healthy!" or "It's small!"—feminists have suggested that there was something problematic about the intense interest in this one aspect of the child. Moreover, it has recently become clear that when babies are born with genitalia that are not categorizable by appearance, the doctors *decide* whether the baby is boy or girl. It seems that a precondition for entrance into a human community is having a body that may be deemed male or female, even though some bodies don't present themselves that way (Findlay 1995).

What is so important about insisting upon this distinction between male and female? In social terms, what is riding on it? Butler argues that this distinction makes possible the discourse and practices that privilege heterosexuality. The founding principle for heterosexuality is the distinction between male and female. But what if the founding principle depends upon reiteration? What if the reiteration brings the founding principle into play—and keeps it in play—rather than the reverse? The enormous range of practices that sustains heterosexuality as normal, preferred, and unremarkable requires and mobilizes another set of practices that are banished, punished, and in other ways declared "outside." The "outside" is, of course, also "inside." What we repress remains; therefore, reiterating our desires is never simple reiteration. Indeed, vehement reiteration of desire may indicate the instability of those desires. The old expression "The lady doth protest too much" captures the insight that statements, including statements of desire and aversion, cannot be taken at face value. Consider, for example, the following common statements: "I could *never* love a woman"; "I can't *imagine* being gay"; "I feel sick if a man approaches me in a bar." Virulent expressions of homophobia can be understood as anxiety-creating desires that are articulated as revulsion and projected onto others. Such statements provide evidence that we need to question "both gender binarism and the inside-outside logic that makes homosexual identity seem like heterosexuality's opposite" (Adams 1993, 31).

Homophobic assumptions—that gay men are effeminate and lesbians are mannish, for example—reify both masculinity and femininity as well as the categories straight and homosexual. At the experiential level, it is easy enough to counter such generalizations. But often these generalizations are refuted in ways that redraw the boundaries between accept-able and not acceptable. Consider the (defensive) remark "Of course gays don't 'have to be' wimps" (read they could be as macho as any (straight) man). Or "many lesbians are femi-nine and even wear make-up and high-heeled shoes" (just like straight women). In these cases, the proof of the normality of (some) gays and lesbians is seen to reside in their con-formity to the very gendered roles that are elsewhere undergoing critique.

In such ordinary statements, we see how the categories male–female, masculine–feminine, gay–straight are all used to sustain each other, thereby constantly constraining, modifying, and confirming the sense of the possible and the impossible. From this per-spective, conventional masculinity is produced through constant reiteration, and those reiterations aim to approximate some masculine ideal that does not exist prior to the reit-erating process. But this ongoing attempt to approximate that ideal represents and pro-duces psychic anxiety and social, political, and economic consequences. How can some-one ever know if he is "being man enough"? Man enough for what, we want to ask? If we substitute woman for man in this phrase, we may be trying to demonstrate that woman can never measure up, or we may be parodying the original phrase to display its meaning and its vacuity. The phrase "being man enough" appears both full of meaning and empty at the same time.

Perhaps this is a useful way to apprehend the concepts of masculinity and femininity. There seems little question that they are charged with meaning, used and reused in multi-ple ways to reward and punish, exclude and include, valorize and undermine. But when we examine them closely, they seem to disappear before our eyes. Women speak of having to become like men to succeed in the corporation. For example, as we saw in chapter 5, they may dress like men, suited up, briefcase in hand. But few of us think that masculinity actu-ally resides in the clothes. Or do we? Consider the enormous interest, humour, and revul-sion generated by those who most obviously flout convention—a man dressed as a woman and displaying "feminine" mannerisms, perhaps. A man cannot simply get up in the morn-ing and decide to wear a skirt: immediately he is labelled a crossdresser, with all that term entails. And his mannerisms: why are such mannerisms seen as feminine, now that they are displayed by a male? But wait, is he a man? Or is he a woman dressed as a man? Is he a woman dressed as a man displaying feminine mannerisms? Is he a woman dressed as a man gazing at a woman dressed as a man who is "acting like" a woman?

At this point, you will probably have thrown up your hands. But consider this poem, written by Mikaela Hughes, when she was six or seven. Her best friend had just moved to Australia, and her cat had just died. At the same time, she had realized that her classmates had assumed that she was a boy.

> I seem to be a boy But really I'm a girl. I seem to be happy But really I am sad. I seem to not have a cat But really I have a cat that is dead. (1996, 146)

Why, then, all this categorization? What on earth does it mean in the end to ask, What is s/he "really"? *Exactly*, say the queer theorists. If you look only at the performance, the categories of sex and gender appear more as a chest of Halloween clothes and props, a cul-tural resource for the mis/use of all. But Judith Butler is careful to point out that sex and gender are not garments to be put on in the morning; in the reiteration of acts, the specif-ic materiality of the body is produced. We may feel ourselves to be male, female, mascu-line, feminine, gay, straight in the depths of our being. In her words, the "activity of this gendering cannot, strictly speaking, be a human act or expression, a willful appropriation, and it is certainly not a question of taking on a mask; it is the matrix through which all willing first becomes possible, its enabling cultural condition" (1993, 7).

Let us return to women who may try to appear like men in their bid to climb the corporate ladder. Dressing the part may be accompanied by attempts to appear unemotional at work. But does that mean that masculinity is coincident with failure to display emotion? These days, at least, there is a lot of attention paid to the idea that men can feel too. The "sensitive new-age guy" may not be a passing phenomenon. Or women may behave like men by taking on the corporate goals and culture. But does masculinity reside in the pursuit of profits and the instrumental use of others? Or women may sleep with women, like men (or at least like those men who sleep with women). But the limits for women's being like men seem to have been crossed in this last example. Indeed, women report that they often risk their jobs if they are known to share their intimate lives with women. Gay men in the corporation may well stay closeted. Loving other men—regardless of their other behaviours—may put them across the line of acceptance, promotion, or employment. Is this because they are, in this respect, like women—that is, like the women who love men, not like the women who love women as men (are supposed to) do? Here we see that, just as sexual boundary making draws upon and uses gender markers, so are the boundaries of masculinity and femininity maintained, in part, through sexual boundary making (Ingraham 1994).

Butler goes further in her theorizing, arguing that just as discourses on masculinity and femininity and discourses on sexuality enable each other in the ways we have seen, so too do they both depend upon and enable the continuous reiteration of other social inclusions and exclusions. In particular she points to the ways in which dominant ideas of normative masculinity incorporate and depend upon images of nonracialized men—that is, white men. In fact, we might ask, do we even have a discourse on masculinity (however full and empty we deem the category to be), or do we have discourses on masculinity intricately bound up with whiteness and racialization? If the latter, this would mean that reiterating one's identity as male depends not just upon the identity female but also upon the identities—the excluded identities—of colour, blackness, brownness, and all that those identities, in turn, are taken to mean.

Consider how often media accounts of the activities of the subgroup in the population identified as youth not only include the (assumed) sex of participants but also their race—when they are not white. *White* usually requires no mention because it is seen to be normative, while "young" "black" "men" are presented as having an identity that distinguishes them from young white men, or old white men, or young black women. Much of their media image partakes of many aspects of normative masculinity: toughness, instrumentality, aggressiveness, and refusing to take direction from others (known in other circles as "being one's own boss"). But somehow, in the process of being racialized, such characteristics take on menacing tones. "Boys will be boys," but these boys are threatening and are excluded from the more benign rendition of that cliché. Given all the data on date rape, wife battery, and child abuse, this can't be because there are no "white" "male" "youth" who are menacing anyone. On the contrary, Statistics Canada's 1994 survey found that "the highest rates of wife assault are among young men 18 to 24 years of age" (Rodgers 1994, 46). How is it that masculinity remains, at least in non-feminist discourse, apparently untainted by such findings?

In a study of recent Canadian trial judgments, the researchers found some clues in the language of the judges (Coates, Bavelas, and Gibson 1994). They found that there is no consensus about the appropriate courtroom language to describe sexual assault in cases where the assailant is not a stranger to the victim. As a result, judges vacillate between using the language of "stranger" rape and the language of consensual sex. A man who entered a woman's bedroom while she was asleep and inserted his penis into her mouth was described in the trial judgment as having "offered" his penis (ibid., 189). Words that are common in discussing love making, like fondle, touch, and intercourse, were regularly used instead of the term sexual assault, the legal words for unwanted encounters. A man found guilty of sexual assault was described as having an "impeccable character" (ibid., 196), leading one to wonder just what he would have had to do to rule himself out of this category. Despite evidence such as this, an editorial in the *Globe and Mail* took the Canadian Panel on Violence Against Women to task for "an avalanche of recommendations, some vague, some silly, some worthy." In particular, the editors urged, "mandatory gender-sensitivity training for judges should be quickly rejected" (1993, D6).

Poststructuralism's focus on the text and queer theory's focus on performance permit an analysis of gendered subjectivity in all areas of human literary and artistic production from scientific documents through legislation to comic strips and television programs. The word games that maintain the boundaries between male and female, masculinity and femininity, need constant reinvention, but their reinvention relies on the fixed idea that men and women are different in ways that are known. But there is a trick here, to return to Judith Butler. The trick is that it is these reinventions (reiterations) that maintain the boundaries by presenting themselves as simple reflections of an underlying reality. For example, observers noted that Kim Campbell would "have to be aggressive to fight Liberal Leader Jean Chrétien, but when women become aggressive they are often labelled hysterical" (Smith 1993, A4). In an article arguing that "sharing the housework isn't a political gesture, it just makes sense," Ken Mark wrote that he recalled "Peter Gzowski's chat with a naval non-commissioned officer on the proper way to iron a shirt. These men are not wimps or sissies just because they know what is the business end of an iron" (1994, A24). Note how the category wimp and sissy is left untouched, presumably to be filled with some behaviour that *will* bring such opprobrium upon some men's heads. In another story entitled "Handywoman: Powerful new role model is plugged in," the reader is introduced to "icons of a new brand of feminism in the nineties—the handy yet feminine woman" (Williams 1994, A24). These reiterations create the exclusions and the inclusions, the hierarchical arrangements that feminists have variously called patriarchal relations, the sex/gender system, or the racialized sex-gendered system.

In our society doctors assign sex at birth, and gender is assumed to follow this assignation, taking hold by the end of the second or third year of life. But this process, neither the first nor the second step, carries the certainty that the culture—including medical culture—assumes. In Patricia Elliot's psychoanalytic understanding, "it is in the nature of sexed identity to be unstable, to be open to question"(1998, 19). Nowhere has this been made more evident than in the accounts and struggles of transgendered people. Under the rubric "transgendered" Eleanor MacDonald includes "all those people whose internally felt sense of core gender identity does not correspond to their assigned sex at birth or in which they were raised" (1998, 4). In her excellent analysis, MacDonald takes issue with most feminist approaches to transgendering—from those who are hostile through oblivious to those who dismiss the problem because "gender shouldn't matter" (ibid., 6). The more recent postmodern emphasis on diversity and contingency that uses poststructuralism and has motivated the development of queer theory is "certainly vastly preferable" (4). Yet here there is a "risk of romanticizing" just what it means to "live on [the] borderlines"(9) when there are "virtually no social spaces" where one is accepted (8). Coming out as transgendered means having one's "gender identity disputed, contested, disbelieved, or fully denied. Having to prove to others that you really are who you say you are" is a daily task for many. "Few among the non-transgendered," MacDonald writes, "have pondered for long the luxury of living in a body that feels at ease and consonant with the self" (1998, 7).

Taking on board the experiences of the transgendered both theoretically and politically forces a reconsideration of categories and identities: how they are made and unmade; how they create inclusions, and provoke exclusions; how they create (unnecessary?) pain; how they produce responsibilities and burdens "for those being categorized and those doing the categorizing" (Kessler 1998, 132). Feeling at home in one's body requires more work for some than for others. But we can all learn from the work that some must do in order to carry on with their lives. For some decades feminism made "woman" the common denominator for "membership" in their social movements and analysis while lesbians and gays made sexual identity (orientation) the focus. Transgendering, however, provides the opportunity to question the notion of identity itself and "the issues of identity boundaries, stability and coherence." What, then, would be the basis for developing relationships for building communities, for mobilizing social movements? In a way consonant with "transversal politics" discussed in Chapter 7, where we reach from ourselves, openly and reflexively, towards others to find shared ground, MacDonald calls for "new exploration of the ethical bases of alliances and formation of communities" (1998, 10).

Gendered understandings inform virtually every aspect of the social world in complex and interrelated ways. Psychoanalytic and poststructuralist perspectives have been the most attentive to this depth and pervasiveness, but they need each other to provide satisfactory accounts of how gender is psychically lodged and linguistically sustained and resisted.

It is not the case, however, that they replace other feminist perspectives in providing explanations for gendered hierarchies. Their utility depends upon the kinds of questions one is seeking to answer. Psychoanalytic theories is just beginning to develop in ways that explain how gender interacts with other social hierarchies—those of class, race, age, and so on—in the process of psychosexual maturation (Abel 1990; Abel, Christian and Moglen 1999; Hamilton 1997). As most proponents of these theories would concede, these approaches generally make no sustained contribution towards understanding the gendered relations of political economy, including capitalism, imperialism, or racism, or towards strategies for the dismantling of these exploitative systems.[13] Strategies for social change at every level, however, need to include the insights of psychoanalysis, namely, that we are constituted–and expect to be constituted—as gendered human beings from the earliest days of infancy and childhood. To undo the equation of masculinity with domination and femininity with subordination, therefore, not only requires more than one generation, but the willingness of adult men and women to revisit their own past with the hope of understanding those basic patterns of self-perception and desire that lead to violent forms of "othering."

Many feminists have also challenged poststructural approaches, generally on two interrelated grounds. By focusing upon reading the texts or observing the performance, poststructuralism fails to distinguish between subjectivity as the constitution of a self (who we are), representations of that self (how we are portrayed), and activity (what we do). What this means, as some critics have argued, is that there isn't theoretical space for asking questions about *causal* relationships between gendered behaviours and attitudes, the depictions of men and women, and what men and women do. The absence of a causal analysis appears to leave feminists without strategic analyses for transforming oppressive and exploitative relationships. This political concern is related to a second problem that many feminists have with poststructuralism: that an understanding of subjectivity as an outcome of discourse—rather than as a site for the constitution of a *self* (Benjamin 1994)—fails to provide a full account of human agency and the potential of people to act individually or collectively to change the social world (Weir 1996).

Neither explanation nor strategic thinking is the strong suit of poststructuralism, and most feminists show little interest in abandoning either. A poststructural approach continues to coexist, then—and I think necessarily—with older approaches and controversies about the interconnections between gendered subjects, gendered representation, and gendered activity.

CONCLUSION

As we discussed in chapter 1, different feminist perspectives provide different understandings of what is most important to changing patriarchal society. Let us take an example. A magazine editor accepts advertisements illustrating women who have dieted to produce the "perfect" body. A young girl reads the magazine and starves herself while another looks for alternative images of robust and cheerful women. How are the different responses to be explained? By the ads, by the presence or absence of alternative images, by variations in early childhood development, by what the reader sees women and men doing in her daily life? Why do popular magazines routinely run such images? Because those who produce them share the dominant valuation in the culture? Because they help sell magazines? Because the advertisers realize profit from all the products designed to produce the body beautiful?

Such questions look for causal explanations. Liberal feminists have engaged in many, often successful, campaigns to pressure the popular media into providing alternative images of women and girls (Macpherson 1994, 149). Their belief in the saliency of education for changing laws and attitudes guides this kind of strategic thinking. What is clear—35 years on from those first protests against beauty pageants—is that issues around sexual objectification resonate among subsequent generations of young women. Naomi Wolf's *The Beauty Myth* (1990) sold millions of copies; her speeches in the United States and Canada drew packed halls; and young women especially, whether self-described feminists or not, respond to her spirited critique of a culture that induces them to diet their way to oblivion. The protests against beauty pageants appear now as the first salvo in a long feminist challenge to a cultural economy that not only rewards and punishes women on the basis of their appearance but also induces them to spend lots of money on their appearance, to take unconscionable risks with their health, and to spend lives in a spiral of guilt-ridden dieting (Kirsch 1995, A3).[14]

Marxist feminists, by contrast, might begin with questions about profits and the dependence of capitalist relations upon the creation of needs. There are multimillion-dollar industries that depend upon women altering their body size through methods ranging from dieting to surgery. Such industries employ women in Canada, and abroad, at very low wages. From this perspective, therefore, an analysis that began with images of women and dieting would extend to the international political economy. But Marxist feminists would also highlight the continuing situation of women's economic dependence upon men, and how these relations of dependence help create the need for women to please men.

Radical feminists challenge the institutions of heterosexism, partly in order to loosen the hold that men have over women. Women have been coerced by man-made law and masculine violence—physical and representational—into heterosexual marriage, into degrading and oppressive work as models in pornography and as prostitutes, and into conforming with the entire heterosexist structuring of society. Why does the young girl looking at the magazine images feel that she should look like them? Does she believe that this will help attract male attention? Radical feminists insist that women must get out from under the power of men, and this involves action on many fronts. They have argued, for example, that men sexually violate women because they absorb violent pornography. Censoring such material, therefore, is justified on the grounds that it will diminish the violence that men wreak upon women.

Marxist feminists do not see censoring pornography as central to eliminating male violence, but focus rather on economic coercion in explaining many manifestations of gender. Women do low-paid gendered work because most of the time that is all that is available. From this perspective, women endure violence in the home because of their economic dependence on men, and men are more likely to act violently in the home when they are exploited at work (Luxton 1980). As the economic circumstances of so many people's lives worsen with cutbacks in social services and rising unemployment and underemployment, increasing numbers of women and children will be in growing jeopardy, including danger from physical violence.

The political discourse especially from the mid 1990s reinvents, with a vengeance, long-standing distinctions between those who are dependent on others and those who fend for themselves. In this rhetoric that provides the fuel for electoral success, increasing numbers of people find themselves with bodies that don't matter, written out of the social and political world. Psychoanalytic understandings of the false distinction between dependence and independence; poststructuralist and queer theory's readings of discourse and performativity; radical feminist insights into men's abuse of women's minds and bodies; liberal feminist insistence on the centrality of education and attitudes—all these, I would argue, contribute to an understanding of contemporary social life and suggest ways to destabilize the late twentieth century's version of the deserving and the undeserving. Finally, as I have indicated in other chapters, Marxist and anti-racist analyses of the contemporary global political economy draw attention to the immense power of those controlling capital to shape the lives of women, children, and men in different ways. In the last chapter we look more closely at feminist analyses of the phenomenon called "globalization," at the international political economy, at the interconnections between the conditions of life for women living in Canada and elsewhere, and at movements for social justice.

NOTES

1. I am very grateful to the author of the article, Maryam Sanati, for confirming that this advice indeed does appear in the little pink book which is entitled "Feeling Naked on the First Tee: An Essential Guide for New Woman Golfers" by Ann Kelly.

2. According to Prentice et al., the first public action of the newly formed Toronto Women's Liberation group was a protest against a winter bikini contest (1988, 353).

3. When Colleen Swanson, wife of Dow Corning's ethics advisor, experienced debilitating ill health, neither of them connected this with her recent breast implants, implants produced and marketed by her husband's employer (Byrne 1995). Yet in a CBC radio interview, John Swanson reported that, in the 1970s, he had discounted warnings in *Ms.* magazine about the danger of silicone breast implants as feminist overreaction. An estimated 150 000 women in Canada had breast implants as of 1992 (*Winnipeg Free Press,* 1992a).

4. I am very grateful to Patrizia Gentile for providing me with a copy of her unpublished paper. She convincingly argues that "the beauty contest 'model' was appropriated by the federal service in order to enforce specific codes of femininity, masculinity and heterosexuality" (1995, 1). See also Gentile 2000 and Kinsman 1995.

5. The Kingston Women's Liberation Movement held an elaborate protest against beauty queen contests at Queen's University in October 1969. Six members of the group entered the contest. When they were introduced, each in turn took the opportunity to address the audience (Adamson 1995, 262–63).

6. I recently heard a report on CBC Radio that cyberbullying among girls especially is well documented in Great Britain, and is now being reported in Canada. An Internet search on "Girls and Bullying" pulled many entries.

7. Reginald Bibby and Donald C. Posterski's *Teen Trends: A Nation in Motion* (1992) cite a 1988 survey on male–female couples, aged 15–24, who live together. Forty-six percent of the respondents said the female partner did all the cooking, cleaning, and laundry, while only 4 percent said the male did most or all of these jobs.

8. In July 1957 a "weeping Miss USA" lost her title when organizers discovered that she was married and the mother of two children. Leona Gage told pageant officials that she and her cousin Barbara Gates had gambled every cent they had to finance her chance at fame and fortune (*Toronto Star* 1957, 1).

9. See Dorothy Smith (1992) for an elaboration of this position.

10. See also Susan Russell's 1978 research in an Ottawa high school. She discovered that boys reported that their grades were improving even when they had deteriorated, while girls continually underestimated their performance (1987).

11. In a letter to *Ms.* magazine, Pam Elliot, co-ordinator of the Lesbian Battering Intervention Project in St Paul, Minnesota, wrote that she had been "besieged with requests nationwide for setting up support services on lesbian battering" (1991, 5).

12. Following her double mastectomy, the late Kathleen Martindale wrote: "I've got an invisible disability. I've become a quick-change artist in gyms and other places where there's no or little privacy. Most people cringe when they see my chest. They say I've been mutilated. In place of breasts with nipples I have a scar which extends from under my left armpit, goes jaggedly across my entire chest, and then ends up under what used to be my right armpit. My lover and I call it 'the zipper.' That's what it looks like, a long, red zipper" (1994, 12). Martindale also had to deal with the fact that there were no support groups for lesbian cancer patients even in Metropolitan Toronto.

13. But see, for example, the last chapter in Jessica Benjamin's *The Bonds of Love* (1988) for an insightful treatment of the relationship between gendered socialization and bureaucracy.

14. Dr. Ron Davis, a Toronto clinical psychologist, estimated at a seminar on eating disorders that "five per cent of university women have full-blown eating disorders" and that more than 90 percent of those with eating disorders are women (Kirsch 1995, A3).

Global Restructuring, Canadian Connections, and Feminist Resistance

On 14 June 2003, *The Globe and Mail* carried a story about Fahima Osman, a 25-year-old Canadian woman studying medicine at McMaster University (Anderssen). The title was "Dream Child," the story was upbeat, as indeed it should have been. The only student of African background in her program, Fahima will be the first Canadian-trained physician in Toronto's large Somali community. Smart, hard-working, compassionate, and persevering, Fahima is generous to her eight younger brothers and sisters who see her as a role model, and upon graduation determined to use her medical skills not just in Canada but in Somalia.

Fahima's story provides an opportunity to look at two concepts—human agency which has been an important theme in this book, and globalization, which helps link the Canadian story to the rest of the world. In the context of her family history and the racism in Canadian society, Fahima's achievement is nothing short of breath-taking. Though by no means the most disadvantaged in the Somalian diaspora, the Osmans arrived penniless in Canada when she was 11. In the Canadian school system Fahima encountered little encouragement. A guidance counsellor once refused to let her retake calculus, suggesting that she was setting her sights too high.

Fahima belongs to a large cohort of immigrant visible minority children whose educational attainment equal or exceed those from non–visible minority groups (Boyd 2002).[1] Family encouragement—family pressure—contributes to explanations for their educational achievements. Their success will change not only the composition of the Canadian population but also the experience of those who come after them and find teachers, doctors, and lawyers who look like them, and believe that they can "do it." The need to explain their success, however, remains. For Fahima, perhaps, encounters with everyday racism helped her to achieve her goals. Such hard work in the face of adversity suggests a form of resistance. For other children, everyday racism feeds other forms of resistance that may lead to dropping out of school, tangles with the law, or political action. Understanding an individual biography is never simple. Why did Mary Wollstonecraft, born in straitened circumstances to parents who didn't much like her, write the books that made her a feminist icon? Why did Fahima Osman pull all-nighters to earn the grades necessary for acceptance into a highly competitive medical school? Obviously we need to know a great deal more about them to offer explanations, and even then, we would be speculating, however intelligently.

REFUGEES, GLOBALIZATION, AND THE CANADIAN STATE

By following Fahima Osman's life backwards to the days before she became a refugee living in Canada, we bump up against the global political economy, the division of the world into haves and have nots, the worldwide movement of people seeking better lives, often fleeing civil wars, famine, poverty, ethnic, racialized and gender persecution, and genocide. The year before she started medical school Fahima went to Somalia as an unpaid intern. Nothing had prepared her for what she saw—starving children, hospitals without basic equipment, women left to die because they could not produce the money for a Caesarean section. As Fahima explained: "it was just a matter of luck that we're born privileged not a kid starving in Africa."

Fahima's father's journey from Somalia included paying 500 Yemen shillings to join 100 other stowaways on an unstable fishing boat bound for the United Arab Emirates where he found a job working for a Canadian oil company. This was an expensive and risky trip; indeed he nearly drowned. But he survived, and eventually his daughter Fahima became a medical student at McMaster. Good for her, good for Canada. But we need to take a second look at his decision to become a stowaway. In the current context of Canadian law, such people, and those who harbour them, have been criminalized; in recent years most of them have been detained as prisoners, and then returned against their will to their country of origin (Chan and Mirchandani 2002, 20). Ironically, many Canadians will read the story of Fahima's father and feel good that he made it to Canada and that his children are doing well—all the while supporting their government's forced deportations of refugees who are not only described as "bogus" refugees, but also people from whom "good" Canadians need protection (Pratt and Valverde 2002; Sharma 2002, 18; Lepp 2002, 90; Thobani 2001).

Anna Pratt and Mariana Valverde argue that the Somalis were among the first group targeted by government legislation in the 1990s, legislation made politically possible by a new discursive environment that saw "the virtual disappearance of the deserving subject of international human rights law, the refugee fleeing persecution in her/his country." Those without identification papers—like most Somalis—now meet "extreme suspicion," even when it is known that such documents are not available because of the conditions in the countries from which they are fleeing (Pratt and Valverde 2002, 146). "Even the victims of certified, televised genocide," they point out, "end up being regarded as 'so-called refugees' as soon as they board a plane for Toronto" (ibid., 147). In a similar vein, Annalee Lepp and the Global Alliance Against Traffick in Women (GAATW) show that migrant sex workers are "cast simultaneously as 'victims' of organized crime, as 'criminals' in violation of immigration and prostitution laws, as potential 'pawns' of the criminal justice system" (ibid., 91).

Canadian Refugee Policy: Feminist Challenges

Regardless of their wishes, their reasons for migrating, or any concern for their human rights, these women face detention and deportation from Canada when tracked down by the authorities (see Box 7-1).

BOX 7-1	Trafficking in Women

In conceptualizing trafficking within the context of transnational migration and as constituting its most abusive form, studies have also emphasized that a number of structural factors contribute to the movement of women and to global trafficking in women. First and foremost are the ongoing destructive effects of globalization. These include the imposition of structural adjustment programs and international trade agreements that squeeze national economies especially in countries of the South, as well as the severe dislocations caused by the transitional economies in Russia and Eastern Europe and by civil/military strife. These have resulted in the growing economic disparities between North and South, the displacement of peoples from rural agricultural communities, environmental devastation, deepening immiseration of marginalized populations, rising unemployment in urban centres, declining real wages, and the feminization of migration. As an International Labour Organization report emphasized in 1996, the feminization of international labour migration is "one of the most striking economic and social phenomena of recent times." Given the unprecedented demand for the cheap labour of "Third World" women, these women have come to assume a central role in their families as wage earners.

Given also the increasing demand for their sexual, reproductive, and domestic services in informal and invisible sectors of the economy in countries of the North, like Canada, these women cite economic factors as the primary reason for their decision to migrate for work or marriage. These factors include the desire to mitigate situations of poverty and indebtedness, secure elevated earnings and long-term financial security, as well as send money home to support and better the lives of their families....

Within a global context in which female movement has escalated and countries of the North like Canada are increasingly closing legitimate forms of migration through stricter border controls and more stringent immigration and refugee policies, recent studies indicate that those women who need to or wish to migrate rely on various parties, including families, acquaintances, or returnees to facilitate their search for work overseas. They also respond to advertisements for jobs overseas published in newspapers in their countries of origin. In the process, they are often put into contact with or are approached by formal agents who arrange for transportation, travel documents, visitors or entertainment visas, and employment in cities like Toronto or Vancouver. Based on the information supplied by agents, some women are aware of the kind of work they are undertaking and the conditions of their verbal contracts (for example, the amount of their debt); others may have knowledge of the nature but not the conditions of their work; and still others are deceived.

Thus, even though the Canadian media often promotes the image of the quintessential "trafficking victim" as a "young Asian woman" sold by family members to or lured by organized crime gangs, transported forcibly across national borders, and sold into "sexual slavery," Global Alliance Against Traffic in Women [GAATW] research in Thailand and recent Canadian studies indicate that this is not the majority experience and does not reflect the complexities of women's migratory experiences....

Despite Canada's self-proclaimed status as a champion of human rights in the international arena, when it comes to the implementation of human rights protections for trafficked and migrant women, there is not a great deal of room for optimism at this particular conjuncture. The Canadian government is obligated as a signatory of the UN Trafficking Protocol to develop a national policy on trafficking. However, it remains to be seen whether it will proceed to further formalize its myopic and repressive policies or whether it will take seriously the various recommendations made by human rights activist and schol-

ars as well as Non-Governmental Organizations (NGOs), such as the Toronto Network Against Trafficking in Women and GAATW Canada, in recent years. At a basic level, this would include signing and implementing the provisions contained in the UN Convention on the Rights of Migrant Workers and Their Families as well as incorporating the "Human Rights Standards for the Treatment of Trafficked Persons" as developed by the Foundation Against Trafficking in Women, the International Human Rights Law Group, and GATTW in Bangkok in its future policies....

This would mean addressing the root causes of migration and trafficking, and a radical rethinking of the Canadian government's enthusiastic support for globalization and trade liberalization policies, which are rarely recognized as responsible for exacerbating the deteriorating socio-economic conditions in countries of the South that contribute directly to the feminization of migration.

Source: Annalee Lepp, *Trafficking in Women and the Feminization of Migration: the Canadian Context* (2002).

Under Canada's immigration act immigrants are accepted for three main reasons: to benefit Canada economically, to reunify families, and "to offer safe haven to persons with a well-founded fear of persecution." In 2001, of the 250 346 immigrants admitted, the economic class accounted for 61 percent, the family class 27 percent, and refugees 11 percent (Li 2003, 25). Women claimants fare badly compared to men in all three of these categories (Tolley 2003, 6; Boyd 2001, 103–23).

About 85 percent of the world's refugees are women and children, but between 1985 and 1994 only 61 women were admitted for every 100 men (Boyd 2001, 112). Children under age 15 represent about half the population in flight, but account for only one-quarter of those admitted (Boyd 1994, 8). The fate of children is overwhelmingly linked to their mothers, and women are excluded from launching successful claims as refugees and immigrants because they have children. Single women also face great disadvantages in humanitarian-based admissions with only 40 women admitted for every 100 men in the same years (Boyd 2001, 112).

During the same period just over half the women admitted as refugees were the principal applicants, compared with 91 percent of the men. There are many reasons for this: given their subordination in their countries of origin women are less likely to meet admission criteria based on education, employment, and social opportunities; refugee services do not usually select women and children for permanent resettlement because they are perceived as only temporarily separated from fathers and husbands. Most important, the United Nations convention on refugees still does not include gender as grounds for persecution (Boyd 2001; 1994, 9).

In response to mounting pressure from refugee advocates, the Canadian Immigration and Refugee Board (IAB) (the body that determines who is declared a Convention Refugee and therefore entitled to protection and resettlement) released guidelines in 1993, strengthened in 1996, to assist its members in assessing claims that those before them face gender-based persecution in their own countries (Rinehart 1995, B6; Boyd 2001, 118). These stood as a model for similar guidelines in the US and Australia. But whether and how much they have improved women's chances of being declared Convention Refugees is still unclear. For example, being opposed to the laws and practices that subordinate women to men in her country of origin is not enough: a woman needs to show that she has a "genuine fear of harm [sufficient] to constitute persecution" (Boyd 2001, 17).

But these guidelines only apply to women seeking refugee status from inside Canada (Boyd 2001, 117). Yet, as Amnesty International confirms, women are subject to rape in wars and to sexual and other abuses as refugees: "Women are raped in custody. They're flogged for violating dress codes. They risk being stoned to death for so-called sexual offenses or they find themselves jailed because of family connections" (Anita Tiessen quoted in the *Globe and Mail*, 1995, A10). In the 1980s women's "particular vulnerabilities" (Thompson 1995) while in flight or in temporary camps were partially recognized in the United Nations Women at Risk program (Boyd 2001, 118). But Nancy Worsfold, executive director of the Canadian Council for Refugees, has faulted the Canadian response for failing to keep its promise to identify women and children in danger abroad and resettle them in Canada. Indeed, "the paperwork for the program is so slow that the UN High Commission for Refugees hesitates to refer women to the Canadian program because the program itself can put women in the [refugee] camps in danger" (*Winnipeg Free Press* 1995; Boyd 2001, 118–20). Just over 1000 people were admitted under this program from 1988 to 1997—some 350 families, small numbers "when compared with the large refugee populations in which women and children predominate" (Boyd 2001, 121).

Within international refugee law, however, experts report the development of new "gender asylum" provisions which interpret "forms of violence against women" within the broad legal systems created by the international community to address human rights abuses. These include the human rights regime which seeks to monitor and deter abuse, and the more limited refugee rights regime which seeks to protect qualifying people who are able to cross borders (Anker and Lufkin 2002, 134–5). Defining gender persecution in human rights terms has made significant headway but some argue that the international community has no right to declare that cultural practices such as Female Genital Mutilation (FGM) constitute a violation of core human rights. There has been more success with refuge law which "does not seek to reform states and does not address root causes [because] its role is [ultimately] palliative" (153–4). Canada provided a precedent when the

Canadian Immigration and Refugee Board found that "the return of a woman to Somalia to face involuntary infibulation [FGM] violated...numerous provisions of the UDHR [Universal Declaration of Human Rights] and the ICCPR [International Covenant on Civil and Political Rights]" (145).

Anker and Lufkin point out since "the legalized refugee regime consists almost exclusively of states in the North determining refugee claims from the South, these purportedly international human-rights-based judgments [may appear] patronizing and hypocritical, [particularly] in gender persecution cases, since violence against women (including intra-family violence) is prevalent throughout the world" (2002, 152–3). While many feminists in the South work to end various practices like FGM, they criticize feminists in the North who want to play a leadership role in the South and fail to acknowledge ongoing practices in their own "enlightened" countries that are oppressive and dangerous for women. However, Uma Narayan demonstrates that if we attend to the specific causes of violence against Third World women, "we can see genuine connections across cultures" and thereby "develop viable strategies for eliminating women's oppression that make credible, general ethical claims" (cited in Quillen 2001, 114–15).

Canada's immigration policies can also place at risk those women who are admitted as immigrants and refugees. For example, as Monica Boyd points out, while a woman could "hypothetically...claim domestic violence as grounds for persecution" she is surely unlikely to do so given the Immigration Review Board's practice of hearing the refugee claims of spouses jointly (Boyd 2001, 117). As dependants, women have been denied access to (admittedly inadequate) resettlement programs, including language training (Man 2002, 26–32). Running through immigration and refugee policies at both the international and national levels are patriarchal assumptions that women will be protected and supported by male family members. How contradictory this is given the need for refugee policies that take into account women's "particular vulnerabilities" that are in fact the consequences of male domination and privilege, and that follow women from their country of origin through flight as refugees and, for the "fortunate" few, to their new home in Canada.

At first glance, Canada's restrictive policies on refugees and immigrants seem at odds with the rhetoric on globalization that encompasses free trade, free exchange of goods and services, and the fantastic development of the Internet. Yet not only do these developments co-exist with the punitive barriers to the movement of people, but the processes involved in globalization have contributed massively to the exponential growth in refuges willing to risk everything for a crack at life in Canada.

According to dominant political and business discourse, the dynamics of "globalization will raise standards of human rights, law, ethics and corporate governance around the world, even in dismal Africa....No pollution, no barriers, no dogmas, no sweatshops..." (Dudley Fishburn quoted in Ng 2002, 74). But in other readings, globalization means social dislocation, increased poverty, environmental degradation, more unpaid work for women, soaring infant and child mortality, declining wages for those who have work, the end of job security, and the decline and privatization of social services. Indeed, some researchers abandon the word globalization and refer instead to "global restructuring" to reflect the critical approaches that investigate the "highly gendered" (Marchand and Runyan 2000, 12), "multi-dimensional, multispeed and disjuncted processes" that are involved in the attempt to construct a "new world order" (ibid., 7).

GENDERING GLOBAL RESTRUCTURING

These broad relations of power in which we are all enmeshed have structured feminist organizing internationally. Third World women have challenged the perspectives and pre-rogatives of Western feminists in every venue including women's international organizations and networks, international forums like the United Nations, and academia. Theoretically much of this work emerged from the "painful debates" between First and Third World feminists about the relevance of feminism internationally, debates which "triggered the articulation of a new gendered political economy by socialist feminists and feminists in the South" and involved a "fundamental critique of economic development" (O'Brien et al. 2000, 35).

According to Deborah Steinstra, "economic justice remains the poor sister of women's transnational organizing" for several reasons: "the complexity of the issues involved, the powerful actors who dominate the global economy, the mystification of economics which prevents many from understanding it...and the disparities between and among women around the world based on class, the international division of labour, ethnicity and colonization" (2000a, 218; O'Brien et al. 2000, 38). Although it was not my original intention, this chapter came to revolve around economic inequalities—how they have been deepened and exacerbated by the victory of the market and by women's stoical and creative resistance. Immersion in contemporary writings of Third World feminists focuses the mind not only on the tremendous and growing inequalities between women and men and among women, but also on the consequences of this for much else including women's health and education, violence against women, women's sexuality, and environmental degradation.[2]

Feminist researchers investigate global restructuring in its many manifestations without succumbing to cynicism or despair that all this is inevitable. Rather, they seek to bring to light the many ways in which women worldwide cope with and resist the changes that affect them so negatively (Marchand and Runyan 2000). Deborah Barndt chose to follow "the journey of the corporate tomato from a Mexican agribusiness to a Canadian supermarket...as a device for examining globalization from above (the corporate agendas) and globalization from below (the stories of lowest-waged women workers in these sectors" (2002a, 82) (see Box 7-2).

Barndt's remark that "tomatoes...are often treated better than the workers" reminds me of the common observation in the English countryside during the enclosure movement in the early days of capitalist agriculture: namely, that the sheep looked better than the people. With the dispossession of peasants from the land, people were forced to find waged work. Yet, wages barely covered their own subsistence (that is, food and drink), let alone support for children or a spouse. Nor had people developed institutions to support themselves through the exigencies of life on earth: care for infants and children, for the sick, for those without work, for those working for wages that were below subsistence. Women faced a double bind, from which they have yet to recover: once they lost access to land they had to work for wages and care for children at the same time. If they didn't do the first, they all starved; if they didn't stay home, their babies would die (Hamilton 1978). Through the great social movements for unions, socialism, social welfare, and feminism, women joined struggles to develop laws and institutions to mitigate the vagaries of the capitalist marketplace. Over time, the liberal belief in the marketplace as the ideal regulator of social life came to be tempered by the acknowledgment of the consequences that accompanied

BOX 7-2	**Women, Work, and Globalization of the Tomato Trail**

The Indigenous migrant workers brought by truck from the poorer states to the Santa Rosa plantation for the harvest represent the most "flexible" members of the workforce. They are so flexible, in fact, that they take their kids out of school, leave their own plots of land behind, and move entire families to horrendous migrant labour camps surrounding the tomato fields. There, women not only bear the burden of backbreaking work under the hot sun, but many carry their babies on their backs and double their picking pace to fill the quotas of their working children. They are literally in foreign territory, as most don't speak Spanish, the dominant language, and can't ask for the support to which they're entitled. They must use their minimal wages to purchase food often sold by the company and find it difficult to maintain their own culinary practices, let alone eat healthily. If they get ill from pesticide exposure, they have difficulty securing medical assistance. Their domestic duties are also more arduous, since their living quarters usually lack basic necessities, such as water and electricity.

As we see within the hierarchy of women working for Santa Rosa, class and race conspire with gender to create different conditions. The mestizo packers brought by the company as a mobile maquila fare much better than the Indigenous field-workers. They make as much as eight times the amount as field-workers, partly because they are flexible (without family responsibilities) and can work 10- to 12-hour days during peak season. Their schedules and assembly line tasks are determined by

company needs and rhythms, and they comply. In turn, the company does not punish them when they take a day off to recover energies, because they are being paid by the hour and can be temporarily replaced. Their ultimate flexibility is in their willingness to leave their families behind and move from one production site to another, the skilled female labour of the tomato business. Some see this as a temporary sacrifice, allowing them to amass savings to buy land, get married, and settle down, but older women have become wedded to the company and have lost all opportunity to create a family, due to their flexibility to meet corporate needs. For many, this is the only way they can contribute to the family wage, and so it is, once again, a sacrifice of family for family.

This paradox was most dramatically illustrated by the story of Irena, [a] transnational migrant worker [who] leaves her family behind in Mexico for four months every year to pick locally produced tomatoes in Canada. While her wage is considerably higher than that of Mexican internal migrants, she must still work during the eight months she is at home, however, leaving her family once again to take care of a couple of invalids as a live-in domestic.

What does flexibility look like at the consumption end of the tomato chain? The epitome of part-time workers, McDonald's employees, especially young women, are sought for their willingness to meet erratic and short shifts, allowing the company to avoid paying benefits. Scheduling is determined by the labour/hour ratio, and workers complain of being asked to leave when restaurant traffic is slow. [T]heir flexibility at work also translates into eating practices that are, at best, equally flexible and, at worst, isolating and unhealthy.

Loblaws' labour strategies in the past decade have also mirrored this trend toward increasingly part-time and ever-more flexible labour. Cashiers, not coincidentally primarily female, have effectively lost full-time status, as concession bargaining has increased the part-time contingent, buying out higher paid full-timers and part-timers alike and rolling back wages to lower starting salaries and longer waiting periods before receiving benefits or raises. While, ironically, unionized part-time cashiers in the stores have more job stability than women working full-time on contract in Loblaws' head office, seniority reigns in scheduling. This means that the younger students who've put in less time with the company may only get four hours a week of work and can be called to work on the weekends when they'd like to be out socializing. It is assumed that, like young McDonald's employees, they will be flexible as part and parcel of their apprenticeship in the business world; low wages and erratic hours go with the territory of youth employment, seen as a sacrifice they make in working their way up the ladder.

While such flexibility may often suit student needs, it most definitely suits corporate interests, as food companies like McDonald's and Loblaws determine labour needs in concert with customer flow and inventory control. The just-in-time production of post-Fordist practices not only extends the scientific management that serves the profit motives of the corporations but is made possible by both flexible labour and new technologies. In the Loblaws case, particularly, the same scanning technology that has allowed global monitoring of inventory has speeded up cashiers' work and increasingly monitored their productivity. Ironically, the very technology that makes them more efficient for the company's bottom line could eventually replace them. This is why unions like the United Food and Commercial Workers claim concession bargaining is a defensive strategy to save jobs, even as those jobs get reduced in time and wage levels. They fear not only that companies like Loblaws will move their operations to their nonunionized lower waged affiliated discount stores but that jobs like cashiers will be eliminated by new technologies that require minimal work at the front end and have consumers scanning their own groceries in big boxes.

Source: Abridged from Deborah Barndt, *Tangled Routes*, Garamond Press, Toronto, 2002. Reprinted with the permission of Garamond Press.

the untrammelled pursuit of profits. But only after the Great Depression of the 1930s, did a social consensus emerge of the role that governments should play, nationally and through building international institutions—in regulating the marketplace and in redistributing resources (Leys 1996).

During the last two decades of the twentieth century, however, we witnessed the re-emergence in world affairs of the unregulated marketplace as the source of all that is worthy. Given that this worldview echoes ideas of the eighteenth century liberals, this era earns the label neo-liberal. Not surprisingly, what caused havoc and misery in the eighteenth century in newly capitalizing societies is now causing misery worldwide. This is "global-ization from below." In a nutshell, the terms under which globalization is occurring serve to make rich countries richer and poor countries poorer, and rich people richer and poor people poorer, wherever they live. The new consensus aggressively pursues the notion that markets rather than national states are "the preferred means for allocating jobs, goods and services" (Armstrong and Armstrong 2002, 49).

Several interconnected developments made it possible for transnational corporations (TNCs) "to begin treating the whole world not just as a single market, but also as a single production site." In order to operate in many different countries they developed "large legal and technical departments to negotiate with governments and engage in 'regulatory arbi-trage,' getting the greatest possible advantage out of the differences between national reg-ulatory regimes" (Leys 2001, 8–11). Tax shelters became crucial, and in response govern-ments competed to provide "business-friendly" environments. But neo-liberal triumph was not inevitable. National governments, in political scientist Colin Leys' words, also adopt-ed neo-liberal domestic policies as a "political project to defeat socialism" (2001, 12). We have seen the most powerful governments in the world back the interests of TNCs by enter-ing into free trade agreements, agreements that met vociferous opposition in Canada from a broad coalition of feminists, labour and environmental activists, and cultural critics, among others. These agreements, including the North American Free Trade Agreement with the US, Canada, and Mexico (NAFTA), not only brought down long-standing tariff barriers to free trade, but engaged in regulating what are called the non-tariff barriers, namely any government program, policy, law, or regulation that might give one country an advantage over another (Cohen et al. 2002, 6–14; Ellwood 2001, 60).

But free trade, like the "free" market is a misnomer: through the World Trade Organization (WTO), the richest countries ensure that their economies are bolstered at the continuing expense of the poorest countries. Perhaps the WTO's greatest (if unintended) consequence has been the mobilization of the largest and most diverse social movement on the contemporary landscape, aimed at nothing less than dismantling the WTO agenda. Everywhere and every time the WTO meets so do the protestors from labour unions, NGOs, political parties, and indigenous communities around the world (Starhawk 2002, 155–59; Foster 2002, 165–68: Kennelly 2002, 160–64; Nagra 2003).

Prior to an informal session of the WTO in Montreal in July 2003, the respected inter-national agency Oxfam garnered over a million names for its petition calling for fair trade practices. "In their rhetoric," Oxfam charges, "governments of rich countries constantly stress their commitment to poverty reduction. Yet [they] use their trade policy to conduct what amounts to robbery against [the] world's poor." The rules of the WTO on "intellectu-al property, investment, and services protect the interests of rich countries and powerful TNCs, while imposing huge costs on developing countries." The Montreal meeting did nothing to dispel Oxfam's concerns, and the agency urged developing countries to unite against the pressures of the rich countries at the WTO's next full session (2003).

The actions of international organizations, including the World Bank and the International Monetary Fund (IMF), have been singled out for their dramatically deleteri-ous effects in Third World countries, in particular, but for less advantaged peoples every-where (Armstrong and Armstrong 2002). During the 1960s and 1970s, developing coun-tries followed the lead of developed countries in accumulating large debts (the United States became the largest debtor nation) (Leys 1996, 21). Beginning in the early 1980s developing countries were forced to turn to the IMF for loans. The IMF makes these loans "highly conditional,…often placing major constraints upon state autonomy" including requirements for liberalization, deregulation, privatisation, and fiscal reform (O'Brien et al. 2000, 162). This conditionality is the focus of what Lee Ann Broadhead calls "the much despised" Structural Adjustment Programs (2002, 180). In order to qualify for loans and other economic aid, countries must show their compliance with the rules of the market-place by cutting government social spending—whether on health, education, or any policy that served to protect people from the workings of the market (Leys 1996, 23), including land distribution and food subsidy programs (Barndt 2002b, 173–76).

Feminists among other critics have challenged the policies of the IMF and the World Bank but this is uphill work. In the assessment of Anne Marie Goetz, the policy discourses of the women's movements and these international agencies

> could not be more different. [While the] driving concern of liberal economics is to improve market efficiency…the driving concern of feminist economics is gender justice, righting the wrongs experienced by women because of their sex, including the derogation of the value of their work, the limits on their rights to property ownership, unequal access to education, employment or positions of public power, and even the denial of women's rights to control their bodies and sexuality. (O'Brien et al. 2000, 47–8)

While neo-liberal assumptions render women's work invisible (World Bank cited in O'Brien 2000, 37), the feminist economics lens reveals the irony of market-driven policies expanding women's work. State cutbacks mean that women everywhere must expand their domestic responsibilities to compensate for decreasing state investment in such matters as children's education and health, care for disabled, and pensions for aging adults. This process transforms what had been public goods and citizenship entitlements into saleable commodities, thus exacerbating "gender biases in household decisions about which children to educate or bring to the clinic, with girls often losing out" (O'Brien 2000, 37). Even more detrimental are the adjustment measures which aim to encourage production for the market and for export. For example, in regions where women dominate agricultural production men may demand increased inputs of women's labour on crops sold for cash and export, "thus undermining the food security of families" (O'Brien 2000 37–8).

In the developed world, as well, the reign of the free market has produced "declining real wages for the least skilled, dramatic increases in inequality of incomes and wealth, higher unemployment and declining levels of collective provision that only yesterday had defined the kinds of societies people wanted to live in" (Leys 1996, 194). Among the casualties of this decline are "support for gender and other kinds of equality," as well as social services and social security, all of which bring "corresponding increases in social distress, marginalization, racism, crime, violence and political alienation" (Leys 1996, 194; Marchand and Runyan 2000, 17–18).

Letting the market reign supreme has been justified politically by arguing that the interests of those seeking profits dovetail with the interests and needs of most people through the so-called "trickle down" effect. If governments and international financial regulators create good conditions for investment, the argument goes, everyone will benefit. In this scenario "women's concerns with social justice" may be interpreted as "attempts to impose market distortions" (O'Brien 2000, 34), as "subjective and value-laden," or as "anecdotal [and] controversial" (ibid., 55–6). At best, as a sympathetic Executive Director of the World Bank noted, gender may be portrayed as a "series of special problems…rather than a social relation which underlies and needs to be addressed" in all economic policy (quoted in O'Brien 2000, 52).

Under the regime of market-driven politics, taxes for most public projects become a bad thing (unless they are to bankroll private investment, the military or security of the state). This belief is surprisingly widely shared. In my first year sociology class, students respond to my question: "What do you think of taxes?" by claiming "Taxes are bad and governments take our money." While it is perplexing that university students who benefit as much as anyone, and more than most, from taxation would hold this view, their complicity is a measure of the success of those building "the new consensus."

Sociologically speaking, taxes represent a relationship between people. No matter how rich we may be, we can't build our own sewer systems, our own universities or our own hospitals. This was the great discovery of previous generations coping with the rise of capitalism and industrialization. Living together must be a collective enterprise. What happens when this idea becomes an object of scorn? Canadians—especially residents of Walkerton in 1999 and Toronto in 2003 during the SARS epidemic—discovered what happened with the erosion of public utility and public health systems. In a global economy, however, not only national taxation systems but a "progressive international income tax" would be "a rational form of insurance against world disorder" (Leys 1996, 195). Such an idea seems utopian in the current political interpretation but as the consequences of a world left to market imperatives become clearer, political responses are in the making.[3]

An excellent issue of *Canadian Woman Studies*, entitled "Women, Globalization and International Trade" (2002), provides a rich and varied account of the effects of global restructuring on women in Canada and throughout the world (Lévesque 2002, 51–54). From this remarkable collection I have selected four themes—land and agriculture, wage labour, social support, and ecology—that reveal how women's lives have deteriorated as well as some examples of how they have resisted. Interestingly, although writers acknowledge that global restructuring produces different effects for women in Canada, and women in the Third World (as well as many differences among women in both locations), many also point out remarkable similarities (Lévesque 2002, 51–54).

Land and Agriculture

Historically, the social relations of capitalism throw people off their land. Their land becomes the site of new capitalist agriculture, and landless people are forced onto the wage labour market. In developing countries women are responsible for up to 80 percent of their country's food production, and unlike men they produce food "often intended for use in their own households and communities." In subsistence economies whole communities would starve without the food produced and processed by women (Storey 2002, 191).

While land concentration has long been a problem, structural adjustment policies have "stripped away mechanisms for community land ownership and counteracted progressive land reform programs." Families and communities can no longer ensure food security. Men leave to find work, and "women are left on their own to scrabble a living for their children" (ibid., 193). Increased trade is heralded as "the magical answer to problems of global malnutrition, despite ample evidence that such trade may actually make access to food more precarious for many of the world's poorest people." In response, Via Campesina, a global movement representing family farms, farm workers, landless peasants, rural women's groups, and indigenous peoples, "advocates taking agriculture completely out of the WTO, NAFTA and other agreements" (194). "Neoliberal trade agreements" they argue, "interfere with socially just forms of agrarian reform and access to land, and hence with the right of women to gain land title, to carry out their traditional responsibilities to the environmental health of the land, and to speak in their own right when agreements are being negotiated" (194–5).

Compare this analysis with a recent endorsement by then-heir apparent to Prime Minister Chrétien, Paul Martin, and Ernesto Zedillo, former president of Mexico, that "from China to Chile, from South Korea to South Africa, there is little disputing any more that private investment is the driving engine behind prosperity and growth." Their only concern was that this investment "too rarely benefits the poorest of the poor" and that, surprisingly (to them), 54 countries were poorer in 2000 than they were in 1990. Their solution is to unblock all remaining impediments to private investment (Martin and Zedillo 2003). One wonders if they have heard, for example, of the recently patented "Terminator" seed that prevents seeds from germinating when replanted. Farmers will now be forced to purchase a fresh supply of seeds every year, giving the corporations total control over seeds. "The immense gain for corporate agriculture comes," in Seema Kulkarni's words, "at the expense of women's capacity to ensure food security for their families" (2002, 198).

With food production treated as an industry like any other, trade provisions about agriculture not only impoverish farmers but also override "the status of food as a human right under the terms of the UN Declaration of Human Rights" (Storey 2000, 194). Around the world, women take responsibility "for guaranteeing the necessities of life to all family members so that trade agreements "that suck resources out of the community and into corporate pockets" affect them more negatively (194).

Farm women in Canada, as elsewhere, report "far too large a reproductive and productive workload that becomes even larger whenever the family is under economic stress" (194). Economic hardship has forced a steep decline in men and women working on the land, and those who remain report increased stress, tension, fatigue, and illness from the erosion of agriculturally focused support programs (Gerrard et al. 2000). Shannon Storey, chair of Canada's National Farmers Union International Program Committee, declares that "farm families in Canada and around the world have had their already challenging lives turned upside down by a vision of global trade that views food as just another commodity in the marketplace" (2002, 190).

Many critics of corporate agriculture not only agree that food production should be left out of large international trade agreements but that local subsistence agriculture and trade are critical to family and community survival and must be protected in order to achieve food security. Women do most of this agricultural work; many credit women's removal from land as key to the destruction of communities. In Kenya, women of the Freedom Corner movement including the Muuungana wa Wanavijiji (Organization of Villagers), along with many other groups in Africa, work towards offering "a subsistence alternative to corporate world trade by growing their own food, by repudiating the production of export crops, reinvigorating regional subsistence trade routes, by defending the land of subsistence producers and the market sites of subsistence traders" (Brownhill and Turner 2002, 176). For Canadian researchers Leigh S. Brownhill and Terisa E. Turner, "Freedom Corner reveals the sophistication of an historically deep movement of dispossessed Kenyan women engaged in defending the freedom to live outside of an increasing commodified world order" (2002, 176).

Those people involved in what has been called the "subsistence perspective" call for "the re-establishment of our sense of individual and collective power over our bodies, beliefs, communities, land, food [and markets] in order to redirect our labour towards the creation of use value, abundance, fertility, and life and away from the production of exchange value, scarcity, violence and death" (Bennholdt-Thomsen et al. 2001, x). In Canada too, some feminists have called for rebuilding lives outside the dominant economic order. Canadian Suzanne Mackenzie led the way in developing feminist geography and, in one of her last articles, she speculated on how people live/will live in other ways by telling the story about how one woman and her neighbours "altered their environments in the course of altering their lives." This woman, Mackenzie writes, "stands some time in the not-too-distant future, and looks back at our cities" (1993, 190). The woman is Suzanne Mackenzie herself whose vision flowed directly from her path-breaking research on how women managed in Canadian towns once the jobs left, and social security nets disappeared (1986; 1987) and people "said there was no money to pay for meeting human needs that could not be met by the market." Mackenzie's story proceeds through recounting conversations that she has heard, and that she invents.

The woman in the story "seems to argue that the environments she and her neighbours are creating [work well]: that is, they enable greater choice by providing flexible resources" (1993, 190). This is Suzanne Mackenzie's vision, part of her legacy to the feminist communities she loved so much:

> The shape of the home and community began to change, including its concrete walls and paths. At first, it was just that things seemed shabbier, the paint peeled, grass grew in deserted supermarket parking lots, the cars were older, there were a growing number of boarded-up buildings. Gradually, the shabbiness became invisible, turned into something else. We put home-made playground equipment in the overgrown parking lots and built a small grandstand in one. People tore down backyard fences...and created block gardens and play spaces. They moved in together, and the whole block used an empty house for a food co-op, play centre, drop-in clinic, and meeting place....A few years ago, we moved all the washing machines that still worked into one house and took turns doing each other's laundry. We even do some cooking that way now, and we use one house as a workshop to make things that other people need and will pay or trade for. We spend most of our time here, working and living....Often it feels we are only hanging on, waiting for something. But then, too, it feels that we are hanging on to what really matters. (199–200)

Remembering earlier days Mackenzie's mother charged that her daughter and her friends had "given up, [that] public money...should be paying for childcare, health care, housing."

But, Mackenzie replies that "we also have to survive. We cannot wait to feed ourselves and the children or love and comfort each other until someone gives us the resources to do it better. [W]e must ask for resources from the basis of what we have built here, an economy built on our immediate human needs. We must extend the resources and the values of serving human needs outwards, to other groups of people, like and unlike us" (1993, 199–200).[4]

For 30 years German eco-feminist Maria Mies has contributed to the theoretical and practical development of this subsistence perspective (Bennholdt-Thomsen et al. 2001, xi). Mies argues that "violence against women is the 'necessary' method for maintaining the exploitative international and sexual division of labour" that is the hallmark of capitalism, and she cites as examples of contemporary violence "mass rapes, dowry killings, forced sterilization, sex tourism" as well as the "use of Third World women as guinea pigs" for drug testing by transnational industries (Mies 2001, 6). When people are dispossessed from their land, they turn to their only alternative, selling their labour power for a wage, and in many parts of the globe this alternative has become increasingly precarious.

Wage Labour

To understand what is happening to wage labour we can return to Marx's insight about the innermost secret of capitalism. Workers appear to get paid for what they produce but in fact get paid for their labour power. The difference between what they produce and what they earn contributes to surplus value, namely profits. But, Marx added, overall wages cannot slip below subsistence, or the workers would die: hence capitalism requires a subsistence wage. But what happens when—as in the current era—the supply of workers greatly exceeds demand, and people cannot support themselves or their families? The point is that for capitalism it doesn't matter, and in a world of market-driven politics, that's what counts (Leys 1996, 193).

During the past 200 years workers formed unions and struggled for better wages and improved working conditions, and men and women developed political parties to fight for legislation that would protect them in sickness, in old age, during pregnancy. Propelled by feminism, women joined these struggles, and in Canada and other developed capitalist societies their wages and working conditions also improved. With the development of capitalism in the rest of the world, many believed (it was an article of faith among liberals and within dominant social scientific theories including modernization and functionalism) that wages would also eventually respond to the demands of workers, producing a gradual improvement worldwide. Instead, a reverse process is in full swing. Capital continues to be diverted from venues where workers are better paid, unions are strong, and where legislation like unemployment insurance and old age pensions provides workers with some security, for places where lower wages produce higher profits. Once a trickle, now a deluge, and male and female workers in many Western industries have been left reeling. Permanent jobs are increasingly replaced by contract employment, leaving people without safety nets, unable to plan their futures, and insecure about the present (Lévesque 2002, 51–4).

Rising rates of unemployment lead governments to offer incentives to industries to relocate in their areas. Call centres have been attracted to New Brunswick, for example, by government incentives, money for training, low payroll and other taxes, low wages, and the relative absence of unions. In her study of these call centres, Joan McFarland noted there are striking differences between them and the maquiladoras—the labour factories that sprang up in Mexico following the NAFTA (2002, 69; Labreque 2002, 100). Yet "both are the outcomes of strategies based on outside investment by footloose industries attracted by government incentives, have similarly structured workforces subject to the same worker 'burnout,' and involve the relaxation of laws and regulations affecting workers' health" (McFarland 2002, 29).

Global capital thrives as it hires poor, Third World, minority, and migrant women—in order to keep labour costs down and productivity up in the name of free trade, global competitiveness, and economic efficiency. Feminists have coined the phrase "the feminization of labour" to describe this aspect of global restructuring which depends on a flexible and casual labour force (Marchand and Runyan 2000, 16–17). The new mantra: be ready when you are needed, day or night, for as many hours as necessary, and expect nothing in return except a low hourly rate (no benefits, no vacation, no child care, no pension, no sick days). At the same time as work benefits hit the dust so did the state supports that men and women had struggled for so valiantly over the preceding century.

Social Support

With the unravelling of social security nets all over the world, women and men become more willing to take any kind of work under any kind of conditions. This is the strategy behind capital's international disciplining of work forces, a strategy dressed up in the language of higher productivity. With the dismantling of social spending on education, health and welfare, women disproportionately lost "good" jobs—not just "good" because they paid better salaries, but because their work helped their families and communities.

In Trinidad Rosetta Khalideen and Nadira Khalideen met women running a small eating establishment with the help of their young daughters. Some of them had once been teachers but as one of them noted "the teaching job doesn't pay anymore...not since the IMF" (2002, 108). The visitors were surprised: was not Trinidad "considered one of the most economically vibrant countries in the Caribbean due to successful economic reforms?" "I wonder where you're getting your story from," came the response. "Go around this island and talk to women here, they'll tell you a whole new side to the story" (2002, 108). As Khaideen and Khalideen subsequently discovered, "[t]he story of global economic restructuring for many Caribbean women...speaks of feminization of poverty, decreased consumption, and increased workloads, reduction in access to social welfare, and the erosion of gains in gender equality" (2002, 108; Marchand and Runyan 2000, 17–18). As elsewhere, women "make do" by working in the informal economy, reducing their families' consumption, and relying on remittances from family members abroad. Indeed, many of those from the Caribbean, the Philippines, and elsewhere who migrate to Canada (many under the Live-in Caregiver Program) send a high proportion of their earnings home. A 21-year-old Filipina caregiver whom I know sends half her modest monthly salary to her parents: this is what is expected, and she knows her family depends on her contribution. Others leave their small children with mothers or husbands, hoping to sponsor their move to Canada once they have completed their three years as live-in caregivers. In all these cases, women make choices from the available menu, and their willingness to migrate from home and loved ones speaks to the closing of opportunity in their own countries and their determination to seek a better life in Canada.

Environmental Impact

Human beings always have left their mark on their environment (Duncan 1996). Yet only in the past hundred years—and at a greatly accelerating rate—have we put the planet Earth in jeopardy. "The water cycle, the composition of the atmosphere, the assimilation of waste and recycling of nutrients, the pollination of crops, the delicate interplay of species"—all these basic life-support systems are in danger, "pushed to the brink" in Wayne Ellwood's words, "by growth-centred economics" (2001, 91). Yet despite tremendous pressure from environmental social movements these issues have not made significant inroads into the growth agenda of multilateral economic institutions (O'Brien 2000). Given that the Earth is our only "home and native land," the continuation of human life cannot be taken for granted, as environmental movements—including eco-feminism—across the globe argue.

Eco-feminists begin with the assumption that there is "a critical connection between the domination of nature and the domination of women" (Barndt 2002, 67). They accept women's affinity to nature but revalue the connection: women's connection with nature makes them more sensitive to violations to the earth, and to what is necessary to preserve life on this planet.[5] Today this call echoes in the words of feminist writers from various parts of the world. In her stinging critique of genetically modified organisms (GMO) Canadian activist/writer Helen Forsey declares: "Through all the talk of butterflies and bacteria, profits and preferences, neutraceuticals and novel foods, margins and marketability, almost no one seems to have noticed that the whole GMO enterprise reeks of patriarchy" (2002, 207). "Man's drive to 'dominate and control,'" she continues, "has always been dangerous to women, to children, and to other living things; but we have regularly been ignored, ridiculed and silenced—for daring to try and point this out" (ibid., 208). Forsey sees the impetus for GMOs as another dangerous male gamble to control life, and while she acknowledges that the position on GMOs does not break down on simple gender lines, she posits that the pro-GMO position is "inherently patriarchal" (208).

Indian feminist Vandana Shiva says bluntly: "globalization is giving rise to new slavery, new holocausts, new apartheid." Like Forsey, Shiva argues not only that genetic engineering is making "our fields sites of biological warfare," but also that "women's worlds are worlds based on protection—of our dignity and self-respect, the well-being of our children, of the earth, of her diverse beings, of those who are hungry and those who are ill" (2002, 16) (see Box 7-3).

| BOX 7-3 | **Violence of Globalization** |

Vandana Shiva, director of the Research Foundation for Science, Technology and Ecology, New Delhi, provided this testimony at the Women's Court held in South Africa on March 8, 2001.

We thought we had put slavery, holocausts, and apartheid behind us—that humanity would never again allow dehumanizing and violent systems to shape the rules by which we live and die. Yet globalization is giving rise to new slavery, new holocausts, new apartheid. It is a war against nature, women, children, and the poor. A war that is transforming every community and home into a war zone. It is a war of monocultures against

diversity, of big against small, of wartime technologies against nature.

Technologies of war are becoming the basis of production in peacetime. Agent Orange, which was sprayed on Vietnam, is now being sprayed on our farms as herbicide along with Round Up and other poisons. Plants and animals are being genetically engineered, thus making our fields sites of biological warfare. And perverse intelligence is being applied to terminate life's cycles of renewal by engineering "Terminator" seeds to be sterile.

As the violence grows, the stress on societies, ecosystems, and living beings is reaching levels of breakdown. We are surrounded by processes of ecological and social breakdown.

Witness the events of our times which are now front page news. Cows in Europe being subject to bovine spongiform encephalopathy (BSE), millions of animals being burnt as foot-and-mouth disease spreads due to increased trade, farmers in India committing suicide in thousands, the Taliban destroying their heritage by vandalizing the Bamiyan Buddhas, a 15-year-old boy shooting his classmates in a Californian high school, ethnic cleansing.

All these are wars of peacetime occurring in our daily lives and the last expression of violence in a system that has put profit above life, commerce above justice....

Cows are herbivores, they are not meant to eat their own carcasses. But, in an industrial system of factory farming globalized under free trade rules of agriculture, it was "efficient" to grind up the meat of infected sheep and cows and turn it into cattle feed. This has spread BSE among cattle—a disease that can be transmitted to humans.

Children should be playing with their friends. Schools are not supposed to be war zones. But a culture of guns and violence, combined with one that has focused so exclusively on commerce and economic growth and material accumulation, has left future generations uprooted and unanchored, afraid and violent. Our children are robbed of childhood. [C]hildren are being pushed into prostitution or warfare, the only options for survival when societies break down. Across the Third World, hunger and malnutrition have grown as a result of structural adjustment and trade liberalization policies.

During 1979–81 and 1992–93, calorie intake declined by three percent in Mexico, 4.1 percent in Argentina, 10.9 percent in Kenya, 10.0 percent in Tanzania, 9.9 percent in Ethiopia. In India, the per capital cereal consumption declined by 12.2 percent for rural areas and 5.4 percent for urban areas. Denying food to the hungry and feeding the markets is one of the genocidal aspects of globalization. Countries cannot ensure that the hungry are fed because this involves laws, policies and financial commitments that are "protectionist"—the ultimate crime in the globalization regime.

Denying medicine to the ill so that the global pharmaceutical industry can make profits is another aspect of genocide. Under the Trade Related Intellectual Property agreement of the World Trade Organization, countries have to implement patent laws granting exclusive, monopolistic rights to the pharmaceutical and biotech industry. This prevents countries from producing low cost generic drugs. Patented HIV/AIDS medicine costs $15 000, while generic drugs made by India and Brazil cost $250–$300 for one year's treatment. Patents are, therefore, literally robbing AIDS victims of their lives.

However, in the world order of globalization dictated by commerce, greed and profits, it is providing cures through affordable medicine that is illegal. India, Brazil, and South Africa have been taken to the WTO Court (the Dispute Settlement Mechanism) because they have laws that allow low cost medicine to be produced. At the World Court of Women, we declare that laws that force a government to deny citizens the right to food and the right to medicine are genocidal.

Globalization is a violent system, imposed and maintained through use of violence. As trade is elevated above human needs, the insatiable appetite of global markets for resources is met by unleashing new wars over resources. The war over diamonds in Sierra Leone, over oil in Nigeria has killed thousands of women and children.

The transfer of people's resources to global corporations also makes states more militaristic as they arm themselves on behalf of commercial interests, and start wars against their own people. Violence has been used by the government against tribal people in areas where bauxite is mined in Orissa and in Koel Karo, where the building of a large dam was stopped. But it is not just non-renewable resources like diamonds, oil and minerals that global corporations want to own. They want to own our biodiversity and water. They want to transform the very fabric and basis of life into private property. Intellectual Property Rights (IPRs) on seeds and plants, animals and human genes are aimed at transforming life into the property of corporations. While falsely claiming to have "invented" life forms and living organisms, corporations also claim patents on knowledge pirated from the Third World. The knowledge of our mothers and grandmothers is now being claimed as inventions of western corporations and scientists. The use of neem (Azarichta Indica) as pesticide and fungicide was claimed to be an invention by the US Drug Administration and W.R. Grace. India challenged it and was able to have the patent revoked. The seeds and plants of basmati have been claimed as inventions by a US corporation called Ricetec. And these are only some examples of biopiracy which will lead to the absurd situation where the Third World pays for knowledge that evolved cumulatively and collectively.

From the Women's Court, we declare that patents on life and patents based on biopiracy are immoral and illegal. They should not be respected because they violate universal principles of reverence for life and the integrity of a culture's knowledge systems.

We will not live by rules that are robbing millions of their lives and medicines, their seeds, plants and knowledge, their sustenance and dignity and their food. We will not allow greed and violence to be treated as the only values to shape our cultures and our lives. We will take back our lives, as we took back the night. We know that violence begets peace and love begets love. We will reweave the world as a place of sharing and caring, of peace and justice, not a market place where sharing and caring and giving protection are crimes and peace and justice are unthinkable. We will shape new universals through solidarity, not hegemony.

Source: This testimony originally appeared in *The Hindu* on March 25, 2001, and was reprinted in *Canadian Woman Studies*, 21/22 (41) 15-16, 2002.

The cultural eco-feminism of Forsey and Shiva appears to fly in the face of postmodern feminism, the drive to "cure" feminism of essentialism, and of the possibility of men and women working together to preserve our world. Yet given the precarious position of the planet and of the lives of the majority of its inhabitants, we could read this as one discourse of resistance, along with many others. Positively, it conjures up a different world where life-affirming behaviours become paramount, and men trade control for stewardship.

Postmodern feminists have developed what may be called social eco-feminism to show how women and nature are wielded together to form "systems of domination." They seek to expose the dualism—women = nature, men = social—that informs these relationships as "an oppressive fiction rather than a fact of nature itself" (Sandilands 1999, 72). In some ways social eco-feminists see the process of gendering as even more pervasive than those who attach gender to biological difference. Consider how the discourse of global restructuring relies on notions of gendered symbols and metaphors "to ward off resistance by variously valorizing globalization, making it appear natural and inevitable, and dampening debate about its effects." As Charlotte Hooper discovered globalization narratives read like "rape scripts," based on the assumption that men and women play out fixed—and inevitable—gender roles of aggressors and victims (cited in Marchand and Runyan 2000, 12). In her analysis of *The Economist*, a major international business magazine, she explored the new tropes of masculinity for the globalized world but also found many examples of old-fashioned sexist language. "Ripe for Rape" ran the headline on a story about Myanmar with its teak forests waiting to be felled, and its gem deposits, and natural beauties, all awaiting exploitation by businessmen (ibid., 68–9). Eco-feminists join with the broader environmental movement, feminist movements, movements of indigenous peoples to expose and reverse these global processes that have brought such misery to people's lives even as they undermine the possibility of future generations inheriting the earth.

RESISTANCE TO GLOBALIZATION

Globalization may seem inexorable and immovable even to activists and researchers. As Deborah Barndt confessed: "My own digging into the tangled routes of the corporate tomato has made me wonder at times how we got here and how we could ever possibly challenge or transform any of the structures or ideas that hold the system in place" (2002, 229). Yet, in her study she breathes life—to use a metaphor—into relationships that might otherwise lie dormant. Once these relationships are made visible we may choose to act more consciously as we locate ourselves within the processes that she delineates. "Any action we take" Barndt counsels, "should be determined in collaboration with [local] groups who are working for environmental and social justice, and this can include working through trade unions, through NGOs that are linking workers, women, and environmentalists in the NAFTA context, or more broadly in the hemisphere" (ibid., 205).

Regardless of where we choose to act we need to know a lot. In her analysis of the garment industry in Canada, Roxanna Ng argues that "drastic measures are needed to ameliorate increasing labour rights violations," and she calls for "research, public education and activism." In order to act strategically people have to understand the processes involved in production, they have to understand the implications for people at every stage of the process (which may well occur in several different countries), and they must develop alliances in order to bring pressure on corporations, national governments and international agencies (2002, 79).

Resistance starts with the understanding that "globalization is about processes that result from actual decisions and practices, rather than forces beyond human control" (Armstrong and Armstrong 2002, 50). As indicated in this chapter, oppressive and exploitative processes elicit strategies for coping and resistance that may range from individual responses through local mobilizations to international actions. As feminists and other social movement activists know, collective resistance is difficult, partly because people are affected in different ways—and because not everyone suffers (at least not in the short term). Some people's advantages accrue from the misery of others. As the editors of the *Canadian Woman Studies* issue on globalization point out, we can "unthinkingly 'benefit' from cheap bananas picked by hungry, poisoned and scared indigenous Guatemalans who have lost their land to transnational corporations, and from inexpensive brand-name clothes produced by women in deplorable conditions in Free Trade zones all round the world" (Artobus et al. 2002, 3).

Canadians with pensions "benefit" when the mining companies that pension funds have invested in avoid the costs of environmental damage their activities cause in New Guinea, Surinam, Kirghizstan, or Costa Rica. Women of the Windward Islands (St. Vincent and the Grenadines) identified a fall in banana prices as contributing directly and indirectly to loss of access to food; health problems; and land not being actively farmed as women became unable to purchase seed and other tools of production. The WTO had ruled against the preferred status their family-raised bananas had enjoyed in European markets over cheaper products produced by multinationals. But the multinationals exploited their workers, overused chemicals, and engaged in monoculture cropping (Storey 2002, 192–3). Such methods produce cheaper bananas, but not forever; workers suffer terribly from the pesticides; and land becomes barren through the massive use of agrochemicals (Barndt 2002b, 199–200).

In Costa Rica, Canadian companies who engage in open-pit mining use the extremely toxic cyanide lixiviation technique which carries serious health risks for workers, and is "deadly" for the local environment. "The contamination of the water and the air" writes Ana Isla "has created much grief for rural women" who experience high levels of birth defects and child mortality (2002, 151). Isla's graphic description of the water of the Agua Caliente river, now "yellow and fetid with the odours of the chemicals" helps make it clear why local men and women actively fight their government and the mining companies in desperate attempts to prevent more mining. Women fighting the mines look for support from Canadian women, especially those "whose stocks, mutual funds, and pension funds directly contribute to the exploitation of nature" in their country (ibid., 154).

How do we acknowledge our own complicity and move to empathize and act alongside others? Feminist activist and writer Cynthia Cockburn decided to answer this question by studying women who work together in the most difficult situations, namely across ethnic differences in zones of conflict: Israeli and Palestinian women, Protestants and Catholics in Northern Ireland, and women in Bosnia-Herzegovina. "Groups act together with a shared purpose," she found, "only by means of conscious and careful processes of boundary-crossing, agenda setting and alliance-building." They put "a great deal of effort" into structuring a democratic space—"small enough for mutual knowledge, for dispelling myths, but big enough for comfort." Through a "careful and conscious handling of identity processes" they try to "sustain their alliances" (2000, 51). Italian feminists have coined the phrase "transversal politics" where each person brings her own experience and identity to the dialogue, but also makes "the imaginative shift that enables her to empathize and cooperate with women who have different membership" (Cockburn 2000, 50; Eschle 2001, 206–8, 212–19, 230–34).

If there are women everywhere who resist, individually and collectively, one must inquire if this constitutes a worldwide women's movement? The answer depends in part on the definition. Cynthia Cockburn says: if a "social movement is the non-powerful, non-wealthy and non-famous using both civil and confrontational means to transform the social world radically," then the answer is "Yes" (2000, 46). Drawing on extensive research Deborah Steinstra describes how "women's movements have taken their strength from the organizing done locally and nationally and translated it into transnational networks; caucuses at United Nations conferences on the environment, human rights, population, social development, women and habitat; strong regional networks; and organizations that deal with particular areas (2000a, 211; 2000b). Paralleling the powerful outreach of international capitalism, supported by national governments, are impressive transnational networks of women working in development. They include Development Alternatives for Women Working in a New Era (DAWN), African Women's Economic Policy Network, and Women in Development Europe; health and reproductive technologies—Women's Reproductive Health Coalition; women's rights as human rights—International Women's Rights Action Watch, the Asia-Pacific Forum on Women, and the Latin American Committee for the Defence of Women's Rights; trafficking in women—the Global Alliance Against Traffic in Women (see Steinstra 2000a and 2000b and O'Brien 2000).

Historically for feminists—going back to Mary Wollstonecraft—redressing economic inequality involves the struggle for women's economic independence, and for two main reasons. First, women's subordinate place in the family—even when they do most of the labour—means that higher family income does not necessarily mean more resources, more education, or more options for them. As Marchand and Runyan note "structural accounts of markets and states barely scratch the surface of the power relations embedded in civil society that enable the process of restructuring" (2000, 225). Third World women have been acutely aware of this as they observe the results of decades of development funding and projects that were channelled by and through men, and not only failed to reach women and their children but also further disadvantaged them. Empowerment has been a key concept in these feminist circles (Chowdry 1995, 36–8; Parpart 1995, 237), as has self-sufficiency and the subsistence perspective. Resources must be in the hands of women if they are to benefit, and the benefits are to flow to their children, especially their girl children. Otherwise, as Seema Kulkarni states, cash crops "mean more money to husbands and increased drudgery for women" (2002, 196).

Second, women's economic independence means the possibility of social and political independence. The story of women's dependence on husbands and fathers is not a happy one: asymmetrical power relations do not mandate violence, disrespect, and entitlement, but they permit all of this. When women are economically independent they are more likely to be in a position to decide whether and whom to marry, whether to stay, whether and with whom to have sex, whether to have children, and how many. In short, they are in a position to share their lives with men, with each other, or to live alone. Economic independence is not enough; it's no panacea but it may well be a precondition. Although waged or salaried work is the most likely route to economic independence in Canada, this can also accrue from owning a business, performing, creating and selling paintings, pottery, or glass, having access to land for growing food for use or sale, or from taxation that provides a guaranteed annual income.

Fighting for women's economic independence may not seem a radical project—except in a patriarchal world. The World Bank, for example, "demurs on assessing justice in gender relations because this is seen as cultural interference [and] the condemnation of inequities in gender relations is assumed to reflect a narrow, highly ideological, Western feminist perspective" (O'Brien et al. 2000, 51). Given the extent and range of women's mobilization in the South, however, there is no longer—if there ever was—any justification for dismissing the struggle for women's empowerment as an invention of Western feminism. Women everywhere decide in their own historical and cultural context what to struggle for, how to define themselves, and what they want.

My account of globalization moved from Fahima Osman through Canada's refugee policy to global restructuring and resistance. Understanding these processes makes it clear that no one manages alone; many of us manage because of the advantages accruing from national and global inequalities; for many others the road is jammed with humanly created obstacles. We need to remember that small things can make a difference. For example, two weeks after her story appeared in the *Globe and Mail* Fahima Osman wrote to the editor to express her wonder at the response she had been receiving from young people who found her story inspirational. "But most importantly," she continued, "you made my community very happy. There is hardly anything positive in the media about Somalis, and they were really proud of the story" (Greenspon 2002, A2).

CONCLUSION

Feminism remains a remarkably open discourse. In the name of feminism, activists and scholars have written grand meta narratives that sought to explain the pervasiveness of patriarchal relationship throughout time and space; they have written small local histories and accounts that display the workings of oppression and resistance in fine detail; they have interrogated every area of life to examine the relationships between men and women, and the discourses that animate social life whether in religious, economic, political, or cultural institutions, or within art, literature, music, and popular culture. They have been open to discourses from all the other progressive social movements in the twentieth century: anti-racist movements, movements of indigenous peoples, environmental, anti-globalization, labour, human rights movements, the list goes on. In the current economic-political environment feminism provides some of the most compelling counter-narratives to the story of triumphant capitalism and the victory of the "free market." Feminism works both to demystify the way things are and to expose the risks to the planet Earth and ourselves should we refuse to change our behaviour. Feminism also works to reveal the possibilities about how we might live with each other in relationships of sharing, reciprocity, pleasure, and delight.

NOTES

1. Feminist demographer Monica Boyd studied the educational attainments of the adult offspring of immigrants by analyzing data from the 1996 panel of the Survey of Labour and Income Dynamics. The sample was comparatively small, and the results complex and very interesting. In summary, "when compared to the overall average of 13.3 years of education for persons age 20–64," those who came to Canada before they were 15 as well as second generation visible minorities have more education than the rest of the Canadian population (2002, 1053).

2. For a similar perspective see Joan McFarland's *From Feminism to Human Rights: The Best Way Forward?* (1998, 50–61).

3. But at the same time, at this writing, US President Bush is seeking a new round of tax cuts designed to enrich wealthy individuals and corporations, reduce even more the resources of the growing numbers of poor people, and produce the $87 billion needed to pursue the war in Iraq and to send people to Mars.

4. For appreciations of Suzanne Mackenzie's pioneering work connecting feminist scholarship and radical politics, see the tributes by Audrey Kobayashi and others in *Gender, Place and Culture: A Journal of Feminist Geography* 6(4).

5. Catriona Sandilands provides an excellent discussion of the history and varieties of eco-feminism (1999).

References

Abel, Elizabeth. 1990. "Race, Class and Psychoanalysis. Opening Questions." In *Conflicts in Feminism*. Ed. Marianne Hirsch and Evelyn Fox Keller. New York and London: Routledge.

Abel, Elizabeth, Barbara Christian, and Helene Moglen, eds. 1999. *Female Subjects in Black and White: Race, Psychoanalysis, Feminism*. Berkeley: University of California Press.

Abele, Frances. 1997. "Understanding What Happened Here: The Political Economy of Indigenous Peoples." In *Understanding Canada: Building on the New Political Economy*. Ed. Wallace Clement, 118–40. Montreal: McGill-Queen's University Press.

———, and Daiva Stasiulis. 1989. "Canada as a 'White Settler Colony': What about Natives and Immigrants?" In *The New Canadian Political Economy*. Ed. Wallace Clement and Glen Williams, 240–77. Montreal: McGill-Queen's University Press.

Abella, Irving. 1982. *None Is Too Many: Canada and the Jews of Europe, 1933–1948*. Toronto: Lester & Orpen Dennys.

Abrams, Philip. 1982. *Historical Sociology*. Somerset, England: Open Books Publishing.

Ackelsberg, Martha. 1997. "Rethinking Anarchism/Rethinking Power: A Contemporary Feminist Perspective." In *Reconstructing Political Theory: Feminist Perspectives*. Ed. Mary Lyndon Shanley and Uma Narayan, 158–177. University Park, Pennsylvania: Pennsylvania University Press.

Adams, Kathleen Pirrie. 1993. "Back to Estrus: Thoughts on Lesbian Bar Scenes." *Fireweed* 38, 2: 29–35.

Adams, Mary Louise. 1994. *The Trouble with Normal: Postwar Youth and the Construction of Heterosexuality*. Toronto: University of Toronto Press.

Adamson, Nancy. 1995. "Feminists, Libbers, Lefties and Radicals: The Emergence of the Women's Liberation Movement." In *A Diversity of Women: Ontario, 1945–1980*. Ed. Joy Parr, 252–80. Toronto: University of Toronto Press.

Adamson, Nancy, Linda Briskin, and Margaret McPhail. 1988. *Feminist Organizing for Change*. Toronto: Oxford University Press.

Agnew, Vijay. 1996. *Resisting Discrimination: Women from Asia, Africa and the Caribbean and the Women's Movement in Canada*. Toronto: University of Toronto Press.

Akyeampong, Ernest R. 1995. "The Labour Market: Year-end Review." In *Perspectives on Labour and Income*. Ottawa: Statistics Canada.

Albo, Gregory, and Jane Jenson. 1989. "A Contested Concept: The Relative Autonomy of the State." In *The New Canadian Political Economy*. Ed. Wallace Clement and Glen Williams, 180–211. Montreal: McGill-Queen's University Press.

———. 1997. "Remapping Canada: The State in the Era of Globalization." In *Understanding Canada: Building on the New Political Economy*. Ed. Wallace Clement, 215–39. Montreal: McGill-Queen's University Press.

Altergott, Marjorie. 1999. "Infant Feeding." In *Encyclopedia of Reproductive Technologies*. Ed. Annette Burfoot, 15–22. Boulder, Colorado: Westview Press.

Anderson, Karen. 1987. "A Gendered World: Women, Men, and the Political Economy of the Seventeenth-Century Huron." In *Feminism and Political Economy: Women's Work, Women's Struggles*. Ed. Heather Jon Maroney and Meg Luxton, 121–38. Toronto: Methuen.

———. 1988. "As Gentle as Little Lambs: Images of Huron and Montagnais-Naskapi Women in the Writings of the 17th Century Jesuits." *Canadian Review of Sociology and Anthropology* 25, 4: 560–76.

———. 1991. *Chain Her by One Foot*. London: Routledge.

———. 1996. *Sociology*. Scarborough: Nelson.

Anderson, Kim. 2000. *A Recognition of Being: Reconstructing Native Womanhood*. Toronto: Second Story Press.

Anderssen, Erin. 2003. "The New Canada: Dreamchild." *Globe and Mail*, 14 June, F1–5.

Andrew, Caroline. 1984. "Women and the Welfare State." *Canadian Journal of Political Science* 17, 4: 667–83.

Anker, Deborah E., and Paul T. Lufkin. 2002. "Refugee Law, Gender and the Human Rights Paradigm." *Harvard Human Rights Journal* 15: 133–154.

Arat-Koc, Sedef. 1989. "In the Privacy of Our Own Home: Foreign Domestic Workers as Solution to the Crisis in the Domestic Sphere in Canada." *Studies in Political Economy* 28 (Spring): 33–58.

Archibald, Kathleen. 1973. "Men, Women and Persons." *Canadian Public Administration* 16 (Spring): 14–24.

Arendt, Hannah. 1951. *Imperialism*. Part 2 of *The Origins of Totalitarianism*. New York: Harcourt, Brace & World.

Armstrong, Christopher, and H.V. Nelles. 1988. *Southern Exposure: Canadian Promoters in Latin America and the Caribbean, 1896–1930*. Toronto: University of Toronto Press.

Armstrong, Jeannette. 1996. "Invocation: The Real Power of Aboriginal Women." In *Women of the First Nations: Power, Wisdom and Strength*. Ed. Christine Miller and Patricia Chuchryk, ix–xii. Winnipeg: University of Manitoba Press.

Armstrong, Pat. 1996. "The Feminization of the Labour Force: Harmonizing Down in a Global Economy." In *Rethinking Restructuring: Gender and Change in Canada*. Ed. Isabella Bakker, 29–53. Toronto: University of Toronto Press.

———. 2001. "Evidence-Based Health-Care Reform: Women's Issues." In *Unhealthy Times: Political Economy Perspectives on Health and Care in Canada*. Ed. Pat Armstrong, Hugh Armstrong and David Coburn, 121–45. Toronto: Oxford.

———, and Hugh Armstrong. 1986. "Beyond Sexless Class and Classless Sex: Towards Feminist Marxism." In *The Politics of Diversity*. Ed. Roberta Hamilton and Michèle Barrett, 108–40. London: Verso.

———. 1988. "Women, Family and Economy." In *Reconstructing the Canadian Family: Feminist Perspectives*. Ed. Nancy Mandell and Ann Duffy, 143–74. Toronto: Butterworths.

———. 1990a. "Lessons from Pay Equity." *Studies in Political Economy* 32: 29–54.

———. 1990b. *Theorizing Women's Work*. Toronto: Garamond.

———. 1994. *The Double Ghetto: Canadian Women and their Segregated Work*. 3rd ed. Toronto: McClelland & Stewart.

————. 2002. "Thinking it Through: Women and Work in the New Milennium." *Canadian Woman Studies/les cahiers de la femme* 21/22 (4/1): 44–50.

————, and David Cockburn, eds. 2001. *Unhealthy Times: Political Economy Perspectives on Health and Care in Canada*. Toronto: Oxford.

————, Mary Cornish and Elizabeth Millar. 2003. "Pay Equity: Complexity and Contradiction in Legal Rights and Social Processes." In *Changing Canada: Political Economy as Transformation*. Ed. Wallace Clement and Leah Vosko, 161–82. Montreal: McGill-University Press.

Arnopoulos, Sheila McLeod. 1979. *Problems of Immigrant Women in the Canadian Labour Force*. Ottawa: Canadian Advisory Council on the Status of Women.

Atrobus, Peggy, Brenda Cranney, Ana Isla, Angela Miles, Patricia E. (Ellie) Perkings, Linda Christiansen Ruffman, Nandita Sharma, Shannon Storey, and Noulmook Sutdhibhasilp. 2002. "Editorial." *Canadian Woman Studies/les cahiers de la femme* 21/22 (4/1): 3.

Atwood, Margaret. 1988. *Cat's Eye*. Toronto: McClelland & Stewart.

Austin, Stephanie. 2001. "Collective Voices: Young Feminists' Experiences at POWER Camp." *Canadian Woman Studies/les cahiers de la femme* 20/21 (4/1): 129–33.

Avery, Donald. 1979. *"Dangerous Foreigners": European Immigrant Workers and Labour Radicalism in Canada, 1896–1932*. Toronto: McClelland & Stewart.

Bacchi, Carol Lee. 1983. *Liberation Deferred? The Ideas of the English-Canadian Suffragists, 1877–1918*. Toronto: University of Toronto Press.

Baines, Beverley. 1993. "Women and the Law." In *Changing Patterns: Women in Canada*. 2nd ed. Ed. Sandra Burt, Lorraine Code, and Lindsay Dorney, 243–78. Toronto: McClelland & Stewart.

————. Forthcoming. "Using the Canadian Charter of Rights and Freedoms to Constitute Women." In *Constituting Women: The Gender of Constitutional Jurisprudence*. Ed. Beverley Baines and Ruth Rubio Marin. Cambridge: Cambridge University Press.

Bair, Deidre. 1990. *Simone de Beauvoir: A Biography*. New York, N.Y.: Summit Books.

Bakan, Abigail B., and Daiva K. Stasiulis. 1995. "Making the Match: Domestic Placement Agencies and the Racialization of Women's Household Work." *Signs* 20, 2: 303–335.

Bakker, Isabella, ed. 1996. *Rethinking Restructuring: Gender and Change in Canada*. Toronto: University of Toronto Press.

————, and Katherine Scott. 1997. "From the Postwar to the Post-Liberal Keynesian Welfare State." In *Understanding Canada: Building on the New Political Economy*. Ed. Wallace Clement, 286–310. Montreal: McGill-Queen's University Press.

Bannerji, Himani. 1995. *Thinking Through: Essays on Feminism, Marxism and Anti-racism*. Toronto: Women's Press.

————. 1999. "A Question of Silence: Reflections on Violence Against Women in Communities of Colour." In *Scratching the Surface: Canadian Anti-racist Feminist Thought*. Ed. Enakshi Dua and Angela Robertson, 261–77. Toronto: Women's Press.

Barber, Marilyn. 1985. "The Women Ontario Welcomed: Immigrant Domestics for Ontario Homes, 1870–1930." In *The Neglected Majority: Essays in Canadian Women's History*. Vol. 2. Ed. Alison Prentice and Susan Mann Trofimenkoff, 102–21. Toronto: McClelland & Stewart.

Barndt, Deborah. 2002a. "'Fruits of Injustice': Women in the Post-NAFTA Food System." *Canadian Woman Studies/les cahiers de la femme* 21/22 (4/1): 82–89.

————. 2002b. *Tangled Routes: Women, Work, and Globalization on the Tomato Trail*. Aurora, ON: Garamond Press.

Barrett, Michèle. 1988. *Women's Oppression Today*. 2nd ed. London: Verso.

————. 1991. *The Politics of Truth*. Stanford: Stanford University Press.

————. 1992. "Psychoanalysis and Feminism: A British Sociologist's View." *Signs* 17 (Winter): 455–66.

————. 1999. *Imagination in Theory*. Cambridge: Polity Press.

————. 1999a. "Virginia Woolf Meets Michel Foucault." In *Imagination in Theory*. Cambridge: Polity Press, 186–204.

Bashevkin, Sylvia. 1989. "Free Trade and Canadian Feminism: The Case of the National Action Committee on the Status of Women." *Canadian Public Policy/Analyse de Politiques* 15, 4: 363–75.

————. 1993. *Toeing the Lines: Women and Party Politics in English Canada*. 2nd ed. Toronto: Oxford University Press.

Bashevkin, Sylvia, ed. 2002. *Women's Work is Never Done: Comparative Studies in Care-giving, Employment, and Social Policy Reforms*. New York and London: Routledge.

Batcher, Elaine. 1987. "Building the Barriers: Adolescent Girls Delimit the Future." In *Women and Men: Interdisciplinary Readings on Gender*. Ed. Greta Hofmann Nemiroff, 150–65. Richmond Hill, ON: Fitzhenry & Whiteside.

Baum, Gregory. 1986. *Liberation Theology and Marxism*. Montreal: McGill University.

Beattie, Christopher. 1975. *Minority Men in a Majority Setting: Middle-Level Francophones in the Canadian Public Service*. Toronto: McClelland & Stewart.

Beauvoir, Simone de. 1952. *The Second Sex*. New York: Knopf.

————. 1954. *She Came to Stay*. Cleveland: World Pub. Co.

Beavers, Suki et al. 2000. Editorial. *Canadian Woman Studies/les cahiers de la femme* 20 (3): 3–5.

Bégin, Monique. 1992. "The Royal Commission on the Status of Women: Twenty Years Later." In *Challenging Times: The Women's Movement in Canada and the United States*. Ed. Constance Backhouse and David H. Flaherty, 21–38. Montreal: McGill-Queen's University Press.

————. 1997. "The Canadian Government and the Commission's Report." In *Women and the Canadian State/Femmes et L'Etat Canadien*. Ed. Caroline Andrew and Sanda Rogers, 12–26. Montreal: McGill-Queen's University Press.

Bell, Brandi Leigh-Ann. 2001. "Women-Produced Zines Moving into the Mainstream." *Canadian Woman Studies/les cahiers de la femme* 20/21 (4/1): 56–60.

Bell, Daniel. 1960. *The End of Ideology*. Glencoe, Illinois: Free Press.

Bell, Laurie, ed. 1987. *Good Girls Bad Girls: Sex Trade Workers and Feminists Face to Face*. Toronto: Women's Press.

Belsey, Catherine. 1980. *Critical Practice*. London: Methuen.

Benjamin, Jessica. 1988. *The Bonds of Love*. New York: Pantheon Books.

————. 1994. "The Shadow of the Other (Subject): Intersubjectivity and Feminist Theory." *Constellations* 1 (2): 231–54.

Bennholdt-Thomsen, Veronika, Nicholas G. Faraclas, and Claudia von Werlhof. 2001. "Introduction." In *There is an Alternative: Subsistence and Worldwide Resistance to Corporate Globalization*. Ed. Veronika Bennholdt-Thomsen, Nicholas G. Faraclas, and Claudia von Werlhof, x–xv. London and New York: Zed Books.

Berg, Maggie. 1991. "Luce Irigaray's 'Contradictions': Post-Structuralism and Feminism." *Signs* 17: 50–70.

Bernard, Wanda Thomas. 2003. "Claiming Voice: An Account of Struggle, Resistance, and Hope in the Academy." In *Seen but not Heard: Aboriginal Women and Women of Colour in the Academy*. Ed. Rashmi Luther, Elizabeth Whitmore, and Bernice Moreau, 69–78. Ottawa: Canadian Research Institute for the Advancement of Women.

Bernstein, Judy, Peggy Morton, Linda Seese, and Myrna Wood. 1972. "Sisters, Brothers, Lovers...Listen...." In *Women Unite!* Toronto: Women's Press.

Bibby, Reginald, and Donald C. Posterski. 1992. *Teen Trends*. Toronto: Stoddart.

Bindman, Stephen. 1990. "Dismissed lesbian suing military." *Toronto Star*, 5 Feb., A3.

———. 1992. "Military gives OK to gays, lesbians." *Calgary Herald*, 28 Oct., A1.

Binkley, Marian. 1995. *Risks, Dangers, and Rewards in the Nova Scotia Offshore Fishery*. Montreal: McGill-Queen's University Press.

Black, Naomi. 1993. "The Canadian Women's Movement: The Second Wave." In *Changing Patterns: Women in Canada*. 2nd ed. Ed. Sandra Burt, Lorraine Code, and Lindsay Dorney, 151–76. Toronto: McClelland & Stewart.

Blackburn, Althea. 1995. "Fighting for the 'Family' Name: A Socio-legal Analysis of the Canadian Response to Same Sex Families in the Charter Era." MA thesis, Queen's University.

Borrows, John. 1994. "Contemporary Traditional Equality: The Effect of the Charter on First Nations Politics." *University of New Brunswick Law Journal* 43: 1–43.

Bose, Anuradha. 1972. "Consciousness Raising." In *Mother Was Not a Person*. Ed. Margret Andersen. Montreal: Black Rose Books.

Bouchard, Brigitte, and John Zhao. 2000. "University Education: Recent Trends in Participation, Accessibility and Returns." *Education Quarterly Review* 6 (4): 24–32.

Boyd, Monica. 1994. "Canada's Refugee Flows: Gender Inequality." *Canadian Social Trends* 32: 7–10.

———. 2001. "Gender, Refugee Status, and Permanent Resettlement." In *Immigrant Women*. Ed. Rita James Simon, 103–24. New Brunswick, New Jersey: Transaction Publishers.

———. 2002. "Educational Attainments of Immigrant Offspring: Success or Segmented Assimilation." *International Migration Review* 36 (4): 1037–60.

———, and Elizabeth Grieco. 2003. "Women and Migration: Incorporating Gender into International Migration Theory." *Migration Information Source*. www.migrationinformation.org/Feature/display.cfm?id=106. (Accessed August 10, 2003.) Washington, D.C.: Migration Policy Institute.

Boyd, Susan. 2003. "From Custody and Access to Parental Responsibilities? What does Bill C-22 Offer to Women and Children?" *Jurisfemme* 22 (1). www.nawl.ca.

Bradbury, Bettina. 1979. "The Family Economy and Work in an Industrializing City: Montreal in the 1870s." Canadian Historical Association *Papers*.

————. 1984. "Pigs, Cows and Boarders: Non-wage Forms of Survival Among Montreal Families, 1861–91." *Labour/Le Travail* 14: 9–46.

————. 1993. *Working Families: Age, Gender, and Daily Survival in Industrializing Montreal.* Toronto: McClelland & Stewart.

Brand, Dionne. 1984. "A Working Paper on Black Women in Toronto: Gender, Race and Class." *Fireweed* 19: 26–43.

————. 1991. *No Burden to Carry: Narratives of Black Working Women in Ontario, 1920s–1950s.* Toronto: Women's Press.

————. 1994. "'We weren't allowed to go into factory work until Hitler started the war': The 1920s to the 1940s." In *'We're Rooted Here and They Can't Pull Us Up': Essays in African Canadian Women's History.* Coordinator, Peggy Bristow. Toronto: University of Toronto Press.

Brant, Beth. 1985. "Coming Out as Indian Lesbian Writers." In *In the Feminine: Women and Words/Les femmes et les mots.* Ed. Ann Dybikowski, Victoria Freeman, Daphne Marlatt, Barbara Pullman, and Betsy Warland. Edmonton: Longspoon Press.

————. 1991. *Food and Spirits.* Vancouver: Press Gang.

Brasile, Monica. 2001. "From Riot Grrrl to *Mamagirl* in Omaha Nebraska." *Canadian Woman Studies/les cahiers de la femme* 20/21 (4/1): 63–8.

Bray, Abigail, and Claire Colebrook. 1998. "The Haunted Flesh: Corporeal Feminism and the Politics of (Dis)Embodiment." *Signs* 24 (1): 35–67.

Bray, M. Phyllis. 1989. "'No Life for a Woman': An Examination and Feminist Critique of the Post-World War II Instant Town with Special Reference to Manitouwadge, Ontario." MA thesis, Queen's University.

————. 1991. "The Long-Distance Commute in the Mining Industry: The Human Dimension." *CIM Bulletin* 84, 953: 62–64.

————. 1993. "The 'Perfect' Mine Wife: The Sancta Barbara Order of Merit—A Retrospective." *Bulletin of the Canadian Institute of Mining and Metallurgy* (March): 99–102.

Briskin, Linda. 1993. "Union Women and Separate Organizing." In *Women Challenging Unions: Feminism, Democracy, and Militancy.* Ed. Linda Briskin and Patricia McDermott, 89–108. Toronto: University of Toronto Press.

————. 1999. "Unions and Women's Organizing in Canada and Sweden." In *Women's Organizing and Public Policy in Sweden and Canada.* Ed. Linda Briskin and Mona Eliasson, 147–84. Montreal: McGill-Queen's University Press.

Briskin, Linda, and Patricia McDermott, eds. 1993. *Women Challenging Unions: Feminism, Democracy, and Militancy.* Toronto: University of Toronto Press.

Bristow, Peggy. 1994. *"We're Rooted Here and They Can't Pull Us Up": Essays in African Canadian Women's History.* Toronto: University of Toronto Press.

Broadhead, Lee-Anne. 2002. "The Gender Dimension to the Search for Global Justice." *Canadian Woman Studies/les cahiers de la femme* 21/22 (4/1): 179–182.

Brodie, Janine. 1989. "The Political Economy of Regionalism." In *The New Canadian Political Economy.* Ed. Wallace Clement and Glen Williams, 138–59. Montreal: McGill-Queen's University Press.

————. 1994. "Shifting the Boundaries: Gender and the Politics of Restructuring." In The *Strategic Silence: Gender and Economic Policy*, 46–60. London: Zed Books.

———. 1995. *Politics on the Margins: Restructuring and the Canadian Women's Movement.* Halifax: Fernwood.

———. 1997. "The New Political Economy of Regions." In *Understanding Canada: Building on the New Political Economy.* Ed. Wallace Clement, 240–261. Montreal: McGill-Queen's University Press.

———, Shelley A.M. Gavigan, and Jane Jenson. 1992. *The Politics of Abortion.* Toronto: Oxford University Press.

Brodribb, Somer. 1992. *Nothing Mat(t)ers: A Feminist Critique of Postmodernism.* Toronto: Lorimer.

Brodsky, Gwen, and Shelagh Day. 1989. *Canadian Charter Equality Rights for Women: One Step Forward or Two Steps Back?* Ottawa: Canadian Advisory Council on the Status of Women.

Brody, Miriam. 1992. "Introduction." *Vindication of the Rights of Woman* by Mary Wollstonecraft, 1–84. London: Penguin Books.

Brouwer, Ruth Compton. 1990. *New Women for God: Canadian Presbyterian Women and India Missions, 1876–1914.* Toronto: University of Toronto Press.

Brown, Rosemary. 1989. *Being Brown: A Very Public Life.* Toronto: Random House.

Brownmiller, Susan. 1999. *In Our Time: Memoir of a Revolution.* New York: Dial Press, Random House.

Brownhill, Leigh S., and Terisa Turner. 2002. "Subsistence Trade and World Trade: Gendered Class Struggle in Kenya, 1999–2002." *Canadian Woman Studies/les cahiers de la femme* 21/22 (4/1): 169–177.

Brunswick, Ruth. 1948. "The Preoedipal Phase of the Libido Development." In *The Psycho-ana-lytic Reader.* Ed. Robert Fleiss. New York: International Universities Press.

Brym, Robert J., with Bonnie J. Fox. 1989. *From Culture to Power: The Sociology of English Canada.* Toronto: Oxford University Press.

Buckner, Philip. 1990. "CHR Dialogue—The Maritimes and Confederation: A Reassessment." *Canadian Historical Review* 71, 1.

Burfoot, Annette. 1999. "Theories of Reproduction—Ancient to Contemporary." In *Encyclopedia of Reproductive Technologies.* Ed. Annette Burfoot, 1–3. Boulder, Colorado: Westview Press.

Burnet, Jean, ed. 1986. *Looking in My Sister's Eyes: An Exploration in Women's History.* Toronto: Multicultural History Society of Ontario.

Burr, Catherine. 1995. "Ontario can't keep employment equity down." *Globe and Mail,* 29 June, A17.

Burstyn, Varda. 1983. "Economy, Sexuality, Politics: Engels and the Sexual Division of Labour." *Socialist Studies/Etudes Socialistes: A Canadian Annual.*

———. 1985. *Women Against Censorship.* Toronto: Douglas and McIntyre.

———. 1990. "The Waffle and the Women's Movement." *Studies in Political Economy* 33: 175–84.

———, and Judy Rebick. 1988. "How 'Women Against Free Trade' Came to Write Its Manifesto." *Resources for Feminist Research* 17, 3: 138–42.

Burt, Sandra. 1993. "The Changing Patterns of Public Policy." In *Changing Patterns: Women in Canada.* 2nd ed. Ed. Sandra Burt, Lorraine Code, and Lindsay Dorney, 212–42. Toronto: McClelland & Stewart.

Butler, Judith. 1993. *Bodies that Matter: On the Discursive Limits of "Sex."* New York: Routledge.

Byrne, John A. 1995. "Informed Consent." *Business Week*, 2 Oct., 104–16.

Cameron, Barb, and Cathy Pike. 1972. "Collective Child Care in a Class Society." In *Women Unite!*, 87–89. Toronto: Canadian Women's Educational Press.

Campbell, Elaine. 1998. "Female Representation in the Senate, The House of Commons, and Provincial and Territorial Legislative Assemblies." Ontario Legislative Library. Current Issue Paper 56. Microlog 99–0599.

Campbell, Marion. 1995. "Separation or Integration: A Case Study, the Ban Righ Board of Queen's University." MA thesis, Queen's University.

Canada Medical Record. 1890. "Co-education." 18: 118–20.

Canadian Parliamentary Guide. 1995. 23 Feb., 201–3.

Canadian Practitioner. 1892. "Higher Education for Women." 17: 257–60.

Canadian Social Trends. 1996. "1996 Census: Count Yourself In!" 40: 29–33.

Canadian Women's March Committee. 2000. "It's Time for Change." *Canadian Woman Studies/les cahiers de la femme* 20 (3): 21–3.

———. 2000. "The National Women's Lobby Interim Report to Canadian Women." Oct. www.canada.marchofwomen.org/en/reports.html (Accessed 7/31/03).

Cannon, Martin. 1995. "(De)marginalizing the Intersection of 'Race' and 'Gender' in First Nations Politics." MA thesis, Queen's University.

Carpenter, Mary. 1996. "Female Grotesques in Academia: Ageism, Anti-feminism and Feminists on the Faculty." In *Anti-feminism in the Academy*. Ed. Vévé Clark, Shirley Nelson Garner, Margaret Higonmat, and Ketv Katrak. New York: Routledge.

Carr, Jim. 1994. "Immigration policy 'racist.'" *Winnipeg Free Press*, 15 Nov., A6.

Carty, Linda. 1994. "African Canadian Women and the State." In *'We're Rooted Here and They Can't Pull Us Up': Essays in African Canadian Women's History*. Coordinator, Peggy Bristow. Toronto: University of Toronto Press.

———. 1999. "The Discourse of Empire and the Social Construction of Gender." In *Scratching the Surface: Canadian Anti-racist Feminist Thought*. Ed. Enakshi Dua and Angela Robertson. Toronto: Women's Press.

Castellano, Marlene Brant. 1989. "Women in Huron and Ojibwa Societies." *Canadian Woman Studies/les cahiers de la femme* 10(2/3): 45–48.

———, and Janice Hill. 1995. "First Nations Women: Reclaiming Our Responsibilities." In *A Diversity of Women: Ontario, 1945–1980*. Ed. Joy Parr, 232–51. Toronto: University of Toronto Press.

Cauchon, Paul. 1992. "Les mouvements de femmes donnent naissance à 'Québec féminin pluriel.'" *Le Devoir*, 1 June.

Cebarotov, E.A. (Nora). 1995. "From Domesticity to the Public Sphere: Farm Women, 1945–86." In *A Diversity of Women: Ontario, 1945–80*. Ed. Joy Parr, 200–31. Toronto: University of Toronto Press.

Chamberland, Line. 1996. "Remembering Lesbian Bars: Montreal, 1955–75." *Canadian Women: A Reader*. Ed. Wendy Mitchinson, Paula Bourne, Alison Prentice, Gail Cuthbert Brandt, Beth Light, and Naomi Black. Toronto: Harcourt Brace.

Chan, Wendy, and Kiran Mirchandani, eds. 2002. *Crimes of Colour: Racialization and the Criminal Justice System*. Peterborough, ON: Broadview Press.

Chase, Gillean. 1996. "Strangers, Sisters." In *To Sappho, My Sister: Lesbian Sisters Write about Their Lives*. Ed. Lee Fleming, 59–68. Charlottetown: Gynergy Books.

Chaykowksi, Richard P., and Lisa M. Powell. 1999. "Women and the Labour Market: Recent Trends and Policy Issues." *Canadian Public Policy–Analyse de Politiques* XXV Supplement 1: S1–25.

Cheal, David. 1991. *Family and the State of Theory*. Toronto: University of Toronto Press.

Chenier, Elise Rose. 1995. "Tough Ladies and Troublemakers: Toronto's Public Lesbian Community, 1955–65." MA thesis, Queen's University.

Chesler, Phyllis. 1972. *Women and Madness*. New York: Doubleday.

Chilly Collective, eds. 1995. *Breaking Anonymity: The Chilly Climate for Women Faculty*. Waterloo: Wilfrid Laurier University Press.

Chodorow, Nancy. 1978. *Reproduction of Mothering*. Berkeley: Berkeley University Press.

———. 1989. *Feminism and Psychoanalytic Theory*. Cambridge: Polity Press.

———. 1999. *The Power of Feelings: Personal Meaning in Psychoanalysis, Gender, and Culture*. New Haven, Connecticut: Yale University Press.

Chowdry, Geeta. 1995. "Engendering Development? Women in Development (WID) in International Development Regimes." In *Feminism/Postmodernism/ Development*. Ed. Marianne Marchand and Jane L. Parpart. London and New York: Routledge.

Chunn, Dorothy. 1995. "Feminism, Law, and Public Policy: Politicizing the Personal." In *Canadian Families: Diversity, Conflict and Change*. Ed. Nancy Mandell and Ann Duffy, 177–210. Toronto: Harcourt Brace.

Clairmont, Donald H., and Dennis William McGill. 1999. *Africville: The Life and Death of a Canadian Black Community*. 3rd ed. Toronto: Canadian Scholars' Press.

Clark, Alice. 1982 [1919]. *Working Life of Women in the Seventeenth Century*. London: Routledge and Kegan Paul.

Clark, Campbell. 2002. "PM scolds Liberal dissenter." *Globe and Mail*, January 28, A1.

Clark, Lorene, and Debra J. Lewis. 1977. *Rape: The Price of Coercive Sexuality*. Toronto: Women's Press.

Clement, Wallace. 1975. *The Canadian Corporate Elite: An Analysis of Economic Power*. Toronto: McClelland & Stewart.

Coates, Linda, Janet Beavin Bavelas, and James Gibson. 1994. "Anomalous Language in Sexual Assault Trial Judgements." *Discourse and Society* 5, 2: 189–206.

Coburn, Judi. 1974. "'I See and am Silent': A Short History of Nursing in Ontario." In *Women at Work: Ontario, 1850–1930*. Toronto: Canadian Women's Educational Press.

Cockburn, Cynthia. 2000. "The Women's Movement: Boundary-crossing on Terrains of Conflict." In *Global Social Movements*. Ed. Robin Cohen and Shirin M. Rai, 46–61. London and New Brunswick: Athlone Press.

Cohen, Marjorie Griffin. 1987. *Free Trade and the Future of Women's Work: Manufacturing and Service Industries*. Toronto: Garamond Press and the Canadian Centre for Policy Alternatives.

———. 1988. *Women's Work, Markets and Economic Development in Nineteenth-Century Ontario*. Toronto: University of Toronto Press.

————, Laurell Ritchie, Michelle Swenarchuk, and Leah Vosko. 2002. "Globalization: Some Implications and Strategies for Women." *Canadian Woman Studies/les cahiers de la femme* 21/22 (4/1): 6–14.

Cohen, Rina. 1994. "A Brief History of Racism in Immigration Policies for Recruiting Domestics." *Canadian Woman Studies/les cahiers de la femme* 14, 2: 83–86.

Collins, Patricia Hill. 1990. *Black Feminist Thought*. London: Harper Collins.

Comack, Elizabeth. 2002. "Do We Need to Syndronize Women's Experiences? The Limitation of the 'Battered Woman Syndrome.'" In *Violence Against Women: New Canadian Perspectives*. Ed. Katherine M.J. McKenna and June Larkin, 277–84. Toronto: Inanna Publications and Education.

Connelly, Patricia. 1978. *Last Hired: First Fired*. Toronto: Women's Press.

————, and Martha MacDonald. 1986. "Women's Work: Domestic and Wage Labour in a Nova Scotia Community." In *The Politics of Diversity*. Ed. Roberta Hamilton and Michèle Barrett, 53–80. London: Verso.

Conrad, Margaret. 1986. "'Sundays Always Make Me Think of Home': Time and Place in Canadian Women's History." In *Rethinking Canada: The Promise of Women's History*. Ed. Veronica Strong-Boag and Anita Clair Fellman, 67–81. Toronto: Copp Clark Pitman.

Cook, Sharon Anne. 1995. *"Through Sunshine and Shadow": The Woman's Christian Temperance Union, Evangelicalism, and Reform in Ontario, 1874–1930*. Montreal: McGill-Queen's University Press.

Coté, Andrée, Elizabeth Sheehy, and Diana Marjury. "Stop Excusing Violence Against Women: NAWL's Brief on Defence of Provocation." www.nawl.ca/provocation.htm. (Accessed: 8/23/03.)

Cowan, Mary Rose. 1993. "When Will Justice Be Done?" *Herizons* 7, 12: 17–23.

Creese, Gillian. 1988. "The Politics of Dependence: Women, Work and Unemployment in the Vancouver Labour Movement Before World War II." In *Class, Gender, and Region: Essays in Canadian Historical Sociology*. Ed. Gregory S. Kealey, 121–42. St John's: Committee on Canadian Labour History.

————, and Daiva Stasiulis. 1996. "Intersections of Gender, Race, Class and Sexuality." *Studies in Political Economy* 51: 5–14.

Currie, Andrea. 1989. "A Roof is Not Enough: Feminism, Transition Houses and the Battle Against Abuse." *New Maritimes* (Sept./Oct.): 16–29.

Currie, Dawn. 1986. "Re-thinking What We Do and How We Do It: A Study of Reproductive Decisions." *Canadian Review of Sociology and Anthropology* 25 (2): 231–53.

————. 1999. *Girl Talk: Adolescent Magazines and their Readers*. Toronto: University of Toronto Press.

Danylewycz, Marta. 1987. *Taking the Veil: An Alternative to Marriage, Motherhood, and Spinsterhood in Quebec, 1840–1920*. Toronto: McClelland & Stewart.

Das Gupta, Tania. 1999. "Anti-Black Racism in Nursing in Toronto." *Studies in Political Economy* 51: 97–116.

deSève, Micheline. 1992. "The Perspectives of Quebec Feminists." In *Challenging Times: The Women's Movement in Canada and the United States*. Ed. Constance Backhouse and David H. Flaherty, 110–16. Montreal: McGill-Queen's University Press.

————. 1997. "Gendered Feelings about Our National Issue(s)." *Atlantis* 21 (2): 111–16.

Devor, Holly. 1997. *FTM: Female-to-Male Transsexuals in Society*. Bloomington: Indiana University Press.

Dewar, Elaine. 1977. "Beyond Sisterhood: Is There Life after Liberation?" *Weekend Magazine, Winnipeg Free Press*, 1 April: 6–8, 10–11.

Dickie, Bonnie. 1993. *A Web Not a Ladder.* National Film Board, Women and Work Series.

Diner, Robyn. 2001. "Things to Do with the "F" Word: The Ironic and Unruly Adventures of Liz Phair and Courtney Love." *Canadian Woman Studies/les cahiers de la femme* 20/21 (4/1): 76–81.

Dodd, Dianne, and Deborah Gorham, eds. 1994. *Caring and Curing: Historical Perspectives on Women and Healing in Canada*. Ottawa: University of Ottawa Press.

Doob, Anthony N. 2002. "Understanding the Attacks on Statistics Canada's Violence Against Women Survey." In *Violence Against Women: New Canadian Perspectives*. Ed. Katherine M.J. McKenna and June Larkin, 55–62. Toronto: Inanna Publications and Education.

Doucette, Joanne. 1989. "Redefining Difference: Disabled Lesbians Resist." *Resources for Feminist Research* 18, 2: 17–20.

Drolet, Marie. 2002. "Wives, Mothers and Wages: Does Timing Matter?" Research Paper No. 186. Ottawa: Statistics Canada.

———. 2003. "Motherhood and Paycheques." *Canadian Social Trends* XX, 19–21.

Dua, Enakshi. 1999. "Beyond Diversity: Exploring the Ways in Which the Discourse of Race has Shaped the Institution of the Nuclear Family." In *Scratching the Surface: Canadian Anti-racist Feminist Thought*. Ed. Enakshi Dua and Angela Robertson. Toronto: Women's Press.

———. 1999. "Introduction." In *Scratching the Surface: Canadian Anti-racist Feminist Thought*. Ed. Enakshi Dua and Angela Robertson. Toronto: Women's Press.

Dubinsky, Karen. 1985. *Lament for a "Patriarchy Lost"? Anti-feminism, Anti-abortion, and REAL Women in Canada*. Ottawa: Canadian Research Institute for the Advancement of Women.

———. 1993. *Improper Advances: Rape and Heterosexual Conflict in Ontario, 1880–1929*. Chicago: University of Chicago Press.

DuBois, Ellen Carol. 1978. *Feminism and Suffrage: The Emergence of an Independent Women's Movement in America, 1848–1869*. Ithaca, New York: Cornell University Press.

Duffy, Ann. 1986. "Reformulating Power for Women." *Canadian Review of Sociology and Anthropology* 23: 22–47.

Duffy, Ann, and Norene Pupo. 1992. *Part-Time Paradox: Connecting Gender, Work and Family*. Toronto: McClelland & Stewart.

Dumont, Micheline. 1992. "The Origins of the Women's Movement in Quebec." In *Challenging Times: The Women's Movement in Canada and the United States*. Ed. Constance Backhouse and David H. Flaherty, 72–89. Montreal: McGill-Queen's University Press.

Duncan, Colin A. M. 1995. "Women of Quebec and the Contemporary Constitutional Issue." In *Gender Politics*. Ed. François-Pierre Gingras, 153–74. Toronto: Oxford University Press.

———. 1996. *The Centrality of Agriculture: Between Humankind and the Rest of Nature*. Montreal: McGill-Queen's University Press.

Echols, Alice. 1989. *"Daring to Be Bad": Radical Feminism in America, 1967–1975*. Minneapolis: University of Minnesota Press.

Ehrenreich, Barbara. 1983. *The Hearts of Men: American Dreams and the Flight from Commitment*. New York: Doubleday.

Eichler, Margrit. 1988. *Families in Canada Today: Recent Changes and Their Policy Consequences*. 2nd ed. Toronto: Gage.

———. 1992. "Not Always an Easy Alliance: The Relationship Between Women's Studies and the Women's Movement in Canada." In *Challenging Times: The Women's Movement in Canada and the United States*. Ed. Constance Backhouse and David H. Flaherty, 71–102. Montreal: McGill-Queen's University Press.

———, ed. 1995. *Change of Plans: Towards a Non-sexist Sustainable City*. Toronto: Garamond.

Eisenstein, Hester. 1984. *Contemporary Feminist Thought*. London: Allen & Unwin.

Eisenstein, Zillah. 1981. *The Radical Future of Liberal Feminism*. Boston: Northeastern University Press.

Eldridge, Laura Lee. 2002. "Going Back Home: From Full-time Paid Work to Full-time Motherhood." MA thesis, Queen's University.

Elliot, Pam. 1991. Letter to editor. *Ms*. 1, 4: 5.

Elliott, Patricia. 1998. "Some Critical Reflections on the Transgender Theory of Kate Bornstein." *Atlantis* 23 (1): 13–19.

Ellwood, Wayne. 2001. *The No-Nonsense Guide to Globalization*. Toronto: New Internationalist and Between the Lines.

Engels, F. 1948 [1884]. *The Origin of the Family, Private Property and the State*. Moscow: Progress Publishers.

Errington, Jane. 1993. "Pioneers and Suffragists." In *Changing Patterns: Women in Canada*. 2nd ed. Ed. Sandra Burt, Lorraine Code, and Lindsay Dorney, 59–91. Toronto: McClelland & Stewart.

———. 1996. *Wives and Mothers, Schoolmistresses and Scullery Maids: Working Women in Upper Canada, 1790–1840*. Montreal: McGill-Queen's University Press.

Eschle, Catherine. 2001. *Global Democracy, Social Movements, and Feminism*. Boulder, Colorado: Westview.

Evans, Patricia M., and Gerda R. Wekerle. 1997. "The Shifting Terrain of Women's Welfare: Theory, Discourse, and Activism." In *Women and the Canadian Welfare State*. Eds. Patricia M. Evans and Gerda R. Wekerle. Toronto: University of Toronto Press.

Evans, Sara. 1979. *Personal Politics: The Roots of Women's Liberation in the Civil Rights Movement and the New Left*. New York: Alfred A. Knopf.

Faderman, Lillian. 1981. *Surpassing the Love of Men: Romantic Friendship and Love Between Women from the Renaissance to the Present*. New York: Morrow.

Fahmy-Eid, Nadia, and Nicole Laurin-Frenette. 1986. "Theories of the Family and Family/Authority Relationships in the Educational Sector in Quebec and France, 1850–1960." In *The Politics of Diversity*. Ed. Roberta Hamilton and Michèle Barrett, 287–302. London: Verso.

Faludi, Susan. 1991. *Backlash: The Undeclared War Against American Women*. New York: Anchor Books.

Fausto-Sterling, Anne. 1993. "The Five Sexes." *The Sciences* (March/April): 20–21.

Feldberg, Georgina, and Marianne Carlsson. "Organized for Health: Women's Activism in Canada and Sweden." In *Women's Organizing and Public Policy in Sweden and Canada*. Ed. Linda Briskin and Mona Eliasson, 347–374. Montreal: McGill-Queen's University Press.

Feminist Review. 1985–86. Vols. 20, 22, 23.

Ferguson, Sue. 2002. "The Daycare Dilemma." *Maclean's* 115 (14): 58–61.

Ferris, Melanie A. 2001. "Resisting Mainstream Media: Girls and the Act of Making Zines." *Canadian Woman Studies/les cahiers de la femme* 20/21 (4/1): 51–55.

Fillion, Kate. 1995. *Lip Service: The Truth about Women's Darker Side in Love, Sex, and Friendship*. Toronto: Harper Collins.

Fillmore, Nick. 1989. "The Big Oink: How Business Won the Free Trade Battle." *This Magazine* 22, 8 (March): 13–20.

Findlay, Deborah. 1995. "Discovering Sex: Medical Science, Feminism and Intersexuality." *Canadian Review of Sociology and Anthropology* 32, 1: 25–52.

Findlay, Sue. 1987. "Facing the State: The Politics of the Women's Movement Reconsidered." In *Feminism and Political Economy: Women's Work, Women's Struggles*. Ed. Heather Jon Maroney and Meg Luxton, 31–50. Toronto: Methuen.

———. 1997. "Institutionalizing Feminist Politics: Learning from the Struggles for Equal Pay in Ontario." In *Women and the Canadian Welfare State: Challenges and Change*. Ed. Patricia M. Evans and Gerda R. Wekerle, 310–29. Toronto: University of Toronto Press.

———. 1999. "Representing Women's Interests in the Policy Process: Women's Organizing and State Initiatives in Sweden and Canada, 1960s–1990s." In *Women's Organizing and Public Policy in Sweden and Canada*. Ed. Linda Briskin and Mona Eliasson, 119–46. Montreal: McGill Queen's University Press.

Finkel, Alvin. 1993. "Populism and Gender: The UFA and Social Credit Experiences." *Journal of Canadian Studies* 27, 4: 76–97.

Firestone, Shulamith. 1970. *The Dialectic of Sex*. New York: William Morrow & Co.

Fiske, Jo-Anne. 1991. "Colonization and the Decline of Women's Status: The Tsimshian Case." *Feminist Studies* 17: 509–35.

———. 1996a. "Gender and the Paradox of Residential Education in Carrier Society." In *Women of the First Nations: Power, Wisdom and Strength*. Ed. Christine Miller and Patricia Chuchryk. Winnipeg: University of Manitoba Press.

———. 1996b. "The Womb is to the Nation as the Heart is to the Body: Ethnopolitical Discourses of the Canadian Indigenous Women's Movement." *Studies in Political Economy* 51: 65–95.

Fleming, Lee, ed. 1996. *To Sappho, My Sister: Lesbian Sisters Write about Their Lives*. Charlottetown: Gynergy Books.

Forbes, Ernest R. 1979. *Maritime Rights—The Maritime Rights Movement, 1919–1927: A Study in Canadian Regionalism*. Montreal: McGill-Queen's University Press.

Forsey, Helen. 2002. "GMOs: Globalizing Male Omnipotence." *Canadian Woman Studies/les cahiers de la femme* 21/22 (4/1): 207–10.

Foster, Jenny. 2002. "Tear Gas in Utero: Quebec City." *Canadian Woman Studies/les cahiers de la femme* 21/22 (4/1): 165–68.

Foster, Susan. 1998. "Choreographies of Gender." *Signs* 24 (1): 1–31.

Foucault, Michel. 1982. "The Subject and Power." In *Michel Foucault, Beyond Structuralism and Hermeneutics.* Eds. H. Dreyfus and P. Rabinow. Chicago: University of Chicago Press.

Fox, Bonnie J. 1989. "The Feminist Challenge: A Reconsideration of Social Inequality and Economic Development." In Robert Brym with Bonnie Fox, *From Culture to Power: The Sociology of English Canada.* Toronto: Oxford University Press.

Freud, Sigmund. 1965. *New Introductory Lectures on Psychoanalysis.* Trans. and ed. James Strachy. New York: W.W. Norton.

Friedan, Betty. 1963. *The Feminine Mystique.* New York: Dell Publishing.

Funston, Pauline. 2000. "Feminism in the Transition House." *Canadian Woman Studies/les cahiers de la femme* 20 (3): 41–2.

Galloway, Priscilla. 1987. "Room to Grow." In *Still Running: Personal Stories of Queen's Women.* Ed. Joy Parr, 108–20. Kingston: Queen's University Alumnae Association.

Gannagé, Charlene. 1986. *Double Day Double Bind: Women Garment Workers.* Toronto: Women's Press.

Gardiner, Judith. 1992. "Psychoanalysis and Feminism: An American Humanist's View." *Signs* 17 (Winter): 437–54.

Gartner, Rosemary, Myrna Dawson, and Maria Crawford. 2002. "Woman Killing: Intimate Femicide in Ontario, 1974–1994." In *Violence Against Women: New Canadian Perspectives.* Ed. Katherine M.J. McKenna and June Larkin, 123–46. Toronto: Inanna Publications and Education.

Gaskell, Jane. 1986. "Conceptions of Skill and the Work of Women: Some Historical and Political Issues." In *The Politics of Diversity.* Ed. Roberta Hamilton and Michèle Barrett, 361–84. London: Verso.

———. 1988. "The Reproduction of Family Life: Perspectives of Male and Female Adolescents. In *Gender and Society: Creating a Canadian Women's Sociology.* Ed. Arlene Tigar McLaren, 146–68. Toronto: Copp Clark Pitman.

Gentile, Patrizia. 1995. "Defending Gender in the Security State: Beauty Contests and Fruit Machines, 1950–1972." Unpublished paper, Carleton University.

———. 2000. "'Government Girls' and 'Ottawa Men': Cold War Management of Gender Relations in the Civil Service. In *Whose National Security: Canadian State Surveillance and the Creation of Enemies.* Eds. Gary Kinsman, Dieter K. Buse, and Mercedes Steedman. Toronto: Between the Lines.

George, Glynnis. 2000. *The Rock Where We Stand: An Ethnography of Women's Activism in Newfoundland.* Toronto: University of Toronto Press.

Gerrard, Nikki, Gwen Russell and Saskatchewan Women's Agricultural Network. 2002. "An Exploration of Health-related Impacts of the Erosion of Agriculturally Focussed Support Programs for Farm Women in Saskatchewan." Saskatoon: Saskatchewan Women's Agricultural Network.

Gershbain, Nikki, and Aviva Rubin. 1994. "The Struggle Beneath the Struggle: Antisemitism in Toronto Anti-racist Movements." *Canadian Woman Studies/les cahiers de la femme* 14, 2: 58–61.

Ghalam, N.Z. 1997. "Attitudes Towards Women, Work and Family." *Canadian Social Trends* 46, 13–17.

Gibb-Clark, Margot, and Sean Fine. 1993. "Will 'slaves to the law' ever be free?" *Globe and Mail*, 27 Nov., A1, A10.

Gibson, Frederick W. 1988. *Queen's University Volume II 1917–1961*. Kingston and Montreal: McGill-Queen's University Press.

Gill, Judy, Diana Chastain, Linda Carmen, Mary Bolton, Jenny Robinson. 1972. Women's Liberation Movement Toronto, Ontario. September 1970. "Sexual Myths." In *Women Unite!* Toronto: Canadian Women's Educational Press, 162–69.

Gillett, Margaret. 1981. *"We Walked Very Warily": A History of Women at McGill*. Montreal: Eden Press.

Globe and Mail. 1976. "McLaughlin's long futile search." 11 Sept.

———. 1993. "Violence is not a women's issue." [Editorial]. 31 July, D6.

———. 1995. "Female refugees suffer abuse." 8 March, A10.

Gordon, Linda. 1976. *Woman's Body, Woman's Right: A Social History of Birth Control in America*. New York: Grossman.

Gorham, Deborah. 1979. "Flora MacDonald Denison: Canadian Feminist." In *A Not Unreasonable Claim: Women and Reform in Canada, 1880s–1920s*. Ed. Linda Kealey, 47–70. Toronto: Women's Press.

———. 1994. "'No Longer an Invisible Minority': Women Physicians and Medical Practice in Late Twentieth-Century North America." In *Caring and Curing: Historical Perspectives on Women and Healing in Canada*. Ed. Dianne Dodd and Deborah Gorham, 183–212. Ottawa: University of Ottawa Press.

Gough, Kathleen. 1973. *The Origin of the Family*. Toronto: New Hogtown Press.

Grant-Cummings, Joan. 1998. "The Global Capitalist Economic Agenda: Impact on Women's Human Rights. *Canadian Woman Studies/les cahiers de la femme* 16 (1): 6–10.

Gray, Stan. 1987. "Sharing the Shop Floor." In *Women and Men: Interdisciplinary Readings on Gender*. Ed. Greta Hofmann Nemiroff, 377–402. Richmond Hill, ON: Fitzhenry & Whiteside.

Green, Joyce. 2003. "Decolonization and Recolonization in Canada." In *Changing Canada: Political Economy as Transformation*. Ed. Wallace Clement and Leah Vosko, 51–78. Montreal: McGill-University Press.

Green, Mary Jean. 2001. *Women and Narrative Identity*. Montreal: McGill-Queen's University Press.

Greenspon, Edward. 2003. "We are bound by our geography." *Globe and Mail,* 28 June, A2.

Grewal, I., and C. Kaplan. 1994. *Scattered Hegemonies: Postmodernity and Transnational Feminist Practices*. Minneapolis: University of Minnesota Press.

Guindon, Hubert. 1988. *Tradition, Modernity, Nation.* Toronto: University of Toronto Press.

Haddad, Tony, and Lawrence Lam. 1988. "Canadian Families—Men's Involvement in Family Work: A Case Study of Immigrant Men in Toronto." In *International Journal of Comparative Sociology* 29, 3/4: 269–81.

Haig-Brown, Celia. 1988. *Resistance and Renewal: Surviving the Indian Residential School.* Vancouver: Tillacum Library.

Hale, Sylvia M. 1988. "Male Culture and Purdah for Women: The Social Construction of What Women Think Women Think." *Canadian Review of Sociology and Anthropology* 25, 2: 276–97.

Hamilton, Roberta. 1978. *The Liberation of Women: A Study of Patriarchy and Capitalism.* London: Allen and Unwin.

———. 1985. "Feminists in the Academy: Intellectuals or Political Subversives?" *Queen's Quarterly* 92, 1: 3–20.

———. 1986. "The Collusion with Patriarchy: A Psychoanalytic Account." In *The Politics of Diversity.* Ed. Roberta Hamilton and Michèle Barrett, 385–97. London: Verso.

———. 1988. *Feudalism and Colonization: The Historiography of New France.* Gananoque, ON: Langdale Press.

———. 1995. "Pro-natalism, Feminism and Nationalism." In *Gender Politics.* Ed. François-Pierre Gingras, 135–52. Toronto: Oxford University Press.

———. 1997. "Theorizing Gender, Sexuality and Family: Feminism and Psychoanalysis Revisited." In *Feminism and Families.* Ed. Meg Luxton. Halifax: Fernwood.

———. 2002. *Setting the Agenda: Jean Royce and the Shaping of Queen's University.* Toronto: University of Toronto Press.

Hammond, Sarah. 2003. "Woman chosen to lead as Queen's revamps engineering department." *The Kingston Whig-Standard,* 23 July.

Hansen, Karen V., and Ilene J. Philipson. 1990. *Women, Class, and the Feminist Imagination.* Philadelphia: Temple University Press.

Harding, Sandra. *The Science Question in Feminism.* Ithaca, New York: Cornell University Press, 1986.

Hartsock, Nancy. 1990. "Foucault on Power: A Theory for Women?" In *Feminism/Postmodernism.* Ed. Linda J. Nicholson, 157–75. New York: Routledge.

Hausman, Bernice. 2001. "Recent Transgender Theory." *Feminist Studies* 27 (2): 465–490.

Heald, Susan. 1997. "Telling Feminist Truths: Research and Writing about Feminist Organizing." *Atlantis* 22 (1): 31–42.

Hekman, Susan. 1999. "Backgrounds and Riverbeds: Feminist Reflections." *Feminist Studies* 25 (2): 427–446.

Henry, Frances. 1973. *Forgotten Canadians: The Blacks of Nova Scotia.* Don Mills, ON: Longman.

Henry, Frances, Carol Tator, Winston Mattis, and Tim Rees. 2000. *The Colour of Democracy: Racism in Canadian Society.* 2nd ed. Toronto: Harcourt Brace.

Herman, Didi. 1995. *Rights of Passage: Struggles for Lesbian and Gay Equality.* Toronto: University of Toronto Press.

Hill, Christopher. 1969. *Reformation to Industrial Revolution.* Harmondsworth: Penguin Books.

Hird, Myra. 2002. *Engendering Violence: Heterosexual Interpersonal Violence from Childhood to Adulthood.* Hampshire, England: Ashgate.

Hochschild, Arlie. 1990. *The Second Shift.* New York: Avon.

hooks, bell. 1988. *thinking feminist, thinking black.* Toronto: Garamond Press.

Horn, Kahn-Tineta. 1991. "Beyond Oka: Dimensions of Mohawk Sovereignty." An Interview with Kahn-Tineta Horn. *Studies in Political Economy* 35: 29–41.

Horowitz, Gad. 1977. *Basic and Surplus Repression in Psychoanalytic Theory.* Toronto: University of Toronto Press.

Hrdy, Sarah. 1981. *The Woman Who Never Evolved*. Cambridge: Harvard University Press.

Hubbard, Ruth. 1990. "The Political Nature of 'Human Nature.'" In *Theoretical Perspectives on Sexual Differences*. Ed. Deborah L. Rhode, 63–73. New Haven, Connecticut: Yale University Press.

Hughes, Mikaela, and Catherine Hughes. 1996. "The Hughes Family Chronicles." In *To Sappho, My Sister: Lesbian Sisters Write about Their Lives*. Ed. Lee Fleming, 135–50. Charlottetown: Gynergy Books.

Humphreys, Helen. 2002. *The Lost Garden*. Toronto: Harper Flamingo.

Iacovetta, Franca. 1992. *Such Hardworking People: Italian Immigrants in Postwar Toronto*. Montreal: McGill-Queen's University Press.

———. 1995. "Remaking Their Lives: Women Immigrants, Survivors, and Refugees." In *A Diversity of Women: Ontario, 1945–80*. Ed. Joy Parr, 135–67. Toronto: University of Toronto Press.

Ibsen, Henrik. 1967. *Four Great Plays by Ibsen*. Trans. R. Farquharson Sharp. Intro. John Gassner. New York: Bantam.

Ingraham, Chrys. 1994. "The Heterosexual Imaginary: Feminist Sociology and Theories of Gender." *Sociological Theory* 12, 2: 201–19.

Irigaray, Luce. 1985a. *Speculum of the Other Women*. Ithaca, New York: Cornell University Press. Trans.: Gilliam C. Gill.

———. 1985b. *This Sex Which is Not One*. Trans.: Catherine Porter with Carolyn Burke. Ithaca, New York: Cornell University Press.

Isla, Ana. 2002. "A Struggle for Clean Water and Livelihood: Canadian Mining in Costa Rica in the Era of Globalization." *Canadian Woman Studies/les cahiers de la femme* 21/22 (4/1): 148–154.

Jackson, Andrew. 2003. "Is Work Working for Women?" Research Paper #22. Canadian Labour Congress. www.clc-ctc.ca.

Jacques, Alison. 2001. "You Can Run But You Can't Hide: The Incorporation of Riot Grrrl into Mainstream Culture." *Canadian Woman Studies/les cahiers de la femme* 20/21 (4/1) 46–50.

Jamieson, Kathleen. 1978. "Sex Discrimination and the Indian Act." In *Indian Women and the Law: Citizens Minus*. Ottawa: Minister of Supply and Services.

Jhappan, Radha. 1996. "Race and Gender Essentialism or a Post-mortem of Scholarship." *Studies in Political Economy* 51: 15–64.

Jiwani, Yasmin. 2002. "Erasing Race: The Story of Reena Virk." In *Violence Against Women: New Canadian Perspectives*. Ed. Katherine M.J. McKenna and June Larkin, 441–55. Toronto: Inanna Publications and Education.

Johnson, Holly. 2002. "Methods of Measurement." In *Violence Against Women: New Canadian Perspectives*. Ed. Katherine M.J. McKenna and June Larkin, 21–54. Toronto: Inanna Publications and Education.

Kaufman, Michael, ed. 1987. *Beyond Patriarchy: Essays by Men on Pleasure, Power, and Change*. Toronto: Oxford University Press.

Kay, Fiona. 1997. "Balancing Acts: Career and Family Among Lawyers." In *Challenging the Public/Private Divide: Feminism, Law and Public Policy*. Ed. Susan Boyd. Toronto: University of Toronto Press.

Kelly, Joan. 1984. "The Social Relation of the Sexes: Methodological Implications of Women's History." In *Women, History and Theory: The Essays of Joan Kelly*. Chicago: University of Chicago Press.

Kennedy, Elizabeth Lapovsky, and Madeline D. Davis. 1995. *Boots of Leather, Slippers of Gold: The History of a Lesbian Community*. New York: Routledge.

Kennelly, Jacqueline J. 2002. "Making Connections: Women's Health and the Anti-globalization Movement." *Canadian Woman Studies/les cahiers de la femme* 21/22 (4/1): 160–64.

Kessler, Suzanne J. 1998. *Lessons from the Intersexed*. New Brunswick, New Jersey: Rutgers University Press.

Khalideen, Rosetta and Nadira Khalideen. 2002. "Caribbean Women in Globalization and Economic Restructuring." *Canadian Woman Studies/les cahiers de la femme* 21/22 (4/1): 108–113.

Killian, Melody. 1972. "Children are Only Littler People." In *Women Unite!* Toronto: Canadian Women's Educational Press, 90–98.

Kinsman, Gary. 1995. "'Character Weaknesses' and 'Fruit Machines': Towards an Analysis of the Anti-homosexual Security Campaign in the Canadian Civil Service." *Labour/Le Travail* 35: 133–61.

———. 2001. "Gays and Lesbians: Pushing the Boundaries." In *Canadian Society*. Ed. Dan Glenday and Ann Duffy, 212–246. Toronto: Oxford University Press.

Kirsch, Vik. 1995. "Eating disorders plague students: Hundreds now affected by dietary chaos says hospital psychologist." *Guelph Mercury*, 27 June, A3.

Klein, Alice, and Wayne Roberts. 1974. "Besieged Innocence: The 'Problem' and Problems of Working Women, Toronto, 1896–1914." In *Women at Work, Ontario, 1850–1930*. Ed. Janice Acton, Penny Goldsmith, and Bonnie Shepard, 211–60. Toronto: Canadian Women's Educational Press.

Klinger, Cornelia. 1998. "Essentialism, Universalism, and Feminist Politics." *Constellations* 5 (3): 333–344.

Knocke, Wuokko, and Roxanna Ng. 1999. "Women's Organizing and Immigration. Comparing the Canadian and Swedish Experiences." In *Women's Organizing and Public Policy in Sweden and Canada*. Ed. Linda Briskin and Mona Eliasson, 87–116. Montreal: McGill-Queen's University Press.

Koedt, Anne. 1973. "The Myth of the Vaginal Orgasm." In *Radical Feminism*. Ed. Anne Koedt, Ellen Levine, and Anita Rapone, 198–207. New York: Quadrangle.

Kome, Penney. 1983. *The Taking of Twenty Eight: Women Challenge the Constitution*. Toronto: Canadian Women's Educational Press.

Kostash, Myrna. 1980. *Long Way from Home. The Story of the Sixties Generation in Canada*. Toronto: Lorimer, 1980.

———. 1996. "Dissing Feminist Sexuality." *Canadian Forum* 75 (852): 13–17.

Kowaluk, Lucia. 1972. "The Status of Women in Canada." In *Mother Was Not a Person*. Montreal: Black Rose Books, 210–20.

Kreps, Bonnie. 1979. *No Life for a Woman*. Produced by Serendipity Films Ltd. for the National Film Board.

Krull, Catherine. 2003. "Pronatalism, Feminism and Family Policy in Quebec." In *Voices: Essays on Canadian Families*. Ed. Marion Lynn, 245–265. Toronto: Thompson.

Kulkarni, Seema. 2002. "A Local Answer to a Global Mess: Women's Innovations to Secure Their Livelihood." *Canadian Woman Studies/les cahiers de la femme* 21/22 (4/1): 196–202.

Kumar, Pradeep. 1993. "Collective Bargaining and Women's Workplace Concerns." In *Women Challenging Unions: Feminism, Democracy and Militancy*. Ed. Linda Briskin and Patricia McDermott, 207–30. Toronto: University of Toronto Press.

Labreque, Marie R. 2002. "Dans le maquiladoras du Yukatan...'Pour qui a vraiment envie de travailler.'" *Canadian Woman Studies/les cahiers de la femme* 21/22 (4/1): 100–7.

Ladurie, Emmanuel Le Roy. 1974. *The Peasants of Languedoc*. Trans. and intro. John Day. Chicago: University of Illinois Press.

Laframboise, Donna. 1996. *The Princess at the Window: A New Gender Morality*. Toronto: Penguin.

Lakeman, Lee. 2000. "Why Law and Order Cannot End Violence Against Women and Why the Development of Women's (Social, Economic, Political, and Civil) Rights Might." *Canadian Woman Studies/les cahiers de la femme* 20 (3): 24–33.

LaMarsh, Judy. 1968. *Memoires of a Bird in a Gilded Cage*. Toronto: McClelland & Stewart.

Lamoureux, Diane. 1987. "Nationalism and Feminism in Quebec: An Impossible Attraction." In *Feminism and Political Economy: Women's Work, Women's Struggles*. Ed. Heather Jon Maroney and Meg Luxton, 51–68. Toronto: Methuen.

LaRoque, Emma. 1996. "The Colonization of a Native Woman Scholar." In *Women of the First Nations: Power, Wisdom and Strength*. Ed. Christine Miller and Patricia Chuchryk, 11–18. Winnipeg: University of Manitoba Press.

Lavigne, Marie. 1986. "Feminist Reflections on the Fertility of Women in Quebec." In *The Politics of Diversity*. Ed. Roberta Hamilton and Michèle Barrett, 303–21. London: Verso.

———, Yolande Pinard, and Jennifer Stoddart. 1979. "The Fédération Nationale Saint-Jean-Baptiste and the Women's Movement in Quebec." In *A Not Unreasonable Claim: Women and Reform in Canada, 1880s–1920s*. Ed. Linda Kealey, 71–87. Toronto: Women's Press.

Lawrence, Bonita. 2002. "Rewriting Histories of the Land: Colonization and Indigenous Resistance in Eastern Canada." In *Race, Space and the Law: Unmapping a White Settler Society*. Ed. Sherene H. Razack, 21–46. Toronto: Between the Lines.

Leacock, Eleanor. 1981. *Myths of Male Dominance*. New York: Monthly Review Press.

———. 1986. "Montagnais Women and the Jesuit Program for Colonization." In *Rethinking Canada: The Promise of Women's History*. Ed. Veronica Strong-Boag and Anita Clair Fellman, 7–22. Toronto: Copp Clark Pitman.

Leah, Ronnie Joy. 1999. "Do You Call Me 'Sister'? Women of Colour and the Canadian Labour Movement." In *Scratching the Surface: Canadian Anti-racist Feminist Thought*. Eds. Enakshi Dua and Angela Robertson, 97–126. Toronto: Women's Press.

Lepp, Annalee. 2002. "Trafficking in Women and the Feminization of Migration: The Canadian Context." *Canadian Woman Studies/les cahiers de la femme* 20/21(4/1) 90–99.

Leslie, Genevieve. 1974. "Domestic Service in Canada, 1880–1920." In *Women at Work, Ontario, 1850–1930*. Ed. Janice Acton, Penny Goldsmith, and Bonnie Shepard, 71–126. Toronto: Canadian Women's Educational Press.

Lett, Dan. 1995. "Safe haven a nightmare for refugees." *Winnipeg Free Press*, 18 Sept., B3.

Lévesque, Andrée. 2002. "Le travail des femmes à l'heure de la mondialization néo-libérale." *Canadian Woman Studies/les cahiers de la femme* 21/22 (4/1): 151–55.

Leys, Colin. 1996. *The Rise and Fall of Development Theory*. London: James Currey.

———. 2001. *Market-Driven Politics: Neoliberal Democracy and the Public Interest*. London: Verso

Li, Peter. 2003. "Understanding Economic Performance of Immigrants." *Canadian Issues/Themes Canadiens* April, 25–26.

Library of Parliament. 2003. Information and Documentation Branch. www.parl.gc.ca/information/about/people/key/Standings. (Accessed July 27.)

Liddington, Jill, and Jill Norris. 1978. *One Hand Tied Behind Us: The Rise of the Women's Suffrage Movement*. London: Virago.

Lippman, Abby. 1989. "Prenatal Diagnosis: Reproductive Choice? Reproductive Control?" In *The Future of Human Reproduction*. Ed. Christine Overall, 182–94. Toronto: Women's Press.

Little, Margaret Jane Hillyard. 1998. *'No Car, No Radio, No Liquor Permit': The Moral Regulation of Single Mothers in Ontario 1920–1997*. Toronto: Oxford University Press.

Lorde, Audre. 1984. *Sister Outsider*. Trumansburg, New York: Crossing Press Feminist Series.

Luther, Rashmi, Elizabeth Whitmore, and Bernice Moreau. 2003. *Seen But Not Heard: Aboriginal Women and Women of Colour in the Academy*. 2nd ed. Ottawa: Canadian Research Institute for the Advancement of Women.

Lowe, Graham S. 1987. *Women in the Administrative Revolution*. Toronto: University of Toronto Press.

Lowe, Mick. 1995. "Joan Kuyek vs. INCO." *Canadian Forum* 74 (Nov.): 14–20.

Lunman, Kim. 2003. "Chretien's 'morally grave' error." *Globe and Mail*, 7 July.

Luxton, Meg. 1980. *More than a Labour of Love*. Toronto: Women's Press.

———, and June Corman. 2001. *Getting By in Hard Times*. Toronto: University of Toronto Press.

MacDonald, Eleanor. 1998. "Critical Identities: Rethinking Feminism Through Transgendered Politics." *Atlantis* 23 (1): 3–12.

MacGregor, Sherilyn. 1994. "Feminist Approaches to Planning Thought and Action: Practical Lessons from Women Plan Toronto." MA thesis, Queen's University.

Mackenzie, Colin. 1988. "New map diminishes Canada." The Globe and Mail, 14 October, A1–2.

Mackenzie, Suzanne. 1986. "Women's Responses to Economic Restructuring: Changing Gender, Changing Space." In *The Politics of Diversity*. Ed. Roberta Hamilton and Michèle Barrett, 81–100. London: Verso.

———. 1987. "Neglected Spaces in Peripheral Places: Homeworkers and the Creation of a New Economic Centre." *Cahiers de Geographie du Québec* 31 (83): 247–60.

———. 1993. "Redesigning Cities, Redesigning Ourselves: Feminism and Environments." In *Limited Edition: Voices of Women, Voices of Feminism*. Ed. Geraldine Finn, 90–202. Halifax: Fernwood.

MacKinnon, Catharine A., and Andrea Dworkin. 1995. "In Defense of Themselves." *New York Times Book Review*, 7 May, 47.

Macpherson, Kay. 1994. *When in Doubt, Do Both: The Times of My Life.* Toronto: University of Toronto Press.

Mahon, Rianne. 1999. "Both Wage Earner and Mother": Women's Organizing and Childcare Policy in Sweden and Canada." In *Women's Organizing and Public Policy in Sweden and Canada.* Ed. Linda Briskin and Mona Eliasson, 238–279. Montreal: McGill-Queen's University Press.

Makin, Kirk. 1999. "Top court restores woman's dream of becoming a forest-fire fighter." *Globe and Mail,* 10 Sept., A1–2.

———. 2003. "Pay-equity goes against Bell." *Globe and Mail,* 27 June, A8.

Man, Guida. 2002. "Globalization and the Erosion of the Welfare State." *Canadian Woman Studies/les cahiers de la femme* 21/22 (4/1): 26–32.

Marchak, Patricia. 1980. "The Two Dimensions of Canadian Regionalism." *Journal of Canadian Studies* 15, 2 (Summer): 88–97.

Marchand, Marianne H., and Anne Sisson Runyan. 2000. "Introduction." In *Gendering and Global Restructuring: Sightings, Sites and Resistances.* Ed. Marianne H. Marchand and Anne Sisson Runyan. London and New York: Routledge.

Mark, Ken. 1994. "Sharing the housework isn't a political gesture, Ken Mark says. It just makes sense." *Globe and Mail,* 16 Feb. A24.

Maroney, Heather Jon. 1987. "Feminism at Work." In *Feminism and Political Economy: Women's Work, Women's Struggles.* Ed. Heather Jon Maroney and Meg Luxton, 85–108. Toronto: Methuen.

———. 1992. "'Who Has the Baby?' Nationalism, Pronatalism and the Construction of a 'Demographic Crisis' in Quebec, 1960–1988." *Studies in Political Economy* 39: 7–36.

Marron, Kevin. 2003. "Debt weighing on grads: post-secondary education costs deter many would-be professionals." *Globe and Mail,* July 21.

Marshall, Barbara L. 2000. *Configuring Gender: Explorations in Theory and Politics.* Peterborough: Broadview.

Marshall, Lisa. 1999. Review of "...But Where Are you Really From." *Canadian Woman Studies/les cahiers de la femme* 19 (3): 185.

Martin, Paul, and Ernesto Zedillo. 2003. "Doing good by doing well." *Globe and Mail,* 1 Aug., A15.

Martindale, Kathleen. 1994. "Can I Get A Witness? My Lesbian Breast Cancer Story." *Fireweed* 42: 9–15.

———. 1995. "What Makes Lesbianism Thinkable: Theorizing Lesbianism from Adrienne Rich to Queer Theory." In *Feminist Issues: Race, Class and Sexuality.* Ed. Nancy Mandell. Scarborough, ON: Prentice-Hall.

Marx, Karl. 1969 [1869]. "The 18th Brumaire of Louis Bonaparte." In Karl Marx and Friedrich Engels, *Selected Works.* Vol. 1: 394–87. Moscow: Progress Publishers.

Marx, Karl, and Frederick Engels. 1969 [1848]. "Manifesto of the Communist Party." In *Selected Works,* 98–137. Moscow: Progress Publishers.

Matthews, Ralph. 1980. "The Significance and Explanation of Regional Divisions in Canada." *Journal of Canadian Studies* 15, 2: 43–61.

May, Kathryn. 2003. "One in four works 50 hours a week, study finds." *Kingston Whig-Standard,* August 24.

McBride, Joy, and Karen McBride. 1996. "Answering to My Sister's Name." In *To Sappho, My Sister: Lesbian Sisters Write about Their Lives*. Ed. Lee Fleming, 175–84. Charlottetown: Gynergy Books.

McCallum, Margaret E. 1986. "Keeping Women in Their Place: The Minimum Wage in Canada, 1910–25." *Labour/Le Travail* 17: 29–56.

McClelland, Susan. 2001. "Child Poverty." *Maclean's Magazine*. September 17. www.maclean's.ca/topstories/article.jsp?content=56960. (Accessed August 22, 2003).

McDaniel, Susan. 1993. "The Changing Canadian Family: Women's Roles and the Impact of Feminism." In *Changing Patterns: Women in Canada*. 2nd ed. Ed. Sandra Burt, Lorraine Code, and Lindsay Dorney, 422–51. Toronto: McClelland & Stewart.

McDonough, Peggy. 2001. "Women and Health in the Global Economy." In *Unhealthy Times: Political Economy Perspectives on Health and Care*, 195–222. Eds. Pat Armstrong, Hugh Armstrong, and David Cockburn. Toronto: Oxford.

McFarland, Joan. 1988. "The Construction of Women and Development Theory." *Canadian Review of Sociology and Anthropology* 25: 299–308.

———. 1998. "From Feminism to Women's Human Rights: The Best Way Forward?" *Atlantis* 22 (2): 50–61.

———. 2002. "Call Centres in New Brunswick: Maquiladoras of the North?" *Canadian Woman Studies/les cahiers de la femme* 21/22 (4/1): 64–70.

McIntyre, Sheila. 1994. "Refining Reformism: The Consultations that Shaped Bill C-49." In *Confronting Sexual Assault: A Decade of Legal and Social Change*. Ed. Julian Roberts and Renate Mohr, 193–326. Toronto: University of Toronto Press.

———. 1995. "Gender Bias within the Law School: 'The Memo' and Its Impact." In *Breaking Anonymity: The Chilly Climate for Women Faculty*. Ed. the Chilly Collective, 211–64. Waterloo: Wilfrid Laurier University Press.

———. 2000. "Tracking and Resisting Backlash against Equality Gains in Sexual Offence Law." *Canadian Woman Studies/les cahiers de la femme* 20 (3): 72–83.

McIvor, Sharon Donna. 1999. "Self-government and Aboriginal Women." In *Scratching the Surface: Canadian Anti-racist Feminist Thought*. Ed. Enakshi Dua and Angela Robertson. Toronto: Women's Press.

McKenna, Katherine M.J. 1994. *A Life of Propriety: Anne Murray Powell and Her Family, 1755–1849*. Montreal: McGill-Queen's University Press.

———, and June Larkin, eds. 2002. *Violence Against Women: New Canadian Perspectives*. Toronto: Inanna Publications and Education Inc.

McLaren, Angus, and Arlene Tigar McLaren. 1986. *The Bedroom and the State: The Changing Practices and Politics of Contraception and Abortion in Canada, 1880–1980*. Toronto: McClelland & Stewart.

Messing, Karen. 1987. "Do Women Have Different Jobs Because of Their Biological Differences?" In *Women and Men: Interdisciplinary Readings on Gender*. Ed. Greta Hofmann Nemiroff, 341–53. Richmond Hill, ON: Fitzhenry & Whiteside.

Michalos, Alex C. 2000. "Evaluation of Equality Policies for the Status of Women in Canada." *Social Indicators Research* 37 (2): 242–77.

Mies, Maria. 2001. "Woman, Nature and the International Division of Labour: Maria Mies Interviewed by Ariel Salleh." In *There is an Alternative: Subsistence and Worldwide Resistance to Corporate Globalization*. Ed. Veronika Bennholdt-Thomsen, Nicholas G. Faraclas and Claudia von Werlhof, 3–14. London and New York: Zed Books.

Miller, Christine, and Patricia Chuchryk. 1996. "Introduction." In *Women of the First Nations: Power, Wisdom and Strength*. Ed. Christine Miller and Patricia Chuchryk, 3–10. Winnipeg: University of Manitoba Press.

Miller, Karen-Lee, and Janice Du Mont. 2000. "Countless Abused Women: Homeless and Inadequately Housed." *Canadian Woman Studies/les cahiers de la femme* 20 (3): 115–22.

Millett, Kate. 1971. *Sexual Politics*. New York: Avon Books.

Million, Dian. 2000. "Telling Secrets: Sex, Power and Narratives in Indian Residential School Histories." *Canadian Woman Studies/les cahiers de la femme* 20 (2): 92–104.

Mills, C. Wright. 1959. *The Sociological Imagination*. London: Oxford University Press.

Mitchell, Juliet. 1971. *Women's Estate*. Harmondsworth: Penguin Books

———. 1974. *Psychoanalysis and Feminism*. New York: Pantheon Books.

Mitchell, Marjorie, and Anna Franklin. 1984. "When You Don't Know the Language, Listen to the Silence: An Historical Overview of Native Indian Women in B.C." In *Not Just Pin Money*. Ed. Barbara K. Latham and Roberta J. Pazdro, 17–34. Victoria: Camosun College.

Mitchinson, Wendy. 1979. "The WCTU: 'For God, Home and Native Land'—A Study in Nineteenth-Century Feminism." In *A Not Unreasonable Claim: Women and Reform in Canada, 1880s–1920s*. Ed. Linda Kealey, 151–68. Toronto: Women's Press.

Modleski, Tania. 1991. *Feminism Without Women: Culture and Criticism in a "Post-feminist Age."* New York: Routledge.

Moghissi, Haideh. 1994. "Racism and Sexism in Academic Practice." In *The Dynamics of "Race" and Gender: Some Feminist Interventions*. Ed. Haleh Afshar and Mary Maynard, 222–34. London: Taylor and Francis.

———. 1999. *Feminism and Islamic Fundamentalism: The Limits of Postmodern Analysis*. London & New York: Zed Books.

Montreal Health Press. 1995. *A Book about Birth Control*. Montreal.

Monture-Angus, Patricia. 1995. *Thunder in My Soul: A Mohawk Woman Speaks*. Halifax: Fernwood Press.

———. 2003. "In the Way of Peace: Confronting 'Whiteness' in the University." In *Seen but Not Heard: Aboriginal Women and Women of Colour in the Academy*. Ed. Rashmi Luther, Elizabeth Whitmore and Bernice Moreau, 33–54. Ottawa: Canadian Research Institute for the Advancement of Women.

Monture-Okanee, Patricia. 1995. "Introduction. Surviving the Contradictions: Personal Notes on Academia." In *Breaking Anonymity: The Chilly Climate for Women Faculty*. Ed. the Chilly Collective, 11–28. Waterloo: Wilfrid Laurier University Press.

Morris, Cerise. 1980. "'Determination and Thoroughness': The Movement for a Royal Commission on the Status of Women in Canada." *Atlantis* 5, 2: 1–21.

———. 1982. "No More than Simple Justice." PhD diss., McGill University.

Morton, Mary. 1988. "Dividing the Wealth, Sharing the Poverty: The (Re)formation of 'Family' in Law in Ontario." *Canadian Review of Sociology and Anthropology* 25, 2: 254–75.

Mosoff, Judith. 1993. "Reproductive Technology and Disability: Searching for the 'Rights' and Wrongs in Explanation." *Dalhousie Law Review* 16, 1: 97–126.

Mosse, Julia Cleves. 1993. *Half the World, Half a Chance.* Oxford: Oxfam.

Nadeau, Mary Jo. 2002. "Who is Canadian Now? Feminism and the Politics of Nation after September 11." *Atlantis* 27 (1): 14–24.

Nagra, Narina. 2003. "Whiteness in Seattle: Anti-globalization Activists Examine Racism within the Movement." *Alternatives* 29 (1): 27–8.

Nakhaie, M.R. 2002. "Class, Breadwinner Ideology and Housework among Canadian Husbands." *Review of Radical Political Economics* 34:137-57.

———. 1997. "Vertical Mosaic Among the Elites: The New Imagery Revisited." *Canadian Review of Sociology and Anthropology* 34(1): 1-24.

Nash, Catherine. 1995. "Siting Lesbians: Sexuality, Planning and Urban Space." MA thesis, Queen's University.

National Council of Welfare. 2002. Ottawa: National Council of Welfare Reports: Poverty Profile 1999.

Nelson, Jennifer J. 2002. "The Space of Africville: Creating, Regulating and Remembering the Urban 'Slum'." In *Race, Space and the Law: Unmapping a White Settler Society.* Ed. Sherene H. Razack, 211–232. Toronto: Between the Lines.

Nett, Emily. 1994. "Demure no more?" *Winnipeg Free Press,* 31 July, A7.

Newman, Peter. 1969. *The Distemper of Our Times.* Toronto: McClelland & Stewart.

Newman, Roger. 1976. "Bank can't find woman qualified to serve as director." *Globe and Mail,* 10 Sept., 1.

Ng, Roxana. 1986. "The Social Construction of Immigrant Women." In *The Politics of Diversity.* Ed. Roberta Hamilton and Michèle Barrett, 269–86. London: Verso.

———. 2002. "Freedom for Whom? Globalization and Trade from the Standpoint of Garment Workers." *Canadian Woman Studies/les cahiers de la femme* 21/22 (4/1): 74–81.

Nicholson, Linda J., ed. 1990. *Feminism/Postmodernism.* New York: Routledge.

Noble, Kimberly. 1991. "Being a bad sport about harassment." *Globe and Mail,* 29 Nov., A18.

Nolin, Nicole. 2002. "Girl Power: From Princess Di to Oprah Winfrey." In *Canadian Communications: Issues in Contemporary Media and Culture.* Eds. Bohdan Szuchewyz and Jeannette Sloniowski, 225–228. Toronto: Prentice Hall.

Nussbaum, Martha C. 2001. "Comment on Quillen's" Feminist Theory, Justice, and the Lure of the Human"." *Signs* 27 (1): 123–35.

O'Brien, Mary. 1981. *The Politics of Reproduction.* London: Routledge & Kegan Paul.

O'Brien, Robert, Anne Marie Goetz, Jan Aart Scholte, and Marc Williams. 2000. *Contesting Global Governance: Multilateral Economic Institutions and Global Social Movements.* Cambridge: Cambridge University Press.

Odette, Francine. 1992. "Body Beautiful/Body Perfect: Challenging the Status Quo. Where Do Women with Disabilities Fit In?" *Canadian Woman Studies/les cahiers de la femme* 14, 3: 41–43.

Ondaatje, Michael. 1992. *The English Patient*. Toronto: McClelland & Stewart.

O'Neil, Maureen, and Sharon Sutherland. 1997. "The Machinery of Women's Policy: Implementing the RCSW." In *Women and the Canadian State/Femmes et L'Etat Canadien*. Ed. Caroline Andrew and Sanda Rogers, 197–219. Montreal: McGill-Queen's University Press.

Ontario Association of Interval and Transition Houses. 2002. "Locked In, Left Out: Impacts of the Budget Cuts on Abused Women and their Children." In *Violence Against Women: New Canadian Perspectives*. Ed. Katherine M.J. McKenna and June Larkin, 413–22. Toronto: Inanna Publications and Education.

Osennontion and Skonaganleh:ra. 1989. "Our World." *Canadian Woman Studies/les cahiers de la femme* 10, 2/4: 7–19.

Ottawa Letter. 1993. "Campbell Sworn in as Prime Minister with Substantially Smaller Cabinet." 21 (28 June): 221–22.

Overall, Christine. 1992. "What's Wrong with Prostitution? Evaluating Sex Work." *Signs* 17, 4: 705–24.

———. 1993. *Human Reproduction: Principles, Practices, Policies*. Toronto: Oxford University Press.

Oxfam. 2003. "Rigged Rules and Double Standards: Trade, Globalization and the Fight Against Poverty." www.maketradefair.com.

Panitch, Leo. 1977. "The Role and Nature of the State." In *The Canadian State: Political Economy and Political Power*. Ed. Leo Panitch, 3–27. Toronto: University of Toronto Press.

Pal, Leslie A. 1993. *Interests of State: The Politics of Language, Multiculturalism, and Feminism in Canada*. Montreal: McGill-Queen's University Press.

Palmer, Hazelle. 1997. *'...But Where Are You Really From?' Stories of Identity and Assimilation in Canada*. Toronto: Sister Vision Press.

Parpart, Jane L. 1995. "Deconstructing the Development 'Expert': Gender, Development and the 'Vulnerable Groups." In *Feminism/Postmodernism/ Development*. Ed. Marianne Marchand and Jane L. Parpart. London and New York: Routledge.

Parr, Joy, ed. 1987. *Still Running: Personal Stories of Queen's Women Celebrating the Fiftieth Anniversary of the Marty Fellowship*. Kingston: Queen's University Alumnae Association.

———. 1990. *The Gender of Breadwinners*. Toronto: University of Toronto Press.

Parsons, Talcott. 1959. "The Social Structure of the Family." In *The Family: Its Function and Destiny*. Ed. R.N. Anshen. New York: Hayner.

Payette, Lise. 1982. *Le pouvoir? Connais pas*. Quebec: Québec/Amérique.

Pepler, D.J., W.M. Craig, and J. Connolly. 1998. *Girls' Aggression: Scenarios and Strategies*. Government of Ontario: Ministry of Training and Education.

Perkins, Patricia E. (Ellie). 2002. "Diversity, Local Economics and Globalization Limits." *Canadian Woman Studies/les cahiers de la femme* 21/22 (4/1): 183–89.

Peters, Evelyn. 1987. "Indians in Regina and Saskatoon, 1982: Some Strategies of Household Organization." PhD diss., Queen's University.

Phillips, David. 1995. "No difference, no deference." *Globe and Mail*, 10 Nov., A20.

Phillips, Susan D. 1991. "Meaning and Structure in Social Movements: Mapping the Network of National Canadian Women's Organizations." *Canadian Journal of Political Science* 24, 4: 755–82.

Philp, Margaret. 1995. "Male–female income gap widens." *Globe and Mail*, 20 Dec., A8.

———. 2000. "Breadwinner now likely to be a woman." *Globe and Mail*, 15 Sept., A3.

Pierson, Ruth Roach. 1986. *"They're Still Women After All": The Second World War and Canadian Womanhood*. Toronto: McClelland & Stewart.

———. 1990. "Gender and the Unemployment Insurance Debates in Canada, 1934–1940." *Labour/Le Travail* 25: 77–103.

———. 1995. "The Politics of the Domestic Sphere." In *Canadian Women's Issues: Twenty-five Years of Women's Activism in English Canada*. Vol. 2. Ed. Ruth Roach Pierson and Marjorie Griffin Cohen, 1–33. Toronto: Lorimer.

Pinterics, Natasha. 2001. "Riding the Feminist Waves: In With the Third?" *Canadian Woman Studies/les cahiers de la femme*, Vol. 20/21 (4/1): 15–21.

Pomerantz, Shauna. 2003. "Lisa Simpson vs. Rory Gilmore." *Good Girl* 5:15.

Porter, John. 1965. *The Vertical Mosaic: An Analysis of Social Class and Power in Canada*. Toronto: University of Toronto Press.

Pratt, Anna, and Mariana Valverde. 2002. "From Deserving Victims to 'Masters of Confusion': Redefining Refugees in the 1990s." *Canadian Journal of Sociology* 27 (2): 135–161.

Prentice, Alison, Paula Bourne, Gail Cuthbert Brandt, Beth Light, Wendy Mitchinson, and Naomi Black. 1988. *Canadian Women: A History*. Toronto: Harcourt, Brace, Jovanovich.

———. 1996. *Canadian Women: A History*. Second edition. Toronto: Harcourt, Brace, Jovanovich.

Prentice, Susan. 1995. "Workers, Mothers, Reds: Toronto's Postwar Daycare Fight." In *Social Welfare Policy in Canada*. Ed. Raymond B. Blake and Jeff Keshen, 258–76. Toronto: Copp Clark.

Quillen, Carol. 2001. "Feminist Theory, Justice and the Lure of the Human." *Signs* 27 (1): 87–122.

Raddon, Mary Beth. 2002. "Follow the Money." *Canadian Woman Studies/les cahiers de la femme* 21/22 (4/1): 221–225.

Ramkhalawansingh, Ceta. 1974. "Women During the Great War." In *Women at Work, Ontario, 1850–1930*. Ed. Janice Acton, Penny Goldsmith, and Bonnie Shepard, 261–308. Toronto: Canadian Women's Educational Press.

Raphael, Mitchell. 2001. "She could learn a few lessons from Anne Murray." *Globe and Mail*, 17 July, B3.

Rayside, David. 1998. *On the Fringe: Gays and Lesbians in Politics*. Ithaca, New York: Cornell University.

Razack, Sherene H. 1991. Canadian Feminism and the Law: The Women's Legal and Education and Action Fund and the Pursuit of Equality. Toronto: Second Story Press.

———. 2002a. "Gendered Racial Violence and Spatialized Justice." In *Race, Space and the Law: Unmapping a White Settler Society*." Ed. Sherene H. Razack, 121–56. Toronto: Between the Lines.

———. 2002b. "Introduction." In *Race, Space and the Law: Unmapping a White Settler Society.*" Ed. Sherene H. Razack, 1–20. Toronto: Between the Lines.

———. 2003. "Racialized Immigrant Women as Native Informants in the Academy." In *Seen but Not Heard: Aboriginal Women and Women of Colour in the Academy*. Ed. Rashmi Luther, Elizabeth Whitmore and Bernice Moreau, 57–66. Ottawa: Canadian Research Institute for the Advancement of Women.

Rebick, Judy. 1994. "Interview with Judy Rebick." *Studies in Political Economy* 44, 39–71.

Report of the Royal Commission on the Status of Women in Canada. 1970. Ottawa: Information Canada.

Resources for Feminist Research. 1990. Special issue: Confronting Hetero-sexuality. 19, 3/4 (Sept.–Dec.).

Rich, Adrienne. 1980. "Compulsory Heterosexuality and Lesbian Existence." *Signs* 5 (Summer): 631–60.

Riddell, W.A. 1928. "Women's Franchise in Quebec a Century Ago." *Transactions of the Royal Society of Canada*, section 2: 85–98.

Riley, Denise. 1987. *"Am I that Name?" Feminism and the Category of "Women" in History*. Minneapolis: University of Minnesota Press.

Rinehart, Dianne. 1995. "Gender protection may harm refugees." *Winnipeg Free Press*, 17 March, B6.

Roberts, Barbara. 1979. "'A Work of Empire': Canadian Reformers and British Female Immigration." In *A Not Unreasonable Claim: Women and Reform in Canada, 1880s–1920s*. Ed. Linda Kealy. Toronto: Women's Press.

Robertson, James R. 1995. *Sexual Orientation and Legal Rights*. Ottawa: Minister of Supply and Services.

Rodgers, Karen. 1994. "Wife Assault: The Findings of a National Survey." *Juristat* 14, 9: 1–22.

Roiphe, Katie. 1993. *The Morning After: Sex, Fear and Feminism*. Boston: Little, Brown.

Rosenberg, Harriet. 1986. "The Home Is the Workplace: Hazards, Stresses and Pollutants." In *Through the Kitchen Window: The Politics of Home and Family*. Ed. Meg Luxton and Harriet Rosenberg, 37–62. Toronto: Garamond.

———. 1987. "Motherwork, Stress, and Depression: The Costs of Privatized Social Reproduction." In *Feminism and Political Economy*. Ed. Heather Jon Maroney and Meg Luxton, 181–96. Toronto: Methuen.

Ross, Becki. 1995. *The House that Jill Built: A Lesbian Nation*. Toronto: University of Toronto Press.

Rudy, Kathy. 2001. "Radical Feminism, Lesbian Separatism, and Queer Theory." *Feminist Studies* 27 (1): 191–222.

Russell, Susan. 1987. "The Hidden Curriculum of School: Reproducing Gender and Class Hierarchies." In *Feminism and Political Economy: Women's Work, Women's Struggles*. Ed Heather Jon Maroney and Meg Luxton, 229–46. Toronto: Methuen.

———. 1989. "From Disability to Handicap: An Inevitable Response to Social Constraints?" *Canadian Review of Sociology and Anthropology* 26, 2: 276–93.

Sadlier, Rosemary. 1994. *Leading the Way: Black Women in Canada*. Toronto: Umbrella Press.

St. Lewis, Joanne. 2003. "In the Belly of the Beast." In *Seen but Not Heard: Aboriginal Women and Women of Colour in the Academy*. Ed. Rashmi Luther, Elizabeth Whitmore and Bernice Moreau, 81–90. Ottawa: Canadian Research Institute for the Advancement of Women.

Sainte-Marie, Buffy. 1993. "Buffy Sainte-Marie: Lyrics of the Land." Interview with Fiona Muldrew and Suzanne McCloud. *Herizons* 7, 2: 30–32.

Saint-Onge, Nicole J.M. 1985. "The Dissolution of a Métis Community: Point à Grouette, 1860–1885." *Studies in Political Economy* 18: 149–72.

Salée, Daniel. 2003. "Transformative Politics, the State, and the Politics of Social Change in Quebec." In *Changing Canada: Political Economy as Transformation*. Ed. Wallace Clement and Leah Vosko, 25–50. Montreal: McGill-Queen's University Press.

———, and William Coleman. 1997. "The Challenges of the Quebec Question: Paradigm, Counter-paradigm, and…?" In *Understanding Canada: Building on the New Political Economy*. Ed. Wallace Clement, 262–85. Montreal: McGill-Queen's University Press.

Salutin, Rick. 1993. "The sexual politics of Kim Campbell's future." *Globe and Mail*, 12 March, C1.

Sanati, Maryam. 2003. "Ladies Who Loft." *Globe and Mail, Report on Business* 20 (2).

Sandilands, Catriona. 1999. *The Good-Natured Feminist: Ecofeminism and the Quest for Democracy*. Minneapolis: University of Minnesota Press.

Sangster, Joan. 1979. "The 1907 Bell Telephone Strike: Organizing Women Workers." *Labour/Le Travailleur* 15.

———. 1989. *Dreams of Equality: Women on the Canadian Left, 1920–1950*. Toronto: McClelland & Stewart.

Satzewich, Vic, and Lloyd Wong. 2003. "Immigration, Ethnicity, and Race: The Transformation of Transnationalism, Localism, and Identities." In *Changing Canada: Political Economy as Transformation*. Ed. Wallace Clement and Leah Vosko, 363–90. Montreal: McGill-University Press.

Schofield, Heather. 2001. "Wealth gap grew wider, StatsCan study finds." *Globe and Mail,* 16 March.

Scotiabank. 2003. "Two-thirds of Canadians think that the cost of a college or university education is becoming out of reach." Press Release, 4 Sept.

Scott, Joan Wallach. 1988. *Gender and the Politics of History*. New York: Columbia University Press.

Scriver, Jessie Boyd. 1984. "Memories." In *A Fair Shake: Autobiographical Essays by McGill Women*. Ed. Margaret Gillett and Kay Sibbald, 1–13. Montreal: Eden Press.

Seccombe, Wally. 1986. "Reflections on the Domestic Labour Debate and Prospects for Marxist-Feminist Synthesis." In *The Politics of Diversity*. Ed. Roberta Hamilton and Michèle Barrett, 190–207. London: Verso.

Seeley, John R., Alexander Sim, and Elizabeth Loosley. 1956. *Crestwood Heights: A Study of the Culture of Suburban Life*. New York: Wiley.

Shadd, Adrienne. 1994. "'The Lord seemed to say *Go*': Women and the Underground Railroad Movement." In *'We're Rooted Here and They Can't Pull Us Up': Essays in African Canadian Women's History*. Coordinator, Peggy Bristow. Toronto: University of Toronto Press.

Shanley, Mary Lyndon, and Uma Narayan. 1997. "Introduction: Contentious Concepts." In *Reconstructing Political Theory: Feminist Perspectives*. Ed. Mary Lyndon Shanley and Uma Narayan, xi–xxi. University Park, Pennsylvania: Pennsylvania University Press.

Sharma, Nandita. 2002. "Immigrant and Migrant Workers in Canada: Labour Movements, Racism, and the Expansion of Globalization." *Canadian Woman Studies/les cahiers de la femme* 21/22 (4/1): 17–25.

Shellrude, Kathleen. 2001. "Coming Between the Lines: A Fresh Look at the Writings of Anti-porn and Whore Feminists." *Canadian Woman Studies/les cahiers de la femme* 20/21 (4/1): 41–45.

Sherfey, Mary-Jane. 1972. *The Nature and Evolution of Female Sexuality.* New York: Random House.

Shiva, Vandana. 2002. "Violence of Globalization." *Canadian Woman Studies/les cahiers de la femme* 21/22 (4/1): 15–16.

Silman, Janet. 1987. *Enough is Enough: Aboriginal Women Speak Out.* Toronto: Women's Press.

Silvera, Makeda. 1985. "How Far Have We Come." In *In the Feminine: Women and Words/les Femmes et les mots.* Ed. Ann Dybikowski, Victoria Freeman, Daphne Marlatt, Barbara Pullman, and Betsy Warland, 68–72. Edmonton: Longspoon Press.

———, ed. 1986. *Fireworks: The Best of Fireweed.* Toronto: Women's Press.

Simmons, Christina. 1991. "Helping the Poorer Sisters: The Women of the Jost Mission, Halifax, 1905–1945." In *Rethinking Canada: The Promise of Women's History.* 2nd ed. Ed. Veronica Strong-Boag and Anita Clair Fellman, 286–307. Toronto: Copp Clark Longman.

Smart, Pat. 1997. "The 'Pure Laine' Debate." *Canadian Forum,* Nov., 15–19.

Smith, Dorothy. 1987. *The Everyday World as Problematic: A Feminist Sociology.* Toronto: University of Toronto Press.

——— 1992. "Whistling Women: Reflections on Rage and Rationality." In *Fragile Truths: Twenty-five Years of Sociology and Anthropology in Canada.* Ed. William K. Carroll, Linda Christiansen-Ruffman, Raymond F. Currie, and Deborah Harrison, 207–26. Ottawa: Carleton University Press.

Smith, Vivian. 1993. "Women welcome victory, 'but it's still not an election.'" *Globe and Mail,* 15 June, A4.

Snider, Laureen. 1994. "Feminism, Punishment and the Potential of Empowerment." *Canadian Journal of Law and Society* 9 (1): 75–104.

Snitow, Ann. 1990. "A Gender Diary." In *Conflicts in Feminism.* Ed. Marianne Hirsch and Evelyn Fox Keller, 9–43. New York: Routledge.

Solie, Karen. 2002. "Review of *The Lost Garden* by Helen Humphreys." *Globe and Mail,* 24 Aug.

Sommers, Christina Hoff. 1994. *Who stole feminism? How Women Have Betrayed Women.* New York: Simon and Schuster.

Spiller, Hortense J. 1987. "Mama's Baby, Papa's Baby Maybe: An American Grammar Book." *dia-critics* 17 (2): 65–81.

Spock, Benjamin. 1957. *Baby and Child Care.* 3rd ed. New York: n.p.

———, and Michael B. Rothenberg. 1985. *Dr Spock's Baby and Child Care.* New York: E.P. Dutton.

Sprague, D.N. 1980. "The Manitoba Land Question 1870–1872." *Journal of Canadian Studies* 15, 3 (Autumn): 74–84.

Srivastava, Sarita. 1996. "Song and Dance? The Performance of Antiracist Workshops." *Canadian Review of Sociology and Anthropology* 33 (3): 291–315.

Stacey-Moore, Gail. 1993. "In Our Own Voice." *Herizons* 6, 4: 21–23.

Starhawk. 2002. "The Bridge at Midnight Trembles: My Story of Quebec City." *Canadian Woman Studies/les cahiers de la femme* 21/22 (4/1): 155–59.

Statistics Canada. 1993. *Women in the Workplace*. 2nd ed. Ottawa: Ministry of Supply and Services.

———. 1995a. "Response to Allegations Made about the Violence against Women Survey." Feb.

———. 1995b. "Unemployment." CANSIM (World Wide Web).

Steenbergen, Candis. 2001. "Feminism and Young Women: Alive and Well and Still Kicking." *Canadian Woman Studies/les cahiers de la femme*, Vol. 20/21 (4/1): 6–14.

Steinstra, Deborah. 2000a. "Dancing Resistance from Rio to Beijing: Transnational Women's Organizing and United Nations Conferences, 1992–96." In *Gendering and Global Restructuring: Sightings, Sites and Resistances*. Ed. Marianne H. Marchand and Anne Sisson Runyan, 209–224. London and New York: Routledge.

———. 2000b. "Making Global Connections Among Women, 1970–99." In *Global Social Movements*. Ed. Robin Cohen and Shirin M. Rai, 62–82. London and New Brunswick: Athlone Press.

Stevenson, Garth. 1980. "Canadian Regionalism in Continental Perspective." *Journal of Canadian Studies* 15, 2: 16–28.

Stevenson, Winona. 1999. "Colonialism and First Nations Women in Canada." In *Scratching the Surface: Canadian Anti-racist Feminist Thought*. Eds. Enakshi Dua and Angela Robertson, 49–80. Toronto: Women's Press.

Stoddart, Jennifer. 1973. "The Woman Suffrage Bill in Quebec." In *Women in Canada*. Ed. Marylee Stephenson, 90–106. Toronto: New Press.

———. 1981. "Quebec's Legal Elite Looks at Women's Rights: The Dorion Commission, 1929–31." In *Essays in the History of Canadian Law*. Vol. 1. Ed. David H. Flaherty. Toronto: University of Toronto Press.

Storey, Shannon. 2002. "Neoliberal Trade Policies in Agriculture and the Destruction of Global Food Security: Who Can Feed the World?" *Canadian Woman Studies/les cahiers de la femme* 21/22 (4/1): 190–195.

Strange, Carolyn. 1995. *Toronto's Girl Problem: The Perils and Pleasures of the City, 1880–1930*. Toronto: University of Toronto Press.

Strong-Boag, Veronica. 1976. *The Parliament of Women: The National Council of Women of Canada, 1893–1929*. Ottawa: National Museums of Canada.

———. 1979. "Canada's Women Doctors: Feminism Constrained." In *A Not Unreasonable Claim: Women and Reform in Canada, 1880s–1920s*. Ed. Linda Kealey, 109–30. Toronto: Women's Press.

———. 1983. "Mapping Woman Studies in Canada: Some Signposts." *Journal of Educational Thought* 17: 94–111.

———. 1986. "'Ever a Crusader': Nellie McClung, First-Wave Feminist." In *Rethinking Canada: The Promise of Women's History*. Ed. Veronica Strong-Boag and Anita Clair Fellman, 178–90. Toronto: Copp Clark Pitman.

———. 1988. *The New Day Recalled: Lives of Girls and Women in English Canada, 1919–1939*. Toronto: Copp Clark Pitman.

———. 1995. "'Their Side of the Story': Women's Voices from Ontario Suburbs." In *A Diversity of Women: Ontario, 1945–1980*. Ed. Joy Parr. Toronto: University of Toronto Press.

Sugiman, Pamela. 1994. *Labour's Dilemma: The Gender Politics of Auto Workers in Canada, 1937–1979*. Toronto: University of Toronto Press.

Swift, Jamie. 1995. *Wheel of Fortune: Work and Life in the Age of Falling Expectations*. Toronto: Between the Lines.

———. 1999. *Civil Society in Question*. Toronto: Between the Lines.

Sydie, Rosalind. 1991. "From Liberal to Radical: The Work and Life of Mary Wollstonecraft." *Atlantis* 17, 1: 36–71.

Tancred, Peta, and Huguette Dagenais. 2001. "Women's Studies, Feminist Studies, Gender Studies: The Academic Arm of the Women's Movement." In *Canadian Society*. Ed. Dan Glenday and Ann Duffy, 191–211. Toronto: Oxford University Press.

Tastsoglou, Evangelia, and Marie Welton. 2003. "Building a Culture of Peace: An Interview with Muriel Duckworth and Betty Peterson." *Canadian Woman Studies/les cahiers de la femme* 22 (2): 115–119.

Tax, Meredith. 1980. *The Rising of the Women: Feminist Solidarity and Class Conflict, 1880–1917*. New York: Monthly Review Press.

Taylor, Barbara. 1979. "'The Men Are as Bad as Their Masters...': Socialism, Feminism, and Sexual Antagonism in the London Tailoring Trade in the Early 1830s." *Feminist Studies* 5, 1: 7–40.

———. 1983. *Eve and the New Jerusalem*. London: Virago.

Teeple, Gary, ed. 1972. *Capitalism and the National Question*. Toronto: University of Toronto Press.

Teghtsoonian, Katherine. 1997. "Who Pays for Caring for Children? Public Policy and the Devaluation of Women's Work." In *Challenging the Public/Private Divide: Feminism, Law and Public Policy*. Ed. Susan Boyd. Toronto: University of Toronto Press.

Tennant, Paul. 1990. *Aboriginal Peoples and Politics: The Indian Land Question in British Columbia, 1849–1989*. Vancouver: University of British Columbia Press.

Thobani, Sunera. 1999. "Sponsoring Immigrant Women's Inequalities." *Canadian Woman Studies/les cahiers de la femme* 19 (3): 11–16.

———. 2002. "War Frenzy." *Atlantis* 27 (1): 5–11.

Thompson, Allan. 1995. "Immigrant women not protected, report says." *Toronto Star*, 23 May, A3.

Tiger, Lionel. 1969. *Men in Groups*. New York: Random House.

Todd, Douglas. 1993. "First openly gay minister ordained." *Vancouver Sun*, 20 Sept., A3.

Tolley, Erin. 2003. "The Skilled Worker Class." Metropolis Policy Brief. Department of Citizenship and Immigration. N. 1, Jan.

Toronto Star. 1957. "Disqualified: 'Miss USA' Mother of 2." 19 July, 1.

Trigger, Bruce. 1991. "Early Native North American Responses to European Contact: Romantic versus Rationalist Interpretations." *Journal of American History* 77, 4 (March): 1195–215.

Trimble, Linda. 1995. "Politics Where We Live: Women and Cities." In *Canadian Metropolitics: Governing Our Cities*. Ed. James Lightbody, 92–114. Toronto: Copp Clark.

Trofimenkoff, Susan Mann. 1977. "Henri Bourassa and the Woman Question." In *The Neglected Majority: Essays in Canadian Women's History*. Ed. Susan Mann Trofimenkoff and Alison Prentice, 106–15. Toronto: McClelland & Stewart.

Turpel, M.E. (Aki-Kwe). 1993. "Patriarchy and Paternalism: The Legacy of the Canadian State for First Nations Women." *Canadian Journal of Women and the Law* 6, 1: 174–92.

Tynes, Maxine. 1987. *Borrowed Beauty*. Porters Lake, NS: Pottersfield Press.

———. 1990. *Woman Talking Woman*. Lawrencetown Beach, NS: Pottersfield Press.

Urquhart, M.C., and K.A.H. Buckley, ed. 1965. *Historical Statistics of Canada*. Toronto: Macmillan.

Valpy, Michael. 1992. "Lives of Canadian girls and women." *Globe and Mail*, 12 March, 2.

Valverde, Mariana. 1991. *The Age of Light, Soap and Water: Moral Reform in English Canada, 1885–1925*. Toronto: McClelland & Stewart.

Vance, Carol, ed. 1986. *Pleasure and Danger: Exploring Female Sexuality*. Boston: Routledge and Kegan Paul.

Vancouver Women's Caucus. 1972. "Lesbians Belong in the Women's Movement." In *Women Unite!* Toronto: Canadian Women's Educational Press.

Van Kirk, Sylvia. 1980. *"Many Tender Ties": Women in Fur-Trade Society, 1670–1870*. Winnipeg: Watson and Dwyer.

———. 1986. "The Role of Native Women in the Fur Trade Society of Western Canada, 1670–1830." In *Rethinking Canada: The Promise of Women's History*. Ed. Veronica Strong-Boag and Anita Clair Fellman, 59–66. Toronto: Copp Clark Pitman.

———. 1987. *Towards a Feminist Perspective in Native History*. Toronto: Centre for Woman Studies in Education.

Vickers, Jill, 1987. "At His Mother's Knee: Sex/Gender and the Construction of National Identities." In *Women and Men: Interdisciplinary Readings on Gender*. Ed. Greta Hofmann Nemiroff, 478–92. Richmond Hill, ON: Fitzhenry & Whiteside.

———, Pauline Rankin, and Christine Appelle. 1993. *Politics as if Women Mattered: A Political Analysis of the National Action Committee on the Status of Women*. Toronto: University of Toronto Press. 1993.

Vienneau, David. 1985. "Feminist movement is dead, REAL Women's group says." *Toronto Star*, 20 Nov., A12.

Vorst, Jessie et al., eds. 1989. *Race, Class, Gender: Bonds and Barriers*. Toronto: Between the Lines.

Vosko, Leah F. 2002. "The Pasts and Futures of Feminist Political Economy in Canada: Reviving the Debate." *Studies in Political Economy 68: 55–83*.

Wakelin, Amy. 2003. "An Elusive Dichotomy: Exploring the Inconsistencies and Contradictions between 'Femininity' and 'Feminism' in Western Culture." Unpublished undergraduate thesis, Department of Sociology, Queen's University.

Walker, Gillian. 1990. *Family Violence and the Women's Movement: The Conceptual Politics of Struggle*. Toronto: University of Toronto Press.

Wallace, Bronwen. 1993. "...I couldn't separate the landscape from how I see my poems moving." Interview in *Sounding Differences: Conversations with Seventeen Canadian Women Writers*. Ed. Janice Williamson. Toronto: University of Toronto Press.

Warskett, Rosemary. 1988. "Bank Worker Unionization and the Law." *Studies in Political Economy* 25: 41–73.

Weaver, Sally. 1993. "First Nations Women and Government Policy, 1970–92: Discrimination and Conflict." In *Changing Patterns: Women in Canada*. 2nd ed. Ed. Sandra Burt, Lorraine Code, and Lindsay Dorney, 92–150. Toronto: McClelland & Stewart.

Weir, Allison. 1996. *Sacrificial Logics: Feminist Theory and the Critique of Identity*. Routledge: New York and London.

Weir, Lorna. 1987. "Socialist Feminism and the Politics of Sexuality." In *Feminism and Political Economy: Women's Work, Women's Struggles*. Ed. Heather Jon Maroney and Meg Luxton, 69–84. Toronto: Methuen.

Weissman, Aerlyn, and Lynne Fernie. 1993. *Forbidden Love*. National Film Board.

Wench Collective. 2001. "Wench Radio: Funky Feminist Fury." *Canadian Woman Studies/les cahiers de la femme* 20/21 (4/1): 69–74.

Wente, Margaret. 1994. "Success stories: Which ones really count?" *Globe and Mail*, 23 July, A2.

Westlund, Andrea. 1999. "Pre-modern and Modern Power: Foucault and the Case of Domestic Violence." *Signs* 24 (4): 1045–1066.

Whitaker, Reg. 1977. "Images of the State in Canada." In *The Canadian State: Political Economy and Political Power*. Ed. Leo Panitch, 28–68. Toronto: University of Toronto Press.

White, Julie. 1993. *Sisters and Solidarity: Women and Unions in Canada*. Toronto: Thompson.

Wiegers, Wanda. 2002. "The Framing of Poverty as 'Child Poverty' and Its Implications for Women." Ottawa: Status of Women Canada.

Wiggins, Cindy. 2003. "Women's Work: Challenging and Changing the World." Ottawa: Canadian Labour Congress. Research Paper #23. www.clc-ctc.ca.

Williams, Dorothy W. 1997. *The Road to Now: A History of Blacks in Montreal*. Montreal: Vehicule Press.

Williams, Pam. 1994. "Handywoman: Powerful new role model is plugged in." *Globe and Mail*, 10 March, A24.

Williams, Patricia. 1991. *The Alchemy of Race and Rights*. Cambridge: Harvard University Press.

Williams, Raymond. 1976. *Keywords*. London: Fontana.

———. 1981. *Culture*. London: Fontana.

Williamson, Janice, and Deborah Gorham, eds. 1989. *Up and Doing: Canadian Women and Peace*. Toronto: Women's Press.

Winks, Robin. 1971. *The Blacks in Canada: A History*. Montreal: McGill-Queen's University Press.

Winnipeg Free Press. 1992a. "Passing the buck." 21 March, A6.

———. 1992b. "Wifebattering not funny, embarrassed MPs declare." 15 May, 14.

———. 1995. "Rules on refugee women faulted." 10 March, A12.

Wolf, Naomi. 1990. *The Beauty Myth*. Toronto: Vintage Books.

Wollstonecraft, Mary. 1992 [1792]. *A Vindication of the Rights of Woman*. London: Penguin.

Wotherspoon, Terry, and Vic Satzewich. 1993. *First Nations: Race, Class and Gender Relations*. Scarborough, ON: Nelson.

Yeatman, Anna. 1997. "Feminism and Power." In *Reconstructing Political Theory: Feminist Perspectives*. Ed. Mary Lyndon Shanley and Uma Narayan, 144–57. University Park, Pennsylvania: Pennsylvania University Press.

Yetman, Lori, and Julie Yetman. 1996. "Peanut Butter and Jam." In *To Sappho, My Sister: Lesbian Sisters Write about Their Lives*. Ed. Lee Fleming, 211–24. Charlottetown: Gynergy Books.

York, Lorraine M. 1994. "Whirling Blindfolded in the House of Woman: Gender Politics in the Poetry and Fiction of Michael Ondaatje." In *Essays on Canadian Writing*, 71–91. Toronto: ECW Press.

Young, Claire, and Diana Majury. 1995. "Lesbian Perspectives." In *Breaking Anonymity: The Chilly Climate for Women Faculty*. Ed. the Chilly Collective, 345–58. Waterloo: Wilfrid Laurier University Press.

Young, Iris Marion. 1990. *Justice and the Politics of Difference*. Princeton: Princeton University Press.

Index